THE EMPEROR NERO

THE EMPEROR NERO

A GUIDE TO THE ANCIENT SOURCES

ANTHONY A. BARRETT, ELAINE FANTHAM,
AND JOHN C. YARDLEY, EDITORS

PRINCETON UNIVERSITY PRESS
Princeton and Oxford

PUBLISHED BY PRINCETON UNIVERSITY PRESS
41 William Street, Princeton, New Jersey 08540

IN THE UNITED KINGDOM: PRINCETON UNIVERSITY PRESS
6 Oxford Street, Woodstock, Oxfordshire OX20 1TW

PRESS.PRINCETON.EDU

Jacket art: Emperor Nero (37–68 AD) Portrait, Engraving, 1882,
Private Collection, J.T. Vintage / Bridgeman Images

ISBN (PBK.) 978-0-691-15651-4

Library of Congress Cataloging-in-Publication Data

Names: Barrett, Anthony, 1941– editor. | Fantham, Elaine, editor. |
Yardley, John, 1942– editor.

Title: The Emperor Nero : a guide to the ancient sources / Anthony A. Barrett,
Elaine Fantham, and John C. Yardley, editors.

Description: Princeton : Princeton University Press, 2016. | Includes
bibliographical references and index.

Identifiers: LCCN 2015048217 | ISBN 9780691156514 (pbk.)

Subjects: LCSH: Nero, Emperor of Rome, 37-68. | Rome—History—
Nero, 54-68—Sources.

Classification: LCC DG285 .E47 2016 | DDC 937/.07092—dc23
LC record available at http://lccn.loc.gov/2015048217

BRITISH LIBRARY CATALOGING-IN-PUBLICATION DATA IS AVAILABLE

This book has been composed in Adobe Jenson Pro and Trajan Pro

Printed on acid-free paper. ∞

PRINTED IN THE UNITED STATES OF AMERICA

1 3 5 7 9 10 8 6 4 2

CONTENTS

Preface vii

Introduction xi

List of Major Events during Nero's Lifetime xxvii

I THE MAKING OF THE EMPEROR 1

II THE NEW EMPEROR 22

III ENEMIES WITHIN 41

IV PARTHIA 77

V BRITAIN AND GERMANY 118

VI THE GREAT FIRE 149

VII THE EMPEROR'S WIVES 171

VIII CONSPIRACIES 190

IX THE EMPEROR AS ARTIST AND SHOWMAN 231

X DEATH 265

Bibliography 287

Index 295

PREFACE

Nero is an inherently fascinating individual, and his reign was witness to a number of highly significant events. The case for a sourcebook therefore seems to be self-evident. In selecting the material to be included in this particular one, we have tried to illuminate those incidents of Nero's life and rule that are either historically significant or just inherently interesting. While few would dispute that these are valid criteria, few also are likely to be in total agreement about which incidents actually meet them. In reality, when selecting episodes that best exemplify the life and career of any historical figure, one cannot help being guided by what are, in the final analysis, essentially subjective principles. This shortcoming we cheerfully concede.

In presenting the material, chosen in part on this subjective basis, we have not been rigidly consistent. For this, we *do* feel that an explanation, albeit brief, is appropriate. For some phases of Nero's reign, we offer a selection of chapters that seem to illustrate events most effectively. But, for other phases, most notably the Parthian campaign and the Pisonian conspiracy, we have provided an almost complete sequence of passages. This has been deliberate. The military events on the Euphrates frontier are largely unintelligible when seen piecemeal; it is only when they are viewed as a whole that anything approaching a coherent picture emerges. The Pisonian conspiracy stands alone in the extant *Annals*, as Tacitus's most detailed lengthy episode, composed as a discrete and almost self-contained extended literary narrative. It also needs to be seen as a whole, not in parts.

The bulk of the material presented here consists of passages from literary sources. We have, however, also made use of "primary sources." The reign of Nero does not abound in significant epigraphical or papyrological material, and we have provided only a very small selection. Nero's coins, on the other hand, are richly varied and numismatically significant, and we have drawn quite heavily on them. They serve two purposes. On the one hand, they provide direct contemporary evidence of how the Neronian regime sought to present itself to the world. But they are also by far the best medium to illustrate the visual Nero. Ancient Roman sculpture survives in abundance, but very few examples survive that have their identifying inscriptions. Consequently, their identification is a highly contested scholarly enterprise, fraught with difficulties, often involving little more than inspired guesswork. And even when a piece of sculpture is confidently identified, one cannot be certain to what extent that portrait has been idealized. By contrast, the images of emperors on official Roman coins present no problems of identification, coming as they do with names and titles. But also it is generally agreed that in this period they are strikingly realistic, warts and all. The numismatic images of Nero depicted in this book offer a vivid, and remarkably honest, record of Nero's transition, like Henry VIII's, from gilded handsome youth to coarse and bloated libertine.

This is not a conventional sourcebook. We have been guided by the principle that much of the writing, especially the historical writing, of antiquity is a baffling mystery to the student and to the general reader (and often to the classical scholar!). We have accordingly provided extensive annotation, far more than is usual in a book of this nature, to explain those individuals, events, and institutions that are likely to be unfamiliar. Our hope is that the resultant text will serve the reader on a number of levels. The serious general reader, already familiar with the broad outlines of Nero's reign, will, we hope, appreciate seeing the actual passages from which his story is derived, and will probably be satisfied to read only the introductions and the translations and generally ignore the commentary. Undergraduates seeking help for regular courses in Roman history will occasionally want to dip into the notes and benefit from the guidance that they provide. Advanced students in more specialized history courses will want to come to grips with some of the problems and issues that are raised in the more detailed sections of the commentary and to pursue the references to their original contexts.

This book reflects the interests and expertise of the collaborators. Anthony Barrett provided the introductory material and the commentary, as well as the numismatic and epigraphic entries, and John Yardley provided the translations of the literary texts. Elaine Fantham, however, undertook general responsibility for all nonnumismatic and non-epigraphic aspects of Chapter IX specifically, and its appendix. All the same, this has been a truly collaborative effort, with all three of us reading over the material of the others and offering emendations and improvements. As is true of all books, its preparation has been both enjoyable and burdensome. The burden was inevitable, but was made lighter by the generous and collegial help and support of others. We are grateful to Professor Paul Russell of the Department of Anglo-Saxon, Norse and Celtic Studies, Cambridge, for his insights on the name of Boudica; to Rachel Robertson, a student at the University of British Columbia, Vancouver, for reading part of the manuscript and giving us a student perspective; and to Simon Malloch of the University of Nottingham, who read through the manuscript in an early phase and saved us from a number of embarrassing errors. Any errors that have crept in since then are entirely our own responsibility. Laura Gagné of the University of Ottawa prepared the index for us. Quinn Fusting of Princeton University Press and her predecessor Hannah Paul have guided the manuscript toward publication with efficiency, patience, and quiet encouragement, and we are grateful to them.

A GUIDE TO USING THIS BOOK

The book begins with a general introduction to the reign of Nero. There follow twelve thematic chapters. Each chapter begins with a brief introduction to the general topic of the sources (in those chapters where there are subdivisions, the various sections are prefaced by their own short introductions).

The translated source material then follows, preceded by short summary captions in italics. In the Chapter on Parthia, where the sources follow a chronological sequence, linking texts summarize very briefly those sections in the sequence that have not been translated.

For the sake of clarity, the discussions of coins and inscriptions are enclosed in boxes.

INTRODUCTION

Nero Claudius Caesar Drusus Germanicus was the fifth Roman emperor and, upon his death in AD 68, the last representative of Rome's first imperial dynasty, the Julio-Claudians. In the popular imagination, he is the quintessential vicious tyrant, with a prodigious appetite for villainy. But the fundamental forces that shaped his reign derived not so much from the vagaries of a willful autocrat as from historical developments a century or so earlier.

The republic that followed the expulsion of the Roman kings at the end of the sixth century BC had become almost unmanageable by the first century BC, being characterized by the excesses of a series of powerful military commanders, culminating in the most famous, Julius Caesar. The death of Caesar, on March 15, 44 BC, ushered in a power struggle, from which his great-nephew and (posthumously) adopted son, Octavian, better known by his later title, Augustus, emerged triumphant, following the defeat in 31 BC of the combined forces of Mark Antony and the Egyptian queen Cleopatra at the Battle of Actium. In 27 BC, in a gesture that marked a key stage in the transition from republic to empire, Augustus surrendered the territories under his control to the Senate and people, and they in turn bestowed on him a huge "province." Its extent varied over the years, but at its core lay Gaul, Syria, and Spain. The governors (*legati Augusti*) of the individual provinces that made up these regions were appointed by Augustus. These "imperial" provinces, with minor exceptions, housed the Roman legions, and since Augustus also appointed the individual legionary commanders (*legati legionis*), he had effective control of the armies. The remaining "public" provinces (often somewhat misleadingly called "senatorial") were administered by senators appointed by lot from a regulated pool of candidates. With the defeat of Cleopatra, Egypt fell to the Romans. It became an imperial possession, governed by a prefect appointed by the emperor and drawn from the equestrian order (the "knights"). This last was, broadly, a social rank with a property qualification lower than that of senators and that could engage openly in commercial business (senators would do so more covertly), although many equestrians were simply landowners. The imperial system also led to a new category of salaried administrators, recruited from the ranks of freedmen (former slaves), who helped the imperial bureaucracy to run the now huge empire. They become an observable phenomenon in the reign of Caligula.

Significantly, Augustus acquired certain constitutional rights of the officers originally instituted to safeguard the interests of the plebeians, the plebeian tribunes, although he did not hold the actual office (a contrivance that allowed the republic to function as a monarchy). His tribunician power (*tribunicia potestas*) gave him important privileges, paralleling some of the privileges he exercised while consul. He was entitled through this *potestas* to summon the Senate and the popular assemblies and to introduce or veto legislation. In many ways, this special power lay at the heart of the new imperial system.

With great skill during a lengthy reign, Augustus sought to present himself as merely a leading citizen, a *princeps*, essentially a republican magistrate, albeit with special authority. The basic weakness of a political organism that was neither true republic nor true monarchy was that there was no clear principle of succession. Augustus clearly hoped to be followed by someone of his own bloodline, but he and his wife of many years, Livia, a Claudian by descent, did not produce together a son who survived childhood. Augustus was in fact succeeded, in AD 14, by Livia's son from her previous marriage, the uncharismatic Tiberius. The dynasty that was established, which ended with Nero, is thus referred to as Julio-Claudian, after the two great families. Tiberius in turn had no surviving son, and upon his death in AD 37, he was followed by the preferred candidate of the praetorians (the imperial guard). Their choice was Gaius Caligula, an emperor whose reputation for depravity arguably rivals Nero's. The great-grandson of both Augustus and Livia, Caligula had an excellent pedigree—he traced his descent on his mother's side through Julia, Augustus's only daughter, while his father was the immensely popular Germanicus, grandson of Livia (which made Caligula the brother of Agrippina the Younger, the mother of Nero). But his rule was reckless and irresponsible, and came to an abrupt end with his assassination in AD 41. Once again, the praetorians intervened, and power fell into the hands of Caligula's uncle, the lame and much scorned Claudius, who proved in fact to be a shrewd and able politician. It was during his reign that Nero came to prominence.

Nero was born Lucius Domitius Ahenobarbus in the imperial villa at Antium (Anzio) on December 15, almost certainly in the year AD 37, during the reign of his uncle Caligula (Chapter I). To what extent his later egregious conduct was predetermined by his family line must remain a matter for speculation. His father, Gnaeus Domitius Ahenobarbus, who died during Nero's infancy, belonged to an old and distinguished family, although he does not seem to have lived up to his forebears; Seneca the Elder comments on his laziness, while Suetonius describes him as despicable in every respect. Nero's mother, Agrippina the Younger, was even better connected, and played the key role in his formative years. She was the great-granddaughter of Augustus, daughter of the highly ambitious Agrippina the Elder and her husband Germanicus, and she was the sister of Caligula. At the time of Nero's birth, she enjoyed privilege and prestige as the sister of the reigning emperor.

By 39, things had turned sour. Agrippina and her sister Livilla were suspected of conspiracy and exiled. At some point after that, Nero's father died, and Nero moved to the house of a paternal aunt, Domitia, to await his mother's recall. Agrippina returned in 41, after Caligula's assassination and the subsequent accession of Claudius, and she was now determined to devote her energies to the promotion of her son's prospects. Following the scandalous fall of Messalina, Agrippina married the emperor Claudius, in 49, and in the following year she persuaded Claudius to adopt her son, who thus acquired the elements Nero and Claudius in his name. In 53, Claudius approved the marriage of Nero to his daughter Claudia Octavia. In the meantime, Agrippina worked to secure the advancement of her favorites, most significantly Sextus Afranius Burrus as commander of the praetorian guard. She also secured the return from exile to Rome of the philosopher Seneca the Younger, reputedly her lover. He was to be Nero's tutor, and he wrote *De Clementia* for the guidance of his pupil.

In 54, Claudius died, reputedly poisoned by Agrippina. The news of his death was suppressed until the succession of the sixteen-year-old Nero could be assured. That it proceeded so smoothly is not surprising, since Agrippina had shrewdly replaced the officers of the guard with her own appointees. Nero was taken to the praetorian camp, where he was enthusiastically proclaimed emperor, and the Senate cooperated by conferring the appropriate imperial powers on him (Chapter II). These beginnings may not have seemed auspicious, but the young emperor soon set minds at rest. He was charming and affable, and he went out of his way to reassure senators of his commitment to maintaining their ancient privileges. In his first speech to them, written for him by Seneca, the young Nero promised to model himself on Augustus, noting that he had not been brought up during civil wars and did not come to his position with resentment or a desire for revenge. He promised to keep his private affairs and state affairs separate, he would not countenance bribery or influence peddling, and, perhaps most encouragingly, he would cut down on the practice of trying cases privately *in camera*.

Tacitus observes that Nero was as good as his word, and several beneficial measures followed. There are reports of debates about the rights of freedmen and about jurisdictional issues between praetors and tribunes, of prosecutions of corrupt officials, and of the reorganization of taxes, much of this happening in collaboration with the Senate and creating the impression for Tacitus that some elements of the old free republic remained. In late antiquity, writers attribute to the emperor Trajan the claim that Nero was superior to all other emperors for a *quinquennium* (five-year period), more likely than not with reference to these first five years.

The initial phase of the new reign was highly promising, and in this early period Nero was willing to be directed by the praetorian commander Burrus and by his former tutor, Seneca. They served to counter the excessive ambitions of Agrippina, who occupied a central position in the first few months, even to the extent of appearing with her son on his precious metal coinage. But control seems to have been ceded very soon to Burrus and Seneca, and it is interesting to note that even in his first emollient speech, written for him by Seneca, as noted, Nero had made an explicit point of distancing himself from some of the practices of the Claudian period. Agrippina's role was gradually diminished, and she eventually became alienated from her son. By the end of 55, she seems to have withdrawn from any active role in political events.

For all its enlightenment, the first *quinquennium* was not free of dark political shadows (Chapter III). In 55, Claudius's natural son Britannicus died, and Nero was suspected of poisoning him, although his guilt cannot be determined. Also, Faustus Cornelius Sulla, Nero's cousin, was exiled as a potential rival in 58. He had close connections to the imperial family and was the husband of Antonia, Claudius's daughter, and might thus have been seen as a threat to Nero. But it was from 59, Nero's fifth year as emperor that things started to go seriously downhill. In that year, Nero determined to rid himself of Agrippina. Why this occurred at this particular time is not fully understood, since Agrippina had not apparently played any major role in affairs of state since 55. Tacitus claims unconvincingly that Agrippina reasserted herself because of her opposition to an affair that Nero was conducting with Poppaea Sabina, at that time the wife of the future emperor Otho. The tradition tells of an elaborate, if perhaps unbelievable, scheme of a collapsing boat that failed to work properly, and has Agrippina swimming to safety, only to be butchered by agents sent by her son to finish her off.

Whether or not there is a causal connection, Nero's conduct after the murder of his mother became far more egregious and far more despotic. The good will that had accumulated in the first five years dissipated. Without the catalyst of Agrippina's interference, Nero found the guidance of Seneca and Burrus no less irksome than he had found his mother's interference, and he increasingly went his own way.

The most striking manifestation of this willfulness was a growing obsession with public performance. Ironically, Nero's interest in poetry had been fostered by Seneca, who had discouraged him from reading the early orators, and he had turned to verses, which he was able to compose with considerable facility; Martial, for one, thought highly of his skill as a poet (*Mart.* 8.70.8). Nero's artistic aspirations now seem to have become obsessive. He founded new games. The *Iuvenalia* of 59, instituted to celebrate the first trimming of his beard, involved theatrical performances. The Quinquennial Games (*Neronia*) of 61 combined in the Greek fashion chariot races and the musical arts. To the shame of traditionalists, Nero began to perform in public, choosing a Greek city, Naples, for his debut, in AD 64 (Chapter IX).

Outside Rome, matters seem generally to have been handled competently. The Rhine frontier remained stable, the serious rebellion of Boudica and its aftermath in Britain in the early 60s was brought to a successful end (Chapter V), and in 63 peace was concluded with Parthia (Chapter IV). But domestically, the reign began a descent into tyranny. Gaius Rubellius Plautus, great-grandson of Tiberius (through his granddaughter Julia), had lived a life of undistinguished obscurity. That said, he seems to have attracted the same dynastic suspicion that brought down Faustus Sulla. In 60, he was obliged to go into exile (Chapter III). Events took an especially serious turn for the worse in 62, when treason trials, which had initially been suspended, were reintroduced in response to the publication of scurrilous verses attacking Nero. The death of Burrus in the same year no doubt accelerated the process of decline. Seneca attempted unsuccessfully to retire; Nero's refusal to accede to his request may have had less to do with any residual respect for Seneca's counsel than with the prestige that the philosopher's name gave his regime. Nero was now dependent mainly on the malign advice of Tigellinus, the sinister commander of the praetorian guard, appointed to replace Burrus. The murders of the exiled Rubellius Plautus and Cornelius Sulla, and the reluctance of the Senate to condemn their deaths, perhaps emboldened Nero in 62 to divorce the popular Octavia in order to marry Poppaea Sabina (Chapter VII). A bogus affair between Octavia and a freedman was concocted to provide grounds. Her subsequent execution represented a landmark in the estrangement of Nero and the traditional nobility, and the consequent bitterness is reflected in the tragedy inspired by her death, the *Octavia*, once assigned to Seneca but more probably Flavian in date. Poppaea was pregnant at the time of her marriage, and in January 63 bore a daughter, Claudia Augusta, who died four months later and was declared a goddess.

Another turning point in Nero's reign occurred in July 64, when much of Rome was destroyed in a devastating fire that began in the area of the Campus Martius and spread between the Palatine and the Esquiline (Chapter VI). Overcrowded streets and timber buildings meant that fire was a constant concern in Rome, but this conflagration was unprecedented in its scale. Only four of Rome's fourteen districts were untouched; three were destroyed completely. Nero's conduct seems to have been beyond reproach. He was in his birthplace, Antium (Anzio), many miles away, when the fire broke out. He returned to the city immediately and personally took measures to counter the blaze, creating firebreaks and setting controlled fires. This last strategy seems to have been misunderstood, and created suspicion that he had deliberately committed arson. He organized schemes to feed the newly homeless, to provide a water supply, and later to remove massive amounts of debris. He set up a compensation scheme for those who had lost their houses. He also took the opportunity to redesign the layout of the Roman streets, making them much wider than before, and to require houses to be built to a much more stringent fire-prevention code. The centerpiece of the new Rome was to be his own residence, the "Golden House" (*Domus Aurea*), a splendid structure situated next to a lake and embraced by quiet groves. Nero's scheme was so ambitious that it fed suspicions that he had burned down the city deliberately. The notion of arson was fostered by rumors that he had watched the conflagration from a tower while dressed up as a performer and had read out his great epic on the fall of Troy, "fiddling while Rome burned," as later generations would characterize his behavior.

In 65, a major conspiracy took place, said by Tacitus to represent every class and rank of Roman society, rich and poor, but centered on Gaius Calpurnius Piso (Chapter VIII). The plot was both poorly organized and poorly concealed, and the revenge was ruthless and virtually indiscriminate. Notable among the victims were the poet Lucan and Nero's former tutor, Seneca, who found himself implicated after the event and committed suicide. Later in the same year, Poppaea died, reputedly kicked to death by Nero while pregnant, but in reality perhaps from a miscarriage. She was granted a public funeral and divine honors (Chapter VII).

Nero did gain some advantage when he established peace with Parthia and marked the event with a grand spectacle (Chapter IX). Tiridates I, the Parthian king of Armenia, was invited to Rome in 66 and was entertained with lavish games. But such spectacles barely concealed the political tensions. In 66, Thrasea Paetus, a Stoic and perhaps the most admired senator of his day, was forced into suicide for his overt lack of enthusiasm for the regime. Nero did, however, feel secure enough to be able to leave Italy and to embark on a tour of the eastern provinces, leaving his freedman Helios to look after affairs in Italy. The trip gave the emperor the opportunity to indulge his philhellenism. He took part in artistic festivals and managed to win every prize. At Corinth, Nero declared the Greeks exempt from taxation, a measure that proved to be short-lived but was enough to establish his popularity in that part of the empire (Chapter IX). But, clearly, all was not well. While in the East, Nero removed from office and put to death three imperial legates, the distinguished Gnaeus Domitius Corbulo, who had given excellent service in Germany and Armenia, and the brothers Scribonius Proculus and Scribonius Rufus, legates of Upper and Lower Germany, respectively.

The fatal threat to Nero would come from the western provinces (Chapter X). Helios anticipated the looming crisis, urging Nero to return to Italy, which he did in late 67. The problems came to a climax in March 68 with the rebellion in Gaul of Gaius Julius Vindex, and the revolt of respected senator and soldier Servius Sulpicius Galba, at that time commanding in Spain. Vindex was in fact defeated and killed two months later, but Nero proved incapable of responding to the crisis effectively, alternating between panic and inertia. Galba eventually showed his hand, openly rebelling against the emperor and reporting to the Senate that he was at their disposal. The unrest spread to Africa, where Lucius Clodius Macer revolted. At the instigation of one of the prefects, the imperial guard switched its support to Galba, and the Senate declared Nero a public enemy. He was obliged to escape to a private villa, where he took his own life with the help of faithful slaves. As his final resting place was being prepared, he supposedly uttered words famous in antiquity as well as now, *qualis artifex pereo* ("what an artist dies in me!").

Nero was clearly neither a competent nor an admirable emperor, but he was especially unlucky in his earliest historical coverage and was discredited by the Flavian emperors who, after some months of turbulence, succeeded him. In this Flavian period, Pliny the Elder called him "poison . . . for the world" (*HN* 22.92) and said of him and the earlier emperor Caligula that they were "the fiery destruction of the human race" (*HN* 7.45), and such judgments in this initial period must have played a major role in shaping the image that emerged in later writers. The negative view of Nero was reinforced by later Christian authors like Tertullian and Lactantius, who vilified him as the Antichrist. That said, after his death, no fewer than three pretenders claiming to be Nero appeared in the East at regular intervals. They received a welcome reception in some quarters, indicating that Nero was not universally unpopular.

LITERARY SOURCES

The study of any historical period is dependent on the range and quality of the sources available. The study of ancient history faces, to a greater or lesser degree, a special challenge, since the source material is often scarce and of dubious value. Hence, a very brief introduction to the topic as it relates to Nero will not be out of place.

Most of the contemporary literary sources for the reign of Nero are now missing and have left traces only in passing references in the surviving authors who made use of them. There are the works written by the members of the imperial family themselves. Claudius, for instance, wrote an autobiography in eight volumes, consulted by Nero but dismissed by Suetonius as nonsense "more lacking in judgment than lacking in style" (Suet. *Claud.* 41.2; Tac. *Ann.* 13.43.4). For the present topic, the most important composition in this category is the memoir of Nero's mother, Agrippina, cited directly by both Pliny the Elder (*HN* 7.46) and Tacitus (*Ann.* 4.53.3). Broadly speaking, however, imperial writings seem not to have been heavily drawn on. The degree to which other contemporary writers are used by our extant sources is much disputed. The Neronian volumes of Tacitus's *Annals* stand out from the rest of that work, and from the two other main sources, Suetonius and Cassius Dio, for the way in which Tacitus actually cites the historians he used (not his practice in the earlier books). None of the writings of two of them, Marcus Cluvius Rufus and Fabius Rusticus, has survived. The historian Cluvius Rufus served as the herald of Nero when he performed in Rome, and was assigned the same duty when Nero went on his Greek tour in 67 (Suet. *Ner.* 21.2; Dio 63.14.3). All of Tacitus's references to him relate to the reign of Nero, although he might well have been cited also in the Caligulan or Claudian chapters now lost. The second writer, Fabius Rusticus, was much admired by Quintilian (10.1.104) and was praised by Tacitus as the most eloquent of the moderns (*Agr.* 10.3). He appears along with Tacitus and Pliny in the will of a wealthy Spaniard, Lucius Dasumius of Cordoba, drawn up in AD 108. He published a history, probably in the Flavian period. Little is known about it, but it was used by Tacitus as a source for the reign of Nero (*Ann.*13.20.2, 15.61.3).

On one occasion (*Ann.* 14.2), Tacitus weighs the contrasting evidence of both Cluvius and Fabius on the question of who instigated the reported incest between Nero and his mother. Despite his general admiration of Fabius, here he follows Cluvius, who assigns the blame to Agrippina. At *Ann.*13.20.2, Tacitus cites these two, along with the elder Pliny, on the issue of whether Nero questioned his praetorian prefect Burrus's loyalty in AD 55. The information from Pliny would have come from a now lost work, his *History*, written in thirty books. That work must also be the source for Pliny's claim, ridiculed by Tacitus, that Claudius's daughter Antonia intended to marry the conspirator Piso (*Ann.* 15.53.3–4). All three of these contemporary sources seem to have been anti-Neronian; unnamed historians mentioned by Josephus (*Ant.* 20.154) as favorable to the emperor have been lost without a trace. Tacitus also cites the memoirs of the general Domitius Corbulo and the testimony of the survivors of the Pisonian conspiracy (*Ann.* 15.73.2). Suetonius and Dio almost certainly drew on some of the same sources, and they do indeed assert that they used several authorities, but, unlike Tacitus, they do not name them.

The works of two writers who lived under Nero and wrote about him have survived. Seneca the Younger (before AD 1–65) spent considerable time in Nero's company before his succession, serving for much of his reign as his tutor and later as his adviser. One of Seneca's extant works, *De Clementia,* was written to offer Nero guidance as ruler, but it yields very little direct historical information. Senecan authorship is claimed for a work set in the early part of Nero's reign, the *Apocolocyntosis,* a witty treatment of the death of Claudius and of his reception in the next world, eulogistically effusive about Nero. Seneca was also a writer of tragedies. One group of manuscripts of his plays includes a work relating to the divorce and execution of Nero's wife, *Octavia.* The play postdates Seneca, since it contains a clear reference to Nero's death, and is so hostile to the emperor that it could not have been performed during his lifetime. It is commonly assigned to the Vespasianic period.

Although the *History* of Pliny the Elder (AD 23/24–79), as noted, is lost, his great encyclopedia, *Naturalis Historia,* has survived. Published in thirty-seven books, it provides information on a vast range of topics from the ancient world. References to Nero and his reign are scattered throughout and are hostile in tone. On one occasion, Pliny drew on the memoir of Agrippina, for the information that Nero was born by a breech birth (*HN* 7.46).

There are three surviving "main" sources for the reign of Nero. Tacitus (mid-50s–after 118) is generally acknowledged to be the premier historian of the Julio-Claudian period. Born about the time that Nero succeeded Claudius as emperor, he pursued a successful career under the Flavians, which he capped with a series of important historical writings. In 97–98, he undertook the *Agricola,* a record of the career of his father-in-law, Gnaeus Julius Agricola. The work is something of an encomium of its subject but also an attack on Domitian, whose despotic regime may well have helped shape Tacitus's general views on the principate. By 100, Tacitus had written his *Histories,* which covered the victories and the rule of the Flavian dynasty (only the first four books and fragments of the fifth survive), and then turned to an earlier period for his final and most famous work, the *Annals,* which was intended to cover the period from the accession of Tiberius in 14 to the death of Nero in 68. We do not know when he began, but he was well into the work in 116, since he appears to allude to Trajan's final victory over the

Parthians at that time (*Ann.* 4.5.2). The *Annals* seems to be designed in three hexads (groups of six books), the first covering Tiberius, the second Caligula and Claudius, and the third Nero. Books 1–6 (5 is very fragmentary) have survived, covering the reign of Tiberius, along with Books 11–16 (11 and 16 are not complete), beginning midway through Claudius's reign and breaking off two years before the end of Nero's. We cannot even be sure that Tacitus had finished the *Annals* when he died.

Tacitus seems to have flourished under the imperial system, even under the despised and oppressive Domitian. Yet there is no doubting the antipathy that emerges from the *Annals*. Tacitus was profoundly opposed to the principate as a constitutional form and was committed to the old aristocratic system of senatorial government. He could, of course, recognize the benefits of an enlightened ruler such as Trajan, but he felt that the system was inherently deleterious. Hence, we should be cautious about his famous claim to write *sine ira et studio*, "without rancor or bias" (*Ann.* 1.1), an echo of the claim made in the *Histories* "without partiality and without hatred" (*Hist.* 1.1). It is indeed the case that he rarely seems to present facts dishonestly. But behind the simple facts lurk his own prejudices. His assignment of motives, and his coverage of rumors and allegedly generally held beliefs, cannot help but make an impact on the reader. That said, Tacitus's bias does not induce him to accept rumors at face value, and on those rare occasions when he cites his sources, he can be critical of them. Generally speaking, while clearly hostile, Tacitus is prepared to report favorable checks on some of the outrages attributed to Nero. As an example, he expresses skepticism about Nero's responsibility for the Great Fire and is the only one of the three main sources to do so.

Tacitus does on occasion refer to the use of direct oral evidence. His use of archival information is not so clear-cut. One potentially important source would have been the deliberations of the Senate. Once senatorial decrees (*consulta*) were passed, copies of their texts were deposited in the treasury, and this was probably true also of their general proceedings, the *acta Senatus*, although we do not know how detailed those proceedings might have been. Scholars such as Ronald Syme have argued that Tacitus's stature as a historian is largely the result of his wide use of senatorial records, and many of the details in the *Annals*, such as the proposals and counterproposals with names attached to them, imply the use of such material. A recently discovered decree has in fact given us the opportunity to compare Tacitus's narrative and the primary evidence. The decree passed by the Senate on December 10, 20, following the trial of Cornelius Piso on a charge of murdering Germanicus (the *senatus consultum de Cn. Pisone Patre*), has come to light in fragments found in Spain, allowing us to test Tacitus's account of the trial and subsequent events. It demonstrates that he drew considerably on the decree and to a large degree represents it faithfully. The difficulty is that while his account undoubtedly derives from that primary source, we do not know whether it comes from his own direct personal consultation or through an intermediary. Perhaps surprisingly, there is only one instance of Tacitus recording a direct scrutiny of the records, in the aftermath of the Pisonian conspiracy, where he says that he finds in the *commentarii senatus* that the consul designate Cerialis Anicius proposed a temple be erected to the Divine Nero (*Ann.* 15.74.3).

Gaius Suetonius Tranquillus was born, possibly in North Africa, in around AD 70. He was an equestrian and held a number of imperial appointments under Trajan and Hadrian, being at one point director of the imperial archives. He wrote prolifically and widely, the twelve *Lives of the Caesars* being his most familiar work. The structure of the individual lives tends to follow a certain pattern, and he will generally describe at the outset each subject's family background, childhood, education, and entry into public life. Then, at the end, he describes the details of the subject's death, often the length of his reign, and his burial, all in broad chronological order. In between, in the body of the text, there are sections dealing with physical characteristics, private pursuits, and involvement in civil and military activities. Here Suetonius generally organizes his material by topic rather than in chronological sequence, assuming that his reader is broadly familiar with the events. Within this scheme, the individualities of each emperor will be brought out; in Nero's case, the emphasis is on how he used his position as emperor as a platform to realize his love of public performance and to pursue his personal artistic ambitions.

Suetonius is a biographer, not a historian. He is generally uninterested in serious political questions if they do not cast light on the personality of his subject, on whom he places his complete focus. (For instance, he does not mention Corbulo, the great general of the Neronian campaigns against Parthia, in *Nero*.) Generally, he is not motivated by the deep hostility that inspired Tacitus. His main weakness is not *ira et studium*, and indeed, in the case of Nero, he does include items that he says do not garner criticism—*nulla reprehensione* (Suet. *Ner.* 19.3). Far more serious is his willingness to lend an ear to the tales handed down by the tradition. He was in fact more than capable of serious research, at times making use of public records and archival sources, and he can be very skeptical of his literary sources. When he conducts his own investigations (such as on the birthplace of Caligula), the results can in fact be impressive. But his skepticism does not prevent him from repeating the frivolous gossip that his sources often transmit, and he cannot resist a juicy anecdote, leaving it to the reader to exercise a judgment that modern historians would feel is the responsibility of the narrator. Suetonius also has a tendency to take isolated and very discrete incidents and to present them as though they reflect the general and consistent behavior of his subjects.

Suetonius probably wrote about Nero very soon after Tacitus wrote his *Annals*. Whether he made use of Tacitus or if the *Annals*, in particular the Neronian chapters, were even available for Suetonius when he wrote his *Nero* are contentious issues. He certainly does not generally seem to have derived his information from Tacitus, instead going back to earlier sources. Nevertheless, he does occasionally seem to make pointed references to his superior research, the most famous instance being in a non-Neronian context, the debate over the birthplace of Caligula (Suet. *Cal.* 8). In his *Nero*, he goes out of his way to say that he had seen autographed copies of Nero's poems with emendations and corrections (Suet. *Ner.* 52), implicitly criticizing the implication of Tacitus that the poems were plagiarized (Tac. *Ann.* 14.16.1).

The third main literary source for Nero is Cassius Dio (ca. 164–after 229), a senator from Nicaea in Asia Minor. His history, in Greek, appears to have covered Rome from the time of the early kings down to Severus Alexander (222–235). He writes very much from a senator's perspective and is extremely hostile to Nero. Dio could not be called an analytical historian; generally, he assembles facts without attempting any kind of deep synthesis, and where he lays out a view it is germane only to the topic at hand and is not part of a reasoned theoretical framework. Throughout his history, Dio very rarely cites his sources, and he makes little endeavor to distinguish between credible and absurd information. His main value generally is that, like Tacitus, he treats Nero's reign annalistically, and he can thus provide us with a sequence of events for the last two years of that reign, information missing from Tacitus's *Annals*, which break off in the middle of AD 66. Unfortunately, however, the original text of Dio for the reign is missing, and we are dependent on the epitomes made in the Byzantine period. Since these epitomes are more selections than summaries proper, important topics that he might have covered seem to be omitted in their entirety. Dio is far more hostile to Nero than Tacitus and Suetonius were.

Elements common to Dio, on the one hand, and to Tacitus or Suetonius, or both, on the other, may derive from their use of the same sources rather than from mutual borrowings. Dio often has details missing from Tacitus; as an example, his unflattering comments about Seneca suggest a source other than the pro-Senecan Fabius used by Tacitus.

As well as the literary evidence, there are also inscriptions, and, for our purposes, one of the most important sources of epigraphic evidence is the record of the Arval brothers. The cult's center was located some four miles west of Rome at the shrine of Dea Dia, although some of its rites were celebrated in the city itself. The college was made up of twelve members, as well as the emperor, and most of what we know about it comes from the record of its own proceedings. At some point, the Arvals started to keep a record in stone, and this record, albeit very fragmentary in places, survives from 21 BC to AD 304. The imperial family has a prominent place in the rituals, and imperial birthdays and other important anniversaries are routinely noted. The Arval record can be useful at a basic level for providing information on such items as the day and month of Nero's adoption by Claudius and at times for showing when prominent individuals were in the vicinity of Rome.

It might be noted that monetary amounts are usually given in the ancient sources in sestertii, and we have adopted that practice generally. It is not possible to cite precise monetary equivalents, but it can be noted that in the Julio-Claudian period soldiers in the legions were paid 900 sestertii (225 denarii) annually, before deductions.

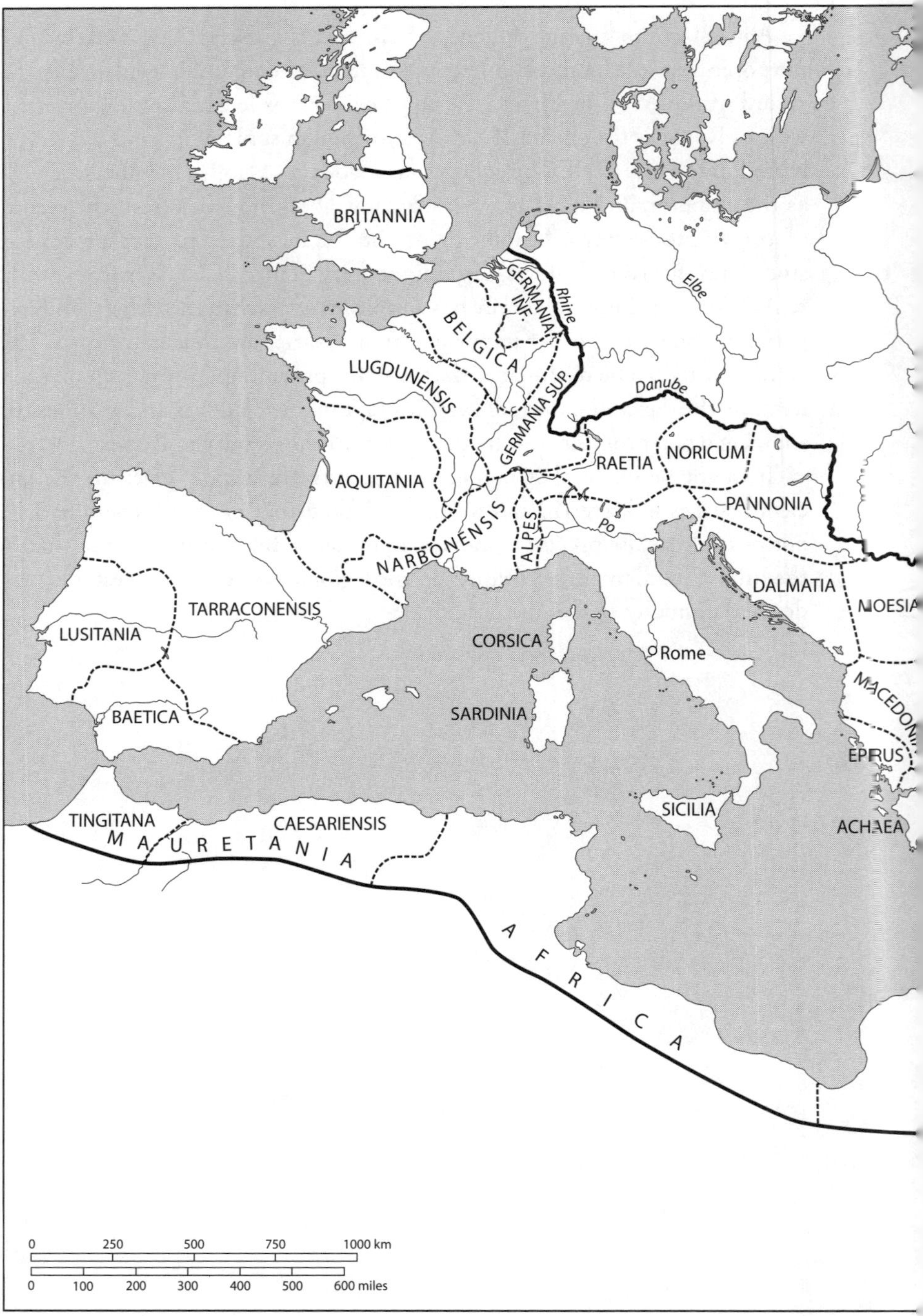

MAP 1. The Roman Empire under Nero

Danube
THRACIA
PONTUS ET BITHYNIA
GALATIA
CAPPADOCIA
ARMENIA
Tigris
ASIA
LYCIA
CILICIA
P A R T H I A
Athens
Euphrates
SYRIA
CYPRUS
CRETA
JUDAEA
ARABIA
CYRENE
AEGYPTUS
Nile

MAJOR EVENTS DURING NERO'S LIFETIME

All dates are AD

37	(Accession of Caligula)
	Probable Birth of Nero
39	Exile of Agrippina
40 or 41	Death of Gnaeus Domitius (father)
41	Accession of Claudius
	Recall of Agrippina
49	Marriage of Agrippina and Claudius
	Betrothal of Nero and Octavia
50	Adoption of Nero by Claudius
53	Marriage of Nero and Octavia
54	Death of Claudius
	Accession of Nero
	Tensions with Parthia
55	Death of Britannicus
58	Exile of Cornelius Sulla
59	Death of Agrippina
60	Rebellion of Boudica
	Exile of Rubellius Plautus
62	Marriage to Poppaea Sabina
	Deaths of Rubellius Plautus and Cornelius Sulla
63	Birth and Death of Daughter, Claudia Augusta
	Submission of Parthians
64	Fire of Rome
	Nero's Performance in Naples
65	Pisonian Conspiracy
66	Marriage to Statilia Messalina
	Death of Petronius
	Tiridates in Rome
	Conspiracy of Vinicianus
	Departure of Nero for Greece
68	Return of Nero to Italy
	Rebellion of Vindex
	Death of Nero

THE EMPEROR NERO

I

THE MAKING OF THE EMPEROR

INTRODUCTION

It has often been observed that the primary weakness of the system established by Augustus was the absence of a clear formula for succession. It is certainly the case that after Julius Caesar every one of the Julio-Claudian emperors seemed at some early stage of his life to have been among the least likely candidates to become emperor. Augustus was an obscure student with a relatively modest family background when he learned that he had been adopted posthumously by Julius Caesar and made his subsequent bid for power. Tiberius enters the historical record as an infant when his parents were fleeing for their lives from Naples during the clashes between Antony and Octavian, and he almost betrayed their presence by crying. Even after his mother had married the future emperor, he spent a period of humiliating self-exile on the island of Rhodes, convinced that he was perpetually sidelined in the competition to succeed. Caligula might not even have escaped with his life had he been older. His two brothers were both put to death as a consequence of the bitter dynastic rivalries instigated largely by Sejanus. Caligula's successor, Claudius, who was neither a natural nor an adopted descendant of Augustus, had spent his youth hidden from public view and was so far from being a serious contender for the principate that he was considered an embarrassment to his family. By the end of Claudius's reign, Nero's father, a man noted for his mediocrity and laziness, was dead, and Nero's mother was in disgraced exile. Even after the succession of Claudius and the recall of Agrippina, Nero would spend his early youth in relative obscurity until the intrusion of his mother into the political scene in Rome.

Like Tiberius, Nero became emperor because of the single-minded and focused ambition of his mother (and, like Tiberius, he resented the idea that he owed his elevation to that agency). After her return from exile, Agrippina acquired a new husband, and presumably also acquired much of his considerable fortune upon his death. We cannot tell if she played any role in the downfall of Claudius's wife Messalina (whose behavior was so reckless that she in all likelihood brought about her own ruin, without any assistance from outside). But it is certainly the case that Agrippina saw the opportunity that the demise of Messalina offered, and exploited it relentlessly. She could provide Claudius with a much needed link to Augustus, since she was his granddaughter in a direct bloodline, and, with her son Nero, she enabled Claudius to take the wind out of the sails of any violent opposition to his reign by holding out the prospect of ultimately being succeeded by a direct Augustan descendant. Claudius was first and foremost a political animal, and if his political survival meant that his own natural son would be forced into a subordinate position, then that was a price he was willing to pay. Hence, after his marriage, which was technically illegal and required a special measure of the Senate because Agrippina was his brother's daughter, he agreed to adopt Nero. The adoption also necessitated a technical dispensation from the law, because Claudius already had a son. Claudius then agreed to his new son's marriage to his daughter Octavia, who was of course technically his sister and in yet another piece of legal legerdemain was adopted by another family to make the marriage legitimate. Claudius was prepared to overcome all of these formidable obstacles for his own self-preservation. Apparently, he did not stop to consider that these survival measures had the fatal flaw that while they made him more secure against external rivals, they generated a new rival in the form of the very individual meant to protect him, his adopted son Nero, and that once Claudius had, in the eyes of his wife, fulfilled his necessary role, she might be inclined, and the ancient sources generally agree that she was inclined, to play out her own role, that of a dynastic black widow spider.

Agrippina had in fact prepared the ground very skillfully. She removed the key supporters of Britannicus from his household staff, leaving him without close advisers and allies in any potential struggle for the succession that might ensue. Most importantly, she had, many years before the issue came to a head, ensured that her own man, Sextus Afranius Burrus, took command of the praetorian guard. Then, in an even more striking display of her capacity for carefully preparing the ground, over time she replaced the officers of the guard, the tribunes and centurions, with her own candidates, not by dismissing or demoting those not in her camp but more skillfully by bribing them with promotions to positions in the legions well away from Rome in the frontier regions. This meant that in December 54 the loyalty of the guard in Rome was a done deal. One can only speculate on how many of these same dislodged officers would still be serving, by then in senior positions, in AD 68, in legions that needed little urging to abandon Nero.

SOURCES

Suetonius provides information about Nero's general nature and appearance.

Suet. *Ner.* 51. Nero was of about average height, with a body that was blotchy and malodorous, hair that was almost blond, a face more agreeable than attractive, grey eyes that were rather weak, a thick neck, protruding stomach, spindly legs, and health that was robust. Indeed, despite his life of most decadent luxury, he was ill only three times during his fourteen-year reign, and even then not seriously enough to give up drinking or his other habits.[1] In his personal grooming and dress, he was so outrageous as to have his hair always layered, and on his Achaean travels even let it grow long behind his head. He also frequently went out into the streets in dining attire, with a napkin tied around his neck and wearing no waistband or shoes.[2]

52. When he was a boy, he engaged in practically all the liberal arts.[3] His mother, however, turned him away from philosophy by warning him that it was not in a future emperor's interests,[4] while his teacher Seneca, in order to prolong his student's admiration for him, steered him away from studying the orators of old.[5]

Suetonius begins the Life of Nero *with an account of the emperor's family background. Romans made much of the notion of inherited family traits and, by putting his focus on the shortcomings of Nero's ancestors, Suetonius seeks to suggest that his character failings were inherited. His narrative takes him down to*

1 Tacitus (*Ann.* 14.22.4) reports under AD 60 that Nero fell seriously ill after bathing in one of the aqueducts, the Aqua Marcia. Later (*Ann.* 14.47.1), he reports that Nero was seriously ill at the time of the death of the distinguished Publius Memmius Regulus in AD 61; this may or may not be a separate occasion from the Aqua Marcia episode.

2 Dio (63.9.1) refers to Nero having long hair at the time he went on his Greek tour. The *Apocolocyntosis* (4.1) speaks of Nero's radiant countenance framed by the flowing locks that encircled his shoulders.

3 We have little information on Nero's early education. The names of two of his tutors, Anicetus and Beryllus, are known, mainly because they reached high station later (Joseph. *Ant.* 20.183; Tac. *Ann.* 14.3.3). They were probably charged with imparting rudimentary skills to the young Nero.

4 Tacitus (*Agr.* 4.3) reports that Agricola was similarly discouraged by his mother from an excessive interest in philosophy.

5 Tacitus (*Ann.* 13.2.1) indicates that rhetoric was the main element in Seneca's curriculum. Suetonius suggests that Nero was directed away from the "early" orators, presumably Cicero and his predecessors and contemporaries, in favor of the more forceful and aggressive style practiced under the principate.

the time of Nero's grandfather, Lucius Domitius Ahenobarbus, consul in 16 BC, whose marriage to Antonia the Elder, daughter of Mark Antony and Octavia, sister of Augustus, was a sure sign of the eminence that the family had acquired by the end of the Republic.

Suet. 5.1. By the elder Antonia, Domitius had as a son Nero's father, who was in every aspect of his life thoroughly detestable.[6] Indeed, while a member of the staff of a young Gaius Caesar in the East, he murdered a freedman of his because the man had refused to drink as much as he was ordered to, and when he was dismissed from the staff, his life was no more disciplined.[7] In a village on the Appian Way, he suddenly brought his team of horses to a gallop and deliberately trampled down a boy, and then in the middle of the Forum in Rome he gouged out the eye of a Roman *eques* for reprimanding him too freely. 2. Moreover, such was his lack of integrity that he not only swindled some bankers out of their payment for items bought for him but also in his praetorship cheated a number of charioteers out of their prize money. When he was the butt of his sister's joking over this, and managers of the racing factions lodged a complaint, he issued a decree that—in the future!—prize money must be paid immediately. A little before Tiberius's death, he was arraigned on charges of treason, adultery, and incest with his sister Lepida.[8] He evaded them through the change of regime and died of dropsy at Pyrgi, having formally recognized Nero, his son by Germanicus's daughter Agrippina.[9]

6 Nero's grandfather, Lucius Domitius Ahenobarbus (consul 16 BC), married Antonia the Elder, daughter of Mark Antony and Octavia, who was the sister of Augustus. His son, Gnaeus Domitius, father of Nero, was born on December 11 (the month and day are attested in the Arval record of AD 57: Smallwood 19.22); Suetonius's characterization of Gnaeus as "in every aspect of his life thoroughly detestable" serves his agenda of putting Nero's character faults in an ancestral context. Elsewhere we get an impression of Gnaeus's lazy insouciance. Seneca the Elder reports that Domitius's own mother was troubled by his lack of ambition, since his priorities seem to have been to build a baths annex to his house and then start to seek out the company of rhetoricians and spend his time declaiming (Sen. *Contr.* 9.4.18).

7 Gnaeus Domitius Ahenobarbus married Agrippina in AD 28 and was consul in 32 (unusually, for the whole year, as noted by Dio 58.20.1). The date of the consulship indicates that he would have been too young for service in 1 BC, and Suetonius may have confused Gaius Caesar's mission with the later one of Germanicus to the East, in AD 17.

8 Gnaeus's last recorded public service was in AD 36, during Tiberius's reign, when he served as commissioner to assess fire damage in Rome (Tac. *Ann.* 6.45.2). Tacitus (*Ann.* 6.47.2) suggests that in AD 37 he was one of the lovers and collaborators of Albucilla and was accused of *maiestas* (treason), largely through the machinations of Macro, commander of the praetorian guard. Only Suetonius mentions the charge of incest.

9 The date of his death is uncertain; it probably occurred in late 40 or early 41 AD.

Nero's birth was noteworthy.

Plin. *HN* 7.8.45. It is unnatural for a child to be born feet first, and for that reason people have called such cases "Agrippas," the birth being "difficult."[10] Such they say was the manner of Marcus Agrippa's birth, he being almost the only example of success among all those born in this way.[11] And yet he, too, is reckoned to have expiated the omen of his inverted birth with his youth made wretched by lameness, with his life spent in warfare and so close to death's door, and with all his progeny bringing misfortune to the earth, especially the two Agrippinas, who bore respectively the emperors Gaius and Domitius Nero, a pair of firebrands to scorch the human race. 46. There was, in addition, his short life span: he was taken off in his fifty-first year, suffering the torments of his wife's adulterous affairs and enduring truly oppressive subservience to his father-in-law.

Nero, too, who was emperor a little while ago and who in his entire principate was the enemy of the human race, was also born feet first, so his mother Agrippina records. It is nature's way for a human to be born head first and taken out for burial feet first.[12]

Nero's parents are divided by deep antipathy.

Dio 61.2.1. The following were omens of Nero's coming rule. When he was born, rays of light surrounded him just before dawn although they came from no observable sunlight.[13] On the basis of this, and from the movement of the stars at that time and their position relative to each other, an astrologer

10 In claiming that people born by breech birth were called "Agrippas," Pliny derives that word from the phrase *aegre partus* ("born with difficulty"), a fanciful etymology found also in Aulus Gellius (*NA*. 16.16.1).

11 Marcus Vipsanius Agrippa was a longtime companion of Augustus. They were raised together in Rome, and Agrippa accompanied the future emperor to Apollonia, returning with him to Rome upon the death of Caesar. A number of important commands followed, most notably at Actium. Although there were tensions when Agrippa was passed over in the succession in favor of Augustus's nephew Marcellus, upon the death of the latter, Agrippa married Augustus's headstrong daughter Julia. Their children included Gaius and Lucius Caesar, and Agrippina the Elder, the mother of Caligula and grandmother of Nero. Agrippa died in March of 12 BC and was buried in the mausoleum of Augustus (Dio 54.28.5).

12 Pliny refers here to the memoirs of Agrippina the Younger (see Introduction). These memoirs are cited only once more; Tacitus found in them the report that Agrippina the Elder unsuccessfully petitioned Tiberius to allow her to remarry (Tac. *Ann*. 4.53.2).

13 See the appendix to this chapter, on Nero's birthdate.

made two prophecies about him: he would rule and he would kill his mother. 2. When she heard this, Agrippina was momentarily so deranged as to cry out the very words "Let him kill me, only let him rule," though she would later have bitter regrets about the prayer.[14] Some people reach such a pitch of folly that, if they anticipate gaining something good that is mixed with something bad, they, in their desire for the better thing, give no thought to the bad, but when the time for that comes, they are distressed and would have preferred not to have accepted even the very best of things. 3. However, with regard to Nero's amorality and lechery, his father Domitius saw them coming, and not from prophecy but from his own character and that of Agrippina. "It is impossible," he said, "for any good man to be born from me and this woman." 4. Time went by, and a snakeskin was found around the neck of Nero while he was a child.[15] This allowed the seers to say that he would acquire great strength from the old, since snakes are believed to throw off old age by discarding it.

Suet. *Ner.* 6.1. Nero was born at Antium nine months after Tiberius's death, on December 15, just as the sun was rising, so that he was touched by its rays almost before he was touched by the earth.[16] With regard to his horoscope, there were many fearful predictions made by many people, added to which was the ominous remark of his father, Domitius, uttered amid the congratulations of his friends, that nothing could have been born from him and Agrippina that was not odious and a scourge on the state. 2. Another clear pointer to the man's unpromising future came on his purification day.[17] When Gaius Caesar's sister asked him to give the baby any name he liked, he fixed his eyes on his uncle Claudius (who soon became emperor, and by whom Nero was adopted) and said he was giving the child his name. How-

14 On the prophecy, see Tac. *Ann.* 14.9.3 (Chapter III).

15 The association between Nero and the snakes appears in different versions in Suetonius and Tacitus.

16 Antium (Anzio) was a colony of some antiquity on the coast south of Rome. It was a popular resort for well-to-do Romans, and a particular favorite of the Julio-Claudians. Augustus liked to stay there, and it was almost certainly the birthplace of Caligula, despite Tacitus's assertion that Caligula was born in a legionary camp (Tac. *Ann.* 1.41.2; Suet. *Cal.* 8). Also, Nero's daughter Claudia Augusta was born there (Tac. *Ann.* 15.23.1). There are traces of an imperial villa with terraces, known as the "Villa Neroniana," which underwent major construction by emperors from Augustus to Septimius Severus, including Nero (Blake [1959], 40; Coarelli [1984], 295–96).

On the date of Nero's birth, see the appendix to this chapter.

17 Nine days after the birth of a boy, a ritual purification was conducted (on the *dies lustricus*), after which he would be given a name.

ever, he did not do this in earnest but as a joke, and Agrippina rejected the name because at that time Claudius was one of the objects of ridicule in the court.[18]

3. Nero was three when he lost his father.[19] His legacy was one-third of the property, but he did not receive even that intact, as the entire estate was appropriated by his co-heir Gaius. And soon afterward, when his mother was also banished, [20] leaving him almost without means and impoverished, he was brought up in the home of his aunt Lepida under two pedagogues, one a dancer and the other a barber.[21] But when Claudius came to power, Nero not only recovered his father's property but also was even further

18 Suetonius is the only source to recount Caligula's supposed role in the naming. It must have been Claudius's *cognomen* "Nero" that was adopted, since the child was given the paternal family *praenomen* Lucius. If Caligula did intervene, his suggestion need not have been insulting. Claudius did suffer humiliations in the latter part of Caligula's reign, but he was treated respectfully at the outset, even holding the consulship in July and August of AD 37.

19 Caligula was co-heir with Nero under Domitius's will, and hence Domitius must have died before Caligula's death at the end of January 41. For Nero to have been three at the time of Domitius's demise, in the most natural meaning of the expression, the death would have to have occurred after December 15, 40 (assuming that Nero was born in 37). This would provide a very narrow range for the death: late December 40–late January 41. It is just possible, however, that when Suetonius called Nero *trimulus*, it might have meant "in his third year," which would mean sometime after December 15, 39. The last mention of Domitius is in the attendance lists of the Arvals, of which Domitius was a member, in October 39; he does not appear in the record in 40 (Smallwood 40).

20 Agrippina was banished to the Pontian Islands for her adultery and for her association with a poorly understood conspiracy, or one of two separate conspiracies, involving the commander of the Rhine legions, Gnaeus Lentulus Gaetulicus, and the widower of Agrippina's sister (and supposedly lover of Agrippina), Marcus Aemilius Lepidus.

The events of 39–40, and particularly the conspiracy or conspiracies in that period, are very confused, but the general narrative of events suggests that Agrippina was banished at some point in the latter part of 39. We do have a fixed chronological point in the Arval record for October 27, 39, where the exposure of the complicity of Gaetulicus (Smallwood 9.19) is noted. For Suetonius's sequence here to be correct, we must assume that Domitius died in late December 39 and that Agrippina's banishment followed very quickly ("soon afterward").

21 After his mother's banishment, Nero went to the home of his paternal aunt Domitia Lepida (Tac. *Ann.* 12.64.4). He would have spent less than two years there, since Agrippina was recalled upon Claudius's accession, presumably early in his reign. Despite Suetonius's claim of "impoverishment," Nero could hardly have lived in penury. Domitia Lepida was a well-to-do woman: she had estates in Calabria (see Tac. *Ann.*12.65.1) and in the Puteoli area, where she had a warehouse, the *horrea Barbatiana* (*Tabulae Pompeianae Sulpiciorum* 42.2, 46.5, 79).

enriched by a legacy from his stepfather, Passienus Crispus.[22] 4. After his mother was recalled and restored to her position, he thrived thanks to her influence and power, so much so that word got out to the general public that men had been sent by Claudius's wife Messalina to strangle him during his siesta because she thought him a rival to Britannicus. A detail added to the story is that those same men were frightened off and took to their heels when a snake emerged from under his pillow. This story arose from the fact that the cast-off skin of a snake was discovered in his bed close to his pillow; nevertheless, following his mother's wishes, he wore the skin on his right arm for some considerable time, set in a golden bracelet.[23] When he finally found the memory of his mother disagreeable, he threw it away and then, when his situation became dire, he looked for it again, without success.

In AD 47, Nero is successfully introduced to the Roman public.

Tac. *Ann.* 11.11.1. It was during this same consulship that the Secular Games were put on, in the eight hundredth year after Rome's founding and the sixty-fourth after their staging by Augustus. . . .[24]

2. When Claudius was seated at the games in the circus, boys from noble families put on the Game of Troy on horseback.[25] Among them were Britan-

22 Agrippina lost her property when she was banished. It was restored upon her recall (Dio 60.4.1), and she also made a very advantageous marriage. Gaius Sallustius Passienus Crispus, a native of Visellium, was a man of considerable learning and wit, and of great wealth, which he acquired from his adoptive father, the great-nephew of the historian Sallust. Passienus held the consulship in 27 and 44 AD and was governor of Asia in 42/43. He was Agrippina's brother-in-law, first married to Nero's elder aunt Domitia, whom he divorced to marry Agrippina. He died at some point in the 40s.

23 For a slightly different version of the snake story, see Tac. *Ann.* 11.11.3.

24 The reference belongs to the year AD 47. The Secular Games, based on a *saeculum* (probably the idea of the oldest possible life span, fixed conventionally by the Romans at 100), were first celebrated as the *Ludi Terentini/ Tarentini* in the year 249 BC, in the Tarentum, a religious precinct in the Campus Martius, and a notional hundred years later, in actuality probably 146 BC, to mark Rome's supposed founding 600 years earlier. The next cycle was neglected, probably because of political turmoil, but Augustus held a celebration in 17 BC, using an Etruscan cycle of 110 years. The ritual program was enhanced by stage competitions and circus games. Applying a cycle of 100 years, Claudius celebrated the games in AD 47, using the Varronian founding date of 753 BC as his starting point. Suetonius (*Claud.* 21.2) claims that Claudius deviously recalculated the date, even though he believed that the Augustan calculation had been correct.

25 The "Game of Troy" was a complex parade game on horseback for young men of important families, often performed on major occasions from the time of its revival by Sulla, though suspended for a time after Augustus as being dangerous. Its origin is un-

nicus, son of the emperor, and Lucius Domitius, who would soon be taken by adoption into the ruling family, with the *cognomen* Nero.[26] The support of the crowd, which was more enthusiastic for Domitius, was taken as an omen. It was also put about that snakes had looked after the boy like guardians during his infancy, a tall tale made up to match the wondrous stories of foreign nations. In fact, Nero, no man to downplay himself, used to recount that no more than one serpent was seen in his bedroom.[27]

12.1. In reality, the support of the people arose from the memory of Germanicus, whose sole male descendant Nero was.[28] And sympathy for his mother, Agrippina, was heightened by the savagery of Messalina. She had always hated Agrippina but at that time was particularly exasperated, being deterred from fabricating charges against her, and finding people to lay them, only by her new infatuation, which bordered on insanity. 2. For she had developed a passion for Gaius Silius, the best-looking of Rome's young men,[29] and so much so that she chased Junia Silana, a woman of noble descent, from her marriage and then assumed possession of her now unattached lover.[30]

After her marriage to Claudius, Agrippina completely dominates her husband and ensures the bethrothal, and later marriage, of Nero and Claudius's daughter, Octavia, and Nero's adoption as Claudius's son.

---

certain. Vergil (*Aen.* 5.548–603) links it to the celebration of the funeral games for the Trojan Anchises, the father of Aeneas, but his account and etymology are not historically based.

26 This is the first mention in the extant *Annals* of Nero, who had presumably been reunited with Agrippina soon after the accession of Claudius, when she was recalled from the exile imposed by Caligula. Their activities between Agrippina's recall and the Secular Games in AD 47 are uncertain. This is also the first mention of Claudius's son Britannicus, but his birth was probably mentioned in the missing portion of the *Annals*.

27 The story about the protecting snakes might well have been circulated by Agrippina, and the degree to which it could be embellished is illustrated by the report of Suetonius (*Nero* 6.4) that the snake's skin was worn by Nero in a golden bracelet.

28 The potency of Germanicus's name had been largely instrumental in securing the accession of his son Caligula, and to some degree of his brother Claudius, and it was still apparently strong then.

29 Gaius Silius was consul designate for the year 49. After putting aside his wife, Junia Silana, he began a notorious affair with Messalina that supposedly led to their marriage, and certainly to the death of both of them.

30 Junia Silana was the sister-in-law of Caligula (through his first wife, Junia Claudilla). As the enemy of Messalina, she was initially a close friend of Agrippina, but Junia later plotted against Agrippina and was subsequently banished. Junia's death is recorded by Tacitus (*Ann.* 14.12.4).

Dio 60.32.1. Once Agrippina was in the palace, she completely dominated Claudius. She was extremely clever at exploiting situations, and by a combination of instilling fear and granting favors, she won over all those who were on good terms with him. Eventually, she saw to it that his son Britannicus was brought up like any of the ordinary citizenry. (His other son, who had been engaged to Sejanus's daughter, was dead.[31])

She then made Domitius Claudius's son-in-law, and later engineered his adoption, too. She succeeded in achieving all this partly by using his freedmen to persuade him and partly by taking steps to have the Senate, the people, and the military shout out in unison what suited her on any particular occasion.

Tac. *Ann.* 12.25.1. In the consulship of Gaius Antistius and Marcus Suillius, the adoption of Domitius was swiftly pushed ahead, [32] through Pallas's influence.[33] Pallas felt bound to Agrippina as the arranger of her marriage, and later because of a sexual relationship, and he now kept urging Claudius to take thought for the good of the state and provide protection for Britannicus in his early years. He cited the parallel of the deified Augustus in whose family, though he had grandsons to rely on, stepsons had a prominent role, and the case of Tiberius, who had children of his own but also adopted Germanicus.[34] Claudius, too, he said, should equip himself with a young man who would assume some of his responsibilities.

2. Convinced by this, Claudius set Domitius, who was three years older, ahead of his own son, making a speech in the Senate along the lines of what

31 Suetonius (*Claud.* 17) relates the story that Drusus, Claudius's son by Plautia Urgulanilla, threw a pear in the air and caught it in his mouth, and thereupon choked on it, a few days after he had been betrothed to the daughter of Sejanus and shortly before receiving the toga of manhood.

32 The year is AD 50. The Arval record (Smallwood 21.58) places the adoption on February 25. After the adoption, the formal legal status of Nero would be exactly the same as that of Britannicus, and since he was older, he would naturally have precedence.

33 Pallas was originally a slave of Antonia, supposedly used by her to carry evidence against Sejanus to Tiberius in Capri (Joseph. *AJ* 18.182). As a freedman, he became influential under Claudius as *a rationibus* ("in charge of accounts," Suet. *Claud.* 28). Here we find him as the promoter of Agrippina's marriage to Claudius and of the adoption of Nero by the emperor. He was honored by the Senate with a major financial award and the *ornamenta praetoria* (Plin. *Ep.* 7.29.2; Tac. *Ann.* 12.53.2). He was killed in AD 62 because of his wealth (Tac. *Ann.* 14.65.1).

34 Augustus had used Tiberius and his brother Drusus as lieutenants while his grandsons (and adopted sons) Gaius and Lucius Caesar were young. Before his own adoption by Augustus in AD 4, Tiberius adopted his nephew Germanicus, even though he had a grown natural son, Drusus. Of course, Tiberius probably had little choice in the matter.

he had heard from the freedman.[35] Experts observed that there had been before this no case of adoption among the patricians of the Claudian family and that they had survived without interruption from Attus Clausus on.[36]

26.1. The emperor was thanked, and the flattery of Domitius was particularly well constructed; and a law was passed that provided for his adoption into the Claudian family with the name "Nero."[37] 2. Agrippina, too, received elevation with the *cognomen* Augusta.[38] When this was done, there was nobody so heartless as not to be touched by sadness for Britannicus's lot. The boy was gradually deprived even of the service of his slaves, and he treated with derision the poorly timed solicitude of his stepmother, aware of its hypocrisy, for they do say that he was not slow-witted by nature. That may be true, or perhaps sympathy for his danger allowed him to keep that reputation without it being put to the test.

Suet. *Ner.* 7.1. While still young, not yet in the later stages of boyhood, he took part in the Troy Game during the circus performances, with self-confidence and a successful result. During his eleventh year, he was adopted by Claudius and entrusted to Annaeus Seneca (who at the time was already a senator) for his education.[39] They claim that the following night Seneca

35 On the relative ages of Nero and Britannicus, see the appendix to this chapter.

36 A distinction is made with the plebeian Claudii Marcelli. Attus Clausus (Appius Claudius Sabinus Inregillensis) was in 500 BC the founder of the *gens* Claudia in Rome (Livy 2.16.4). See Chapter II, n.57.

37 Domitius's father was dead, and Domitius was consequently *sui iuris* (not subject to the jurisdiction of a third party); hence a formal law was needed for the adoption (*arrogatio*). An investigation would be carried out by the pontiffs, and upon completion the adoption would be confirmed in the presence of the pontiffs by a *lex curiata* (a law enacted in the appropriate assembly, the *comitia curiata*).

38 The conferring of this title was a conspicuous honor. Agrippina was the first woman so distinguished while her husband was still alive. Livia, and possibly Antonia, had received the title during their own lifetimes. Interestingly, Claudius refused the same title for Messalina.

39 Little is known of the early life and career of Annaeus Seneca before he became the tutor of Nero in 49. He was born in Cordoba, the capital of the province of Hispania Baetica, the son of Seneca the Elder, about the beginning of the century. A somewhat sickly child, for much of his early life he lived in Rome, where he was raised by an aunt. In the early 30s, he visited Egypt when his aunt's husband was appointed prefect, and, with her help, he was able to achieve a quaestorship, probably under Tiberius, and was launched into a legal career. He had an ambivalent relationship with Caligula, and there were suggestions of literary rivalry between the two (Suet. *Cal.* 53.2; Dio 59.19.7–8). Early in Claudius's reign, he was caught up in the machinations of Messalina and exiled to Corsica on the grounds of adultery with Julia Livilla, Agrippina's sister, spending over seven years

dreamed that it was actually Gaius Caesar that he was teaching, and Nero soon gave some authority to the dream by his brutal nature, of which he gave evidence as soon as he could. Because his brother Britannicus had, after Nero's adoption, called him "Ahenobarbus," as he normally did, he tried to persuade the father that Britannicus was not really his child.[40] Furthermore, when Lepida, his aunt, was indicted, he gave crushing testimony against her in her presence, to please his mother, who was trying to secure the defendant's conviction.[41]

Dio 60.32.5. Nero grew in power, but Britannicus received no respect and no attention. In fact, Agrippina drove out or even killed those who treated him well, and in particular she murdered Sosibius, who had been put in charge of Britannicus's upbringing and education, alleging that he was plotting against Nero.[42] Following that, she handed Britannicus over to people of her own choosing and maltreated him as much as she could. She would not allow him to associate with his father or go out into the streets but kept him in a sort of prison without chains.

Tac. *Ann.*12.41.1. In the consulship of Tiberius Claudius (Claudius's fifth) and Servius Cornelius, Nero was granted the *toga virilis* before his time so that he would appear ready for a political career.[43] And Claudius happily

---

there (Sen. *Helv.* 19.2.4–7; Dio 60.8.5, 61.10.1). He was restored from his exile through the pressures of Agrippina (Tac. *Ann.* 12.8.3) and was appointed Nero's tutor. He became deeply involved in politics after this point, initially as an ally of Agrippina and later as a rival. He had a close relationship with Nero, but the bond weakened after the death of Burrus, and he eventually became estranged from the emperor and died as a consequence of the Pisonian conspiracy (see Chapter VIII). He was a celebrated literary figure, very fashionable in his own day, known for his philosophical and scientific essays, his letters, and his tragedies (perhaps recited rather than performed).

40 Suetonius seeks to exonerate Britannicus by suggesting that the form of greeting came from force of habit. But Nero was adopted in 50, and the incident of the name is placed by Tacitus in 51 (Tac. *Ann.* 12.41.3), so there had been ample time for Britannicus to familiarize himself with the correct appellation. The point of the insult is that by addressing Nero by his old family name, which would have been legally given up when he entered the Claudian family, Britannicus ignored his adoption.

41 Only Suetonius claims that Nero actually testified against Lepida.

42 Sosibius was instrumental in bringing down the powerful Valerius Asiaticus, and was rewarded, on the instigation of Vitellius, with one million sestertii (Tac. *Ann.* 11.1.1, 4.3). He would presumably have had a role in bringing up Titus, who was raised in court alongside Britannicus (Suet. *Tit.* 2).

43 At around the age of fourteen (the precise age could vary considerably), the Roman boy underwent the formal ceremony of manhood, exchanging his purple-edged toga (*toga*

acceded to the sycophantic request of the Senate that Nero enter the consulship in his twentieth year[44] and that in the meantime he hold consular power outside the city as consul designate[45] and be given the title "Prince of the Youth."[46] 2. There was, in addition, largesse for the soldiers along with gifts for the people, all made in Nero's name. Moreover, at the games in the Circus—put on to win over the favor of the masses—Britannicus rode past in the procession wearing the boy's toga while Nero did so in triumphal dress.[47] The people were supposed to see one in the insignia of a commander and the other in the clothes of a boy, and to anticipate on that basis the future prospects of each. At the same time, any centurions and tribunes commiserating with Britannicus's lot were removed on spurious grounds, and some with the pretense of promotion. [48] In the case of freedmen, too, anyone whose loyalty remained untainted was ejected when opportunities like the following arose. 3. When the two met, Nero greeted Britannicus by

---

praetexta) for the plain white one, the "toga of manhood" (*toga virilis*). The year is AD 51. Nero had passed his thirteenth birthday. His relatively early ceremony was paralleled later in the cases of Domitian and Commodus.

44 Gaius and Lucius Caesar had received a similar privilege of advanced designation for the consulship. Private citizens could hold the consulship at thirty-two if they were *nobiles*, but children of the imperial family did so at an earlier age. Germanicus held the consulship at twenty-seven.

45 Proconsular *imperium* had been exercised outside the city and was now exercised by the *princeps* within the city, too. Thus, Nero was given this privilege, but it did not of course equate him with the *princeps*.

46 During the republic, the expression *principes iuventutis* ("Princes of the Youth") was used in the patrician cavalry, in which members served only when they were young. By the late republic, the term was found also in the singular. With the establishment of the principate, "*princeps*" became exclusively associated with Augustus, who took over the phrase *princeps iuventutis* essentially to designate his successors. After they assumed the *toga virilis*, Gaius and Lucius Caesar were both acclaimed *principes iuventutis* (Augustus *RG* 14.4–5).

47 During the republic, the *vesta triumphalis* was the accoutrement not only of those awarded a triumph but also of senior magistrates on important occasions; it was later worn also by the emperor. Caesar was entitled to it at public events, and it was used by Caligula at the dedication of a temple and by Nero in receiving Tiridates (Dio 44.4.2, 6.1; 59.7.1; 63.3.3). In Nero's case, the privilege derived presumably from his proconsular *imperium*.

48 It was possible for Roman soldiers to move back and forth between service in the legions and in the praetorian guard. Service in the latter would provide an excellent base from which to move into a higher legionary rank. Agrippina had already secured the praetorian command for her loyal supporter Burrus, and replacement of the middle ranks proved to be a shrewd maneuver, since the guard would remain loyal to her and later refuse to take part in her murder (see Chapter III).

name, but Britannicus called Nero "Domitius."[49] Agrippina brought this to her husband's notice with bitter complaints, saying it was the start of internal dissension: the adoption was being disregarded, the vote of the senators and the command of the people repudiated within their home. Unless the evil influence of those inculcating such hostility were checked, she added, it would erupt with disastrous consequences for the state. Disturbed by these veiled charges, Claudius punished all the finest tutors of his son with exile or execution, putting the stepmother's appointees in charge of the boy.

FIGURE 1. *RIC*² Claudius 75, Silver Denarius. Obverse: AGRIPPINAE AVGVSTAE, "To Agrippina Augusta." Reverse: NERO CLAVD(ius) CAES(ar) DRVSVS GERM(anicus) PRINC(eps) IVVENT(utis), "Nero Claudius Caesar Drusus Germanicus, Prince of the Youth." From the collection of Andreas Pangerl/romancoins.info.

Sometime after AD 50, Rome witnessed a remarkable numismatic innovation when gold and silver issues from the Roman mint bore portraits with the traditional image of the emperor on the obverse and, for the very first time, his wife on the reverse, identified with the title she had just received, Agrippina Augusta (*RIC*² Claudius 80–81).

Beginning in AD 51, there was a further numismatic innovation: gold and silver issues now carried images of either Claudius or Agrippina (with her title of Augusta) on the obverse, and of Nero on the reverse, with his title of "Prince of the Youth" (see Figure 1), alluded to also by Tacitus in the preceding passage. No parallel coin issue honored Britannicus.

49 See Suetonius for an account of the same incident.

FIGURE 2. *RIC*^{2} Claudius 76, Gold Aureus. Obverse: NERO CLAVD(ius) CAES(ar) DRVSVS GERM(anicus) PRINC(eps) IVVENT(utis), "Nero Claudius Caesar Drusus Germanicus, Prince of the Youth." Reverse: SACERD(otum) COOPT(atus) IN OMN(ia) CONL(egia) SUPRA NUM(erum), "Co-opted as a supernumerary into all colleges of the priests." From the collection of Andreas Pangerl/romancoins.info.

This special issue of Claudius is valuable in providing information that does not appear in the literary sources. The obverse shows a young head of Nero and records his status as "Prince of the Youth." But the reverse provides the additional information that he was co-opted into the priestly colleges. There were four important ones: (1) the pontiffs, the most important college, since it included the senior priesthood, that of Pontifex Maximus, as well as the flamens, who were responsible for individual gods; (2) the augurs, who read the divine signs before any major undertaking; (3) the *quindecemviri sacris faciundis*, a board of fifteen, charged mainly with interpreting the Sibylline books; and (4) the *septemviri epulonum*, a board of seven who had charge of sacrificial banquets. Nero's appointment was supernumerary, in addition to the usual complement on each board. The reverse legend (see Figure 2) encircles two priestly implements, a *simpulum*, on a tripod, and a *lituus*, on a dish (*patera*). The *simpulum* was a ladle used for libations at sacrifices and was associated with the college of pontiffs. The *lituus* was the curved staff used by the augurs to mark out parts of the sky. The pairing is common on Roman coins. The appearance of Nero, rather than the emperor, on the obverse was a striking public declaration of how securely the succession had been determined.

Agrippina fears that Claudius might be regretting his decision to promote Nero and hastens plans to eliminate him.

Tac. *Ann.*12.64.2. But Agrippina was especially frightened. She was alarmed at a remark of Claudius's—which he had let drop when he was drunk—that it was his fate to suffer, and then to punish, the sexual misconduct of his wives. She decided to take action and take it quickly, though first she destroyed Domitia Lepida, and for typically female motives. Lepida was a daughter of the younger Antonia; Augustus had been her uncle; she was first cousin once removed to Agrippina; and she was the sister of Agrippina's former husband Gnaeus—and so she thought herself on Agrippina's level of distinction.[50] 3. Nor was there a great difference in beauty, age, and wealth; and both were immoral, disreputable, and violent, rivals no less in vices than in the blessings granted them by fortune. But the bitterest rivalry between them was over whether aunt or mother would have the greater influence on Nero, for Lepida was trying to win over the young man's mind by cajoling and liberality; Agrippina, by contrast, was grim and threatening—able to give her son an empire, unable to stand him as emperor.

65.1. The charges brought against Lepida, however, were those of having made the emperor's wife the object of magical spells and causing disturbance of the peace in Italy by not keeping her troops of slaves in Calabria sufficiently under control. On these grounds, she was condemned to death, despite Narcissus's vigorous opposition,[51] for Narcissus was becoming ever more suspicious of Agrippina, and he was said to have remarked among his cronies that, whether it was Britannicus or Nero who acceded to power, his death was

50 The year is AD 53. Domitia Lepida was the cousin of Agrippina (Nero's mother) and the daughter of Antonia, herself the daughter of Mark Antony and Augustus's sister Octavia. Lepida was thus the great-niece of Augustus, although Tacitus makes a slight error in that she was in fact the daughter of the elder, not the younger, Antonia. She was the sister of Nero's father, Domitius. Her first husband was Valerius Messala Barbatus, and by him she bore Messalina, the wife of Claudius; her second husband was Faustus Cornelius Sulla, and her third, Gaius Appius Junius Silanus, was executed in AD 42, probably at the instigation of her daughter Messalina. Lepida had taken in Nero at the age of three, after the death of his father and the exile of Agrippina (see Suetonius).

51 Narcissus was probably the most powerful of the freedmen (former slaves who had attained their freedom) of Claudius, under whom he held the office of *ab epistulis* (in charge of correspondence). He was entrusted with important tasks, such as when he was dispatched to Boulogne to quell an incipient mutiny in AD 43 on the eve of an invasion of Britain (Dio 60.19.2–3). He played a key role in the death of Messalina when it was discovered that she had gone through a form of marriage with Gaius Silius, and he supposedly held a brief command over the praetorian guard during the crisis. He was despised by Agrippina (he had supported a rival as Claudius's next wife after Messalina's fall). Narcissus was in Sinuessa seeking a cure for his gout when Claudius died. He was imprisoned shortly afterward and then executed.

certain, but that Claudius had done so well by him that he would lay down his life in his service. 2. Messalina and Silius had been condemned, he said, and there were similar grounds for another accusation should Nero become emperor. If Britannicus were the successor, as emperor he would have nothing to fear.[52] But now the whole royal house was being rent asunder by his stepmother's intrigues, which would be a greater crime than if he had said nothing about the sexual impropriety of the earlier wife. Not that there was even a lack of sexual impropriety now, he added, since she had Pallas as her lover—just so no one could doubt that honor, morals, and her body all meant less to her than supreme power! 3. Uttering these and similar comments, he would embrace Britannicus and pray for him to acquire the strength of age as quickly as possible.[53] Let him grow up, he would say, stretching out his hands at one moment to the gods, at another to the boy himself; let him drive off his father's enemies and even take revenge on his mother's killers.

Tac. *Ann.* 12.69.1. Then, in the middle of the day, on October 13, the doors of the palace suddenly opened.[54] With Burrus accompanying him, Nero came out to the cohort that, following regular military routine, was on guard duty. There, at the prompting of the commanding officer, he was cheered and placed in a litter. They say that some had hesitated, looking around and asking where Britannicus was, but presently, as no one suggested an alternative, they went along with the choice that was on offer. 2. Nero was carried into the camp, and after a few preliminary words appropriate to the occasion, he promised largesse on the scale of his father's generous distributions[55] and was hailed as emperor.

52 The meaning of this passage is far from clear, and the translation is based on the following interpretation of Woodman (2004), 243, n.91: If Nero came to power, Narcissus would have the same grounds for accusing Agrippina as he had for accusing Messalina, namely, ambition for power, and would accordingly have to be silenced by Agrippina. If Britannicus succeeded, he, as the new emperor, would owe nothing to Narcissus and might put him to death as the man who brought about his mother Messalina's death.

53 In Suetonius (*Claud.* 43), it is Claudius who makes the belated display of affection to Britannicus. Tacitus might have preferred a version that showed a freedman, rather than Claudius, playing the active role.

54 Suetonius (*Ner.* 8) gives the exact time, between the sixth and the seventh hour. The attendance of the praetorian cohort, along with the commander Burrus, would be a clear sign that Nero was the new *princeps*. Any lingering support for Britannicus was clearly muted.

55 Claudius had promised each praetorian 15,000 sestertii.

APPENDIX

Nero's Birthdate

The reconstruction of Nero's life and reign depends on the correlation of the data provided by the sources, particularly Tacitus, Suetonius, and Dio. This process is complicated greatly by the fact that these sources regularly date events by reference to Nero's age, and while they thus enable us to place those events in a sequence, there is unfortunately no consensus on when Nero was born. This is a very specific problem, and in some ways a minor one, but it does have an impact on many of the questions that arise in Nero's reign. Also, the evidence for Nero's birth does manifest many of the characteristics of source problems that typify Nero's reign in general, and it provides a useful case study for students of the reign.

Accordingly, it will be helpful to set out the evidence provided by each author:

Tacitus

Tac. *Ann.* 12.41.1 (AD 51). In the consulship of Tiberius Claudius (Claudius's fifth) and Servius Cornelius, Nero was granted the *toga virilis* before his time.

Tac. *Ann.* 12.25.2. Claudius set Domitius [i.e., Nero], who was three years older, ahead of his own son [i.e., Britannicus].

Tac. *Ann.* 12.58.1. In the consulship of Decimus Junius and Quintus Haterius [=AD 53], Nero, now aged sixteen, married Claudius's daughter Octavia.

Tac. *Ann.* 13.6.1–2 (end of AD 54). At the year's end, there were disturbing rumors of another incursion of the Parthians. . . . How could an emperor scarcely past seventeen shoulder this burden or stave off the crisis?

Suetonius

Suet. *Ner.* 6.1. Nero was born at Antium, nine months after Tiberius's death, on December 15, just as the sun was rising, so that he was touched by its rays almost before he was touched by the earth.

Suet. *Ner.* 6.2. When Gaius Caesar's sister asked him [Nero's father] to give the baby any name he liked, he fixed his eyes on his uncle Claudius (who soon became emperor and by whom Nero was adopted) and said he was giving the child his name [i.e., Claudius].

Suet. *Ner.* 8.1. He was seventeen when the information about Claudius [i.e., his death] was made public.

Suet. *Ner.* 57.1. He died in his thirty-second year, on the same date that he had murdered Octavia.

Dio

Dio 61.2.1. When he [i.e., Nero] was born, rays surrounded him just before dawn although they came from no observable sunlight.

Dio 61.3.1. Nero was seventeen when he took power.

Dio 63.29.3 (June 68). Nero had lived thirty years and nine months, and of this had ruled for thirteen years and eight months.

Historia Augusta

SHA: *Verus* 1.8. Lucius [Verus] was born in Rome during the praetorship of his father on December 15, on the same day as the Nero who became emperor.

It should be noted that, ironically, we at times know the precise day and month of the birth of a member of the imperial family without being certain of the year. This happens because the anniversaries of their birthdays were regularly celebrated and to this end recorded in inscriptions, whereas it was not felt necessary to indicate the individual's age. In the case of Nero, we are even given the point in the day when the birth occurred. Nero's birth was a remarkable one, of course, not only for its historical significance but because it was a breech birth that his mother survived (Plin. *HN* 7.8). The most explicit statement on *when* it occurred is provided by Suetonius (*Ner.* 6.1), who informs us that it happened at Antium, just before dawn, nine months after the death of Tiberius (which occurred on March 16, 37), on the eighteenth day prior to the Kalends of January; hence, in our terms, at about 7 AM, December 15, 37. Dio (61.2.1) also records the information that the birth occurred just before dawn. The day is confirmed by the Arval record (Smallwood 16.8, 21.30) and is consistent with the statement in *SHA*, *Verus* 1.8, that Lucius Verus was born on December 15, on the same day as Nero. The epigraphic confirmation of the day perhaps adds some credence to Suetonius's information on the year. Suetonius is indeed supported by Tacitus (*Ann.* 13.6.2), where concerns are recorded at the end of the first year when Nero came to power (AD 54) that the governing of the state was under the control of a young man hardly past his seventeenth birthday. Moreover, Dio (63.29.3) notes that Nero lived for thirty years and a certain number of months and days. The precise number varies with each epitimator, but all are in harmony with a birth in 37 AD. It is generally believed that Nero died on June 9, on the testimony of Jerome (*Chron.* p.36) that Nero ruled for thirteen years, seven months, and twenty-eight days.

The preceding information is explicit and generally not inconsistent with what is known of Nero's birth and later life. But it is contradicted by other references in the very same authors. Suetonius (*Ner.* 8.1) and Dio (61.3.1) both claim that at the time of Claudius's death (October 13, 54), Nero was seventeen years old. This would require a birthday in December 36. It is possible that both authors at this point are relying on a source that got the year wrong, being misled by the fact that Claudius's death happened late in the year. It is also possible that there is a confusion, often found in ancient references to age, between inclusive and exclusive counting, and that the source meant that Nero was in his seventeenth year (but had not reached his seventeenth birthday) in October 54. The year 36 receives some support from the claim in Suetonius (*Ner.* 57.1) that Nero died in 68 (June) in his thirty-second year (*tricensimo et secundo aetatis anno*). In other words, he had passed his thirty-first birthday in December 67. Also, Tacitus (*Ann.* 12.58.1) records the marriage of Nero and Octavia as the earliest event of AD 53 and gives his age as sixteen (*sedecim annos natus*). It is possible, of course, that Tacitus placed the marriage at the beginning of the year for dramatic effect rather than in its proper chronological sequence. A major objection to the year 36 is that Suetonius (*Ner.* 6.2) clearly places the birth in the reign of Caligula, which did not begin until 37. Also, Tacitus (*Ann.* 12.41.1) says that in 51 the *toga virilis* was conferred on Nero before the normal time. If Nero had been born in 36, he would have reached his fourteenth birthday, the traditional age of manhood, in December of the previous year, AD 50.

There is even some evidence for a birthday in 39. Suetonius (*Ner.* 7.1) claims that Nero was adopted by Claudius in his eleventh year (*undecimo aetatis anno*). The adoption is dated to the year 50 by Tacitus (*Ann.* 12.25.1), and the month and day, February 25, are provided by the Arval record (Smallwood 21.53). Nero would need to have been born in December 39 to be in his eleventh year on February 25, 50. But by December 39, Caligula was out of Rome on his northern campaign, and Nero's mother, Agrippina, had been sent into exile because of her adulterous and possibly conspiratorial conduct.

A final piece of evidence is the claim by Tacitus (*Ann.* 12.25.3) that Nero had three years' seniority over Britannicus. The latter was probably born on February 12, 41, twenty days after Claudius assumed office (Suet. *Claud.*

27.2), which would accord well with a birth date for Nero in December 37. That date is likely since in early 55 Britannicus is said to be close to completing his fourteenth year. But caution must be applied, since Suetonius says in the same passage that Britannicus was born in Claudius's second consulship, which fell in 42.

All in all, the year 37 for Nero's birth seems to have the greatest authority, and that year is assumed tentatively throughout this book. It is to be noted, however, that at times what is relevant is not the true date of birth but the date that the source in question *believed* was the true date of birth.

II

THE NEW EMPEROR

INTRODUCTION

Optimus est post malum principem dies primus ("the best day following a bad ruler is the first") declared Curtius Montanus in AD 69 (Tac. *Hist.* 4.42). The essential truth of this observation is demonstrated on several occasions in Roman history. In 37 AD, Romans were spellbound when the young Caligula entered the city and with a dignified humility declared to the Senate that he would rule along Augustan lines. While senators may not have started to feel doubts by as early as the following day, they certainly did within a couple of years. In some ways, the reign of Nero was a reprise of Caligula's. While he was amenable to supervision by Agrippina, or to the joint guidance of Seneca and Burrus, Nero showed himself from the very outset, in December 54, capable of enlightened and statesmanlike judgment. With the murder of his mother in March 59, he felt he was his own man and liberated himself from the stern and sober advice that had served him so well. His reign from that point on was a descent into often arbitrary tyranny. It seems remarkable that Romans would have hoped that the youthful Nero would bring a golden age of enlightened government, given their previous experience under Caligula. Even those who knew Nero well seem to have deceived themselves, including men such as Seneca, who appears to have believed that his *De Clementia,* dedicated to Nero in 55, would be a manual of conduct to which the young emperor would subscribe.

The inevitable disappointment came more slowly in Nero's case than in Caligula's, and the first few years of the Neronian regime were marked by deference to the senatorial order and sobriety in the management of the state. It is difficult to determine exactly how government in this early period operated, since much of it was at the level of Nero's private *consilium* (council of close advisers), and in the nature of things most of what played out there would remain hidden from public view. Tacitus speaks of Seneca and Burrus as partners, equally influential, each in his own way (Tac. *Ann.* 13.2.1), but at the political level, especially in directing Nero's relations with the Senate, it seems more likely that it was Seneca who was the senior partner. As a sign of this, we learn that in the very first piece of business that Nero transacted, the deification of his "father" and predecessor Claudius, it was Seneca who wrote the eulogy for him, and this practice was repeated on later occasions, so that in a way Nero became Seneca's mouthpiece. Claudius's funeral was followed the next day by a major speech delivered by Nero before the Senate, in which he promised to rule by the principles established by Augustus and to avoid the practices that had aroused such bitterness under Claudius, especially the blurring of the public and private aspects of the principate. The Senate decreed that the speech be inscribed in gold and read when the new consuls entered office at the beginning of the new year. Perceptive older members might have pondered over the equally sycophantic response to Caligula's first efforts at governing.

This general observation of an initial period of responsible government is perhaps complicated rather than helped by the notion found in the fourth-century writer Aurelius Victor's *Liber de Caesaribus* and the anonymous *Epitome de Caesaribus*, at one time also mistakenly attributed to Victor, that the emperor Trajan identified a *quinquennium* (five-year period) of good administration by Nero. The evidence is late, and there can be no certainty that Trajan did indeed make such a judgment. It seems to suggest a formal initial five-year period of rule. This did not exist, although it can be said that the murder of Agrippina in 59 (just under five years after the start of his rule) did informally mark a shift in the reign. Also, while Trajan might have found much to admire in the first five years of Nero's reign, it is remarkable that he would have ranked him more highly than he ranked all the other emperors from Augustus down to Nerva. Moreover, Trajan is not represented as admiring Nero's good government as such. Aurelius Victor says that he excelled *augenda urbe maxime* ("especially in his expansion of the city"), and the anonymous author of the *Epitome* is more specific in noting that in this period he constructed an amphitheater and baths. Scholars have tended to become more and more cautious about using Trajan's supposed assessment of Nero's first five years.

SOURCES

The *Quinquennium*

Aur. Vict. *Caes.* 5.1–2. In this way, Lucius Domitius (that certainly being his name, as his father was a Domitius) became emperor. Although in his youth he was under the control of a stepfather for a period appropriate to his age, he nevertheless was so great for a span of five years, especially in his expansion of the city, that Trajan with justification would claim that all the emperors were far different from him—for five years!

Anon. *Epit. de Caes.* 5.1–3. Domitius Nero had Domitius Ahenobarbus as his father and Agrippina as his mother, and he ruled for thirteen years. 2. For a five-year period, he seemed tolerable. As a result of this, some have recorded that Trajan was accustomed to saying that the *principes* as a group were far different from Nero—for a five-year period. 3. Here in the city, he constructed an amphitheater and baths.

The accession of Nero is celebrated throughout the empire.

P.Oxy. VII.1021 (Greek. Smallwood 47). Having fulfilled his service to his ancestors, the manifest god Caesar has also gone to join them, and the anticipated and hoped-for Emperor of the world has been appointed; and the good spirit of the world, Nero, who is the greatest source of good things, has been made Emperor. Accordingly we should all show our gratitude to all the gods by wearing garlands and sacrificing oxen.

In the first year of Nero Claudius Caesar Augustus Germanicus, on the 21st day of the month New Augustus.

We know that, upon the death of Augustus, it was Tiberius who wrote to the *legati* of the imperial provinces to inform them about it (Tac. *Ann.* 1.7.3). It may be that in the case of Claudius's death and Nero's accession it was Agrippina who ensured that the necessary authorities were informed. In Egypt, the communication would have gone to Alexandria and then been sent from there to local officials. This fragment of papyrus was found in the Egyptian city of Oxyrhynchus. The local official, the *strategos,* seems to have made his own copy of the text, since the papyrus copy looks like a rough draft, with several corrections.

New Augustus (*Neos Sebastos*) was the old Egyptian month of Hathyr (November–December), and the date given here, the twenty-first day, if correctly transcribed, would be November 17 in the modern Western calendar. This would mean that it took thirty-five days for the message to travel from Rome to Alexandria to Oxyrhynchus. Caution must be exercised, however. Papyri and stone inscriptions are seldom clear-cut, and wear and tear make transcription difficult and at times impossible. Greeks used letters of the alphabet for numbers, and 21 is based on a reading of κα′ (20 followed by 1), but the α is barely legible, and almost any number in the twenties is possible.

Nero honors the memory of Claudius.

Tac. *Ann.* 13.3.1. On the day of the funeral, Nero proceeded with the eulogy of Claudius.[1] While he held forth on the antiquity of his family, and his ancestors' consulships and triumphs, he and everyone else remained serious.[2] His comments on Claudius's cultural pursuits, and the fact that during his rule there had been no mishap in external affairs, also received a favorable hearing.[3] But when he turned to Claudius's foresight and wisdom, no one could hold back his laughter. And yet the speech, being a composition of Seneca's, had a large measure of sophistication, the man being possessed of a talent that charmed and was well adapted to the contemporary ear.[4]

2. Older people, whose spare time is spent comparing past and present, observed that Nero was the first of all the holders of the supreme power to have needed another man's rhetoric, for the dictator Caesar was a match for the best orators, and Augustus had a ready and articulate delivery, and one befitting an emperor.[5] Tiberius, too, had a skillful manner of weighing his

1 Nero's display of filial piety was something of a conventional pose. During a smooth transition of power, it was considered right and proper for a ruler to show deference to his predecessor, no matter how unpopular he had been. Hence, Caligula would even ask for divine honors for the widely disliked Tiberius, a request that was quietly and diplomatically shelved. Claudius was granted a *funus censorium* ("censor's funeral"), which would have been particularly fitting in his case because he had held the censorship (Tac. *Ann.* 13.2.3; cf. *Ann.* 12.69.2, Dio 60.35.2).

2 The founder of the Claudian *gens* was Appius Claudius Sabinus, who, by conventional dating, was consul in 495 BC. Tacitus (*Ann.* 4.9.2) provides his Sabine name, Attus Clausus. Suetonius (*Tib.* 1.2) states that the Claudians could boast twenty-eight consuls, five dictators, seven censors, seven triumphs, and two ovations.

3 Suetonius (*Claud.* 41–42) lays out Claudius's literary activities, which began at an early age and continued through his principate. When still young, he began a history, with the encouragement of Livy, completing two volumes, and later he undertook a second history, starting with the end of the civil wars, of which he completed eight volumes. He wrote an eight-volume autobiography and a defense of Cicero, as well as two works in Greek, twenty volumes on the Etruscans, and eight on Carthaginian history. He invented three new letters of the alphabet and wrote a book about them (they were abandoned after his death). A new wing of the museum of Alexandria was opened in Claudius's honor and named after him.

4 Tacitus seems not to have been impressed by Seneca. The reference to his "charming" (*amoenum*) talent sounds condescending, and he implies that Seneca's appeal did not last beyond his contemporaries. In Tacitus's early book on oratory, the *Dialogus*, Seneca is not even mentioned. Quintilian (*Inst.* 10.1.125) makes a distinctly unenthusiastic defense of Seneca.

5 Cicero claims that his friend Atticus said that Julius Caesar was the most elegant of Latin orators, and there was no one to whom he should take second place (*Brut.* 252, 261). Tacitus (*Dial.* 21.5) and Quintilian (*Inst.* 10.1.114) speak highly of his abilities, but in more muted tones. Suetonius (*Aug.* 86.1) says that Augustus's style was clear and elegant, and free of artifice.

words and was able to express his sentiments with force or with deliberate ambiguity. Even Gaius Caesar's disturbed mind did not spoil the power of his speaking.[6] In Claudius, too, when he was delivering a prepared speech, one would not find elegance lacking.[7] 3. In Nero's case, he turned his lively intellect elsewhere right from his early years—to engraving, painting, singing, and chariot driving.[8] Sometimes, too, in his verse composition he demonstrated that he had the basic elements of literary skill.

Nero lays out his program of government.

Tac. *Ann.* 13.4.1. The charade of sorrow completed, Nero entered the Curia and, after some preliminary remarks on the authority of the senators and the consensus of the military, he observed that he had advice and examples available to make his administration exceptional.[9] His youth had not been steeped in civil wars or domestic strife, he said, and he brought with him no animosities, no wrongs to be righted, and no thirst for revenge.[10] 2. He then sketched the outlines of his coming principate, disassociating himself especially from matters that had recently caused burning resentment.[11] He would not be a judge in all cases, he said, with informers and defendants confined in one house where the influence of a few would be at work.[12] There would be no bribery in his home, no room for influence peddling. His house and the state

6 Suetonius (*Cal.* 53.2) describes Caligula's style as flowing and elegant.

7 Suetonius (*Claud.* 4.6) quotes Augustus as commenting that he was astonished by how impressive Claudius's speeches were, given his problems with ordinary conversation.

8 It is to be noted that Tacitus does concede that Nero possessed a native intelligence, but feels that he squandered his talents.

9 Nero (or Seneca) lists the Senate first out of deference, although it is the second group, the military, in the form of the praetorian guard, that had been the key player. The "advice" is an oblique reference to Seneca and Burrus, and prime among the "examples" would be Augustus. Suetonius (*Ner.* 10.1) suggests that he specifically mentioned Augustus. Dio (61.3.1) records that this speech was so well received that the Senate ordered that it be inscribed on a silver column and read out annually.

10 Nero here can in a sense distance himself from Augustus, whose youth had been bedeviled by civil wars, and from his other predecessors, who had been beset by domestic strife (to which Augustus also had not been immune).

11 The format laid out by Nero, with its careful division of powers and responsibilities, is very close to that prescribed by Augustus.

12 Nero may well have broadly kept to this undertaking. The Pisonian conspirators are recorded as being tried by him in AD 65 (see Chapter VIII), but the only earlier instance of an *in camera* hearing mentioned in the sources is that of Fabricius Veiento, who had been trafficking in imperial privileges (Tac. *Ann.* 14.50.2). There is no other explicit case recorded for his reign. The contrast with Claudius is striking. Claudius's reign had been characterized by a number of *in camera* hearings, of which the most notorious was probably the trial of Valerius Asiaticus in AD 47 (Tac. *Ann.* 11.1–3).

were separate.[13] The Senate should retain its ancient functions; Italy and the "public" provinces should address themselves to the tribunals of the consuls. They would grant them access to the Senate, while he himself would see to the armies that were his charge.[14]

Nero's early actions match the program he laid out.

Tac. *Ann.* 13.5.1. Nero did not break his word either, and many measures were implemented on senatorial authority. Pleading a case for payment or gifts was to be disallowed, [15] and quaestors designate would not be obliged to give gladiatorial shows.[16] The second of these Agrippina opposed as being a reversal of Claudius's legislation, but the senators carried it nonetheless. (They used to be summoned to the Palatium just so that Agrippina could be present, standing at a doorway added at the back and separated from the proceedings by a curtain, which kept her out of sight but did not prevent her hearing.[17] 2. In fact, when representatives of the Armenians were pleading the cause of their people

13 A major offender in this sphere had apparently been Messalina. Dio (60.17.5) speaks of foreigners buying citizenship through her or through the imperial freedmen.

14 Nero alludes to an ancient custom whereby deputations would present themselves to consuls or other magistrates when seated in the Assembly, and the consuls would then grant them access to the Senate (Livy 29.16.6).

15 The issue of the rights of advocates to receive a fee for their service was a complex and ongoing one. The *Lex Cincia* of 204 BC, which prohibited the acceptance of a fee, was revived by Augustus in 17 BC (Dio 54.18.2). Claudius took a more pragmatic position and fixed the fee at 10,000 sestertii (Tac. *Ann.* 11.7.4). Tacitus here speaks of the Senate, without imperial interference, reverting to the old Cincian law, but the gesture may have proved impractical. This may explain why, according to Suetonius (*Ner.* 17), Nero at some point seems to reaffirm Claudius's measure. Even this commonsense approach was not a success, to judge from the huge sums apparently amassed through lawyers' fees.

16 Tacitus (*Ann.* 11.22.2) records the motion, put forward under Claudius, that this obligation be placed on the quaestors. Suetonius here says that Nero lifted the obligation, and he observes (*Dom.* 4.1) that Domitian reintroduced it. But it is possible that in practice it did not disappear under Nero: the *Life of Lucan* (anonymous, possibly by Suetonius) states that Lucan, when quaestor (which would have been under Nero), put on a show "according to established tradition."

17 The Roman Senate met in a number of locations in addition to the official Curia. These included the library of Apollo on the Palatine, adjoining the imperial palace (Suet. *Aug.* 29.3), initially to accommodate Augustus when he was elderly. Agrippina's privilege was seen as a remarkable one. Dio (57.12.3) observes that even though Livia was practically in charge of the empire, she never committed the impropriety of entering the Senate chamber. There are several recorded instances where interested parties were permitted to observe the proceedings by standing at the formal entrance of the house. The four sons of Marcus Hortalus watched while their father pleaded for financial relief and he was subjected to a dressing down by Tiberius. Nero would later claim (Tac. *Ann.* 14.11.1) that Agrippina had tried to enter the actual chamber.

before Nero, she was preparing to mount the emperor's tribunal and preside with him, and would have done so but for Seneca, who, while the others were paralyzed with fear, advised the emperor to go to meet his mother as she approached. Thus, disgrace was obviated by a show of filial devotion.)[18]

FIGURE 3. *RIC*[2] Nero 2, Silver Denarius. Obverse: AGRIPP(ina) AVG(usta) DIVI CLAVD(ii) NERONIS CAES(aris) MATER, "Agrippina Augusta, wife of the deified Claudius, mother of Nero Caesar." Reverse: NERONI CLAVD(io) DIVI F(ilio) CAES(ari) AVG(usto) GERM(anico) IMP(eratori) TR(ibunicia) P(otestate), "To Nero Claudius, son of the deified one, Caesar Augustus Germanicus, Imperator, with Tribunician Authority." EX S(enatus) C(onsulto), "By a decree of the Senate." From the collection of Andreas Pangerl/romancoins.info.

As Claudius's designated successor, Nero had appeared on some striking Claudian coins. The issues that heralded his own reign were if anything even more innovative. Gold and silver coins that appeared from the Roman mint during Nero's first year, beginning in late 54, depict facing busts of Nero and his mother. The legend identifying Agrippina as Agrippina Augusta, the wife of Claudius and the mother of Nero, appears on the obverse, and Nero's own legend is reserved for the back of the coin, together with the familiar motif of the oak wreath

18 This incident is dated by both Tacitus and Dio to late 54. An embassy had arrived in Rome as a consequence of the Armenian crisis (see Chapter IV). It was apparently not anticipated that Agrippina would have a formal role in the ceremony. She was in fact accustomed to receiving delegations at the same time as Claudius, the most striking being the formal surrender of Caratacus in 51, when she sat on a neighboring dais as Claudius received the British leader (Tac. *Ann.* 12.37.4 [wrongly dating it to 50]; Dio 60.33.7). The tense situation on the occasion described here was cleverly resolved by Seneca (Dio 61.3.3–4 credits Burrus also). Dio saw the event as a turning point, when Seneca and Burrus were able to supplant Agrippina as the chief counselors of Nero.

(the *corona civica,* originally an oak wreath bestowed on a soldier for saving the life of a comrade in action), emphasizing tradition, with the legend *ex sc* (*ex senatus consulto*: "with senatorial authority") (see Figure 3). This arrangement conveys a remarkable association of emperor and mother, hinting that Agrippina was promoting herself as a kind of unprecedented co-ruler alongside her son. The absence of "consul" in Nero's title suggests (but cannot prove) that the dies were cut for this type before January 1, 55, when he assumed the consulship.

Gold and silver imperial coinage did not normally carry the legend SC, which was generally reserved for the lower-value coinage. The significance of the legend has been much debated, but it is possible that its appearance on some Neronian precious metal issues is meant to convey deference to the Senate.

FIGURE 4. *RIC*[2] Nero 7, Silver Denarius. Obverse: NERONI CLAVD(io) DIVI F(ilio) CAES(ari) AVG(usto) GERM(anico) IMP(eratori) TR(ibunicia) P(otestate) COS (Consuli), "To Nero Claudius, son of the deified one, Caesar Augustus Germanicus, Imperator, with Tribunician Authority, Consul." Reverse: AGRIPP(ina) AVG(usta) DIVI CLAVD(ii) NERONIS CAES(aris) MATER, "Agrippina Augusta, wife of the deified Claudius, mother of Nero Caesar." EX S(enatus) C(onsulto), "By a decree of the Senate." From the collection of Andreas Pangerl/romancoins.info.

Agrippina's declining influence over Nero has been detected in his coins of AD 55. A gold and silver series issued in January 55, in the first year of the reign but after the assumption of Nero's first consulship, still shows Nero and Agrippina on the obverse, but the heads on this slightly later issue are now "jugate," both facing the same way (right), with Nero's superimposed over his mother's (see Figure 4). Moreover, Nero's legend now appears on the obverse, while Agrippina's is restricted to the reverse, which depicts the deified Claudius on a chariot pulled by elephants. It has been argued that this series, following the initial one with facing heads, indicates a subtle downgrading of Agrippina's status. But one should be cautious. Issues of the "initial" series, although technically limited to only the first two and a half months of 54, are far commoner than the "second," which were minted during the first nine and a half months of 55. This suggests, as one might have expected, that although the dies were cut in late 54 for the first series, the coins produced continued to be issued through the following year, so that, for practical purposes, the two series were contemporaneous. It would be a curious measure to demote an individual by according her what was still an outstanding honor with a barely discernible diminution from a slightly earlier honor. It is certainly the case that when the jugate type was introduced by Ptolemy II of Egypt in the third century BC to celebrate his marriage to his sister, Arsinoe II, the type was intended to convey an honor (Müller [2009], 353–64).

One of the most striking portraits of Nero around the time of his accession comes from Aphrodisias in the province of Asia. This city, with a strong tradition of loyalty to the Julio-Claudians, constructed a Sebasteion (Augusteum), a special shrine dedicated to Aphrodite (Venus, the founder of the Julian line) and to the emperors and the people. It contains reliefs of the imperial family, including the one illustrated in Figure 5. This depicts a youthful Nero dressed as a soldier but wearing civilian footwear. He is receiving a laurel crown from the right hand of a female figure, who carries in her left hand a cornucopia, representing plenty, the symbol of Demeter. The female figure is generally identified as Agrippina, possibly correctly (another relief from the same building depicts Claudius clasping the hand of a female figure thought also to be Agrippina), but the identification would mean that Aphrodisias was making a very overt statement about Agrippina's role in the succession. It could be that the figure is a personification of Rome or the like.

Tac. *Ann.* 13.10.1. That same year, Nero petitioned the Senate for a statue in honor of his father, Gnaeus Domitius,[19] and for consular insignia for Asco-

19 The "same year" is AD 54. This chapter is the last entered by Tacitus for that year. The general good mood that Nero's enlightened promises provoked was enhanced by the diplomatic successes that he achieved in Parthia (see Chapter IV). The Arval record shows

FIGURE 5. Relief from the Sebasteion, Aphrodisias, Caria. From the Aphrodisias Archives.

nius Labeo,[20] whom he had had as a guardian. He also refused the offer of solid silver or gold statues for himself. Furthermore, despite a vote of the fathers that the calendar year should commence with the month of December (the month in which Nero was born), he kept the first of January as the start of the year because of its venerable religious associations.[21] 2. Nor were charges entertained in the case of the senator Carrinas Celer (who was accused by a slave),[22] or of the Roman knight Julius Densus, the charge against whom was based on his support for Britannicus.[23]

11.1. In the consulship of Claudius Nero and Lucius Antistius, [24] when the magistrates swore the oath to uphold the legislative measures of the emperors, Nero forbade his colleague Antistius to swear to uphold the measures he himself had passed.[25] This drew fulsome praise from the senators, who hoped that his young mind, elated by the glory arising from even trivial gestures, might immediately proceed to more substantial ones. 2. Then came his

---

that Domitius's birthday, December 11, was celebrated in 55 (Smallwood 19.29); the record for 54 is missing. It is likely that Nero's request was made on the occasion of the birthday (see Suet. *Ner.* 9.1). By now, Domitius had been dead some fifteen years.

20 Asconius is not otherwise known, but he may be related to the famous grammarian and historian Quintus Asconius Pedianus. A child was placed *in tutela* (in guardianship) upon the death of the *paterfamilias*. Asconius had presumably been appointed either upon the death of Domitius or upon the death of the wealthy Crispus Passienus, Agrippina's second husband.

21 In fact, the tradition of beginning the official year on the calends of January was not an ancient one but had been established in 153 BC. On Nero's birthday, see the appendix to Chapter I.

22 Carrinas is otherwise unknown. Normally, slaves were not allowed to testify against their masters. The restriction was lifted in cases involving treason (*maiestas*) or incest.

23 Julius Densus is also unknown. His case illustrates that trials in the Senate did not exclusively involve juries of peers; there are several instances of knights being tried in the Senate. Presumably, Densus's case involved an attempt to revive the *maiestas* law.

24 We now pass into AD 55. Claudius assumed the consulship at the beginning of his reign, and Nero followed his example. He held the office for two months of the year (Suet. *Ner.* 14).

25 The oath to uphold the acts (*acta*) of the *princeps*, and of his predecessors (unless they were deliberately excluded from the formula), was taken first by the magistrates and then by all the senators. It developed from the oath recorded for the year 45 BC, which took the form of pledging to take no action against the official acts of Caesar (App. *BC* 2.106), and was reinforced by the triumvirs at the beginning of 42 BC (Dio 47.18.3). Dio records that in 29 BC the Senate ratified the acts of Octavian (51.20.1). Tiberius took the oath to uphold the acts of Augustus (Dio 57.8.5), but he refused the request of the Senate that it do the same for his own (Tac. *Ann.* 1.72.1; Dio 57.8.4).

clemency toward Plautius Lateranus, who had been demoted from his rank for adultery with Messalina.[26] Nero restored him to the Senate, committing himself to leniency in a string of speeches that Seneca, by putting them in Nero's mouth, brought to public attention, either to attest to the nobility of his instruction or to showcase his talent.

Suetonius turns to Nero's positive traits.

Suet. *Ner.* 9.1. He began his reign with a display of filial piety. He gave Claudius a splendid funeral, at which he delivered a eulogy and declared him a god.[27] To the memory of his father, Domitius, he paid the greatest honor. . . .[28]

He founded a colony at Antium,[29] for which he enlisted veterans of the praetorian guard and added to them the richest of the senior centurions, who were obliged to leave their homes.[30] He also built a harbor there, which was a very expensive operation.[31]

26 Plautius Lateranus was accused of adultery with Messalina in 48. He was spared the death penalty by Claudius because of the distinguished services of his uncle but was expelled from the Senate (Tac. *Ann.* 11.30.2, 36.4). He would return to the Senate in 55 (Tac. *Ann.* 13.11.2) and later join the Pisonian conspiracy of 65 against Nero (Tac. *Ann.* 15.49.3, 60.1; see Chapter IV). His property was then confiscated and supposedly given later to the Christian church, preserving his memory in the name of the Lateran cathedral. His uncle was Aulus Plautius, commander of the expeditions against Britain.

27 Despite Suetonius's assertion, divine honors were the monopoly of the Senate, although they were presumably granted upon the petition of the emperor. Throughout his reign, Nero described himself on his coins as divi filius, son of one who had been deified. At Suet. *Claud.* 45, there is a suggestion that Nero did not treat the deification with respect (see also Plin. *Pan.* 11.1).

28 Tacitus (*Ann.* 13.10.1) observes that Nero petitioned the Senate for a statue of Domitius, and he suggests that this occurred near the end of the year. If so, Suetonius has not been punctilious in restricting himself to the program laid out by Nero at the very outset of the reign.

29 Antium held a special place in Nero's affections, since he was born there. There was already a colony there, but it had lost many of its settlers, who had moved away, and there was a further unsuccessful attempt to boost its population in AD 60 (Tac. *Ann.* 14.27.2–3).

30 Members of the praetorian guard were able to retire after sixteen years of service. Their better pay (two denarii a day at the time of Tiberius's accession) would have made them welcome in the colony. Legionary senior centurions (*primipili*) were relatively well paid, and they received a bonus upon their retirement (Suet. *Cal.* 44.1; Dio 55.23.1).

31 The date and nature of the harbor at Antium have been much debated. It may have been built in connection with the imperial villa there or may have had a broader function as a safe haven for grain ships from Egypt.

FIGURE 6. *RIC*[2] Nero 394, Brass Sestertius. Obverse: NERO CLAVD(ius) CAESAR AVG(ustus) GER(manicus) P(ontifex) M(aximus) TR(ibunicia) P(otestate) IMP(erator) Pater P(atriae), "Nero Claudius Caesar Augustus Germanicus, Chief Priest, with Tribunician Authority, Imperator, Father of the Country." Reverse: CONGI(arium) I DAT(um) POP(ulo) S(enatus) C(onsulto), "The first donative given to the people. By a decree of the Senate." From the collection of Andreas Pangerl/romancoins.info.

The donative made in AD 54 was commemorated in sestertii issued later in the 60s, as the mature obverse portrait on the sestertius in Figure 6 makes clear. On the reverse, Nero sits on a platform at the left. Above him and facing him stands Minerva, holding an owl in her right hand and a spear in her left. To her left stands Liberalitas, holding a token for the donative. In front of Nero, a seated assistant hands out a donation to someone who is clearly a Roman citizen, as indicated by his toga. He has one foot on the platform and is holding out his right hand to receive the donation while folding his toga with his left hand to receive it. A child stands behind him.

Tacitus (*Ann.* 13.31.2) records a donative of 400 sestertii made in AD 57. This may be the one referred to by Suetonius, who seems, however, to place it in 54, at the beginning of the reign. Tacitus's reference may in fact be to a second (separate) donative, also commemorated in coins similar to the one illustrated in Figure 6 but with the legend CONG II.

The legend SC on the coin should be taken to represent a real or symbolic role for the Senate in the issuance of the coin. It does not imply a role of the Senate in the donative.

Suet. *Ner.* 10.1. To underline his good character even more convincingly, he declared that his rule would follow the principles of Augustus, and he let slip no opportunity to show his generosity and clemency, and even his affability.[32] The heavier indirect taxes he either abolished or reduced.[33] Rewards for informers under the Papian law he cut to a quarter of their former amount.[34] He distributed 400 sestertii to every man among the common people,[35] for each senator who was of very high birth but left destitute he established an annual salary, amounting to 5,000 sestertii in some cases,[36] and for the praetorian cohorts there was a monthly allowance of cost-free grain.[37] 2. Furthermore, when called on to sign the warrant for the execution of a man condemned to death (as was normal practice), he declared: "How I

32 In his account of this episode, Tacitus does not specifically mention the name of Augustus (Tac. *Ann.* 13.4.1), but his presence is implied. There was something of a tradition for emperors to aspire to the Augustan precedent, especially to make a contrast with a recently deceased predecessor, as did Caligula at the funeral of Tiberius (Dio 59.3.8). In particular, of course, they would want to be associated with the Augustan ideals of generosity (*liberalitas*) and clemency (*clementia*) (Suet. *Aug.* 41: *liberalitas*; Suet. *Aug.* 51: *clementia*).

33 Suetonius refers here to *vectigalia, indirect* taxes, such as those levied on goods upon entry and departure. Tacitus (*Ann.*13.50.2–3) suggests that Nero wanted to go further than what Suetonius suggests and considered abolishing *vectigalia* totally because of the outrageous exactions of the *publicani,* who collected the dues. He was dissuaded by his advisers because of the financial chaos it would create (the military treasury was financed from *vectigalia*) and because of the near certainty that it would lead to a demand for the abolition of *direct* taxes, paid only outside Italy as *tributum*. As a consequence, Nero limited himself to controlling the excesses of the tax collectors (Tac. *Ann.* 13.51.2). Tacitus (*Ann.* 13.31.2) reports that he removed the buyer's tax of 4% on the purchase of slaves, but it was simply levied on the vendor, who added it to the price.

34 The *Lex Papia-Poppaea* marked the final stage of the legislation enacted by Augustus to encourage marriage and legitimate procreation. Those who did not marry or produce children were barred from inheritances, while a fruitful marriage resulted in advantages in a public career. The legislation created enormous hardships, prompting Tiberius to set up a committee to try to sort out the legal difficulties (Tac. *Ann.* 3.28.3). Clearly, under Nero, the problems persisted, and his measures were designed to discourage legal actions.

35 Julius Caesar had been the first to make distributions of cash to the populace instead of the traditional public gifts of wine or oil, and after him cash donations became regular imperial practice.

36 Tacitus (*Ann.* 13.34.1) records instances of senators helped financially by Nero. M. Valerius Messala Corvinus, great-grandson of the famous orator of the republican period and partner of Nero in the consulship of AD 58, received an allowance of 500,000 sestertii annually to subsidize his "honest poverty." Tacitus also gives the names of Aurelius Cotta and Quintus Haterius Antoninus, even though they had squandered their family patrimony. No other cases are known, and Suetonius may have exaggerated somewhat.

37 The cost of grain was normally deducted from the praetorians' pay. The measure mentioned here seems to belong to the aftermath of the Pisonian conspiracy when, Tacitus reports, the troops (almost certainly the praetorians) were rewarded with a donative of 2,000 sestertii each and remission of the price of grain (*Ann.* 15.72.1; see Chapter IV). It has been suggested that in 65 Nero in fact made a one-off remission of the grain charge for that particular month (see Bradley [1978] *ad loc.*). But this would have been a modest reward.

wish I had never learned to read and write!"[38] He greeted people of all classes by name without hesitation and accurately.

When the Senate gave thanks to him, he replied: "Do that when I've deserved it." He allowed even the plebs to come to his exercises on the Campus,[39] and quite frequently gave declamations in public.[40]

He also read out his poetry, not just at home but in the theater as well.[41] Such was everybody's delight over this that public thanksgiving was offered by decree for his recitation, and the relevant parts of his poetry were dedicated to Capitoline Jupiter inscribed in letters of gold. . . .

15.1. In dispensing justice, he did not readily reply to plaintiffs except in writing and on the following day.[42] His standard practice in trying cases was to avoid continuous pleadings and to have each detail of the suit discussed in turn by the parties involved.[43] Whenever he withdrew to consult advisers,[44]

38 Seneca (*Clem.* 2.1.2) reports that, when pressed by Burrus to record his permission for the execution of two robbers, Nero declared that he wished he had never learned to write. Suetonius mentions only one condemned criminal, probably a simplification rather than the result of using a different source. The anecdote provides interesting evidence of the involvement of the emperor, even if only as a formality, in routine judicial executions.

39 The Campus Martius was a traditional place of exercise. Nero, like Caligula and Claudius before him, seems to have enjoyed a good relationship with the ordinary people, whatever problems they both encountered with other levels of society.

40 As an academic exercise, young Romans were given the task of delivering "declamations," set pieces on contrived legal issues and unlikely historical scenarios. Suetonius seems to suggest that Nero continued the practice as emperor, although Tacitus (*Ann.* 13.3.2) considers him inferior to his imperial predecessors as an orator.

41 The recitation, where acquaintances would be invited to listen to someone's work, was a well-established tradition of Roman life. It appears that Nero went beyond the normal boundaries and gave recitals in theaters.

42 The role of the emperor in legal proceedings is a well-established phenomenon, but our knowledge of the actual functioning of his court is very limited before the time of Trajan. The imperial trials do not seem to have followed fixed rules of procedure, unlike the regular praetorian courts. Suetonius seems to suggest that Nero sent personal notes to the parties in a case, which would clearly have involved a considerable investment of time if done conscientiously, and no other reference is made to the practice.

43 It seems that the procedure in imperial trials mentioned here—laying out the case in individual points rather than in a single speech—was actually introduced by Nero, probably to speed up the process. It seems to have proved a lasting innovation. Pliny the Younger refers to proceeding in court *kata kephalaion* (taking up the main points one by one) as a way of getting immediately to the truth (*Ep.* 6.22.2). Suetonius speaks of "standard practice," but there is little direct evidence for trials actually conducted by Nero (see Tac. *Ann.* 4.2).

44 The emperor had a body of legal advisers to assist him, and they could offer advice on the possible outcome, but he would be under no obligation to follow that advice, and he had complete discretion in determining the penalty to be applied.

he would never discuss anything openly in a general meeting with them; rather, he would silently and in seclusion read the opinions given in writing by each and then pronounce a verdict based on his personal feelings as though it were a majority decision.[45]

2. For a long time, he did not allow sons of freedmen into the Senate house, and he denied public office to those allowed in by former emperors.[46] Candidates in excess of the number of seats available he put in charge of legions to console them for the delay caused by the deferment.[47] He often conferred the consulship for a six-month period. If one of the consuls died toward the first of January, he appointed no replacement,[48] expressing disapproval of the old case of Caninius Rebilus, who was consul for a single day.[49] He conferred triumphal insignia on a number of people of quaestorian rank and on some from the equestrian order, and not exclusively for military accomplishments.[50] Speeches that he sent to the Senate on certain topics

45 This passage shows that the practice of Nero was to receive written, rather than oral, submissions. Suetonius (*Aug.* 93) shows that Augustus tried a case without advisers.

46 By the *Lex Visellia,* the sons of freedmen were not allowed admission into the equestrian order until the third generation. The emperor could grant dispensations to those not of the senatorial order to enable them to enter a senatorial career, and the expression "for a long time" suggests that such dispensations were later made by Nero. There is no clear example of public office being withheld from those granted such by previous emperors.

47 Tacitus (*Ann.* 14.28.1) refers to this happening as a single incident under the year 60. Twelve praetors would have been elected to the office in what, to judge from the outcome, was a genuine election; three are recorded as unsuccessful, and in normal circumstances they would have waited until a later round, but in this instance they were given military commands. Of course, the year 60 was witness to serious military crises in Britain and Parthia, and this episode almost certainly reflects a one-off arrangement rather than the general policy implied by Suetonius.

48 The procedure established under the republic was that, if a consul left office in the course of the year, he was replaced by a "suffect" (Latin *suffectus,* "replacement"). Augustus institutionalized the system and required resignations in the course of the year to increase the number of suffects and thus the pool of potential administrative officers. From 5 BC, it became regular for consuls to resign in the course of the year, and the actual term could be relatively short. Suetonius's claim that Nero sought to maintain a six-month period where possible cannot be confirmed, since we do not have complete consular records for his reign.

49 C. Caninius Rebilus held the consulship for one day in 45 BC, thus prompting many humorous quips by Cicero that Caninius did not manage to get any sleep during his consulship or that Cicero wanted to visit him during his term but night fell (Macrob. *Sat.* 7.3.10). A "one-day" term did not happen again until the one-day consulship of Roscius Regulus in 69 AD.

50 The culminating achievement of a military campaign, the "triumph" that followed a major victory in the field, was, from AD 19 on, the prerogative of the emperor and his

he would often have read out by a consul, ignoring the fact that it was a quaestor's responsibility.[51]

16.1. He devised a new structure for the city's buildings and ensured that before apartment buildings and private houses there stood colonnades, from the terraces of which fires could be fought, and he erected these at his own expense. He had also intended to extend the city walls as far as Ostia and bring seawater into the old city with a canal. . . .[52]

Dio 61.3.1. Nero was seventeen when he took power.[53] He entered the camp, and reading aloud what Seneca had written out promised them everything that Claudius had granted them.[54] The address that he read out to the Senate, also drafted by Seneca, was of much the same tenor, so that a vote was passed that it be inscribed on a silver tablet and always read out at the start of the new consuls' term of office. The senators, then, were also prepared for a good reign, as if they had some contract assuring it.

In the first year of Nero's new power as emperor, Seneca wrote two highly contrasted works. The Apocolocyntosis, *a parody of Claudius's official deification, is in fact anonymous, but almost certainly written by Seneca.* De Clementia, *the other work published in the same year, was more earnest and more substantial. It was ostensibly in praise of the merciful nature of the young emperor, whose love of his citizens was reciprocated by them, but in reality it aimed as much to show Nero what he ought to become as what he was. Ironically, this work must have been composed at a time when many in the court believed that Nero had already ensured the death of his younger brother Britannicus by poisoning (Chapter III).*

---

family. Less well-connected commanders had to remain content with triumphal *insignia*. Tacitus (*Ann.* 15.72.2) records that, after the Pisonian conspiracy, Nero assembled the Senate and bestowed the triumphal *insignia* on the ex-consul Petronius Turpilianus, the praetor designate, Cocceius Nerva, and the praetorian prefect Tigellinus "as if it involved a military campaign."

51 Of the twenty quaestors elected each year, two had the special designation "quaestor of Augustus," being chosen personally by the emperor to represent him in the Senate during his absences. One of their duties would be to carry imperial messages to the Senate.

52 It has been argued that the incorporation of Ostia within the city boundary was to make up for the land that was taken over by the Golden House, but the Ostia reference here may be linked to Nero's plan to build a canal between that city and Puteoli, traces of which survived to Tacitus's own day (see Suet. *Ner.* 31.3; Tac. *Ann.* 15.42.2).

53 Dio most likely made a mistake with Nero's age, since he was in fact almost certainly sixteen when Claudius died (see Chapter I appendix).

54 Dio alone provides the information that Seneca wrote Nero's original address to the praetorians, as well as the one delivered to the Senate.

De Clementia 1.1. I have set out to write about clemency, Nero Caesar, so as to take on the role of a mirror and demonstrate to you that you will reach the greatest pleasure of all. For although the true profit of righteous deeds is to have performed them, and no reward for virtuous actions is worthy of them beyond the actions themselves, it gives one pleasure to consider and survey a good conscience, and then to cast one's eyes on that vast mob, fractious, quarrelsome, and uncontrollable (which will by its lack of control bring about others' ruin and its own, if it breaks this yoke of yours), and to converse with oneself like this:

2. "Have I of all mortals found favor and been chosen to fulfill on earth the function of the gods? Am I the arbiter of life and death for its peoples? Has whatever destiny and status in life anyone possesses been placed in my hands? Does Fortune announce from my lips whatever she wishes to be granted to each man among mortals? Do peoples and cities draw reasons for rejoicing from my responses? Does no area flourish anywhere unless by my wish and favor? Will these thousands of swords that my peace restrains be drawn at the nod of my head? Which nations are to be utterly laid low, which deported elsewhere, which granted liberty and which have it taken from them, which kings are to become slaves and whose heads to be encircled with the royal diadem, which cities are to be destroyed, and which are to rise up—does all this rest on my decision?"

3. In this great power that I have over the world, anger has not prompted me to unjust punishments, nor has youthful impulsiveness, nor the rashness and arrogance of men (which have often driven patience even from the most tranquil breasts), nor even that quality often to be found in great empires, pride in displaying one's power through intimidation. My sword is sheathed—in fact is fastened in the sheath. My thrift in spilling even the meanest blood is great, and no one, though he lack all else, fails to find favor with me as a human being.

4. I keep my severity hidden but my mercy ready at hand. I hold myself back as if I am going to be accountable to those laws that I have brought out into the light from neglect and darkness. I am moved by the early years of one man, and the advanced years of another. I have shown pity to one because of his high rank, to another because of his low status. Whenever I had found no reason for mercy, I spared myself such action. Today, should the immortal gods demand it, I am ready to account for the human race."

5. This, Caesar, you can boldly declare: everything that has come into your charge and protection is being diligently cared for; nothing has been taken from the state either by force or by stealth because of you. You have set your heart on the rarest quality not so far bestowed on any emperor:

integrity. You do not waste your efforts, and that exceptional goodness of yours has not found ungrateful or malicious critics. You are now receiving your thanks. No one man has ever been so dear to any one person as you are to the Roman people—you are its great and lasting good! 6. But you have set a huge burden on your shoulders; no one speaks now of the deified Augustus or the early days of Tiberius Caesar, nor in wishing to imitate you does any man seek a model apart from you; what is demanded for their taste is your principate. This would be difficult if your goodness were not natural but assumed. Indeed no one can wear a mask for long, and feigned qualities quickly lapse back into their real nature, whereas those based on truth, which come from a solid base, so to speak, advance simply with time to a greater and superior condition.

III

ENEMIES WITHIN

INTRODUCTION

Apart from the rebellions in AD 68 that brought him down, Nero faced at least two external conspiracies during his reign, those of Piso and Vinicianus (Chapter VIII). But, throughout his reign, he also had to deal with threats, or perceived threats, from within the imperial family.

PART ONE: MALE RELATIVES

In a monarchical system that does not have deep historical roots, and especially one where there is no clear and generally recognized successor, usually in the form of the oldest natural son, a ruler will face not only the usual challenges from rival families seeking to wrest power from him but also challenges from claimants within his own family. Hence, it was not gratuitous cruelty that drove the Mughal emperors or the Parthian Arsacids, upon their succession, to murder their own brothers. Nero might be said to have adopted a delayed version of the Mughal method. His position as emperor was not based on any clear-cut dictate of the line of succession. He was technically the previous emperor's eldest son, but that was through adoption rather than blood, and adoption by a predecessor who in any case had seized power from his nephew in what amounted to a military putsch.

In this period, all emperors had a healthy suspicion of members of the old aristocratic families, such as the Junii Silani, who might pose a threat to their position. Apart from this broad concern, Nero identified three individuals from within his own family network as especially dangerous. Since our sources are generally determined to represent Nero as an arbitrary tyrant, we have to be cautious about the portraits they present of his potential opponents, but there is no evidence that any of his three putative rivals had any ambitions to replace him.

The most prominent of these, Britannicus, could hardly have avoided being drawn into dynastic politics. The son of Claudius and Messalina, he most probably was born on February 12, 41 (see Chapter I appendix), and received the *cognomen* (title) of Britannicus after Claudius's victories in Britain. Little is known of his childhood, except that he was tutored by Sosibius and brought up along with Titus, the future emperor (Suet. *Tit.* 2; Tac. *Ann.* 11.1.1; Dio 60.32.5). When Claudius married Agrippina, Britannicus found himself in an awkward situation. Nero was adopted by the emperor, and Britannicus thus became the younger son, his junior status emphasized when Nero received the *toga virilis* in 51 (Tac. *Ann.* 12.41.1). At the games held in that year, Britannicus wore only a *toga praetexta,* while Nero was allowed the accoutrements of a *triumphator.* Agrippina aggravated the situation, reputedly removing loyal freedmen from Britannicus's staff and replacing them with her own appointees (Tac. *Ann.* 12.26.2). Shortly before his death, Claudius supposedly relented and made the decision to give Britannicus priority, which provoked Agrippina to murder her husband. Following his father's death, Britannicus was passed over for the succession, and even his right to half of his father's property was disallowed.

Tacitus claims (*Ann.* 12.69.1) that when Nero was hailed as emperor by the praetorians after Claudius's death, a few of the troops were puzzled by the absence of Britannicus. It seems unlikely that any of them would have been inclined to inquire about the two other supposed rivals. Faustus Cornelius Sulla was Nero's cousin, the son of Domitia Lepida, Nero's paternal aunt. His father was Domitia Lepida's second husband, Faustus Cornelius Sulla, a descendant of the great dictator and himself consul in AD 31. The younger Faustus was half-brother of Messalina, daughter of Domitia Lepida and her first husband, and he thus became brother-in-law of Claudius (his mother was also the emperor's cousin). Claudius arranged the marriage of his daughter Antonia to Faustus, who in recognition of his new status received a consulship in AD 52. Antonia bore him a son (Dio 60.30.6[a]).

Gaius Rubellius Plautus's family came from Tibur and was originally equestrian. His father, Gaius Rubellius Blandus, suffect consul in AD 18, was an ambitious man who made a highly advantageous marriage with Julia, the daughter of Drusus, son of Tiberius and Livilla, the sister of Claudius (Julia had previously been married to her cousin Nero Drusus, the brother of Caligula); Tacitus (*Ann.* 6.27.1) sarcastically comments that the marriage to Rubellius added to the city's mourning because Julia had made such a disadvantageous match. Julia died the victim of Messalina's intrigues. Her son lived a life of relative obscurity.

Of the three potential rivals, Britannicus would clearly have been seen to represent the greatest danger, and Nero acted against him first. In the general euphoria of the beginning of the reign, it may have been felt that Britannicus was not in any danger. Certainly, at the end of 54, an attempt to charge a Roman knight, Julius Densus, because of his loyalty to Britannicus, failed (Tac. *Ann.* 13.10). This situation seems to have changed when Agrippina began to fall out with Nero and made a show of transferring her loyalty to Britannicus, which supposedly provoked Nero to murder him early in AD 55. This was the year when Britannicus might have been expected to assume the *toga virilis.*

Once he had decided on murder, Nero reportedly had a stroke of luck in that the poisoner Locusta was available. She had supposedly performed sterling service in the demise of Claudius, and was fortuitously in detention (perhaps for Claudius's murder) with the praetorian guard. She was drawn into Nero's service and experimented with poisons on various animals, finally obtaining success with a pig. At a dinner attended by various grandees, which included Agrippina and Titus, Britannicus was offered a very hot drink and asked for it to be cooled, whereupon cold water laced with the poison was added. He perhaps should have known better, since the same technique is cited in the supposed poisoning of Alexander the Great (Justin 12.14.9). The effect was immediate, and Britannicus began to gasp for breath. He was removed on a litter and died soon after. The funeral was arranged very quickly, that night (according to Tacitus) or the next day (according to Dio and Suetonius), and Nero made a public statement, probably written by Seneca, expressing conventional platitudes and lamenting the loss of a brother. Nothing more was said, and no report was made to the Senate. In *De Clementia,* published shortly afterward, Seneca asserts that Nero is unstained by the spilling of blood, which certainly vindicates Nero's official version, although the exoneration suffers a blow from Seneca's deathbed pronouncement, when he lists Britannicus among Nero's murder victims (Tac. *Ann.* 15.62.2). It should also be noted that so high was Nero's stock that, according to Tacitus, people generally condoned Britannicus's murder as an example of a Realpolitik, in which the state must be protected from the danger of destructive rivalries (*Ann.* 13.17.2).

The ancient sources are unanimous that Britannicus was murdered, the earliest claim being the brief and assertive statement of Josephus, and the most detailed indictment being the narrative of Tacitus, whose sympathies are readily apparent and who cites the view expressed by Agrippina that Britannicus was the "rightful and worthy heir" (*Ann.* 13.14.2) and by contemporary authors that he was the sole survivor of the Claudian family (*Ann.* 13.17.2). That said, the unanimity of the ancient sources on both the broad charge and many of the details is not of great significance, given the enormous difficulty of either proving or refuting a charge of murder by poisoning. Scholars have questioned their version of events since the mid-nineteenth century (Stahr [1867], 257). Britannicus was epileptic and may well have suffered a severe epileptic fit; the darkening of the body in fact suggests tetanoid epilepsy. No known poison except strychnine, identified only some two hundred years ago, will darken the face. The resemblance between the accounts of the last night of Britannicus and that of Claudius, including the detail of an unsuccessful first dose of poison, suggests that both drew from a common stock of stories of poisonous deaths. The truth about culpability is in fact less important than the perception. The very belief that Nero was responsible would suffice to create an atmosphere of fear. Agrippina may well have become increasingly on her guard. According to Dio (61.7.5), even Seneca and Burrus were alarmed by Nero's action and from this point on lost their serious interest in public business, choosing to concentrate on their own survival. The one person supposedly happy about it all was Locusta, who got a free pardon for all her past misdemeanors as well as a country estate as a bonus. Nero supposedly sent pupils to her. But her past was bound to catch up with her eventually, and she would die shortly after Nero, when Galba eliminated many of his predecessor's favorites.

Faustus Cornelius Sulla and Rubellius Plautus did not represent immediate threats, although they were constantly under a cloud of suspicion. Eventually, they would both be exiled and afterward put to death.

SOURCES

Tensions between Nero and Agrippina escalate, and she hints that she will champion Britannicus.

Tac. *Ann.* 13.14.2. After this, Agrippina charged headlong into fearful threats, not stopping short of declaring in the emperor's hearing that Britannicus was now grown, the rightful and worthy heir to his father's power, which was currently wielded by an adopted interloper as a result of wrongs done by his mother. 2. She had no objection, she said, to the exposure of all the ills of that unhappy house, her own marriage first of all, and her use of poison.[1] The one precaution taken by heaven and by herself was leaving her stepson alive! She would go to the camp with him, she said.[2] The daughter of Germanicus

1 The notion that Agrippina would be willing to have her supposed role in the murder of Claudius made public, and that this information would somehow ingratiate her with his son, is highly implausible.

2 The "camp" refers to the *Castra Praetoria*, the barracks of the praetorian guard, the key group in determining any dynastic change in Rome. Sejanus was responsible for organizing the guard into one single camp, just outside the Viminal Gate. The praetorians were loyal to the house of Germanicus, as Burrus will later intimate to Nero when he tries to recruit them to help in the murder of his mother (see Tac. *Ann.* 14.7.4).

should be heard on one side, the cripple Burrus and the exile Seneca on the other,[3] men laying claim to the governance of the human race—with a mutilated hand, of course, and a professorial tongue! At the same time, she threw up her hands, showered abuse on him, and called on the hallowed Claudius, the shades of the Silani below, and all the crimes she had committed for nothing.[4]

Nero decides to murder Britannicus.

Tac. *Ann.* 13.15.1. Nero was worried by this, and the day was also approaching on which Britannicus was to complete his fourteenth year.[5] He pondered at one moment on his mother's impetuosity, at the next on the strength of character of the boy himself,[6] which had lately been put to the test and demonstrated in a trifling incident but one that had gained Britannicus widespread approval. 2. During the festal days of Saturn, one of the games that Nero's companions played was drawing lots for the "kingship," and the lot had fallen to Nero.[7] He therefore gave the others various commands that would not cause embarrassment, but he ordered Britannicus to get to his feet, go to the middle of the group, and begin a song. He was expecting to provoke laughter at the expense of a boy who had no experience even of sober gatherings, much less drunken ones.[8] Britannicus, however, confidently launched into

3 Nothing more is known about Burrus's handicap. Seneca had been exiled because of his affair with Julia Livilla, Agrippina's sister (Tac. *Ann.* 13.42.2; Dio 61.10.1). He was recalled, shortly after Agrippina's marriage to Claudius, to be Nero's tutor (Tac. *Ann.* 12.8.2).

4 The reference is to Lucius and Marcus Junius Silanus. Lucius had been betrothed to Claudius's daughter Octavia and was disgraced through Agrippina's machinations in order to make way for Nero, which led to his suicide (Tac. *Ann.* 12.8.1; see Chapter I). Marcus, consul in AD 46, was identified by Tacitus as the first victim of Agrippina after the accession of Nero (Tac. *Ann.* 13.1.1).

5 Britannicus was probably born on February 12, 41 (see Chapter I appendix). His fourteenth birthday, in AD 55, would be important, since fourteen was the common age for the *toga virilis* to be assumed, either at the time of the birthday or in the following March. This would make Britannicus a far more viable alternative to Nero.

6 Tacitus earlier damned Britannicus with faint praise, claiming "they do say that he was not slow-witted by nature" (*Ann.* 12.26.2).

7 The Saturnalia began on December 17 and lasted until December 23, involving much boisterous fun. Considerable license was permitted, and many of the traditional Roman conventions were turned on their heads. In some respects, such as the giving of gifts, the festival anticipated the celebration of Christmas. Lucian, in *Saturnalia*, lays out the rules for celebrations, including the appointment of the "king." The reference here must be to the festivities in December 54.

8 Tacitus either dismisses or is unaware of the tradition recounted by Suetonius that Nero was jealous of Britannicus's singing voice.

some verse in which there were allusions to his own removal from his father's home and from supreme power. The result was an awakening of sympathy for him that was the more obvious since the gaiety of the night had banished all insincerity.

Suet. *Ner.* 33.2. He tried to murder Britannicus with poison, as much from envy of his voice, which was more pleasant than his, as from fear that he might at some point enjoy greater popularity with the people because of the memory of his father.[9]

Nero acquires poison and administers it during a banquet.

Tac. *Ann.* 13.15.3. Awareness of the ill will he himself had incurred increased Nero's hatred, and he was now also under pressure from Agrippina's threats. But there was no viable charge, and he did not dare give an order openly for his brother's death. He therefore set to work in secret and ordered a poison to be prepared. He used the services of Julius Pollio,[10] tribune of a praetorian cohort, in whose care the condemned poisoner called Locusta—a woman with a great reputation for her criminal acts—was being detained,[11] for arrangements had been made long before for all closely associated with Britannicus to have no scruples or loyalty.

4. Britannicus was given his first dose of poison by his very own tutors, but because of a bowel movement he excreted it—it was too weak, or perhaps

9 This section appears in the part of Suetonius's *Vita* that puts its focus on the cruelty of Nero and presents a series of deaths where the total focus is on the supposed role of the emperor. Given Nero's pretensions to artistry, it is perhaps inevitable that hostile sources would suggest artistic jealousy as a contributory cause for his hostility toward some of his victims. Tacitus (*Ann.* 15.49.3) claims that he was similarly jealous of Lucan. In Nero's case, the supposed jealousy may arise from the story of Britannicus's better-than-expected performance at the Saturnalia celebrations, as described by Tacitus (*Ann.* 13.15.2). The second, political motivation suggested by Suetonius can be no more than supposition on the biographer's part, but it does convey a very good insight into the political tensions within the court. Britannicus would be seen as an obvious focus for any discontent with Nero.

10 An inscription reveals a Titus Julius Pollio as procurator of Sardinia (*CIL* X 7952), and it is possible that this is the same Pollio rewarded for his services in the following year, when he presumably succeeded Vipsanius Laenas, who was convicted of extortion at that time (Tac. *Ann.* 13.30.1).

11 Locusta is introduced in Tac. *Ann.* 12.66.2 as the person who provided the poison that was used against Claudius. Townend (1960), 110–11, argues that Locusta's role in the Britannicus episode was a doublet inadvertently introduced from her role in the murder of Claudius. But it is not unreasonable that a successful poisoner might find her services needed on subsequent occasions.

had been diluted so its effect would not be immediately lethal. 5. But the time the crime was taking taxed Nero's patience. He threatened the tribune and ordered the poisoner's execution; while they were keeping an eye on public opinion, he claimed, and preparing to defend themselves, they were putting his security on hold. At this, they promised a death as swift as from a sword thrust, and a poison was brewed close to the emperor's bedroom, its virulence guaranteed by the previously tested toxins it contained.

Suet. *Ner.* 33.2. He acquired the poison from one Locusta, who had been an informer against some poisoners, but when its efficacy proved slower than he had expected, producing only diarrhea in Britannicus, he had the woman summoned and beat her with his own hand, claiming she had given the boy a counteragent, not poison. Locusta's excuse was that she had given a smaller dose to cover up the crime and avert animosity against Nero. "Of course," he replied, "I'm afraid of the Julian law!" and he made her prepare, before his eyes in his bedroom, a concoction as prompt and fast-working as she could.[12] 3. He then tried it out on a goat, and after the animal lasted five hours he had it remixed time and again and put it before a pig. The pig died instantly, and Nero then ordered the mixture to be taken into the dining room and given to Britannicus, who was dining with him.

Tac. *Ann.* 13.16.1. It was the custom for emperors' children to take their meals sitting with the other young nobles at their own, less copiously provided table, in sight of their relatives.[13] There Britannicus was dining and, since a chosen member of his staff would taste what he ate and drank, the following ruse was found so that the protocol would not be broken or the crime betrayed by the deaths of both individuals.

2. Britannicus was handed a drink that was innocuous, and also very hot, and that had gone through the tasting process. Then, when it was refused because of its heat, poison was added in some cold water, and that spread so effectively throughout the boy's body that the powers to speak and to breathe

12 There was no *Lex Julia* that covered poisoning; either Suetonius or Nero has it wrong, unless the reference was to the general *Lex Julia de Vi*. The legislation covering poisoning was the *Lex Cornelia de Sicariis et Veneficiis*.

13 Suetonius mentions that Claudius followed the custom of having the imperial children to dinner, along with the children of distinguished men. The children sat, rather than reclined, in keeping with tradition (Suet. *Aug.* 64.3; *Claud.* 32). Valerius Maximus (2.1.2) mentions that this used to be the practice for women also. Suetonius (*Tit.* 2) states that the future emperor Titus was among the participants when Britannicus died, and became ill himself through eating the poison.

were both taken from him. 3. There was alarm among those sitting around him, and the less discerning scattered, but those with a keener understanding remained fast in their seats, staring at Nero. He, reclining and seemingly unaware of the situation, remarked that this was a regular occurrence connected with the epilepsy with which Britannicus had been afflicted since early infancy, and that his sight and senses would gradually return. 4. But from Agrippina, for all her efforts to control her expression, came a fleeting glance of such panic and confusion that it was clear that she knew just as little as Britannicus's sister Octavia. She was beginning to realize, in fact, that her last support had been removed, and a precedent had been set for murdering a family member. Octavia, too, despite her tender years, had learned to hide grief, affection, and all the emotions. And so, after a brief silence, the revelry of the banquet recommenced.

Britannicus is given a hasty funeral.

Tac. *Ann.* 17.1. The one night saw Britannicus's killing and his funerary pyre in tandem, for preparations (which were modest enough) for his funeral had already been put in place.[14]

He was, however, interred in the Campus Martius, [15] during a downpour so violent that the masses took it as a sign of the gods' anger over a crime that even many men could forgive, when they considered the ancient animosities between brothers, and the indivisibility of regal power.[16] 2. Many authors of the period record that, on numerous days prior to the death, Nero took advantage sexually of the young Britannicus—and his end might therefore be seen as neither too early nor cruel. And that was despite its being hurriedly brought on the last of the Claudian bloodline[17] (amid the sacred observances of the table, [18] without his being given even the time to embrace his sisters,[19]

14 Suetonius explicitly and Dio by implication suggest that the funeral took place the next day, although Tacitus is supported by the claims that Nero made in his edict.

15 Britannicus was interred in the Tomb of Augustus in the Campus Martius. Tacitus perhaps refers to the tomb obliquely to avoid the impression that Britannicus was honored.

16 Fraternal strife was a common theme of ancient legend. The most familiar in the Roman tradition was, of course, that of Romulus and Remus. Philo (*Leg.* 68) indicates that a similar justification was made for Caligula's execution of Tiberius Gemellus.

17 Britannicus was the last male born into the great Claudian family (his sisters Octavia and Antonia were still alive). Nero did have a degree of Claudian blood but could claim full Claudian kinship only by adoption. Similarly, upon Nero's death, the Julian line died out.

18 By "sacred observances," Tacitus is referring to the custom at a meal of making ritual libations to the Lares and Penates.

19 In the previous section (16.4), Tacitus implies that of the two sisters only Octavia was present at the banquet.

and before the eyes of his enemy), who was defiled by sexual misconduct before he was by poison.

3. Nero defended the hurried obsequies in an edict, declaring that it was the established practice of their ancestors to remove from the gaze of the people bitterly untimely funerals, and not hold them back with encomia and ceremony.[20] But with his brother's aid now lost to him, he added, all his remaining hopes rested in the state, and the senators and people should give all the more support to their emperor as the lone survivor of a family born to the supreme power.

Suet. *Ner.* 33.3. When Britannicus fell dead at the first taste, Nero lied to his guests, saying that he had been seized by one of his habitual bouts of epilepsy, and the next day, in pouring rain, he hurriedly gave him a commonplace funeral.[21] As for Locusta, he rewarded her for the service she had done him with a pardon and large country estates, and he even sent students to her.[22]

Dio 61.7.4. After treacherously murdering Britannicus with poison, Nero smeared the boy's body with gypsum when it became livid from the effects of the poison. But there was a heavy rainfall as it was being taken through the Forum and, as the gypsum was still wet, the rain washed it all away so that the monstrous deed was not only heard about but actually seen.[23]

5. After Britannicus's death, Seneca and Burrus no longer paid any serious attention to affairs of state but were content with looking after things passably well and holding onto their lives. As a result, Nero openly began to do anything he wanted without any fear.

Joseph. *Ant.* 20.135. Agrippina feared that, when he reached manhood, Britannicus would take over the reins of power from his father and so, wishing to seize the supreme command for her own son, she took measures, it was said, to bring about Claudius's death. She immediately sent Burrus, the commander of the soldiery, and along with him the military tribunes and those

20 Servius (*Aeneid*, xi. 143) and Seneca (*Brev. Vit.* 20.5) observe that the funerals of those who died prematurely took place at night. Before receiving the *toga virilis*, Britannicus would have counted as a child.

21 Suetonius and Dio seem to have used a common source in that both refer to the funeral taking place in heavy rain.

22 Suetonius is the only source to suggest that Locusta was rewarded with estates.

23 Dio may here be referring to the practice of smearing the face of the departed with powder. Servius (*Aen.* 9.485) fancifully traces the etymology of a class of undertakers, *pollinctores*, as derived from the powder (Latin *pollen*) that they applied to dead bodies to conceal the pallor.

freedmen with the greatest power, to take Nero away to the camp and hail him as emperor. Having gained the imperial command in this way, Nero eliminated Britannicus with poison, in a manner unperceived by most, but not much later he quite openly murdered his own mother, repaying her like that not only for bearing him but also for enabling him to gain supreme authority over the Romans through her machinations.[24] He also killed Octavia, to whom he was married, and many distinguished men, on the grounds that they were plotting against him.

Gaius Rubellius Plautus's connection with the Julio-Claudian family gave him a high profile, whether he sought it or not. In 55, Junia Silana, the enemy of Agrippina, accused her of urging Rubellius to foment rebellion with the intention of marrying him if the rebellion proved successful. The accusation got nowhere, but Nero felt insecure enough to banish him to Asia in 60.

Tac. *Ann.* 14.22.1. It was during this period that a blazing comet appeared, which, in the view of the common people, presages a change of ruler.[25] Thus, as though Nero had already been deposed, people began to ask who might be selected. And the man frequently on the lips of all was Rubellius Plautus, whose noble blood came, on his mother's side, from the Julian family. Plautus held to the ideas of his ancestors, [26] being austere in appearance, and moral and reclusive in his private life, but the more cloistered he became through fear, the greater the reputation he acquired. 2. The prevailing rumor was intensified by an interpretation (just as unwarranted) put on a lightning bolt. Nero was dining in his villa, called the Sublaqueum,[27] near the Simbru-

24 Josephus's comment is of special interest because of his own friendship with the future emperor Titus, who was raised with Britannicus and was present at the banquet, where he, too, fell ill. Josephus reflects the version of events that was clearly current in court circles when he published his narrative in the early 90s. His account adds strength to the claim (Chapter I) that Agrippina had removed the freedmen who were sympathetic toward Britannicus and had also, apart from maneuvering the appointment of Burrus as commander of the praetorians (Josephus's "soldiery"), filled the lower ranks of the guard with her own appointees (Tac. *Ann.* 12.26.2, 41.2).

25 The period is AD 60. Seneca (*QNat.* 7.17.2, 21.3, 29.3) mentions this comet and reports that it took away the bad reputation of comets, since it was not accompanied by any evil. Comets presaged the deaths of Augustus (Dio 56.29.3) and Claudius (Plin. *HN* 2.92; Suet. *Claud.* 46; Dio 61.35.1).

26 Rubellius was associated with Stoicism (Chapter VIII), and Tacitus here seems to suggest that his ancestors were similarly inclined.

27 There is no town of Sublaqueum known from ancient sources, and Tacitus introduces the villa in terms that suggest it was not well known. Frontinus refers to a *villa Sub-*

ine lakes, when the meal was struck and the table shattered, and because this had happened in the territory of Tibur, homeland of Plautus's family on his father's side, people believed that Plautus was being designated as the successor by divine will. He also had widespread support from the sort of men who have a voracious (and often misguided) ambition to be ahead of others in espousing new and risky causes. 3. Worried by this, Nero drafted a letter to Plautus, telling him to consider the peace of the city and distance himself from those who were spreading malicious gossip. Plautus had ancestral lands throughout Asia, Nero said, and there he could enjoy his youth in safety and without trouble. And so Plautus retired there with his wife, Antistia, and a few close friends.[28]

In 55, Faustus Cornelius was cleared of conspiring to become emperor but continued to fall under suspicion. In 58, he was accused of plotting against Nero and this time was obliged to go into exile in Massilia.

Tac. *Ann.* 13.23.1. After that, Pallas and Burrus were accused of conspiring to have Cornelius Sulla summoned to imperial power because of his distinguished lineage and family connection with Claudius, whose son-in-law he was through his marriage to Antonia.[29] The man responsible for the charge was a certain Paetus, who was notorious for his dealings with the treasury in confiscated goods, and at that time he was clearly caught in a lie.[30] 2. However, Pallas's proven innocence brought people less pleasure than his arrogance brought indignation, for when the names of the freedmen who were his alleged accomplices were given, Pallas replied that, at home, he never communicated anything except by a nod or a wave of the hand, and if further explanation were necessary, he used writing so as to avoid conversing

---

lacensis of Nero (*Aq.* 93). It seems that it takes its name (literally, "located under the lake,") from its proximity to the three lakes formed by the Anio (Plin. *HN* 3.109).

28 Rubellius was married to Antistia Pollitta, daughter of Lucius Antistius Vetus, consul in 55. She and her father died by suicide some four years after Rubellius's death (Tac. *Ann.* 16.10–11; see Chapter VIII).

29 In the heated political atmosphere that prevailed after the death of Britannicus and during the worsening situation of Agrippina, there were many ready and willing to denounce their opponents. Burrus, the commander of the praetorian guard, and Pallas the freedman were close allies of Agrippina. The charge made against them that they conspired with Faustus is on the surface absurd.

30 The accuser is otherwise unknown. It seems that he was trafficking in confiscated property, perhaps buying it in bulk and selling it at a profit, or buying up the debt and recovering the funds plus a premium from the debtor.

with them. Although he was also in the dock, Burrus joined the judges in expressing his opinion.[31] A sentence of exile was imposed on the accuser, and the records he used to retrieve the forgotten claims of the treasury were incinerated.

13.47.1. Such was the extent to which Nero sought to cloak his shameful and criminal acts.[32] He was especially suspicious of Cornelius Sulla, whose slow-wittedness he took as being its opposite, regarding him as a clever man putting on an act.[33] Graptus, one of the imperial freedmen who—because of his experience and old age—was an expert in the house of the emperors from Tiberius's time, intensified Nero's fears with the following lie.

2. The Mulvian Bridge was, in that period, famous for its nightlife, and Nero used to frequent the place so he would have greater leeway for his lechery outside the city.[34] Now Graptus fabricated the story that a trap had been set for him on his return journey along the Flaminian Way, that Nero had a fortuitous escape because he came back by another route to the Gardens of Sallust, and that the man responsible for the plot was Sulla.[35] (Graptus hit on this story because it so happened that the uproarious behavior of some young people—a widespread phenomenon at the time—had earlier struck groundless panic into a number of the emperor's servants on their way home.) 3. No slave or client of Sulla's had actually been identified, and the man's nature, which was universally despised and incapable of any enterprising act, was at odds with the accusation. Even so, Sulla received orders to quit the country, just as if he had been found guilty, and to remain within the confines of the walls of Massilia.[36]

31 The role of Burrus is strangely anomalous. He was not a senator, and he must be assumed to be sitting as an assessor in a case that the *princeps* is holding in private.

32 "Such was the extent": Tacitus's account of the exile of Faustus follows the description of Nero and Otho's rivalry for Poppaea in AD 58.

33 For all that Faustus Cornelius Sulla was a victim of Nero, Tacitus cannot refrain from commenting on his observed weakness of character.

34 The Mulvian (or Milvian) Bridge stood on the Via Flaminia at a crossing over the Tiber, about two miles from the city. It has given its name to the nearby battle in which the emperor Constantine I defeated his opponent Maxentius in AD 312. He granted toleration to Christianity throughout the empire in the following year.

35 The Horti Sallustiani, north of the Quirinal Hill, were laid out by the historian Sallust and became an imperial possession under Tiberius.

36 Massilia (modern Marseille) was founded by Greeks (from Phocaea in Asia Minor) in what later became Gallia Narbonensis and was a comfortable place of exile during the Roman period.

In 62, Rubellius and Faustus are put to death.

Tac. *Ann.* 14.57.1. After Seneca's downfall, undermining Faenius Rufus's position with a charge of friendship with Agrippina was easy.[37] Tigellinus's power, moreover, was growing daily, and he now felt that his evil qualities, on which his power entirely depended, would be more appealing to Nero if he could put the emperor under obligation by association in crime. He therefore proceeded to pry into his fears. Discovering that his anxieties were focused mostly on Plautus and Sulla—both recently removed from Italy, Plautus to Asia and Sulla to Narbonese Gaul—he began commenting on their noble birth and the fact that both had armies close to them (Plautus in the East and Sulla in Germany). 2. He had not the conflict of interest that Burrus had, said Tigellinus—Nero's safety was his only concern! And for that, all possible precautions were being taken against treachery in Rome by his action on the spot. But how could distant insurrections be quelled? The Gallic provinces were all agog at the name of the dictator,[38] and the peoples of Asia were no less excited by the fame conferred by having Drusus as a grandfather.[39] 3. Sulla was poor, hence his excessive recklessness, and he was faking apathy until he found an opportunity for some bold stroke. As for Plautus, with his great wealth, he did not even feign a desire for tranquility. Instead, he ostentatiously aped the Romans of old, even adopting the arrogant teachings of the Stoics, which made men mutinous and ambitious.[40]

4. There was no further delay. Five days later, before any rumor arrived to cause alarm, Sulla was killed as he was reclining for dinner, after assassins had sailed to Massilia. His head was brought back to Nero, who poked fun at the premature greyness that disfigured it.

58.1. That Plautus's assassination was being planned was less of a secret: more people were concerned for his safety, and the length of the land and sea journey and the time interval involved had given rise to rumor. 2. The lie

37 On Faenius Rufus, see Chapter VIII. Rufus is not referred to again until AD 65 (see Tac. *Ann.*15.50.3).

38 It seems unlikely that the name of Faustus's ancestor, the dictator Sulla, who held office in 82/81 BC, carried much weight a century and a half later.

39 Rubellius Plautus was the son of Julia, daughter of Drusus, the son of Tiberius. It is not clear why Asia should have been excited by the name, since his grandfather Drusus had achieved only modest distinction outside Italy, and that was in Illyricum. Nor did he achieve enough to be generally admired in all the provinces of the empire.

40 This is the first reference by Tacitus to the notion that Stoicism could be a source of opposition to the emperor; see Chapter VIII.

being put about was that Plautus had headed for Corbulo, who was then in charge of mighty armies, and who would himself be in a particularly parlous situation if the famous and blameless were targeted for murder.[41] Furthermore, it was said that Asia had taken up arms in support of the young man, and that soldiers sent to do the deed, being neither strong in numbers nor inwardly committed, had been incapable of carrying out their orders and had joined the revolt.

3. These idle speculations were enhanced, as happens with rumor, by credulous people with time on their hands, but, thanks to some swift winds, a freedman of Plautus arrived ahead of the centurion and delivered to Plautus instructions from his father-in-law, Lucius Antistius.[42] 4. Antistius told him to avoid a cowardly death while there was still a way out. He would, through the sympathy generated by his great name, find good men to help, and would enlist brave allies. Meanwhile, no assistance should be rejected. He needed to drive off sixty soldiers, the number then en route, and while the news was being carried back to Nero and while a second force was on its way, much could transpire that could develop into war. In short, said Antistius, either Plautus's salvation would be gained by such a plan or he would have to suffer nothing worse for showing spirit than playing the coward.

59.1. This, however, made no impression on Plautus. Either he could see no future for himself as an unarmed exile or he was tired of his fluctuating hopes. Or possibly it was because of his love for his wife and children, thinking the emperor would be more lenient to them if he had no worries to bother him. There are some who record that a second message arrived from his father-in-law reporting that he was facing no terrible danger, and also that his philosophy teachers, Coeranus and Musonius—the former of Greek, the latter Tuscan, stock—urged him to await death with resolution rather than live in incertitude and fear.[43]

2. At all events, he was found in the middle of the day stripped for physical exercise. Such was his condition when he was cut down by the centurion, before the eyes of the eunuch Pelago, whom Nero had set over the centurion

41 There is an element of deliberate irony in Tacitus's words, since Corbulo would later be summoned to Greece while Nero was on his grand tour there, and be ordered to commit suicide.

42 The reference is cryptic, but it is shown in the next section that a centurion had been sent to execute Plautus. Consul in AD 55, Lucius Antistius committed suicide in 65, along with his daughter Politta, Plautus's widow.

43 Coeranus is identified as a philosopher in the Index to Book 2 of Pliny's *Natural History*. He was clearly Greek, but is otherwise unknown. Musonius was a distinguished Stoic, exiled following the Pisonian conspiracy (see Chapter VIII).

and his unit like a royal minister over retainers. 3. The head of the murdered man was brought back, and at the sight of it Nero said (I shall quote the emperor's actual words): "Why, Nero < . . . >."[44]

Dio 62.14.1. Nero used his relatives' sufferings as a basis for mirth and joking. Thus, when he had put Plautus to death and looked at his head when it was brought to him, he said: "I didn't realize he had such a big nose"—as though he would have spared him had he had prior knowledge of this.

PART TWO: MOTHER

The abrupt announcement that Tacitus makes at the beginning of *Annals* 14 that Nero has now decided to murder Agrippina comes as a great surprise. She has been absent from the *Annals* since 13.21 (AD 55) and is barely mentioned in the other literary sources during the intervening period. In the meantime, she seems to have had relatively little contact with Nero and to have played no part in the political life of Rome. Suetonius says that Nero felt intimidated by "her threats and violent behavior," but he provides no examples, and it is possible that he is referring to the recollection of her behavior during her earlier ascendancy. Tacitus provides the implausible explanation that Nero was nagged into the deed by Poppaea (see Chapter VII), who saw Agrippina as a block to her marriage to the emperor. But Agrippina's death did not have any immediate impact on Poppaea's situation; she still had to wait another three years to marry Nero. Poppaea's supposed role in early 59 seems to have been to provide a plausible explanation for Nero's conduct, for which no explanation is otherwise forthcoming, as well as the attractive opportunity to demonstrate that Nero had become, like Claudius before him, the dupe of the women in the court. Dio's explanation, that Poppaea was indeed behind Agrippina's murder and acted because she had discovered that Nero had acquired a new mistress who was his mother's double, is even more outlandish. In late 55, Agrippina was only forty-three years old (or thereabouts), having lived her adult life at the center of political intrigue and power. It seems unlikely that she would simply have retired. The intrigue and plotting may well have continued—there is no way of knowing—and Nero will later portray her as plotting against him. But if it did continue, it went underground, hidden from the public and from historical sources. Of course, the explanation may not be political at all but hidden deep in Nero's psyche and known only to himself.

44 Some of the text is missing, but the joke can be recovered from an anecdote in Dio 62.14.1, where Nero comments that he had not realized that Plautus had such a big nose.

Once Nero had decided in early 59 that he would eliminate his mother, he had to find the means. Especially after the suspicious death of Britannicus, she would have been on her guard against poisons. A direct physical attack would have been difficult, since she enjoyed the loyalty of the praetorian guard. Tacitus reports that Nero found a willing helper in Anicetus, his former tutor and now prefect of the fleet based at Misenum. Anicetus's plan to build a collapsing ceiling in Agrippina's bedroom (Suet. *Ner.* 34.2) was apparently leaked and had to be abandoned. He was subsequently inspired by a theatrical performance in which a mechanical ship opened up to disembark animals, and he set about constructing a collapsible seagoing vessel.

The murder was scheduled for the festival of Minerva (March 19–23, 59), which Nero customarily spent at Baiae on the Bay of Naples. Agrippina was invited to join her son and was treated hospitably. She was given an affectionate farewell as she boarded the sinister vessel for the return journey. Tacitus's narrative of the murder (*Ann.* 14.3–13) is generally similar to that provided by Suetonius (*Ner.* 34). The two also share much in common with Dio (61.12–14) and are not inconsistent with the *Octavia* (125, 310–57, 955). The description of the disaster at sea is dramatic and entertaining but must be viewed with considerable skepticism. Apart from the general implausibility of such an excessively ingenious vessel, there are a number of troubling details. The account seems to merge the two notions of the collapsing bedroom and the collapsing ship. Creperius Gallus is described as being near the helm, but he is all the same crushed by the canopy that collapsed onto the sofa. Agrippina and Acerronia are supposedly saved by the sides of the sofa, which would have required them to be lying in curious positions. The reported conduct of the crew raises serious questions. Those in the know supposedly stood at one side to tip the boat over, clearly a suicidal gesture. They also displayed an amazing indifference to secrecy, as when they clubbed Acerronia to death in the belief that she was Agrippina: they could have avoided detection better by simply throwing Agrippina overboard. It is possible that a clue to the true sequence of events is provided in a passing comment of Suetonius (*Ner.* 34.2) but recorded nowhere else, namely that, in order to persuade Agrippina to return by the mechanical ship, Nero had her own vessel deliberately rammed on the inbound journey to Baiae. After Agrippina's death, Nero maintained tight control over the news of the event, which would have led to considerable speculation. Had there been a collision at sea, whether accidental or deliberate, this could have become confused and distorted into the subsequent story of the collapsing boat. According to Tacitus, Agrippina herself was afterward in no doubt that the ship had collapsed. But these doubts are expressed in her private thoughts, to which Tacitus could hardly have had access.

Whether or not Nero, Seneca, and Burrus did in fact hold an emergency meeting after Agrippina's initial escape, their reported reactions seem plausible. Seneca characteristically took the cowardly way out, leaving it to Burrus to find a solution. Burrus's observation that the praetorians were devoted to the whole of the imperial house testifies to the enduring popularity of Agrippina's father, Germanicus, and also to the effectiveness of Agrippina's earlier maneuverings to replace officers of the guard with her own followers (Tac. *Ann.*12.41.2–3).

SOURCES

Agrippina resorts to incest to maintain control over Nero.

Tac. *Ann.* 14.2.1. According to Cluvius's account,[45] Agrippina was so far driven by her desire to hold onto power that at the midpoint of the day, when Nero—even at that hour—was flushed with wine and feasting, she quite often appeared before her inebriated son all dressed up and ready for incestuous relations.[46] People close to them began noticing the salacious kisses and the sweet talk that is usually the precursor to sexual relations, and to counter female charms Seneca sought to enlist a woman's aid. He brought in the freedwoman Acte, who was worried about both her own parlous situation and the disgrace facing Nero.[47] Acte was to report to the emperor that the incest was common knowledge, since his mother boasted of it, and that his soldiers would not accept the sovereignty of a depraved emperor. 2. Fabius Rusticus claims that the desire for such relations was not Agrippina's but Nero's, and it was then frustrated by the freedwoman's ploy.[48] But the other sources give the same version as Cluvius, and popular opinion leans that way, too. Possibly, Agrippina really did envision such a ghastly act, or perhaps contemplating this sexual deviation seemed more plausible in her case. After

45 On Cluvius, see the Introduction.

46 Tacitus here introduces a discussion that is unusual in that he cites the sources for the competing interpretations. At its heart is the claim that Nero had an incestuous relationship with his mother.

47 Acte was an imperial slave from Asia (Dio 61.17.1); she represented a major relationship in Nero's life. Suetonius (*Ner.* 28.1) claims that Nero was prepared to marry her and that he bribed some ex-consuls to testify that she was of royal blood. Agrippina saw the affair as a threat to her own influence over her son. Acte remained loyal to Nero to the end and interred his remains. She outlived him and became prosperous, owning many slaves and property at Puteoli and Velitrae.

48 Suetonius (*Ner.* 28.2) recounts the incest claims and aligns himself with the minority interpretation of Fabius.

all, she had had illicit intercourse with Marcus Lepidus as a girl because of her lust for power;[49] with that same craving, she had abandoned herself to the appetites of Pallas;[50] and she had been trained in all manner of immorality through marriage to her uncle.

Dio 61.11.3.Now Agrippina was afraid that the woman [Poppaea] might become Nero's wife (for he had begun to develop an overwhelming passion for her), and she had the brazenness for a truly diabolical course of action.[51] As if it were not enough for her monstrous record that she had seduced her uncle Claudius with the licentious charms of her glances and kisses, she tried also to make Nero her slave in the same manner.

4. However, whether this did actually take place or whether it was made up as suiting their characters I do not know, but I do record what is acknowledged by everybody, namely that Nero was truly devoted to a certain courtesan for the very reason that she resembled Agrippina, and that, when teasing the girl herself and showing her off to others, he would say that he was having sex with his mother.[52]

Suet. *Ner.* 28.1. Apart from his "pedagogy" with freeborn boys and his illicit sex with married women, he also raped the vestal virgin Rubria.[53] With the freedwoman Acte, he almost entered into a state of legal marriage, after

49 Marcus Aemilius Lepidus had been the husband of Drusilla, sister of Caligula, and was a favorite and possibly designated successor of that same emperor. His affair with Agrippina, the sister of his late wife, in her early twenties at the time, was viewed as incestuous. He was executed by Caligula in 39, probably for involvement in the conspiracy of Gnaeus Lentulus Gaetulicus, and Agrippina was reputedly forced to carry his ashes back to Rome (Dio 59.22.7–8).

50 On Pallas, see Chapter I. Agrippina supposedly had an affair with him.

51 Dio agrees with Tacitus that Agrippina opposed Poppaea's marriage and also sees this as the motive for Agrippina's murder.

52 Dio's account of the reputed incest differs from that of Tacitus in that he adopts the Cluvian version of events and assigns the responsibility to Agrippina, although he does express some general skepticism about whether it happened at all. Dio sees the incest purely in terms of sexual rivalry. He seems to use the same source as Suetonius in suggesting that Nero had a mistress who resembled his mother. The story looks suspiciously like a doublet of the claim that Nero had girlfriends and boyfriends who resembled the late Poppaea (see Chapter VII).

53 The rape of a vestal constituted a very serious crime, with serious punishment for the perpetrator. Suetonius (*Dom.* 8.4) reports that the consensual lovers of vestals were banished and those of the chief vestal were beaten to death, except for an ex-praetor who owned up before conviction and was allowed exile. Nero's crime is not recorded elsewhere (but see Aur. Vict. *Caes.* 5.11.5).

bribing some men of consular rank to commit perjury by saying that she was born of royal stock.[54] Castrating the boy Sporus, he attempted to make a woman of him, and after a formal wedding ceremony with dowry and veil, the boy was escorted in a crowded procession to the palace, where Nero kept him as his wife.[55] A rather witty joke made by someone is still current, to the effect that things could have gone well for humankind if Nero's father, Domitius, had had a wife like that.

2. This Sporus, adorned with the attire of the imperial ladies and carried in a litter, Nero took as his companion around the courts and markets of Greece and subsequently, at Rome, around the Sigillaria,[56] time and again showering him with fond kisses. No one doubted that he wanted sexual relations with his mother but was discouraged by her critics, who feared that a strong-willed and headstrong woman might gain undue influence from this sort of activity—and it was all the more credible after he enlisted among his sleeping partners a prostitute who was said to look very much like Agrippina. One time, too, when he was riding in a litter with his mother, they say that he committed incest with her and was found out by the stains on his clothing.[57]

Nero decides to murder Agrippina and opts for a collapsing boat.

Dio 61.12. When Sabina found out about this, she persuaded Nero to do away with his mother, saying that she was plotting against him.[58] According

54 It would be impossible for Nero to marry Acte, a freedwoman, and the slur here seems to be that in his relationship he treated a social inferior in such a way that it was tantamount to marriage. A similar relationship existed between Vespasian and Caenis (Suet. *Vesp.* 3).

55 Sporus is famous as Nero's lover, and Suetonius suggests that the affair began when Sporus was very young. He remained with Nero until the emperor's death. His association with Otho caused the latter some unpopularity (Dio 64.8.3), and he was also involved with Nymphidius Sabinus (Plut. *Galb.* 9.3). He did have self-respect, committing suicide rather than obeying Vitellius's orders to perform in a rape scene onstage (Dio 65.10.1).

56 During the Saturnalia, clay dolls (*sigilla*) were familiar presents (Macrob. *Sat.* 1.11.46–50) and gave their name to a market, Sigillaria, where eventually general Saturnalia gifts could be purchased.

57 In the story of the incest, Suetonius seems to follow essentially the version of Fabius, reported by Tacitus (discussed earlier). Dio also recounts the story of the Agrippina look-alike.

58 Dio's logic here is not clear. He reports that Nero reputedly committed incest with his mother from sexual jealousy. Poppaea as a consequence sought to eliminate Agrippina. This makes sense only if we add the motivation reflected by Tacitus, that the incest was part of a power play. Clearly, Dio, like Tacitus, can see no valid reason why Nero should have decided on the murder of his mother in 59 and, also like Tacitus, ascribes it to the plotting of Poppaea.

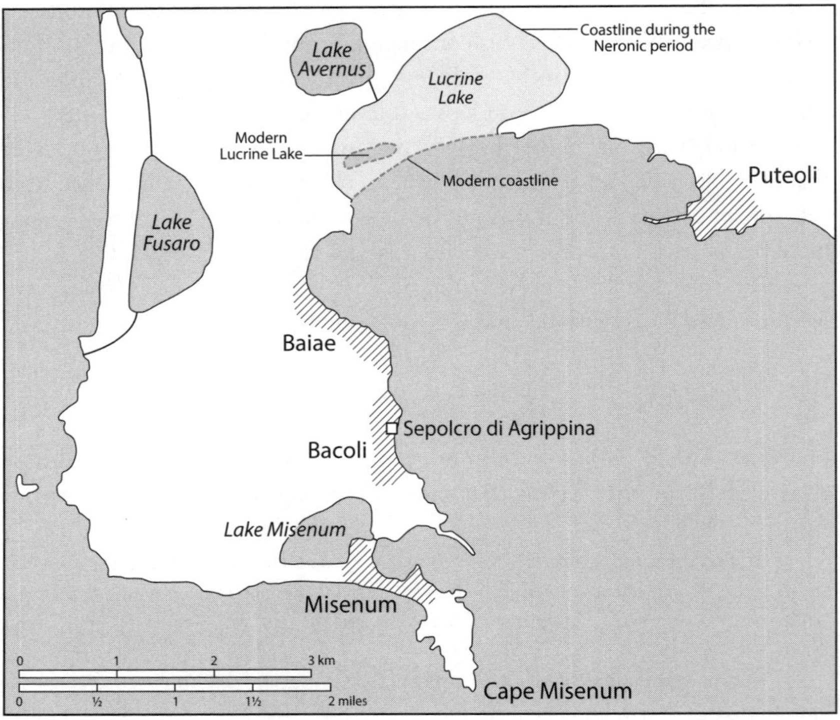

MAP 2. Bay of Naples

to many credible witnesses, Seneca also egged him on, either wishing to cover up that charge that was being made against himself or else from a desire to lead Nero into impious blood guilt so that he would quickly be destroyed by both gods and men.[59]

Tac. *Ann.* 14.3.1. Nero accordingly avoided private meetings with her and applauded her for taking a break whenever she left for her gardens or her estate at Tusculum or Antium.[60] Concluding finally that she was a real problem wherever she was kept, he decided to kill her off, considering only the question of whether to use poison, the sword, or some other violent means.[61] 2. At first, he favored poison. If, however, it were administered at the imperial dinner, the incident could not be ascribed to chance, since Britannicus had already met a similar end, and it was evidently difficult to suborn servants of a woman whose own criminal experiences made her wary of treachery. Besides, she had already built up her body's immunity by the prior taking of counteragents. As for death by the sword, no one could find a method of concealment, and he [Nero] was afraid that someone chosen for such a heinous crime might disregard his orders.

3. It was the freedman Anicetus who came up with the brilliant idea. He was prefect of the fleet at Misenum, had been the young Nero's tutor, and was hated by Agrippina with a loathing that was mutual. [62] Anicetus explained that a vessel could be constructed with a section designed to fall apart on the open sea, pitching the unsuspecting woman overboard. Nothing offered such latitude for accident as did the sea, he said, and, if Agrippina were overtaken by shipwreck, who would be so unreasonable as to attribute

59 Dio is alone in assigning guilt in this matter to Seneca, ascribing this claim to a number of "credible" sources. No other extant authority mentions such a claim, which on the surface seems absurd, and Tacitus by implication rejects it, either because of its absurdity or possibly because it was rejected by one of the sources he is known to have used for this episode, the pro-Senecan Fabius Rusticus.

60 Tusculum was located on the Alban Mount in Latium; it was a summer resort much favored by Rome's wealthy classes and housed a number of fine villas. Antium (see Chapter I) was much favored by the imperial family and was the birthplace of Caligula and Nero.

61 Suetonius (*Ner.* 34.2) says specifically that there were three attempts to poison her.

62 Anicetus had probably been "tutor" in the sense of accompanying Nero to his classes. He had clearly prospered in the emperor's service; the prefect of the fleet was usually an equestrian, but there are instances of freedmen holding the position under Claudius (Plin. *HN* 9.62) and later after Nero's death (Tac. *Hist.* 1.87.2). Tacitus (*Ann.* 4.5.1) reveals that there were two fleets off Italy, at Ravenna and Misenum, and one off Gaul at Forum Iulii (Fréjus).

to crime the mischief done by wind and waves? The emperor would then also grant the deceased a temple, altars, and everything else for demonstrating filial devotion.

Suet. *Ner.* 34.1. Nero was annoyed at seeing his mother examining too critically what he said and trying to reform him, but initially he went only so far as to make repeated attempts to rouse resentment against her by pretending that he was going to renounce his imperial position and retire to Rhodes.[63] Soon afterward, he stripped her of all her honors and power, took away her personal guard of Roman and German soldiers, and sent her packing from the Palatium, where she lived with him. After that, he had no scruples about harassing her, secretly sending men to annoy her with lawsuits while she was staying in Rome and to make her the butt of abuse and ridicule as they passed by her on land or sea when she was resting in her country retreat. 2. Frightened, however, by her threats and violent behavior, he decided to do away with her.[64] After three attempts with poison, and realizing that she had already immunized herself with antidotes, he tampered with the panels in her bedroom ceiling so that they would be loosened by a special device and come crashing down on her at night as she slept.[65]

Dio 61.12.2. But they shrank from acting openly, and they could not get rid of her covertly with poisons, since she took excessive precautions against all of them. But when they saw in the theater a ship that came apart automatically and let out some wild animals, and then reassembled itself again into good shape, they quickly saw to the construction of another such vessel. 3. When the ship was built and Agrippina subjected to Nero's cajoling (he did everything to flatter her so that she would not suspect anything and take measures against him), he did not dare take any steps in Rome in case the

63 There is no other evidence for Nero's supposed intention to abdicate. He had shown favor for Rhodes while still just a youth, when he spoke in favor of the restoration of its freedom (Suet. *Ner.* 7.2), which was in fact granted by Claudius (Tac. *Ann.* 12.58.2; Suet. *Claud.* 25.3); see also Smallwood 412a,b.

64 Agrippina had threatened to make Britannicus emperor and had sought an alliance with Octavia. She was also accused of plotting to have Rubellius Plautus replace Nero. These actions belong to 55, and we do not have any evidence that they continued up to 59.

65 Tacitus (*Ann.* 14.3.2) and Dio (61.12.2) speak generally of an intention to poison Agrippina but do not provide the specific details of Suetonius. The collapsing bedroom ceiling device is not mentioned by Tacitus or Dio; Suetonius separates it from the collapsing boat, yet Tacitus's account of the caving-in of the lead-weighted canopy that initiated the planned disintegration of the boat seems to draw from it.

unholy crime attracted public attention. He went deep into Campania, taking his mother with him, and made a trip on that same ship, which he had decked out with great finery in order to fill her with enthusiasm for constantly using it.

Nero sets the murder plot into motion.

Tac. *Ann.* 14.4.1. The plan's ingenuity won approval, and the timing helped, too, as Nero used to celebrate the festival of the Quinquatrus[66] at Baiae.[67] To this spot he enticed his mother, frequently remarking that one should tolerate the outbursts of parents and try to soothe their anger—all of this to generate a rumor of their reconciliation, which Agrippina would swallow with the gullibility of a woman receiving good news. 2. When she arrived, Nero went to the shore to meet her (she was coming from Antium). He welcomed her with outstretched hands and an embrace, and took her to Bauli. (This was the name of a villa lapped by the waters of an inlet between the promontory of Misenum and the lake of Baiae.) 3. At anchor among the others was one particularly fine vessel—apparently a further mark of respect for his mother, for she had been used to sailing in a trireme with a crew of marines. She was also now invited to dinner, so that there should be darkness, too, to hide the crime.[68]

4. It is well established that there was an informer, and that when Agrippina heard of the plot she could not decide whether to believe it and used a litter as her transport to Baiae. There some sweet talk alleviated her concerns, and she was warmly welcomed and seated above Nero himself. As conversation flowed freely, Nero alternating a juvenile chattiness with an earnest expression as he apparently communicated some serious points, the dinner party became a protracted affair. Nero then escorted Agrippina as she departed, hanging on her gaze and clinging closely to her. Either he was putting

66 The Quinquatrus, the fifth day after the Ides (reckoned inclusively), began the festival of Minerva, celebrated on March 19–23. The Arval brethren held sacrifices on March 28, 59 (Smallwood 5–9); the occasion is not specified, but the rites may well have been intended to celebrate Nero's safe delivery from the plot on his life.

67 Baiae in Campania, with its thermal bathing facilities and favored location, was a popular resort of the Roman upper classes, associated with luxury and louche living; Martial (*Ep.* 1.62.6) speaks of one lady who "arrived there a Penelope and left a Helen." It was in this area that Caligula staged one of his most famous spectacles, his bridge over the Bay of Naples.

68 According to Suetonius (*Otho* 3.1), Otho was the host at this dinner (discussed earlier).

the finishing touch to his charade or the last sight of his mother going to her end made even his heart falter, inhuman though it was.

5.1. As if to furnish proof of the crime, heaven provided a night bright with stars and peaceful, with a tranquil sea. The ship had not gone far. Two of Agrippina's companions were with her: Crepereius Gallus stood near the helm,[69] and Acerronia was leaning over the feet of her mistress (who was lying down),[70] cheerfully talking about the son's change of heart and the mother's reinstatement in his good graces. Then a signal was given, the ceiling covering the spot collapsed, weighted as it was with a large quantity of lead, and Crepereius was immediately crushed to death. Agrippina and Acerronia were protected by the sides of the bed that jutted up above them and that happened to be too strong to crumple under the weight. 2. The disintegration of the vessel did not follow, either; there was general confusion, and most of the sailors, unaware of the plot, kept obstructing the conspirators.[71] The oarsmen then thought it best to throw their weight on one side and capsize the ship like that, but they could not reach a quick consensus about dealing with the emergency, and others countered their efforts, making it possible for the victims to slip gently into the sea. 3. Acerronia, misreading the situation, cried out that she was Agrippina and that the emperor's mother should be helped, whereupon she was battered to death with poles, oars, and any marine implements that came to hand. Remaining silent, Agrippina decreased the chance of recognition (though she did receive one wound to the shoulder). Then, swimming off, she met some skiffs that took her to the Lucrine Lake, and from there was transported to her own villa.[72]

69 Crepereius Gallus was a member of an influential provincial family from the colony of Pisidian Antioch. An equestrian, he had risen in the service open to that order, presumably in part through the patronage of Agrippina (Levick and Jameson [1964]).

70 Acerronia was possibly the daughter of Proculus, consul of AD 37 and thus sister of Gnaeus Acerronius Proculus, who was appointed to the governorship of Achaea sometime after AD 44, also possibly with Agrippina's support (*PIR*^{2} A32–34).

71 Dio (61.13.3) asserts that the ship did collapse as intended and deposited Agrippina in the sea, at which point she swam to shore unaided. He also says that Anicetus was onboard to ensure a smooth operation.

72 There has been much inconclusive debate about the location of the villa where Agrippina died. While visiting Nero at Baiae, she stayed at her villa located at Bauli, traditionally (but not conclusively) identified with the village of Bacoli, south of Baiae (Barr. 44 F4). Because Agrippina landed after the accident at the Lucrine Lake, north of Baiae, some have speculated that she had a villa there also, since the Lucrine Lake would be an odd choice of destination if she then had to travel past Baiae, where Nero was staying, to go to her villa at Bauli. But we do not know if the fishermen who rescued her were familiar

Suet. *Ner.* 34.2. The plan was poorly kept secret by those a party to it, and he [Nero] then conjured up the idea of a collapsible boat to bring about her death either through a wreck or by its superstructure falling on her.[73] Then, feigning reconciliation, he invited her to Baiae, with a most affectionate letter, to celebrate the festival of the Quinquatrus with him. He next charged his trierarchs to damage, with an apparently accidental collision, the galley on which she had come, and he spun out their dinner together. When she was ready to return to Bauli, Nero offered her the vessel fitted with the device as a replacement for the damaged one and cheerfully accompanied her, even kissing her breasts at their parting. 3. He spent the time that followed awake in great anxiety, waiting for the outcome of his enterprise.

Dio 62.13.1. Upon arriving at Bauli, he put on dinners on a very lavish scale for many days, and at them entertained his mother very indulgently. If she were absent, he would pretend to miss her greatly, and when she was there, he made a great fuss over her, telling her to ask him for anything she wanted and freely making her many gifts without her asking. 2. Matters were at that stage when he embraced her one night after dinner, at about midnight, drawing her close to his chest, kissing her eyes and hands, and saying, "Mother, may you have strength and health. My life and my rule depend on you." He then put her in the hands of a freedman, Anicetus, ostensibly to escort her home on the vessel that he had prepared. 3. But the sea would not countenance the tragedy that was to be acted out on it, nor would it accept to take on itself the spurious charge of the unholy crime: the ship came apart and Agrippina fell into the water, but she did not die.[74]

Octavia 310–30. This age, too, has seen the horrific evildoing of a son, when the emperor sent his mother to sea, a victim of deception, on a deadly bark. Given their orders, the sailors hasten to leave the peaceful port, and the sea resounds, beaten by their oars. The bark is carried forward into the deep, and

---

enough with the coast around Bauli to risk a night landing. The Lucrine Lake was famous for its fine oysters, and Strabo (5.4.6) notes that it provided excellent moorage. The rescuers may have been oystermen from the Lucrine area. Moreover, the fact that Agrippina was buried by the road to Misenum, south of Baiae, suggests that she did travel south, past Baiae, from her initial landing place.

73 Tacitus (*Ann.* 14.3.3) attributes its invention directly to Anicetus, prefect of the fleet based at Misenum.

74 Here Dio's version differs from Tacitus's in that Dio claims that the mechanical ship did actually collapse. They both relate the story about the death of Acerronia Polla.

as it glides along, its timbers shiver and, sinking, it splits open and sucks in the sea. A deafening cry mingled with female lamentations rises to the stars. Grim death wanders before their eyes; everyone seeks for himself escape from destruction. Some, naked, cling to planks from the shattered craft, and with them cut a way through the waves, while others head for shore by swimming, and fate sinks many in the deep. The Augusta rends her clothes and tears her hair, and waters her cheeks with tears of sadness.[75]

Agrippina survives the attempt and reaches her coastal villa, where she is finally murdered.

Tac. *Ann.* 14.6.1. There Agrippina reflected on the motive for the duplicitous letter of invitation, and for her particularly respectful treatment. Also, she noted, the ship had been close to shore, had not been driven by the winds, and had not struck any rocks, and yet it had collapsed from the top like some apparatus on land. She also thought about Acerronia's murder and at the same time looked at her own wound, and she realized that the only way of dealing with the plot was by seeming not to recognize its existence. 2. She sent her freedman Agermus to report to Nero that, because of the benevolence of the gods and Nero's own good fortune, she had escaped a serious accident. Despite his alarm over the danger his mother had faced, she added, she begged him to postpone the visit he was anxious to make—she had need of rest for the moment. 3. Meanwhile, feigning nonchalance, she applied medication to her wound and lotions to her body. She ordered a search for Acerronia's will and had her belongings sealed up—her one act that was not a pretense.[76]

7.1. Nero was waiting for news that the deed was done when word came that Agrippina had escaped with a slight wound and had been close enough to danger for no doubt to be left about who was responsible. 2. He was petrified, declaring that she would be there at any moment, intent on swift revenge. She would arm her slaves or incite the soldiery; she would get to the Senate and the people, laying at his door the shipwreck, her wound, and the killing of her friends. And what help was there for *him*? Unless Burrus and Seneca could come up with something. . . . He had had them summoned

75 The "Augusta" is, of course, Agrippina. She received the name and title during the reign of Claudius.

76 Agrippina placed Acerronia's possessions and papers under seal to prevent anything from being removed before her will was executed. No doubt, Agrippina had been named as a beneficiary. It is not clear why Acerronia's possessions and will were stored in Agrippina's Campanian villa or why the will should have been difficult to locate.

immediately, though whether they had no prior knowledge of the plot is unclear.[77]

3. Both were silent for a long while. Either they feared that trying to hold him back would fail, or else they believed that things had gone so far that Nero was done for unless Agrippina were stopped. Then Seneca took the lead to the extent of looking at Burrus and asking whether soldiers should be ordered to kill her. Burrus replied that the praetorian guards had sworn loyalty to the entire house of the Caesars, and that, remembering Germanicus, they would take no violent action against his progeny.[78] Anicetus should live up to his promise, he added.

5. With no hesitation, Anicetus asked to be put in charge of the crime. Responding to his request, Nero declared that this was the day on which he was given an empire, and the giver of such a great gift was his freedman. Anicetus should go swiftly, he said, and take with him the men most ready to follow orders. On being told that Agermus had arrived with a message from Agrippina, Nero took the initiative and provided the scenario for an accusation of his own. He threw a sword at Agermus's feet as the freedman delivered the message entrusted to him, then ordered him clapped in irons as though caught in a treasonous act. He would fabricate a story of his mother plotting the emperor's assassination and then committing suicide from shame when the crime was detected.

8.1. Meanwhile, news had spread of Agrippina's perilous episode, which was represented as an accident, and as people learned of it, they all rushed to the shore. Some clambered up the embankments, some boarded the closest skiffs, others waded into the sea as far as was physically possible, and some stood with arms outstretched.[79] The whole shoreline was filled with the noise of moaning, prayers, and cries as people asked various questions or gave vague replies. A huge crowd surged to the spot with torches, and when it was known that Agrippina was safe, they prepared to offer their

77 Dio (61.12.1) claims that Seneca had previously advocated murdering Agrippina, which seems unlikely. Dio was presumably using a source hostile to Seneca.

78 Agrippina had, of course, replaced officers of the guard with her own supporters (Tac. *Ann.*12.41.2). Philo (*Leg.* 30) says that Caligula ordered Gemellus to commit suicide to keep praetorians from being involved in the execution of a member of the imperial family.

79 If these events took place at the Lucrine Lake, the reference might be to the sandbar reinforced by masonry and topped by a road that ran between the lake and the Bay of Baiae and was the line of communication between Puteoli and Baiae (Strabo 5.4.6). But embankments were commonly erected in the locality in connection with land reclamation (Hor. *Od.* 2.18.20). The reaction of the local populace is an indication that, outside Rome at least, Agrippina commanded much popularity.

felicitations, until they were scattered by the sight of a column of men, armed and menacing.

2. Anicetus cordoned off the villa and broke down the door. He threw aside any slaves in his way until he reached the bedroom door. Before it stood only a few attendants; the rest had been frightened off, terrified by the break-in. 3. In the bedroom, there was a dim light and one of the maids, and Agrippina, who was growing more and more worried that nobody had come from her son, not even Agermus. Things would look different had her plan gone well, she thought; as it was, there was only solitude broken by sudden uproar, and indications that it had gone very badly.

4. Her maid then began to leave. "Are you deserting me, too?" asked Agrippina, and, looking around, she saw Anicetus, who was accompanied by the trierarch Herculeius and by Obaritus, a centurion of the marines.[80] If Anicetus had come to visit the patient, she said, he could report that she was recovered. If he had come to commit a crime, she did not believe her son was involved—he had not given the order for parricide. 5. The assassins stood around the bed, and the trierarch took the lead, striking her on the head with a club. The centurion then drew his sword to deliver the deathblow. "Strike me in the belly," she cried, thrusting out to them her womb, and was finished off by a welter of stab wounds.[81]

Suet. *Ner.* 34.3. But upon learning that the whole thing had gone awry and that she had escaped death by swimming, he [Nero] was at a loss what to do next. When Agrippina's slave Lucius Agermus joyfully reported that she was safe and sound, Nero unobtrusively threw a dagger down beside him and ordered him seized and tied up on a charge of having been bribed to kill him, and then ordered his mother killed, the story being that she had committed suicide to avoid punishment for the crime that had been brought to light.

Dio 62.13.3. Though she was in the dark and was full of drink, and despite the fact that the sailors using their oars on her had actually killed her traveling companion Acerronia Polla, Agrippina still survived. 4. Reaching her home, she feigned ignorance of the plot and did not talk of it. Instead, she

80 A trierarchus was the commander of a ship in the Roman fleet. The centurion Classicus would have commanded the marine soldiers onboard. Tacitus uses the term *classiarii* to distinguish them from the praetorians, who were thought to be too loyal to Agrippina.

81 The *Octavia* (369–72) and Dio (61.13.5) add the dramatic detail that she nominated her womb as the place that had borne Nero. It has been argued that the scene is inspired by Aeschylus, *Choephoroi* 896, where Clytemnestra bares her breast and invites Orestes to strike it.

quickly sent a message to her son and declared that what had happened to her was accidental and that she was sending to him what was, of course, the good news of her safety. Hearing this, Nero could not contain himself; he punished the man who had been sent to him as if he had come to murder him, and he immediately sent off Anicetus with the sailors to deal with his mother. 5. (He would not entrust her killing to the praetorians.) When Agrippina saw them, she knew why they had come. She jumped from her bed, tore open her clothes, and laying bare her stomach said: "Strike this, Anicetus, because this was what bore Nero."

Octavia 361–77. Impious man that he is, he is furious and aggrieved that his mother was snatched from the sea and is still alive, and then he doubles his monstrous crime. He rushes to commit his pitiful mother's murder and allows the atrocity no delay. The henchman who is sent executes his orders: he opens up his mistress's breast with his sword. As she dies, the unhappy lady asks the agent of her murder to bury his frightful sword within her womb, and says: "It is this, this that you must strike with the sword—this that bore such a monster." After these words that mingled with her final groan, she finally gave up her unhappy soul amid the cruel wounds.

Nero reacts to his mother's death.

Tac. *Ann.* 14.9.1. On these events, there is agreement. As for whether Nero looked at his dead mother and praised the beauty of her corpse, there are some who have recorded it and some who deny it.[82] She was cremated that same night on a dining couch in a paltry funeral, and during the whole of Nero's reign, the burial ground was not heaped in a mound or granted an enclosure.[83] (Later on, through the devotion of her servants, she was given a modest tomb alongside the road to Misenum and close to the villa of Caesar the dictator, which, from its lofty elevation, looks out over the bays below.)[84] 2. When Agrippina's pyre was set alight, her freedman, a man named

82 There is an interesting contrast in the presentations of Tacitus and Suetonius. Tacitus stresses the disagreement of the sources over this incident. Suetonius (*Ner.* 34.4) attributes the account to "not untrustworthy" authorities. Dio 61.14.1–4 recounts the incident as factual.

83 The memory of Agrippina's burial is preserved in the remains of a theater building near Bacoli known as the *Sepolcro di Agrippina.* To add insult to injury, she was cremated on a dining room couch instead of the traditional funeral bier.

84 Seneca (*Ep.* 51.11) observes that Marius, Pompey, and Caesar all had villas in the Baiae area.

Mnester, ran himself through with a sword, though whether it was from affection for his patroness or from fear of execution is moot.

3. That such would be her end Agrippina had believed many years earlier and had made light of it. When she consulted the Chaldaeans about Nero, they replied that he would be emperor and kill his mother.[85] "Let him kill me," she replied, "as long as he comes to power."

10.1. As for Nero, it was only after the crime had been committed that its enormity came home to him. He spent the rest of the night petrified and silent at one moment, but more often rising to his feet in panic and dementedly awaiting the dawn that he thought would bring his undoing.[86]

Suet. *Ner.* 34.4. Things more horrific than this are added in not untrustworthy authors: that he rushed off to inspect the murdered woman's corpse, fondled her limbs, criticizing some and praising others, and, meanwhile, becoming thirsty, took a drink. However, although encouraged by the felicitations offered him by the soldiers, the Senate, and the people, he was never able to bear, either then or thereafter, the consciousness of his guilt, and he often admitted that he was pursued by his mother's ghost and the Furies' whips and blazing torches. In fact, he tried, with a sacrifice performed by Magi, to call up her shade and placate it, and furthermore, in his journey through Greece, he did not dare attend the Eleusinian Mysteries, at the beginning of which a call is made by the herald for the removal of all the impious and wicked. [87]

Dio 62.14.1. So it was that Agrippina, daughter of Germanicus, granddaughter of Agrippa, and a descendant of Augustus, was murdered by her own son, on whom she had conferred the supreme power and for whom she had killed other men, and in particular her uncle. 2. When told that she was dead, Nero did not believe it; because of the enormity of the crime, he was overcome with disbelief. He therefore wanted to see for himself what she had suffered. He stripped her entire body naked and examined her wounds, and finally made a comment more execrable than the murder itself. "I did not know I had such a beautiful mother," he said.

85 The term "Chaldeaeans," an ancient people of Babylonia, was frequently used as a synonym for astrologers. Dio (61.2.2) also reports the same prophecy, attributing it to an unnamed astrologer. Tacitus (*Ann.* 6.22.4) had earlier observed that he would later relate a prophecy about Nero's reign made by the son of the famous soothsayer Thrasyllus.

86 It is to be remembered that these dramatic events had taken place in the course of a single night. His mother took her leave just before midnight.

87 There is no other evidence that Nero visited Eleusis on his tour of Greece.

3. And then he gave money to the praetorians, clearly so they would wish for many such acts to occur in the future, and he wrote to the Senate listing other things of which he knew she was guilty. In particular, he said that she had plotted against him and committed suicide when she was found out.[88] 4. Although he sent such information to the Senate, he was still deeply agitated at night, to the point of suddenly jumping out of bed, and in the daytime he became fearful just at the sound, coming from the area where his mother's bones lay, of trumpets ringing out some noisy military music. He accordingly moved elsewhere, and when the same thing happened to him there, he would again, in a frenzy, go somewhere else.

Nero is encouraged by the official reaction to Agrippina's death.

Tac. *Ann.* 14.10.2. It was the obsequiousness of the centurions and tribunes, orchestrated by Burrus, that first encouraged him to hope; they grasped his hand and congratulated him on evading the unforeseeable danger of his mother's criminal act.

His friends then visited the temples and, the example set, the adjacent towns of Campania bore witness to their joy with sacrifices and ambassadorial missions; [89] and Nero, with a contrary pretense, was dejected, apparently displeased with his own deliverance and in tears over his mother's death. 3. However, unlike men's expressions, the appearance of landscapes does not change, and the grim sight of that sea and shoreline was continually before his eyes (and there were those who believed that the sound of a trumpet could be heard in the surrounding hills, and lamentations coming from his mother's tomb). Nero therefore withdrew to Neapolis and sent a letter to the Senate. The gist of it was that Agermus, one of Agrippina's closest freedmen and his would-be assassin, had been caught with a sword and that Agrippina, conscience-stricken over the crime she had engineered, had paid the penalty.

11.1. Nero added "crimes" from earlier times. She had entertained hopes of joint rule, he declared, and of having the praetorian guard swear allegiance to a woman, with the Senate and people subjected to the same humiliation.[90]

88 Dio is the only source to report that Nero gave money to the praetorians; such generosity was likely, indeed was almost *de rigeur*, in situations where the loyalty of the praetorians was particularly crucial.

89 One of these missions is recorded by Quintilian (*Inst.* 8.5.15): Julius Africanus, a noted orator of Gallic origin, declared that on this occasion Nero's Gallic provinces entreated him to bear his good fortune with courage.

90 Joint rule would have been constitutionally impossible for a woman in Rome, and Nero is clearly trading on the resentment felt about Agrippina's patent desire for indirect

When she was disappointed in this, her resentment against the military, the senators, and the plebs had led her to oppose the cash distributions for the soldiers and the people,[91] and to hatch plots against illustrious men. What an effort it had been, he said, for him to stop her bursting into the Curia and giving replies to deputations from foreign peoples![92]

2. He followed this with a sidelong attack on the Claudian period, attributing to his mother all the enormities of that regime and claiming that her extermination was for the public good. He even discussed the shipwreck, though there was no one to be found who was stupid enough to think it accidental—or to believe that a lone man had been sent with a weapon by a shipwrecked woman to smash his way through the emperor's bodyguard and navy! 3. As a result, it was no longer Nero (whose villainy surpassed all criticism) but Seneca who was the subject of nasty rumors—with a declaration like that he had signed his confession![93]

12.1. But it was with an amazing spirit of rivalry among the notables that public prayers were officially authorized at all the couches, and the Quinquatrus—the period when the "plot" was brought to light—was to be celebrated with annual games.[94] A gold figure of Minerva was also to be set up in the Curia with a statue of the emperor next to her, and Agrippina's birthday was to be placed among the days unfit for public business.[95] It had been Thrasea Paetus's practice to let earlier instances of sycophancy pass by remaining silent, or with a brief indication of assent, but on this occasion he

---

power. Caligula had included his sisters in the traditional oath of loyalty sworn to the emperor (Suet. *Cal.* 15.3), but the suggestion here is that Agrippina sought to go much further. Of course, since the charge involves Agrippina's future intentions, it cannot be disproved.

91 Agrippina had attempted to encourage frugality in Nero, but there is no evidence that she blocked donatives.

92 This is a considerable exaggeration. Agrippina had sought only to listen to meetings of the Senate (Tac. *Ann.* 13.5.1). On Agrippina's attempt to meet the Armenian deputation, see Chapter II, n.73.

93 Seneca regularly gave Nero help in writing his speeches, as for instance in his eulogy on Claudius's death (Tac. *Ann.* 13.3.1) and his early speeches advocating leniency (Tac. *Ann.* 13.11.2). Quintilian (*Inst.* 8.5.18) identifies this letter as a work of Seneca and quotes from it Nero's declaration that he could scarcely believe that he had survived and that he took no joy from it.

94 Public prayers (*supplicationes*) were originally days of fasting in times of distress. Images of the gods were placed on a couch, and a table with food was set up before it. The Arval brethren had a special session on March 28, 59, to offer prayers for the safety of the emperor (Smallwood 22.5–9).

95 These so-called *dies nefasti* were those on which the praetor could not pronounce judgment in the law courts. Agrippina's birthday was November 6.

walked out of the Senate, thus exposing himself to danger, but without providing the others with an impulse to assert their independence.[96]

2. There were also, at the time, frequent but meaningless prodigies. A woman gave birth to a serpent, and another was killed by a lightning bolt while making love with her husband. The sun was suddenly darkened, and the fourteen districts of the city were struck by lightning.[97] But all of this was far from being the result of divine intervention—Nero extended his reign and crimes for many years thereafter!

3. To deepen resentment against his mother, and to make it clear that his own clemency was increased by her removal, he reinstated in their ancestral homes two illustrious ladies, Junia and Calpurnia,[98] as well as the ex-praetors Valerius Capito and Licinius Gabolus. These had earlier been banished by Agrippina. He even allowed the ashes of Lollia Paulina to be brought back and a tomb erected for her,[99] and Iturius and Calvisius, men whom he had himself recently relegated, he relieved of their punishment. In the case of Silana, she had passed away on her return to Tarentum from her distant exile, at a time when Agrippina, whose hostility was the cause of her downfall, was already losing influence or had relented.[100]

13.1. Nero nevertheless hung back in the towns of Campania, nervously wondering how he should enter the city and whether he would find the Senate fawning and the plebs supportive. He did, however, have all the worst characters—and no palace ever had a richer crop—telling him that the name of Agrippina was detested and that his popularity with the people had been boosted by her death. Proceed with confidence, they told him, and feel their veneration in person. At the same time, they begged permission to go ahead

96 This is the first allusion in the *Annals* to Thrasea Paetus, the famous Stoic victim of Nero (see Chapter VIII).

97 This eclipse is mentioned by Dio, and by Pliny (*HN* 2.180), who reports that it was seen in Rome on April 30 at midday and by Corbulo in Armenia three hours later.

98 Junia Calvina was at one time married to Lucius Vitellius, brother of the later emperor, and was said to be a woman of great charm (Sen. *Apocol.* 8.2). She was exiled after her brother's suicide (Tac. *Ann.* 12.4.1, 8.1). She lived until near the end of Vespasian's reign (Suet. *Vesp.* 23.4). Calpurnia was forced into exile by Agrippina, supposedly because Claudius had praised her beauty (Tac. *Ann.* 12.22.3).

99 Lollia Paulina was the wife of Caligula, and after his death was a contender for marriage to Claudius, after the death of Messalina. Agrippina saw her as a rival and brought about her death.

100 Junia Silana was probably the daughter of Marcus Junius Silanus and sister of Junia Claudilla, wife of Caligula; she was married to Gaius Silius before his affair with Messalina. Thwarted in a later marriage attempt by Agrippina, she sought to slander Agrippina before Nero and was exiled (Tac. *Ann.* 11.12.2, 13.19–22).

of him. 2. And, in fact, they found a warmer welcome than they had promised, with the people coming to meet him in tribes, [101] the Senate in festive garb, wives and children marshaled by sex and age, and spectators' seats erected along the route he would be taking, just as triumphs are viewed. So now he approached the Capitol with pride, [102] as victor over a servile people, and gave his thanks—and then let himself loose on all the forms of depravity that, though repressed with difficulty, respect for his mother (such as it was) had managed to check.

The private, unofficial reaction was not so supportive.

Suet. *Ner.* 39.1. Nero was tolerant of nothing more than he was of people's curses and insults, and he showed himself especially forgiving in the case of those attacking him verbally or in verse. 2. Many of these compositions, in Greek and Latin, were posted in public or circulated, such as the following:

> "Nero, Orestes, Alcmeon, mother-killers all."[103]
>
> "A new enumeration: Nero killed his own mother."[104]
>
> "Who says Nero is not of the great line of Aeneas?
>
> One carried off his father; the other his mother."[105]
>
> "While our man tunes his lyre-string,
> and while the Parthian strings his bow,
>
> Ours will be Paean, the other the Far-shooter."[106]

101 The divisions of the Roman people as instituted by King Servius. He established four city and twenty-six rural tribes. Their number was later raised to thirty-five.

102 The victorious general would mount the Capitol during a triumph, a tradition contributing to the irony of the present situation.

103 Dio (61.16.2[2]) places this line in the context of Nero's return to Rome in 59 after the murder of his mother. The Argive Alcmeon's mother, Eriphyle, accepted a bribe to persuade her son to participate in the expedition against Thebes. He returned to kill her. Orestes, son of Clytemnestra, killed his mother and her lover to avenge their murder of his father, Agamemnon.

104 "Nero killed his own mother" is conveyed in Greek as *Neron idian metera apecteine*. Greek numbers are represented by letters of the alphabet. The numerical value *neron* is the same as the rest of the line *idian metera apecteine*, namely 1005, suggesting that Nero = matricide.

105 Aeneas, the founder of the Roman nation and of the Julian line, was glorified for having carried his father from the burning ruins of Troy.

106 Parthians were celebrated for their skill at archery.

"Rome will become one house. Move to Veii, Citizens of Rome, unless that house seizes Veii, too!"

However, he did not seek out the authors, and when a number of them were reported to the Senate by an informer, he would not allow them to be given a particularly harsh punishment. 3. The Cynic philosopher Isidorus loudly criticized him, as he passed in the street, for doing a good job of singing the misfortunes of Nauplius but putting his own advantages to poor use. And Datus, an actor in Atellan farces, in a certain song "Farewell, father; farewell, mother" aped a person drinking and another swimming, an obvious allusion to the deaths of Claudius and Agrippina, and in the last line ("Orcus guides your feet") he showed by a gesture that he was referring to the Senate.[107] Nero did no more than banish the actor and the philosopher from Rome, either pooh-poohing all insults or trying to avoid provoking people's ingenuity by showing resentment.[108]

FIGURE 7. *RIC*[2] Nero 399, Brass Dupondius. Obverse: NERO CLAVD(ius) CAESAR AVG(ustus) GERM(anicus) P(ontifex) M(aximus) TR(ibunicia) P(otestate) IMP(erator) P(ater patriae), "Nero Claudius Caesar Augustus Germanicus, Chief Priest, with Tribunician Authority, Imperator, Father of the Country." Reverse: MAC(ellum) AVG(usti). S(enato) C(onsulto), "Market of Augustus. By a decree of the Senate." From the collection of Andreas Pangerl/romancoins.info.

Dio (61.18.3) records that among the measures that followed Agrippina's death in 59 Nero dedicated a food market. It may well have been part of his program of winning popular support. The edifice, located on the Caelian Hill, was on a monumental scale and is illustrated on

107 Orcus is god of the underworld. Isidorus and Datus are not otherwise known.

108 Suetonius and Dio (61.16.3) are in agreement that Nero's reaction was restrained, Dio saying that he took no legal action.

his coins (see Figure 7), which depict an elaborate two-story building, with a central domed section flanked by colonnades at the bottom and housing a loggia on the upper section.

The legend SC refers to a possible role of the Senate in issuing the coin, not in the construction of the market.

Dio 61.16.1 (Loeb 8.70). When Nero entered Rome following the killing of his mother, people treated him with respect in public, but privately, when they could safely speak freely, they would be tearing him to pieces. For instance, they hung a leather bag at night from a statue of his, thereby suggesting that he should be stuffed into it; and, again, they threw into the Forum a baby and tied on it a little tablet that read: "I am not going to rear you in case you murder your mother."

2a. When Nero came into Rome, they pulled down the statues of Agrippina. But failing to cut through one in time, they threw a rag over it so it would appear to be veiled, after which somebody immediately composed the following inscription and fixed it on the statue: "I am ashamed, and you *have* no shame."

2.2. And in many places it was possible to read the same inscription:

"Nero, Orestes, Alcmeon, mother-killers all."[109]

It was also possible to hear people saying this very thing: that Nero did away with his mother. 3. For there were many who denounced certain people for gossiping to that effect, and their aim was not so much to destroy them as to attack Nero. As a result, Nero would not entertain any charge of this sort; either he did not want the rumor to gain greater circulation or by now he did not care about what people said. 4. However, in the middle of the sacrifices for Agrippina that took place following a decree, there was a total eclipse of the sun, during which the stars appeared.[110]

Furthermore, the elephants that pulled the chariot of Augustus entered the Circus, reached the seats of the senators, stopped there, and went no further.[111] 5. And then in addition to all that there was something that one would have most certainly judged as a sign from heaven: a thunderbolt once entirely burned up his dinner as it was being brought to him, taking away his food like some harpy.

109 This line is also cited by Suetonius (discussed earlier).

110 This is clearly the eclipse mentioned in Tac. *Ann.* 14.12.2.

111 A chariot carrying the image of Augustus.

IV

PARTHIA

INTRODUCTION

Any attempt to reach a proper understanding of Rome's relations with Parthia during Nero's reign will be fraught with difficulties. Most of what we learn about the Parthians comes from Greek and Roman sources, which are invariably hostile. In the case of our main source, Tacitus, we have the additional problem that although he may on occasion treat events outside of Italy in considerable detail, his grasp of geography and topography, as well as his understanding of the strategic issues, are seriously limited. In both of his accounts of the two major theaters of operation of the Neronian period, Britain and Parthia, both treated in considerable detail, there are fundamental problems of chronology and geography that have evaded satisfactory explanation.

The Roman writer Justin refers to the view that the world was divided between two powers, the Romans and Parthians (*Epit.* 41.1.1), and while this claim is much exaggerated, it is certainly the case that the great empire of Parthia occupied the attention of Rome for much of its history from the late republican period onward. Parthia was formed from what was originally a province (satrapy) of the Persian Achaemenid empire, the dynastic period of the empire named after King Achaemenes, of the early seventh century BC. Nothing is known of its history in this Achaemenid period. Assyrian sources of the seventh century mention a region called Partakka or Partukka; whether this is identical with later Parthia is disputed. The earliest certain occurrence of the name is as "Parthava," in the famous Bisitun inscription of the Persian king Darius I, dated to about 520 BC. The region was joined to Hyrcania (now Gorgan in Iran) under Alexander the Great and ruled as a satrapy by the Seleucid rulers (named after Seleucus, one of Alexander's generals). According to a (disputed) tradition, the founder of the independent Parthian empire was Arsaces I, who rebelled and instituted his own rule in the latter half of the third century BC, establishing the Arsacid dynasty as traditional rulers of Parthia. The Persian plateau was not, however, totally conquered until the time of Mithridates I (171–138 BC). At its height, the Parthian empire extended its sway from the Caspian Sea to the Persian Gulf, and was bounded in the west by the Euphrates and in the East by the Indus.

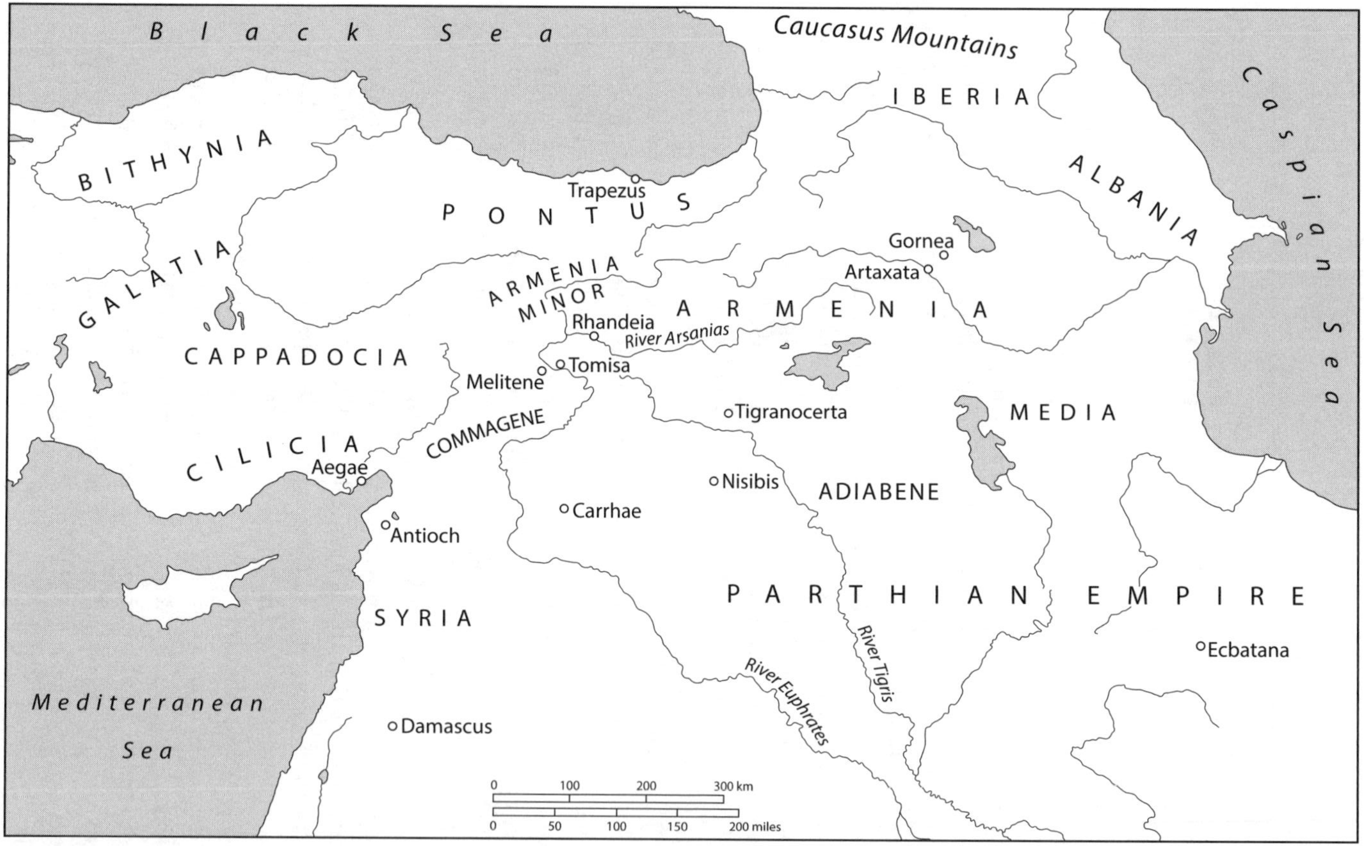

MAP 3. The Eastern Frontier under Nero

The earliest formal contact between the kingdom and a Roman official was friendly. In the second half of the 90s, Sulla, in Asia Minor to deal with the threat of King Mithridates of Pontus, traveled to Cappadocia and on to the Euphrates, where he accepted an offer of friendship from an envoy of the Parthian king (Livy *Per.* 70.7; Velleius 2.24.3). This happy situation would not endure. In the last generation of the republic, the Roman generals Lucullus and Pompey saw themselves as heirs to Alexander the Great and undertook the conquest of the Hellenistic kingdoms of the East, establishing the Euphrates as the demarcation between the two empires of Rome and Parthia. This left a Rome-dominated Asia Minor, where the regions adjoining the sea became generally Roman provinces and the interior was ruled by pro-Roman client rulers. Marcus Crassus took the situation one stage further when he chose Parthia as the arena in which to win military glory that would place him on a par with his two colleagues Pompey and Caesar. Crassus enjoyed some initial successes, but he was finally crushed in 53 BC at the major Battle of Carrhae. The defeat did little to curb Roman imperial appetites in the area, and Julius Caesar was planning to lead an army of sixteen legions into the kingdom when he was assassinated in 44 BC. Caesar's project was revived by Mark Antony, who invaded Parthia in 36 BC with an enormous army of 100,000 troops. He was forced to retire in ignominy.

Augustus handled the Parthian issue with considerable skill. He was faced with an imperialist urge at home, which he managed to satisfy with the vague expectation that Parthia would one day be crushed, a notion much reflected in the literature of the time. But he was above all a pragmatist. He demanded from the Parthians the return of prisoners and standards taken in previous campaigns, and these were recovered in 20 BC in a huge diplomatic coup. Augustus appreciated that for all its size and wealth Parthia was internally weak. Ethnically and culturally diverse, with mixtures of Greek and Iranian elements, it was essentially a feudal society with a king who was suzerain over a number of vassals in the form of powerful noble families. Their loyalty to the central ruler was often suspect, and at various periods they enjoyed considerable local autonomy. As a result, the Parthian army lacked the Roman army's discipline and staying power, and was almost totally deficient in siege craft. Added to these problems were the constant incursions from the seminomadic people to the East. This feudal and balkanized structure of Parthia meant that, in fact, after the death of the expansionist King Mithridates II (88 BC), the policy of Parthia was essentially defensive. It lacked the internal order and coherence required for it to behave otherwise. The conflicts between the Romans and Parthians, despite the efforts of the Romans to depict them otherwise, were generally instigated not by the Parthians but rather by the Romans, who had ambitions to extend their conquests beyond the Euphrates.

Augustus recognized that the key to Roman–Parthian relations was Armenia, the mountainous state south and southwest of the Caucasus and east of the Euphrates, bordering on Parthia (the area west of the Euphrates was defined by the Romans as Armenia Minor). The Parthians had a long-standing claim on Armenia, which ran counter to Rome's desire to maintain the area as a protectorate. Caught between two great empires, it played a role similar to that of Poland between Germany and Russia in more modern times. With an Iranian aristocracy, it had a certain affinity with Parthia, but it also had a powerful sense of independence and identity, which the Romans were able to exploit. Augustus's reduction of the total number of legions to twenty-eight and the preoccupation with military crises in Germany and Pannonia precluded any adventures in Armenia. He instead followed a double-headed strategy of military pressure and diplomacy, and was able on a number of occasions to install his nominee on the Armenian throne, and once even on the Parthian. But he did little to back them with serious support, and for all intents and puposes acquiesced on those occasions when the Armenians rejected his candidates.

This policy was essentially continued by his successor, Tiberius. When, early in his reign, Armenia was threatened, Tiberius sent out Germanicus, the grandfather of Nero, who installed Zeno/Artaxias on the throne, bringing stability until Zeno's death in AD 32. In early 37, the aggressive Parthian king Artabanus was reputedly planning an invasion of Syria. The legate of Syria, Lucius Vitellius, moved his army up to the Euphrates and overawed the Parthians, who decided to yield in the face of superior force and decisive action. During Claudius's reign, the region once again became a scene of conflict. In AD 47, a Parthian embassy came to Rome and, invoking their long-established alliance, asked Claudius to send them a king. This he did, in the person of Meherdates, although he gave his appointee little help, and Meherdates soon fell, to be replaced by the Arsacid Vologaeses, who proceeded to appoint one brother as king of Media and sought to establish another, Tiridates, as king of Armenia.

Pharasmanes, king of the Caucasian kingdom of Iberia (corresponding roughly to the eastern and southern parts of modern Georgia), had from AD 35 supported the claim of his brother, Mithridates, to the throne of Armenia. Pharasmanes' son Radamistus, with the acquiescence of the Romans, usurped the throne from this same Mithridates, his uncle. The Romans had troops in Armenia, but when Mithridates sought their protection, the commander surrendered him to Radamistus for a bribe. Radamistus subsequently murdered him, along with his sons. Radamistus's hold on Armenia was tenuous. This situation was exploited by the Parthians, who invaded in AD 52 or 53, driving out Radamistus and taking the fortress cities of Artaxata and Tigranocerta. The Parthians in turn were forced to retire because of the severe winter conditions, and Radamistus reentered the country, only to be forced out again, this time by an internal rebellion in support of Tiridates (Tac. *Ann.* 12.44–51).

This was the complex situation that confronted Nero at the time of his accession. The military strength of Rome was located in Syria, which housed four legions, and its legate could call on the assistance of the client monarchs in the neighboring regions. This was the first time since Mark Antony that Rome had committed major resources and efforts to dealing with Parthia. Despite the detailed information that we are given on Rome's relations with Parthia during Nero's reign, it is difficult to define a coherent Roman policy in the region. At its core, there seems to be a conviction that an invasion of Parthia was not to be countenanced, nor was annexation of Armenia, and that Tiridates, the brother of Vologaeses, should be allowed to rule Armenia if he was willing to receive the throne from Nero. It would take twelve years for the issue to be resolved, with the grand celebration held in Rome in AD 66 to mark Tiridates' arrival there. There is no doubt that Armenia was the great "foreign policy" success of Nero's reign. But if this was indeed Rome's policy, it does not seem to have been a policy pursued consistently, as will become clear in Tacitus's narrative, especially at *Annals* 15.6, when the Roman general Caesennius Paetus seems to speak of outright annexation by Rome, declaring that, "It would be he, Paetus, who would impose on the conquered peoples tribute and laws and, instead of a phantom king, Roman jurisdiction."

In the end, Roman will prevailed, and the king established in Armenia was there essentially as a vassal of Rome. But for all that, he was a Parthian, and an Arsacid. And it is to be noted that according to John of Antioch (*Fr.* 104), the false Nero who came on the scene during the reign of Titus expected support from the Parthians on the grounds that they were indebted to him (i.e., supposedly Nero) for his having returned Armenia to them (cf. Dio 66.19.3).

SOURCES

The Parthians carry out raids in Armenia, and the Romans wonder how Nero will cope with the crisis. Client kings are instructed to muster in the frontier area. Internal domestic disputes oblige the Parthians to abandon their designs in Armenia. The development is treated as a great success in Rome, and a victory is celebrated.

AD 54

Tac. *Ann.* 13.6.1. At the year's end, disturbing rumors arrived of another incursion of the Parthians and of their raids on Armenia after the expulsion of Radamistus (who, after often taking control of the realm and then becoming a fugitive, had now also abandoned the war).[1] 2. As a result, in a city avid for gossip, questions were being asked.[2] How could an emperor scarcely past seventeen shoulder this burden or stave off the crisis? What support was to be expected from a man ruled by a woman?[3] Could battles, the blockading of cities, and all the other military operations also be conducted by teachers? 3. Others felt differently; what had transpired, they said, was better than calling on Claudius, enfeebled with age and indolence, to undertake the hardships of a campaign, a man who would be taking orders from slaves![4] In fact, Burrus and Seneca were known for their broad experience, and, people asked, how far could their emperor be lacking in strength when Gnaeus Pompey took on the burden of the civil wars in his eighteenth year[5] and Caesar Octavianus in his nineteenth? [6] 4. At the highest level of government, more was achieved by authority and policy than by weapons and physical strength. Nero would give proof positive that he was relying on friends who were honorable (or otherwise) if, setting jealousy aside, he were to select an outstanding com-

1 Tacitus resumes his account of eastern affairs from the end of *Annals* 12.51, beginning his narrative at the very end of AD 54 (Nero was almost certainly seventeen on December 16, 54). As is often the case when dealing with events outside Rome, and especially when dealing with Parthia, Tacitus abandons the strictly annalistic format and allows his narrative to continue beyond the year's end, indicating at the close of *Annals* 13.9 that he has done just that.

2 This next passage is presented by Tacitus almost in the form of a *controversia*, an artificial legal disputation used in the rhetorical schools.

3 Tacitus here suggests that by the end of 54, despite the contretemps involving the Armenian ambassadors (see Chapter II, n.73), there was a public perception that Agrippina still exercised enormous influence.

4 Claudius had in fact launched and participated in the highly successful invasion of Britain in AD 43, and the suggestion here is that by the end of his reign some ten years later he was a spent force.

5 Pompey the Great was born in 106 BC; he received his first command in 84 BC, when he was actually 23: Velleius Paterculus (2.53.4) observes that some authorities negligently made an error of five years in calculating Pompey's career. He had already served under his father in 87 BC and had possibly taken part in the capture of Asculum two years earlier. But these last two hardly constitute commands.

6 Augustus was born in 63 BC. In the *Res Gestae* (1.1), he refers to assuming military command at the age of nineteen; he did not in fact conduct regular operations until 43 BC.

mander rather than a rich man relying on favor gained through influence-peddling.

AD 55

Tac. *Ann.* 13.7.1. As people passed these and other such observations around, Nero ordered the young men recruited in the neighboring provinces to be brought up to supplement the legions of the East and for the legions themselves to be deployed closer to Armenia.[7] He further ordered the two veteran kings Agrippa and Antiochus to make ready forces for an offensive into Parthian territory,[8] and bridges were also to be built over the Euphrates. Nero assigned Lesser Armenia to Aristobulus[9] and the area of Sophene to Sohaemus, both of them also receiving royal diadems.[10] 2. And then, opportunely, a rival to Vologaeses emerged in the person of his son Vardanes,[11] and the Parthians left Armenia, apparently postponing hostilities.

Responsibility for Armenia is assigned to Domitius Corbulo, with command over the provinces of Cappadocia and Galatia. There are no legionary troops there, and the Third Legion (Gallica) and the Sixth (Ferrata) are transferred from Syria. The legatus *of Syria, Ummidius Quadratus, is concerned about his own*

7 The "young men" would be Roman citizens residing in the provinces. Legions were manned by citizens, the auxiliaries by allied noncitizens.

8 Nero's strategy is in some ways a vindication of the Roman policy of maintaining a number of "client" rulers in the frontier area; that said, in the end, the rulers enumerated here saw no direct service. Marcus Julius Agrippa (II) was the son of Julius "Herod" Agrippa, the close friend and adviser of Caligula and of Claudius, who died in AD 44. Originally granted Chalcis by Claudius, the younger Agrippa's territories had subsequently been enlarged by both Claudius and Nero.

Antiochus IV was made king of Commagene by Caligula and then possibly dismissed by him. He was apparently restored by Claudius, and his territory was enlarged by the addition of part of Cilicia. He was removed by Vespasian in AD 72 on suspicion of collaboration with the Parthians.

9 Aristobulus was the son of Herod of Chalcis, whose kingdom he subsequently acquired. After his reign, Armenia Minor, which lay west across the Euphrates from Armenia and had a coastline on the southeast of the Black Sea, seems to have been incorporated into the empire by Vespasian.

10 Sohaemus was granted Sophene in the southwest of Armenia, separated by the Euphrates from Cappadocia. Josephus (*AJ* 20.158) states that Sohaemus was made king of Emesa in Syria in this year (AD 54), and he says nothing of Sophene. Sohaemus was later a supporter of Vespasian.

11 The bane of the Parthians was internal dissent, often involving rival members of the ruling family. Nothing further is known about Vardanes.

status and meets Corbulo at Aegeae. His concerns are justified. Representatives of the two legati *are sent to Parthia to receive hostages, and the Parthians opt to entrust them to Corbulo's representative.*

ILS 9018 (Smallwood 51a). [The Sixth Legion F]errata, which [spent the winter] in [Greater] Armenia [under] Gnaeus Domitius [Corbulo], legate [of Nero Caesar] Augustus with propraetorian power, [dedicated this monument] in honor of . . . Asper *primipilus*, son of Publius, of the tribe Scaptia.[12]

> The transfer of the sixth legion from Syria to Armenia has left a physical memento in the form of this fragmentary inscription on a marble plaque that would have stood in Armenia, presumably near the base of the Sixth Legion, but through time found its way to Metropolis near the city of Cyzicus, where it resides. It was accompanied by a Greek version, now very fragmentary. The identity of the person honored is not known, but, as is standard in inscriptions, the names of his father and his tribe are recorded. Corbulo, as was normal for governors of imperial provinces, administered with the authority of a praetor, not consul, since as the subordinate of the *princeps* he had to occupy a lower rank.
>
> The Sixth Legion Ferrata ("the ironclads") was first raised in Gaul by Caesar in 52 BC. It served under Antony and after Actium came under the command of Octavian, who transferred it to Syria in 30 BC. It was still part of the regular garrison of Syria when Corbulo received his command. It would later move to Italy, where it supported Vespasian, but was shortly afterward sent back to the East. It received the title of *Fidelis Constans* ("Loyal and Steadfast") from Septimius Severus.

Tac. *Ann.* 13.8.1. In the Senate, however, all was celebrated with hyperbolic proposals. Members voted public thanksgiving to the gods and triumphal dress for the emperor on the thanksgiving days,[13] that he enter the city in

12 Primipilus, the senior rank of centurion, is a restoration for a word almost completely missing from the inscription.

13 The news of the success in Parthia would have arrived in Rome in a period when there was already general euphoria following the highly positive initial impression created by Nero. The *vesta triumphalis* was worn not only by those awarded a triumph but also by senior magistrates on important occasions and then by the emperor. Caesar was entitled to use it at public events, and it was worn by Caligula at the dedication of a temple and later by Nero when receiving Tiridates (Dio 44.4.2, 6.1; 59.7.1; 63.3.3).

ovation, and that he be granted a statue on the same scale as that of Mars the Avenger, and in the same temple.[14] But the routine sycophancy apart, they were happy that Nero had given Domitius Corbulo responsibility for securing Armenia and that an avenue was apparently being opened up for merit.[15]

2. The troops in the East were divided in the following manner. Some of the auxiliaries, along with two legions, were to remain in the province of Syria under its governor, Quadratus Ummidius.[16] Corbulo would have an

14 The temple of Mars Ultor was the traditional venue for the celebration of victories and therefore highly appropriate in this case.

15 Tacitus postpones until this point reference to what was a key factor in the success achieved by the Romans, the command given to [Gnaeus] Domitius Corbulo. He greatly admires this individual, even down to his imposing physique and his eloquent tongue. Corbulo's mother, Vistilia, had married six times (Plin. *HN* 7.39), and, as a consequence, Corbulo had a number of important family connections (he was the half-brother of Caesonia, Caligula's wife).

Corbulo's initial career is not easy to determine, since it is difficult to distinguish between his activities and those of his father in that early phase, but we know that he served in Germany under Claudius in AD 47, when he held his first command (Tac. *Ann.* 11.18.2; see Chapter V) and achieved major successes. His generalship there, which would set the tone for the rest of his career, was marked by the restoration of legionary discipline, previously allowed to slacken, and by the severity of his punishments. He was suspected, however, of stirring up trouble among the Chauci and was called back across the Rhine, although he was all the same awarded the *ornamenta triumphalia*. Tacitus's caustic comments on his treatment are reminiscent of Tiberius's recall of Germanicus from Germany and the bestowal of supposedly empty honors (Tac. *Ann.* 2.42.1). Corbulo later held the governorship of Asia, perhaps in AD 52/53. In the current crisis, he was appointed to a special legateship of Cappadocia, the rugged area in eastern Anatolia annexed by Rome in AD 17 and in this period normally falling under the authority of the legate of Syria. It may well be that he was also on this occasion given command over Galatia, the region bordering Cappadocia to the west, since he is later recorded as raising troops there (Tac. *Ann.* 13.35.2). His mandate was limited to ensuring the stability of Armenia and its status as an independent kingdom.

After his sterling work in dealing with the Parthians, Corbulo was, in 67, summoned by Nero to Greece, where he committed suicide to avoid execution. One of his daughters, Domitia Longa, later married the emperor Domitian.

One anecdote attached to Corbulo (although the reference may be to his father) is that he reduced Cornelius Fidus, the son-in-law of Ovid, to tears by calling him a plucked ostrich (*struthocamelum depilatum:* Sen. *Dial.* 2.17.1).

16 Gaius Ummidius Quadratus was praetor in AD 18, but for reasons unknown his career then slowed down, and he did not reach the consulship until about AD 40. Under Claudius, he became governor of Illyricum, and by 51 was governor of Syria. He had to intervene in Judaea several times to deal with local unrest, and he was drawn into the strife over Armenia. He died while still in office, probably sometime shortly before AD 60. His career is attested in an inscription from Mt. Cassino (*ILS* 972).

equal number of citizen and allied forces, plus the infantry and mounted troops wintering in Cappadocia.[17] The allied kings had instructions to take orders from either commander, depending on the requirements of the war, but their support leaned more toward Corbulo. 3. To capitalize on his reputation (which is of utmost importance in new ventures), Corbulo marched swiftly, but was met at the city of Aegeae in Cilicia by Quadratus.[18] He had come there fearing that, if Corbulo entered Syria to take over his troops, he would have all eyes turned on him,[19] for Corbulo was a man of large physique and flamboyant speech, and, beyond his experience and intelligence, he made an impression even with his unimportant attributes.

9.1. In fact, both men sent messengers to King Vologaeses, advising him to choose peace over war and supply hostages, thereby maintaining the deference to the Roman people customarily shown by earlier kings.[20] To allow himself to prepare for war on his own terms or else to remove suspected rivals by calling them hostages, Vologaeses put in their hands the leading members of the Arsacid house. 2. They were accepted by the centurion Insteius, who had been sent by Ummidius and happened to be there first, visiting the king on that business.[21] When this came to Corbulo's notice, he ordered Arrius Varus, prefect of a cohort, to go and take possession of the hostages.[22]

This led to a quarrel between the prefect and the centurion, and, not to prolong this spectacle before foreigners, the hostages and Roman officers who were escorting them were left to decide the matter. They preferred Corbulo, whose renown was fresh and who enjoyed some sort of popularity even with the enemy. 3. The result was friction between the generals. Ummidius

17 Syria normally housed four legions—the Third (Gallica), Sixth (Ferrata), Tenth (Fretensis), and Twelfth (Fulminata)—with close to five thousand men each. These were divided equally between Ummidius and Corbulo.

18 Aegeae, founded originally by the Macedonians and later a naval base, was located near the mouth of the river Pyramus on the Gulf of Issus in Cilicia in southern Asia Minor (Barr. 67 B3).

19 It was perhaps inevitable that the divided command in the campaign against the Parthians would create rivalries and confusion over zones of responsibility.

20 Tacitus (*Ann.* 12.10.2) states that the Parthian deputation to Claudius speaks of the great respect that the Parthians felt for Rome.

21 Insteius may possibly be the Insteius Capito who is mentioned later by Tacitus as Corbulo's camp prefect in AD 58 (*Ann.* 13.39.1). If so, it almost certainly means that at this time he was a senior centurion (*primipilus*), reasonably so, in view of the importance of his mission. He would presumably have been later assigned to Corbulo and promoted to the senior post of camp prefect.

22 Arrius Varus would later make secret reports on Corbulo and be rewarded by Nero with a promotion to senior centurion (Tac. *Hist.* 3.6.1). He later became a supporter of Vespasian.

protested that the gains made by his plans were taken from him; Corbulo for his part claimed that the king had been brought to offer hostages only when he himself had been chosen as commander for the war and thereby transformed Vologaeses' hopes into fear. To settle their quarrel, Nero had a proclamation made that laurel was being added to the imperial fasces because of the successes of Quadratus and Corbulo.[23] These events I have put together, though they actually extended into the next consulship.

Tacitus now returns to Rome, picking up events from the beginning of AD 58. The Parthian narrative is resumed at 13.34. The sequence of events is far from clear, but it seems that Corbulo spent the period between 55 and 58 getting his troops into condition, raising levies in his province and strengthening his army with the addition of another legion. While the Parthian King Vologaeses is caught up in a revolt in Hyrcania, Corbulo urges Tiridates to seek his throne from Nero. Tiridates in turn tries unsuccessfully to lure Corbulo into a trap, then rejects his proposal, and hostilities break out. Corbulo captures the old Armenian capital Artaxata.

AD 58 Nero's Third Consulship

Tac. *Ann.* 13.34.2. The war between Parthia and Rome over the possession of Armenia had been dragging on after a feeble start,[24] but at the beginning of that year it was prosecuted with vigor.[25] Vologaeses would not permit his brother Tiridates to be deprived of a kingdom that he had given him or to possess it as a gift of a foreign power, and Corbulo thought it in keeping with the greatness of the Roman people to recover territory earlier won by Lucullus and Pompey.[26] Furthermore, the Armenians, whose loyalty was dubious,

23 The imperial fasces were the symbolic axes bundled in rods borne by the twelve attendants (lictors) assigned to Augustus in 19 BC and retained by his successors. They were wreathed with laurels for victories won under the emperor's auspices.

24 It is not clear what Tacitus's precise meaning is here. There had been no actual war with Armenia since the accession of Nero. Perhaps he is going back earlier, to AD 52 or 53, when the Parthians drove Radamistus out of Armenia.

25 Tacitus resumes the account of the Parthian campaign, which he left in AD 55. We now find ourselves at the beginning of 58. We have to assume by inference from what Tacitus says here that in the intervening period King Vologaeses had been offered the throne of Armenia for his brother Tiridates, provided the latter would accept it as bestowed by Rome. The Parthians seem to have been obdurate on the principle that Tiridates would not recognize the right of the emperor to bestow the kingdom from Rome.

26 During the republic, the Romans had achieved a major success in Armenia. Tigranes (II) the Great had built his kingdom into a major power, but he became drawn into the war between Rome and his father-in-law, Mithridates. Lucullus inflicted the first of a

were inviting in the armies of both sides, although they were geographically and culturally closer to the Parthians, with whom they were also connected by intermarriage and to whom, in addition, they inclined through their ignorance of liberty.

Corbulo spends the winter of 57–58 getting his troops into shape.

Tac. *Ann.* 13.35.1. Corbulo, however, had more trouble coping with the lethargy of his troops than with enemy treachery. The legions transferred from Syria, listless after a long peace, had little tolerance for camp fatigues.[27] It was clear that there were veterans in that army who had not done sentry duty or the night watch, and who looked on the rampart and ditch as something unfamiliar and strange. Without helmets and without breastplates, they were sleek and prosperous, having spent their service only in towns.[28]

2. Corbulo therefore discharged those disadvantaged by age or ill health, and requested reinforcements. Troop levies were then held throughout Galatia and Cappadocia,[29] and a legion was added from Germany,[30] together with auxiliary cavalry and cohorts of infantry. 3. The entire army was kept under canvas, despite a winter so severe that the ground, covered with ice, would not afford a place for tents without digging.[31] Many had limbs frostbitten from the intense cold, and some died on watch. The case was noted of

---

series of defeats on him in 69 BC, but it was Pompey who finally subdued him and obliged him to become a Roman ally. Pompey, in fact, owed much of his success to the kind of internal dispute that would frequently come to the aid of the Romans, in that Tigranes's son had rebelled against his father.

27 The legions of Syria had been divided equally between Corbulo and Ummidius (Tac. *Ann.* 13.8.2), with Corbulo receiving the Third and Sixth, and Ummidius retaining the Tenth and Twelfth. But a vexillation of the Tenth is also recorded as serving with Corbulo (Tac. *Ann.* 15.40.2).

28 It was clearly the practice in Syria for legions to wear civilian clothing when they were not on campaign.

29 Roman citizens in these two provinces would be recruited for the legions, and noncitizens would serve in the auxiliaries. Galatia had been incorporated into the empire, with its territory enlarged, upon the death of its last king, Amyntas, in 25 BC (Dio 53.26.3).

30 The reference to a legion sent from Germany is very puzzling, since no German legion is attested as taking part in the eastern campaign. The Fourth Legion, Scythica, is mentioned as being present in Cappadocia in AD 62 (Tac. *Ann.* 15.7.1), and it is possible that Tacitus or his source has confused that legion with the Fourth Legion, Macedonica, which was stationed at Mainz in Germany at that time. But Tacitus makes no reference to it or indeed to any non-Syrian legion in the current campaign.

31 Tacitus presumably refers here to the winter of 57–58. Roman legions would sleep under canvas while on campaign; in winter, they would remain in their legionary fortresses. The tactics described here show Corbulo to have been a ruthless disciplinarian.

a soldier who, carrying a load of firewood, had his hands frozen to the point where they stuck to his load and fell off, leaving his arms as stumps. 4. Corbulo himself, lightly dressed and bareheaded, was regularly in the marching line and among the working parties, giving praise to the stouthearted and consolation to the sick, and setting an example for all. Then, because many could not bear the harshness of the climate and campaign and were beginning to desert, Corbulo looked to severity as a remedy. He did not treat the first or second offenses with leniency, as happened in other armies: anyone leaving the standards was summarily executed. That this was beneficial, and more effective than clemency, became clear from the results: there were fewer desertions from that camp than from those where leniency was shown.

Summary of Tac. *Ann.* 13.36–38. Tiridates carries out a number of swift raids, avoiding a major engagement. In response, Corbulo plans an attack on several fronts. Antiochus is ordered to invade the area bordering his kingdom. Pharasmanes executes his son Radamistus to show his support of Rome. Negotiations between Corbulo and Tiridates are fruitless [*not translated*].

Corbulo brings about the surrender of a number of important Armenian strongholds, including Artaxata.

Tac. *Ann.* 13.39.1. Corbulo, meanwhile, to prevent the war dragging on to no purpose and to force the Armenians to defend their own possessions, prepared to destroy their fortresses. The strongest in that prefecture, which was called Volandum,[32] he kept for himself; the minor ones he assigned to his legate Cornelius Flaccus and to the camp prefect Insteius Capito.[33] 2. Then, after examining the fortifications and making appropriate arrangements for the assault, he encouraged his troops to chase from his home this vagrant enemy, prepared neither for peace nor for war, and who, by his flight, admitted his perfidy as well as his cowardice. They should think about the spoils as well as the glory, he said.

3. Corbulo next divided his army into four parts. One he grouped in tortoise formation and brought forward to undermine the rampart; a second he ordered to move ladders up to the walls; and a large contingent he ordered to launch firebrands and spears from the engines. The slingers and throwers

Conditions would be particularly harsh because the winter camps seem to have been in Armenia, not in Cappadocia (as implied in Tac. *Ann.* 13.36.1).

32 The fort of Volandum is unknown, although from Tacitus's account we can place it south of the Araxes River and west of Artaxata (Barr. 89 G1).

33 Cornelius must have been a legionary legate, but is otherwise unknown. Insteius may be the centurion mentioned in 13.9.1.

were allocated a position from which to shoot their projectiles over a considerable distance, so that fear would be equally spread among the enemy and no unit would be able to bring assistance to those in difficulties. 4. Such was the fervor and drive of the army that, by the third part of the day, the walls had been stripped of defenders, the barriers of the gates demolished, the fortifications taken by scaling, and all adults slaughtered—with not a soldier lost and a mere handful wounded. The horde of noncombatants was auctioned off, and the rest of the plunder went to the victors. 5. The legate and the prefect were just as fortunate. Three fortresses were stormed in one day, and of the others some capitulated in terror and others surrendered through the decision of the inhabitants.

6. This inspired them with confidence for an attack on the tribal capital, Artaxata.[34] The legions were not led there by the shortest route, however: crossing the river Araxes (which laps the city walls) by the bridge would put them in range of projectiles. They went over it at a distance, using a ford of some width.

Summary of Tac. *Ann.* 13.40. Tiridates makes an unsuccessful attack on the Roman forces [*not translated*].

Tac. *Ann.* 13.41.1. Corbulo established his camp on the spot and considered whether to march on Artaxata by night, with his legions unencumbered by baggage, and lay siege to the city, for he assumed Tiridates had withdrawn there. Scouts then brought word that the king was on a lengthy journey and that it was unclear whether he was heading for the Medes or the Albani.[35] Corbulo therefore waited for dawn, sending ahead his light infantry in the meantime to invest the walls and commence the blockade at a distance. 2. In fact, the townspeople of their own accord threw open the gates and put themselves and their possessions at the mercy of the Romans. That move saved their lives. Artaxata was put to the torch, destroyed and leveled to the ground since, because of the size of its walls, it could not be held without a strong garrison, and we did not have forces enough to split between strengthening the garrison and prosecuting the war. On the other hand, if

34 Artaxata had been founded by the Armenian king Artaxias, supposedly on the advice of Hannibal, on the left bank of the Araxes River in 186 BC. It was the capital of Armenia.

35 The Medes were a people akin to the Persians; they inhabited the mountainous area southwest of the Caspian. By "Media" Tacitus is referring strictly to Media Atropatene (Barr. 69 H2), in the northwest, distinguished from Greater Media.

The Albani were a group of tribes in modern Dagestan/Georgia. Tacitus (*Ann.* 14.26.1) suggests that Corbulo in fact went to Media.

the town remained untouched and unguarded, there was no advantage or glory forthcoming from its capture. 3. There was, in addition, a seemingly god-sent prodigy. Up to this point, everything had been brightly illuminated by the sun. Suddenly, however, the area enclosed by the walls was covered with a black cloud and cut off by flashes of lightning, so that it was believed that the gods were attacking and the town was being consigned to destruction by them.[36]

4. Nero was hailed as *Imperator* because of this success, and following a senatorial decree prayers of thanksgiving were held. There were statues voted to the emperor, and arches and repeated consulships; and the day on which the victory was won, on which it was announced, and on which it had been discussed in the Senate were all to be set among the festal days.[37] Other measures of this sort were also put to the vote, so outrageous that Gaius Cassius, who had supported the other honors, declared that, if thanks given to the gods were to be commensurate with the blessings of fortune, a whole year would be insufficient for their prayers. Accordingly, he said, there should be a distinction made between holy days and business days; that is, days on which they could hold religious observances without suspending human activity.[38]

Dio's Account

Dio, unlike Tacitus, places all his Parthian narrative together, just after the account of the Fire of Rome in AD 64, and presents it in retrospect. Dio is even more enthusiastic about Corbulo than Tacitus is. The otherwise close re-

36 A solar eclipse of April 30, 59, is mentioned by Pliny (*HN* 2.180) as having been seen by Corbulo in Armenia. The Tacitean description here does not properly suit an eclipse, but the account may have been much distorted in the sources. It is therefore possible that Corbulo spent the winter in Artaxata and did not destroy the town until the following spring. Syme (1958), I.391.2, argues that, because the narrative breaks off after the destruction of Artaxata, that event marks the end of the campaigning year and occurred in 58.

37 The fall of Artaxata was the first great military success of Nero's reign. The acclamation of *Imperator*, traditionally made to a successful commander in the field, was now enjoyed exclusively by the emperor, for victories won by his legates. Nero accepted that particular honor, but the record shows clearly that he did not accept the continuous consulships.

38 Gaius Cassius had been consul in 30 and was later appointed as legate of Syria in 44. He was an eminent legal scholar and author of several books on civil law. Banished by Nero in 65 (Tac. *Ann.* 16.9.1), he was recalled by Vespasian. He was the brother of Lucius Cassius Longinus (see *Ann.* 6.15.1). Cassius was sarcastically suggesting that care should be taken lest the festive days become so numerous that there would not be any days left for the conduct of business.

semblance between Dio and Tacitus in the narrative of events in Armenia suggests that both made use of Corbulo's memoirs but that Dio did not make use of the hostile account from which Tacitus clearly drew at times. Where he provides more detail than Tacitus, that detail may well be taken from the memoirs.

Dio 62.19.1. While he was doing this, a report reached him from Armenia together with a laurel crown to mark another victory,[39] for Corbulo had brought together the scattered military units and given them the training that had been neglected.[40] Then even the report concerning Corbulo was sufficient to alarm King Vologaeses of Parthia and the Armenian leader Tiridates.

19.2. Corbulo, like the first Romans, not only had an illustrious pedigree and great physical strength but was also intellectually gifted, and he showed great courage, fairness, and integrity in his dealings with everybody, friends and foes alike. 3. This was why Nero sent him off to the war in place of himself and put in his charge a force greater than he would anyone else—he was as confident that Corbulo would crush the barbarians as he was that he would not revolt against him. Corbulo disappointed him in neither respect, 4. but he upset everyone else in one sole regard, namely that he maintained his loyalty to Nero: people so wanted to have him as emperor instead of Nero that they reckoned this to be his only bad quality.[41] Corbulo, then, effortlessly took Artaxata, and he razed the city to the ground.[42]

Tigranocerta now falls to Corbulo, as well as the Fortress of Legerda. The Parthians are much preoccupied by a revolt of the Hyrcanians, who send envoys to the Romans.

AD 59–60

Tac. *Ann.* 14.23.1. After the destruction of Artaxata, Corbulo felt that he should capitalize on the fresh panic to seize Tigranocerta: by destroying it,

39 Dio takes as his starting point the fall of Artaxata, probably late in 58 (Tac. *Ann.* 13.41), and then summarizes events down to the ending of military action.

40 Dio here echoes Tac. *Ann.* 13.35.2, where Tacitus notes that Corbulo added a new legion, Scythica IV, and in Cappadocia brought the Syrian legions up to fighting capability.

41 There is some irony in this account, in that Corbulo would be forced to commit suicide after the failed Pisonian conspiracy in 65.

42 Almost certainly in 58. Dio, with Tacitus (*Ann.* 13.41.2), probably reflects Corbulo's commentaries in observing that Artaxata was burned to the ground.

he could heighten the enemy's fears, or by sparing it he could gain a reputation for clemency. He therefore set off for the town.[43] The army was not on an offensive footing—he did not want to quash hopes of pardon—but he did not relax his guard either, knowing as he did the volatility of the race, which, reluctant in the face of danger, was treacherous when offered opportunities.

2. The barbarians' reaction differed with their temperament: some came to him with entreaties, and others deserted their villages and dispersed into the wilderness, while there were also those who hid themselves and their dearest possessions in caves. The Roman commander accordingly varied his approach, showing compassion toward suppliants, swiftly pursuing fugitives, and dealing ruthlessly with those who had occupied hiding places—he filled the mouths and exits of the chambers with brushwood and twigs and burned them out. 3. And then Corbulo himself came under attack from the Mardi (practiced marauders who had mountains to defend them against an invader) as he was skirting their territory.[44] He sent in his Iberians and plundered their country, spilling foreign blood to punish the enemy's effrontery.[45]

24.1. Though Corbulo and his army sustained no losses in the battle, they were beginning to experience exhaustion from food shortages and their labors, being reduced to staving off hunger with animal flesh. In addition, there was a lack of water, an intense summer heat, and long marches, lightened only by the endurance of the commander, who bore as much as—and more than—the rank and file. 2. They then reached a cultivated region, where they harvested the crops and took by assault one of two strongholds in which the Armenians had sought refuge (the other, which repulsed the first attack, was reduced by siege). 3. Passing from there into the lands of the Tauronites, Corbulo managed to avoid an unexpected danger. Not far from his tent, a barbarian of some distinction was discovered with a weapon, and under torture the man gave a detailed account of a plot against the commander, identifying

43 Tacitus resumes his narrative from 13.41. This section covers the campaigns of AD 59–60.

Tigranocerta had been founded sometime after 80 BC by Tigranes I to replace Artaxata as the capital of Armenia. Its initial population consisted mainly of Greeks forced to resettle there after an invasion of Cappadocia. The partially completed city was almost totally destroyed by Lucullus in 69 BC. Its location is unknown; a strong candidate is Arzan in the eastern Tigris basin (Barr. 89 D3).

44 The Mardi were a nomadic people found in Armenia and Media. They were partially conquered by Alexander the Great and appear as enemies of the Romans at the time of Lucullus. They have been seen by some as ancestors of the modern Kurds, but the identification is far from confirmed.

45 The Iberians would be the troops of King Pharasmanes, who had given up his own dynastic ambitions in Armenia.

himself as its instigator and naming his accomplices. There followed the conviction and execution of those who, under a pretense of friendship, had been plotting treachery.

4. Not much later, representatives sent from Tigranocerta brought news that the city's defenses were open to Corbulo and that their fellow citizens were ready to follow his orders, and at the same time they handed over to him a golden crown as a gift of welcome.[46] The Roman accepted it respectfully, and the city suffered no loss. Unharmed, they would adopt a compliant attitude all the more readily, he thought.

25.1. The fort of Legerda, however, which a group of defiant young warriors had closed against him, was not taken without a fight. The enemy ventured to do battle before the walls; furthermore, when they were driven back within their fortifications, they could be forced to yield only when faced with a siege mound and an armed assault.[47] 2. These ends were achieved the more easily because the Parthians were distracted by the Hyrcanian War. The Hyrcanians had sent representatives to the Roman emperor with a petition for an alliance, calling attention to the fact that, as a pledge of their friendship, they were obstructing Vologaeses. As the representatives were returning, Corbulo, fearing they might be surrounded by enemy patrols after crossing the Euphrates, gave them an armed guard and escorted them to the shores of the Red Sea. [48] From there, they returned home, steering clear of Parthian territory.

Dio 62.20.1. After doing this, he marched on Tigranocerta,[49] sparing all the lands of peoples who submitted to him but devastating those of peo-

46 Frontinus (*Strat.* 2.9.5) reports a different account, that Tigranocerta was besieged and held out stubbornly until Corbulo executed one of the enemy nobles, Vadandus, and hurled his head into the city by siege machine. It fell by chance in the middle of a council that the residents were holding and terrified them into submission.

47 Legerda is mentioned by Ptolemy (*Geog.* 5.13.19), although his text here is far from certain; it was a fortress near the north Tigris, possibly Lidjia on the upper slopes of the Taurus, west-northwest of Tigranocerta (Barr. 89 C2). It should be noted, however, that the name is an emendation of the word *legerat* in Tacitus's manuscript.

48 The reference to the Red Sea can generally mean the modern Red Sea or the shore of the Persian Gulf. The former can be ruled out here. Furthermore, it is hard to see how there could be a route between the shore of the Persian Gulf and the Caspian Sea that did not cross through Parthian territory, and it has been argued that there has been confusion here between the Red Sea and the Caspian Sea. Corbulo, in control of Armenia, could easily have sent the Hyrcanians by the southern end of the Caspian.

49 Dio's "marched in the direction of Tigranocerta" and Tacitus's "He therefore set off for the town [Tigranocerta]" (*Ann.* 14.23.1) clearly reflect a single source.

ples who offered resistance; and he took possession of the city, which voluntarily surrendered. He was also responsible for other magnificent and glorious accomplishments, which included bringing Vologaeses, formidable though he was, to accept peace terms appropriate to the great prestige of Rome.

In AD 60, Tiridates tries to recover Armenia from the East but is repulsed. Nero, meanwhile, sends out Tigranes, a descendant of Archelaus of Cappadocia, to take the throne. Corbulo leaves a small garrison with Tigranes and goes to Syria. Client rulers are given military authority over Armenia's border areas.

Tac. *Ann.* 14.26.1. Furthermore, Tiridates was now advancing into the fringes of Armenia by way of Media. In response, Corbulo sent his legate Verulanus ahead with the auxiliaries,[50] and then he followed with the legions by forced marches, thus obliging the Parthian to withdraw a long way and abandon his hopes for war. Those he found opposed to us he subjected to wholesale slaughter and burning, and he was proceeding to take control of Armenia when Tigranes, chosen by Nero to assume the throne, arrived on the scene.[51] Tigranes was a member of the Cappadocian nobility, and a grandson of King Archelaus, but a long period as a hostage in Rome had brought him into a state of abject submissiveness. 2. And his welcome there was not unequivocal either, since there still remained some support for the Arsacids, though most people, from a loathing for the high-handedness of the Parthians, preferred a king given them by Rome. Tigranes was also provided with military assistance—a thousand legionaries, three cohorts of allies, and two squadrons

50 Verulanus is otherwise unknown, unless he is the Severus Verulanus mentioned in Tac. *Ann.* 15.3.1, who would later hold a consulship, probably in AD 66.

51 The uncle of this man, Tigranes V, had been appointed king of Armenia by Augustus (*RG* 27.2) and was later executed under Tiberius for *maiestas* (Tac. *Ann.* 6.40.2). The nephew, Tigranes VI, was the great-grandson of Herod the Great (Joseph. *AJ* 18.5.4) and great-grandson (Tacitus is casual in referring to him as grandson) of Archelaus, last king of Cappadocia. He had spent much of his life in Rome, where he was held as a hostage. His link with the ruling family of Armenia was a tenuous one. The family of his grandfather, Alexander, son of Herod, had renounced Judaism and settled in Armenia. Tigranes must have been highly regarded by Nero, but Tacitus has little respect for him, and his tenure proved to be a short one. The appointment of Tigranes seems to suggest a move away from the policy of accepting a Parthian candidate to rule Armenia provided that he do so under the nominal blessing of Rome. This may reflect a confused policy in Rome at a time when Nero was breaking out of the orbit of Seneca and Burrus. The arrival of Tigranes seems more or less to have coincided with Corbulo's appointment to Syria (discussed later) and departure from Armenia for that province.

of cavalry. In addition, to facilitate his defense of his new kingdom, various portions of Armenia were instructed to accept submission to whichever king they were contiguous to—Pharasmanes, Polemo, Aristobulus, or Antiochus.[52]

Corbulo withdrew into Syria, which, left vacant by the death of the legate Ummidius, had now been assigned to him.[53]

52 Corbulo made extensive use of client kings for the defense of Armenia's borders. Tacitus's language ("accept submission") suggests that the general reference here is probably to military authority in the border areas of Armenia rather than to the assignment of territory. Note that in giving Aristobulus and Sohaemus territories to actually rule over, he specifies "both of them also receiving royal diadems." Of the kings who had been asked to provide help at the outset of the crisis in AD 54 (Tac. *Ann.* 13.7.1), the services of Antiochus of Commagene and of Aristobulus are called on once again. Agrippa II and Sohaemus ruled kingdoms some distance from the theater of operations, in Chalcis and Emesa, respectively, and had presumably returned there once the crisis passed.

Two other kings appear to be used at this stage. Pharasmanes of Iberia had initially supported the claim to Armenia made by his son, Radamistus. Later, to ingratiate himself with the Romans, he had put Radamistus to death and taken some sort of military action against Armenia on his own initiative, not on the instructions of Corbulo. Tacitus (*Ann.* 14.23.3) suggests that he sent troops to aid the Romans against the Mardi. He would have been an ally to be handled with caution, and it is surprising that he was given military authority in part of Armenia. Polemo (II) was the grandson of Polemo I, who had received his kingdom of Pontus and Armenia Minor from Antony, and Augustus had added the kingdom of Bosporus. Armenia Minor, however, was transferred initially to Antiochus of Commagene by Augustus (Dio 54.9.2), subsequently by Caligula to King Cotys of Thrace (Dio 59.12.2), and finally, as Tacitus (*Ann.* 13.7.1) shows, to Aristobulus by Nero. Polemo II received Pontus and the Bosporan kingdom from his childhood friend Caligula (Dio 59.12.2). Although he lost his Bosporan realm, he did receive part of Cilicia (Dio 60.8.2). At some point after 63 and the end of the Armenian crisis, Nero incorporated Pontus within the empire (Suet. *Ner.* 18). Polemo is one of the more important client kings, and yet there is no other mention of his supposed role in the campaign. Moreover, the area of Armenia contiguous to his kingdom was not under threat. It is important to note that the presence of both Pharasmanes and Polemo is based on an emendation made in 1672 by J. F. Gronovius of *pars nipuli* in Tacitus's manuscript to *Pharasmani Polemonique*.

53 Corbulo had been operating as special legate in Cappadocia (and Galatia). In AD 60, he was appointed to the regular and prestigious governorship of Syria. It had been intended that Ummidius Quadratus, who had clashed with Corbulo, would be replaced by Publius Anteius in AD 55 (Tac. *Ann.* 13.22.1), but Anteius was detained in Rome, possibly because he was an ally of Agrippina. He seems to have been involved in some sort of shady trafficking in property that had legally been confiscated by the state but not collected. He committed suicide in AD 61 (Tac. *Ann.* 16.14.3). We do not know when Ummidius died, and some plausibly read the *sibi* of Tacitus's phrase *sibi permissam* ("assigned to him") as a reference not to Corbulo but to Syria, to mean that the province "had been left to its own devices."

In AD 61, irresponsible raids by Tigranes provoke a Parthian response. The Parthians put the Hyrcanian problem to one side and prepare to take Armenia for Tiridates. Corbulo sends two legions to support Tigranes and proceeds to strengthen the frontier defenses along the Euphrates. Tigranocerta holds out against the Parthians, who, under the threat of invasion by Corbulo, agree to send an embassy to Nero. Corbulo informs Rome that Armenia needs to be the responsibility of a separate military commander, and Caesennius Paetus is appointed to that position.

AD 61–62

Vologaeses resolves to assist Tiridates and settles his differences with the Hyrcanians.

Tac. *Ann.* 15.1.1. Meanwhile, Vologaeses, king of Parthia, had learned of Corbulo's exploits and discovered that Tigranes, a foreigner, had been placed on the throne of Armenia; and at the same time he wanted to avenge the expulsion of his brother Tiridates, which was an insult to the dignity of the Arsacids.[54] However, when he considered Roman greatness and his past respect for the treaty, which had remained unbroken, he was drawn in two different directions at once.[55] He was hesitant by nature and was also encumbered by the defection of a mighty people, the Hyrcanians, and the numerous campaigns arising from it.[56]

2. In fact, he was still wavering when news of a further insult galvanized him into action. Upon emerging from Armenia, Tigranes had inflicted damage

54 The account of events on the eastern frontier is resumed from the end of *Ann.* 14.26, where Tacitus had carried them down to the end of AD 60. We now resume in the spring of AD 61, and this section must cover two years, 61–62, since Paetus did not arrive until 62 (Syme [1958], 392). Tacitus describes the final settlement with Parthia in some detail because of its historical significance. The military and diplomatic events are very complex.

55 The treaty of friendship that Augustus had reached in 20 BC, and that had resulted in the recovery of Roman standards taken in battle by the Parthians, had been renewed by Artabanus (Tac. *Ann.* 2.58.1). It was also renewed when Germanicus was in Syria and again at the end of Tiberius's reign and the beginning of Caligula's. It had never been formally broken. Respect was symbolically important. When in AD 49 Parthian ambassadors went to Rome to seek the return of Meherdates, Claudius noted the deferential attitude shown by the Parthians toward Rome (Tac. *Ann.* 12.11.1).

56 Hyrcania was a fertile area south of the Caspian, bounded on the east by the Oxus. It was annexed to the Persian empire, probably by Cyrus the Great, but preserved its national consciousness and involved itself in the factional disputes in Parthia (Tac. *Ann.* 6.36.4, 43.2). Some of the Parthian kings were of Hyrcanian origin.

on the bordering tribe of the Adiabeni too extensively, [57] and for too long, for his action to be simply predatory raiding, and the chiefs of the Parthian races were infuriated. They had now become so despised, they said, that it was not even from a Roman general that they were under attack but from an overambitious hostage treated for years by the Romans as one of their slaves.[58]

Tac. *Ann.* 15.3.1. When Corbulo heard this from reliable reports, he sent two legions under Verulanus Severus and Vettius Bolanus to assist Tigranes, [59] but secretly instructed them to act at all times with deliberation rather than speed. This was because he wanted to be in a state of war rather than fighting one,[60]and he had also informed Nero by dispatch that Armenia needed its own commander for its defense, and that Syria would be in more serious danger if Vologaeses attacked. 2. In the meantime, he deployed his remaining legions along the bank of the Euphrates, put a makeshift company of provincials under arms, and with armed detachments closed the points of entry open to the enemy.[61] And because the region lacked water, he established forts at the springs, and some of the streams he hid from view under piles of sand.

57 Adiabene was a Parthian vassal state in the Tigris region (Barr. 91 E2), the northern part of Assyria between the Tigris and the mountains of Kurdistan, although confusingly the elder Pliny sometimes uses it to refer to the whole of Assyria (*HN* 5.66). Its ruler Izates (AD 36–50s) was much involved in Parthian dynastic politics (Tac. *Ann.* 12.13.1) and converted to Judaism, partly from political motives (Joseph. *AJ* 20 *passim*).

58 Tigranes did have a connection with the royal house of Parthia, but it was tenuous. He was not popular with the Armenians; he had spent too long at Rome and was considered a foreigner (Tac. *Ann.* 14.26.1). He also seems to have proved himself incompetent, since his deliberately provocative raids outside Armenia on Parthia went counter to the Roman policy at this time of seeking some degree of accommodation with their rivals.

59 Verulanus Severus is presumably the Verulanus mentioned in an early part of the campaign (Tac. *Ann.* 14.26.1); he would later be consul, probably in AD 66. Little is known of the earlier career of Vettius Bolanus; he possibly did not come from a consular family, but his later career was distinguished. He would go on to be consul in AD 66, governor of Britain in 69–71, and proconsul of Asia in about AD 78–80. He is praised by Statius in a poem dedicated to Bolanus's son, Crispinus (*Silv.* 5.2.30–67).

60 It might of course have been suspected that Corbulo wished to protract his command by avoiding a decisive outcome. But he seems to have been constrained from the outset by instructions from Rome to show strength but keep open the chance of accommodation with Parthia.

61 The province of Syria regularly housed four legions. With the removal of two of them, three would have remained available to Corbulo, since Tacitus notes that one more legion was added, from Germany, in 58, although no legion from Germany is known to have taken part in Corbulo's campaign. The Fourth Legion (Scythica) was sent from Moe-

Awaiting Nero's decision on the special appointment to Armenia, Corbulo reaches a truce with the Parthians, and both sides withdraw their forces from Armenia. Tigranes departs.

Summary of Tac. *Ann.* 15.4. Tigranocerta holds out against attacks by the Adiabeni [*not translated*].

Tac. *Ann.* 15.5.1. Despite his success, Corbulo felt he should not press his luck, and he sent off a deputation to Vologaeses to deplore the violence brought against the province and the fact that a king who was his ally and friend was under siege, along with Roman cohorts.[62] He would do better to raise the siege, said Corbulo, or he, too, would pitch his camp in enemy territory!

2. The centurion Casperius,[63] who had been chosen for this deputation, came to the king at the town of Nisibis, thirty-seven miles from Tigranocerta, and there delivered his instructions in strongly worded terms.[64] 3. Vologaeses had a long-standing and firmly held principle of avoiding armed confrontation with the Romans and, in addition, things were not running well for him. The siege was a failure; Tigranes was secure, thanks to his manpower and supplies; those who had undertaken the assault on the town had been routed; legions had been sent into Armenia; and others were on the Syrian border ready to launch an offensive. As for his own situation, his cavalry was weakened from lack of forage, for the sudden appearance of a swarm of locusts had left nothing in the way of grass or foliage. 4. Vologaeses therefore concealed his unease and, assuming a more conciliatory approach, replied that he would send spokesmen to the Roman emperor about his petition for Armenia and strengthening the peace.[65] He ordered Monaeses to quit Tigranocerta, and proceeded to pull back himself.

sia, not Germany. The fortification of the Euphrates would be seen as a provocative act by the Parthians.

62 The violence presumably refers to desultory raids that Tacitus has not deemed important enough to record.

63 Under Claudius, Casperius tried to mediate between Pharasmanes and Mithridates (see the Introduction to this chapter) in the castle of Gorneae in Armenia (Tac. *Ann.* 12.45.2; Barr. 88 C4).

64 Nisibis was a major city in northeast Mesopotamia, on the river Mygdonius (Barr. 89 D3). It was strategically important, being in the frontier area between Parthia and Armenia. It featured widely in the campaigns of Lucullus. The precise figure of thirty-seven miles does not in fact help in locating Tigranocerta and may well be an error. The Barrington Atlas (Barr. 89 D3) locates Tigranocerta about sixty miles north of Nisibis.

65 Tacitus is rather cryptic here, but the implication is that Vologaeses will now agree to what he had earlier rejected (13.34.2): to contemplate Tiridates' going to Rome to seek

6.1. Most praised this as a magnificent achievement brought off by the king's fear and the threats of Corbulo. Others explained it as a secret agreement whereby Tigranes would also leave Armenia after both sides abandoned hostilities and Vologaeses departed.[66] 2. Why else, they asked, had the Roman army been withdrawn from Tigranocerta? Why had they abandoned in peacetime what they had defended in war? Was it better to have wintered on the fringes of Cappadocia in hurriedly erected huts rather than in the capital of a kingdom they had just succeeded in holding? Armed conflict had been deliberately postponed, they said, so Vologaeses could clash with someone other than Corbulo, and so Corbulo would not further jeopardize the glory he had earned over the years. 3. For, as I have observed, Corbulo had requested that Armenia have its own commander for its protection, and the news was that Caesennius Paetus was close at hand.

Dio 62.20.2. When he heard that Nero had distributed Armenia to others and that Adiabene was being laid waste by Tigranes,[67] Vologaeses prepared to campaign in person against Corbulo in Syria, and into Armenia he sent Monobazus, king of Adiabene, and the Parthian Monaeses.[68]

3. These pinned down Tigranes in Tigranocerta. They were doing him no harm by their blockade, however, and, indeed, whenever they engaged him, they were beaten back both by Tigranes' men and the Romans present with him; and, in addition, Corbulo was keeping a strict watch on Syria. Vologaeses therefore relented and abandoned the expedition.[69]

---

recognition of his position in person. It is not clear why the negotiations broke down, but we have to assume that the Parthian envoys discovered that the Roman attitude had hardened.

66 There were suspicions that Corbulo had secretly agreed to remove Tigranes, who now drops completely out of the narrative. This could suggest that Corbulo was not comfortable with the new aggressive policy now being promoted by Rome and that the abandonment of Tigranes would be a way of resisting that policy without overt disobedience. This would create a complex scenario. It is of course possible that Tigranes simply left of his own accord.

67 Dio is in agreement with Tacitus (*Ann.* 15.1.1–2, not included in the translated passages) in saying that Vologaeses had a reaction to two developments, the appointment of Tigranes to Armenia and his raids against the Adiabeni.

68 Tacitus (*Ann.* 15.1.1–2) notes that Monobazus of Adiabene rebuked the Parthians for leaving his kingdom exposed by the surrender of Armenia but says nothing about his personal participation in the incursion into Armenia. He does mention the Parthian general Monaeses as commanding in that incursion and the presence of some units from Adiabene (*Ann.*15.2.4).

69 Tacitus (*Ann.* 15.5.3–4) also sees the failure of the siege of Tigranocerta as the primary reason for Vologaeses' willingness to come to terms.

4. He sent a message to Corbulo and succeeded in gaining an armistice on the condition that he again send an embassy to Nero and that he raise the siege and withdraw his troops from Armenia. Even then, Nero did not furnish a reply that was either swift or clear, but he sent Lucius Daesennius Paetus to Cappadocia to obviate any revolutionary activity around Armenia.[70]

Paetus arrives on the scene. He is determined to pursue an aggressive policy and starts his raid into Armenia as winter approaches. Despite bombastic reports to Rome, he has to be rescued by Corbulo. The Parthians withdraw from Armenia, and Corbulo in turn abandons positions established across the Euphrates. there are premature celebrations in Rome.

AD 62

Tac. *Ann.* 15.6.3. Soon Paetus was there.[71] The troops were then divided, with the Fourth and Twelfth legions, plus the Fifth (recently summoned from Moesia),[72] put under Paetus's command, along with the auxiliaries from Pontus, Galatia, and Cappadocia.[73] The Third, Sixth, and Tenth legions, and the troops earlier serving in Syria, would remain with Corbulo. All else they would share, or divide up, according to the exigencies of the moment. 4. But Corbulo could not stand a rival, and Paetus, for

70 Like Tacitus (*Ann.* 15.4–6), Dio provides no explanation for why the parleys broke down, and the obscurity of both accounts suggests that the issue was not properly laid out in the common source.

71 Caesennius Paetus served as consul ordinarius for AD 61 and in that same year was given Corbulo's old special command in Cappadocia, where he served until 63. As described by Tacitus, his term was a disastrous one and led to a humiliating defeat. Despite the setback, Paetus was appointed governor of Syria by Vespasian in AD 70, and probably died in 73. He was instrumental in organizing Commagene into a province (Joseph. *AJ* 7.219).

Paetus's arrival is best placed in AD 62. Tacitus refers to Corbulo wintering in Cappadocia (*Ann.* 15.6.2), presumably with reference to the winter just past. But the chronology of this period is very confused. It is possible that Paetus arrived in Cappadocia in summer 61, was defeated a year later, and then wintered in 62–63. But it also may be that he did not arrive there until 62.

72 The Fifth Legion (Macedonica) was stationed in Macedonia until AD 6 and then transferred to Moesia. In 61/62, it was transferred to Armenia, but was still in Pontus when Paetus assumed his command. It later took part in the Jewish War, and in 71 it was returned to Moesia.

73 Corbulo had already been engaged in the levying of auxiliaries in Galatia and Cappadocia (Tac. *Ann.* 13.35.2). Presumably, King Polemo would have raised auxiliaries in Pontus.

whom being second to him should have been glory enough, kept disparaging Corbulo's achievements. There had been "no bloodshed or spoils," he would say, and the "storming of cities" that Corbulo often referred to applied in name only.[74] It would be he, Paetus, who would impose on the conquered peoples tribute and laws, and, instead of a phantom king, Roman jurisdiction.[75]

7.1. Vologaeses' representatives, whom I mentioned earlier as having been sent to the emperor, returned at about this same time, emptyhanded, and so the Parthians turned to open warfare.[76] Paetus did not demur. He took two legions—the Fourth, which Funisulanus Vettonianus commanded at that time, and the Twelfth, which was under Calavius Sabinus[77]—and entered Armenia accompanied by a grim omen. 2. For on their way over the Euphrates, which they crossed by a bridge, the horse carrying the consular insignia took fright for no apparent reason and escaped to the rear of the troops.[78] Furthermore, a sacrificial animal that was standing beside the winter quarters, which were under construction, burst through the half-finished works in flight and ran out from the rampart. Soldiers' javelins also burst

74 The unusual circumstances of the operations, as well as Corbulo's dread of being eclipsed, meant that there was almost bound to be a repetition of clashes of the kind that had occurred between Ummidius and Corbulo. Later, Corbulo will be given an overall command in order to avoid such problems. Paetus is technically correct in that military outposts had been taken but Artaxata and Tigranocerta had surrendered voluntarily.

75 Paetus here speaks of what seems to be an intention to incorporate Armenia into the empire, a plan that appears to run counter to what Corbulo had been striving to achieve. This could suggest an appointment by an independent-thinking Nero that would lead to a more aggressive policy in Armenia than the one being promoted by Seneca and Burrus, who by now had begun to fall from grace. This new policy might have been marked by the rejection of the terms offered by the envoys sent to Rome by Vologaeses, mentioned by Tacitus (*Ann.* 15.5.4).

76 Tacitus suggests that the Parthians began an aggressive campaign in AD 62, but the possibility that Paetus had already taken preemptory military action cannot be discounted. It is interesting to note that the diplomatic efforts of the Parthians were unsuccessful. We are not told what terms they had tried to obtain, but clearly they did not find Nero amenable.

77 Funisulanus is recorded in inscriptions (*ILS* 1005, 1997) as pursuing a highly successful civil and military career under Domitian. Calavius is unknown. These two were Paetus's appointees. Corbulo had sent Verulanus Severus and Vettius Bolanus as commanders of the legions (Tac. *Ann.* 15.3.1).

78 Plutarch notes that a horse of Crassus similarly fell in the Euphrates (*Crass.* 19.5), and Julius Obsequens (69) records the collapse of a caparisoned horse in the presence of Pansa during his consulship (43 BC) as a bad omen (he died in battle). Strictly speaking, this was the only omen that occurred when Paetus led his forces into Armenia. The others happened when they were already established there. It is likely that they entered Armenia from Cappadocia near Melitene to travel south to Tigranocerta.

into flames, a prodigy of significance because, in combat, the enemy (i.e., the Parthians) fights with projectiles.

8.1. Paetus, however, disregarded the omens and, although he had not yet adequately fortified his winter quarters or made any provision for his grain supply, he hurriedly marched his army over the Taurus range.[79] His aim, he kept saying, was to retake Tigranocerta and lay waste the areas that Corbulo had left untouched.[80] 2. He did take a number of strongholds and acquire a measure of glory and plunder[81]—but failed to exercise moderation in the pursuit of glory, or circumspection in the pursuit of the plunder. With forced marches, he overran areas that could not be held, only to lead back his army when the provisions that had been captured had rotted and winter was coming on. Then, as though the war were over, he wrote a letter to Nero framed in grandiose terms but devoid of substance.

9.1. Meanwhile, Corbulo secured the bank of the Euphrates—which he had never neglected—with more closely spaced guard posts. In addition, to ensure that enemy cavalry squadrons would not obstruct his establishing a bridge on the river—for they were already racing about on the nearby plains, an impressive sight—he drew a line of sizable ships, connected with planking and built up with turrets, across the river. From these, using catapults and ballistas, he drove back the barbarians, whom rocks and missiles could reach at a range that arrows shot back in response could not match. 2. Then the bridge was completed, and the hills on the far side were taken over by the allied cohorts and subsequently by the legionary camp.[82] Such was the speed of the Romans, and such their show of strength, that the Parthians abandoned their preparations for invading Syria and directed all their hopes toward Armenia. This was where Paetus was, ignorant of the looming threat and with the Fifth Legion stationed far off in Pontus,[83] and the remaining legions

79 The quarters would have been for the winter of AD 62–63. This would seem to place Paetus's march in autumn 61, since he had spent the first part of the year in Rome, as consul. It is assumed that here Tacitus is following the hostile commentaries of Corbulo.

80 Tigranocerta had been abandoned by Roman troops, and Tacitus's text makes it quite clear here that Tigranes made no effort to maintain it.

81 Tacitus is not an impartial observer, but Paetus clearly could not have engaged the Parthians in a major campaign, since the next chapter indicates that they were focusing their attention on the frontier with Syria, not on Armenia. They did not turn to Armenia until later.

82 Corbulo clearly established a Roman bridgehead on the Parthian side of the Euphrates, a major bone of contention. Vologaeses made the removal of the fortifications his key demand for coming to terms with the Romans.

83 The Fifth Legion (Macedonica) had been transferred from Moesia. It seems that Paetus felt it was not needed immediately and was keeping it in Pontus, where it could more easily be provisioned.

he had weakened by indiscriminately granting leave to his men. Then word came that Vologaeses was approaching with a large army, ready to attack.[84]

Summary of Tac. *Ann.* 15.10.1. Paetus disperses his forces and faces pressure from the Parthians. He has to protect his wife and son with a cohort of troops [*not translated*].

Tac. *Ann.* 15.10.4. They say that Paetus was only with difficulty made to acknowledge the enemy pressure to Corbulo. And there was no haste on Corbulo's part—as the dangers mounted, credit for relieving Paetus would also grow.[85] He did, however, give orders for a thousand men from each of the three legions, along with eight hundred auxiliary cavalry and a similar number from the cohorts, to prepare for the march.

Summary of Tac. *Ann.* 15.11. Vologaeses inflicts a defeat on the Romans, and Paetus again requests help from Corbulo [*not translated*].

Tac. *Ann.* 15.12.1. Corbulo was undaunted. He left some of his troops in Syria to hold the structures erected on the Euphrates, and, taking the shortest route that would not be devoid of provisions, he headed for the region of Commagene, then Cappadocia, and from there Armenia. Accompanying the army—apart from the usual war apparatus—was a large number of camels laden with grain, so Corbulo could ward off both hunger and the enemy.[86]

84 It is remarkable that Paetus knew nothing of the threat posed by the Parthians. The removal of their forces from the Syrian border would have signaled the near certainty that they would now turn their attention to Armenia. It is possible that Corbulo made no effort to alert Paetus to the change in circumstances, as hinted in the next section.

85 Tacitus speaks of two appeals from Paetus to Corbulo, (a) the earlier passage, which he attributes to reports on the situation ("they say"), presumably in sources that were hostile to Corbulo and to which Tacitus had access, and (b) a follow-up appeal, related in the next chapter, which finally galvanized Corbulo to action. Dio (62.21.4) claims that Paetus "kept sending" requests for help. Corbulo's hesitation may have nothing to do with his hostility toward Paetus but may rather reflect the danger, of which he remained conscious, that the Parthians could turn their attention back again to Syria.

86 Corbulo's qualities as a commander are illustrated here. He does not leave the Euphrates unguarded since a surprise Parthian attack was always a risk. He does not march directly north through Parthian territory, where securing supplies would be difficult and he would be exposed to attack, but takes the longer route through the Roman-held territory of Commagene and Cappadocia. He also appreciates the necessity of taking supplies with him. It must have been late in 62 when his mission was launched.

Summary of Tac. *Ann.* 15.12.2–14. Vologaeses blockades the forces of Paetus, who agrees to withdraw from Armenia and surrender his supplies to the Parthians [*not translated*].

Tac. *Ann.* 15.15.1. Meanwhile, Paetus set a bridge on the river Arsanias, which flowed past the camp.[87] He pretended to be making a path for himself, but in fact the Parthians had ordered it built as evidence of their victory—it was to them that it was useful, as our men set off in the opposite direction. 2. Rumor added that the legions had been sent under the yoke and had suffered other indignities appropriate to a defeat, which had been imitated by the Armenians,[88] for they entered the fortifications before the Roman column left, and they stood at the roadside identifying and removing slaves or beasts of burden that had been captured earlier. Even clothing was seized and weapons withheld, the frightened soldiers yielding them so there would be no grounds for a fight.

3. Vologaeses piled up the arms and corpses of the slain as a testimonial to our defeat but stopped short of watching the legions in flight; after indulging his pride to the fullest, he was seeking a reputation for moderation. He forded the river Arsanias on an elephant, and all members of his entourage charged over on their powerful horses, for the rumor had arisen that—because of the treachery of its builders—the bridge would give way under their weight.[89] In truth, those who had the temerity to set foot on it found it strong and reliable.

87 The Arsanias is mentioned by the elder Pliny (*HN* 5.84, 6.128) as one of the main tributaries of the Euphrates, and indeed it may well be its main eastern branch (cf. Barr. 89 B2). Dio (62.21.1) gives the name of the camp as Rhandea, which would presumably be on the northern bank, since the Parthians had to cross the river to reach it. Plutarch (*Luc.* 31.4–5) records that Lucullus crossed it on his northward march from Tigranocerta to Artaxata.

88 Romans were obsessed by the recollection that in 321 BC Roman soldiers were trapped by the Samnites in the pass of the Caudine Forks and forced to go "beneath the yoke." Spears were held in an archway, and defeated troops were forced to march under it in a humiliating display of submission (Livy 9.6.1–4). Dio says nothing of this recent supposed disgrace, but Suetonius (*Ner.* 39.1) reports it as a fact, citing it as one of the two great external disasters of Nero's reign, the other being the Boudican rebellion. This is the sole reference to the events of the Parthian campaign in Suetonius's *Nero*. It seems curious that Vologaeses, who, Tacitus goes on to say, was seeking a reputation for moderation, would have inflicted this pointless humiliation on the Romans or that Paetus's subsequent career could have survived it.

89 Dio (62.21.4) says that Vologaeses, and the elephant, actually crossed the river by the bridge.

16. It is well established, however, that those under siege had such quantities of grain at their disposal that they set fire to their granaries. On the other hand, according to Corbulo's account, the Parthians, short of provisions and their forage exhausted, were on the point of raising the siege (and Corbulo himself was no more than three days' march away, he says).[90] 2. He adds that a sworn undertaking was given by Paetus before the standards, and in the presence of men whom the king had sent to witness it, that no Roman would enter Armenia until the arrival of Nero's letter stating whether he agreed with the peace treaty.[91] 3. While this account was intended to increase Paetus's disrepute,[92] the other details are not unclear: Paetus covered a distance of forty miles in one day,[93] leaving wounded men all along the route, and the panic-stricken retreat was no less unsightly than if the men had turned tail in battle.

4. Corbulo met them with his own forces on the bank of the Euphrates, but he avoided such a display of insignia and weapons as would make a humiliating contrast between them.[94] The units were downcast and deploring the lot of their comrades, and they could not even hold back their tears; greetings could barely be exchanged because of the weeping. Gone was the will to compete in valor, gone the striving for glory, which are the inclinations of successful men; pity reigned alone, and it was stronger in the lower ranks.

17.1. Next came a brief conversation between the commanders. Corbulo complained that his efforts had been wasted, that the war could have been ended if the Parthians had been routed. Paetus responded that everything remained unchanged for the two of them—they should turn the eagles around and together invade Armenia, now weakened by the departure of

90 Tacitus is explicit that he is here using Corbulo's own account, which clearly tries to paint Paetus in the darkest possible terms. The earlier expression "it is well-established" he seems to identify as coming from another source, equally hostile to Paetus. Tacitus (*Ann.* 15.14.3) says that the supplies were to be surrendered to the Parthians. Corbulo's claim that the Parthians were considering lifting the siege is plausible, since winter would be approaching and the opportunities for supplies would be limited.

91 Dio (62.21.2) states that Paetus swore he would abandon Armenia to Tiridates; Tacitus's claim that he agreed that no Romans would enter Armenia would have meant that Paetus had gone well beyond his competence and had imposed an unauthorized restriction on Corbulo. On the other hand, Dio's assertion that Paetus agreed that Nero would give Armenia to Tiridates seems like a misleading summation of what might have been a nuanced suggestion. Tacitus's reference to an expected communication from Nero suggests that some offer of compromise, along the lines of what was finally agreed, was expected.

92 It is noticeable here that while Tacitus is a great admirer of Corbulo, he is aware that his memoirs are not going to be without bias.

93 A daily march of forty miles would be remarkable, in fact double the normal rate.

94 Corbulo would presumably have been at Melitene.

Vologaeses.[95] 2. Such were not the orders he had from the emperor, said Corbulo. He had left his province from concern over the danger facing the legions and, as the Parthians' intentions were unclear, he would head back to Syria. Even so, he would still have to pray for the best of luck in order for his infantrymen, exhausted from the long distances covered, to overtake spirited cavalrymen, who would outpace them over the easy terrain of the plains.[96]

Paetus then wintered in Cappadocia.[97] 3. Messengers from Vologaeses were meanwhile dispatched to Corbulo to tell him to dismantle his forts across the Euphrates and make the river the boundary between them as before. Corbulo had a demand, too, that Armenia be cleared of its various garrisons. In the end, the king acquiesced; the fortifications that Corbulo had established beyond the Euphrates were demolished, and the Armenians were left without a ruler.[98]

18.1. At Rome, meanwhile, trophies and arches were being erected in the middle of the Capitoline Hill for victory over the Parthians.[99] Decreed by the Senate when the war was still undecided, they were not even now discontinued, attention being paid to appearances, despite knowledge of the facts.[100]

In spring 63, quite different reports reach Rome from Paetus and Vologaeses. Rome sees through the pretenses of Paetus but refuses the approaches of Vologaeses, who is now willing to accept that Tiridates should accept the crown from Rome but without having to travel to the city. Conduct of the war is handed over to

95 Paetus's suggestion seems on the surface highly implausible and may represent the version that he sought to propagate in Rome after his return.

96 Corbulo uses the argument that his *provincia* was limited to Syria, and he technically could not move his troops into another zone without the permission of the emperor. This does not seem very persuasive. His other arguments, that the intentions of the Parthians were not clear (implying that they might well have intended to move against Syria) and that his troops would be too exhausted to attempt such a mission, are more plausible.

97 This would have been the winter of AD 62–63.

98 After a fairly detailed exposition of the preceding military events, Tacitus describes the final negotiations in very cursory terms, perhaps because, for reasons that are not clear, the truce broke down. Dio (62.22.2–3) adds that the negotiator for Vologaeses was Monaeses and that the terms were to be validated by Nero upon receipt of an embassy (covered by Tacitus in the next section).

99 Tacitus here refers to the custom of setting up a pile of captured arms as a victory memorial, a practice adopted by the Romans from the Greeks and first recorded toward the end of the second century BC.

100 The Senate would have been obliged to depend on the dispatches of Paetus, with their tone of exaggerated confidence. In fact, the news of his humiliation did not reach them until the next year (see Tac. *Ann.* 15.24.1), so the criticism here is somewhat misplaced. Also, the "arches" may be a confusion with the victory arches decreed to mark the fall of Artaxata in AD 59.

Corbulo, who is given a general military command, while the civil administration of Syria is handed over to Gaius Cestius.

AD 63

Tac. *Ann.* 15.24.1. Meanwhile, at the start of spring, representatives of the Parthians arrived with King Vologaeses' instructions and a letter that ran along the same lines. The claims to sovereignty over Armenia that he had so often insisted on earlier he was now dropping, Vologaeses said. The gods, arbiters of all peoples, no matter how powerful, had delivered possession of it to the Parthians, not without some humiliation for the Romans. 2. Recently, he had blockaded Tigranes, and then released Paetus and his legions unharmed when he could have crushed them.[101] He had given sufficient proof of his power and also demonstrated his clemency. Tiridates would not have refused to come to Rome to accept his diadem either, he said, had he not been held back by the religious taboos of his priesthood. He would, however, come before the standards and statues of the emperor, there to inaugurate his reign in the presence of the legions.[102]

25.1. Such was the letter of Vologaeses, and Paetus's account, suggesting that matters were still undecided, contradicted it.[103] A centurion who had arrived with the representatives was therefore questioned on the Armenian situation, and he replied that all the Romans had quit the country. 2. Aware now of the mockery implicit in the barbarians asking for what they had already seized, Nero consulted the leading men of Rome on whether they preferred a dangerous war or a dishonorable peace.[104] It was war, without question. With

101 Vologaeses gives an inflated account of his achievements. As part of the agreement with Corbulo, he had evacuated Armenia.

102 The elder Pliny (*HN* 30.16–17) claims that Tiridates was a Magian, who refused to travel by water. He was willing to go to a neighboring military camp in Syria or Cappadocia, where legionary standards and the image of the emperor would be stored. This refusal to come to Rome was a major stumbling block in the negotiations, and Nero was clearly unwilling to give up his opportunity for a *coup de théâtre*. Tiridates later did overcome his scruples about coming to the city.

103 Tacitus has of course summarized and simplified the Parthian offer of terms and has perhaps presented the interpretation he has placed on it rather than the actual terms. Paetus's letter must presumably be different from the one reported in Tac. *Ann.* 15.8.2, and we must assume that he sent a second report giving a different version of events from the one provided by Vologaeses. The implication is that he claimed that the Romans were still in control of Armenia.

104 These "leading men" would have been a body of leading citizens with no formal constitutional position, made up from among the friends of the emperor. The Parthian view was somewhat misrepresented. They did not regard Armenia as won and did not ask for it back, and in fact were making a point of not asking for it (Tac. *Ann.* 15.24.1).

his many years' experience of the Roman troops and the enemy, Corbulo was put in charge of the campaign, so there would be no further bungling through another's inexperience—they had had enough of Paetus.[105]

3. The representatives were therefore sent back with their mission not accomplished but bearing gifts to raise hopes that Tiridates would not fail with the same request if he petitioned in person.[106]

Gaius Cestius was entrusted with the civil administration of Syria,[107] and Corbulo with the military forces, which were reinforced by the addition of the Fifteenth Legion, under Marius Celsus, brought in from Pannonia.[108] Tetrarchs, kings, prefects, procurators, and praetors in charge of neighboring provinces were sent written instructions to take orders from Corbulo,[109] whose powers were increased roughly to the level of those the Roman people had granted Gnaeus Pompey for the war on the pirates.[110] 4. Although Paetus

105 Tacitus places the military preparations, the campaign, and the negotiations in AD 63. That would pack a lot of activity into a single year, and it may be that events should be extended over two years, AD 63 and 64, with military operations beginning in that second year (see Vervaet [2000], 264–67).

106 Tacitus here suggests a nuanced and subtle element in the negotiations; the Roman gesture as he reports it does not make great sense. Dio (62.22.3) seems to offer a more satisfactory narrative, that Nero explicitly made an offer to Tiridates if he would come to Rome in person.

107 Gaius Cestius was consul in AD 42; in 63, he became legate of Syria, where he died (Tac. *Hist.* 5.10.1). Tacitus does not make clear whether Cestius went to Syria as Corbulo's assistant or as *legatus Augusti*, with the limitation that command of the legions was assigned to Corbulo. Certainly by AD 66 we find Cestius acting as a regular *legatus*, with command of troops restored to him, since he is then engaged in a major military intervention with considerable forces in Judaea (Joseph. *BJ* 2.499–500).

108 Marius Celsus would later go on to hold a consulship in AD 69. The Fifteenth Legion was probably raised by Octavian in 41–40 BC and stationed in Pannonia from AD 9. It is mentioned as being in Pannonia during the mutinies that broke out following the death of Augustus (Tac. *Ann.* 1.23.5). Transferred to Syria, it was later used in the Jewish Wars.

109 Tetrarchs had in principle been originally the rulers of roughly one-quarter of a country, but at this period the term is used generally for the ruler of a small state in the East. Prefects are presumably the officers in charge of cohorts of troops established within some provinces. Procurator was the term now used for the administrators of the small administrative areas, such as Judaea, not strictly provinces in themselves but under the aegis of the legates of large contiguous provinces. The use of "praetor" is interesting here; it may be applied as a general term covering the governors of imperial and public provinces in the area, or perhaps it is being used pointedly. All imperial provinces were governed by legates *pro praetore*, as only the emperor had proconsular power in the imperial provinces. Bithynia and Asia, however, were public provinces governed by proconsuls. It may be that they did not come under Corbulo's jurisdiction.

110 The *Lex Gabinia* of 67 BC conferred on Pompey an extraordinary command over the whole of the Mediterranean to enable him to deal with the problem of pirates. He

feared worse upon his return, Nero was satisfied merely with a facetious rebuke, the gist of which was that he was pardoning Paetus immediately in order that a man so prone to panic might not fall ill from chronic worry.[111]

Dio 62.21.1. Vologaeses marched on Tigranocerta and repelled Paetus, who had come to its aid. When Paetus fled, he gave chase, cut down the garrison that had been left by him on the banks of the Taurus, and then blockaded him in Rhandea, close to the river Arsanias.[112] 2. But he could not get near the defensive wall because he lacked heavy-armed soldiers and was not well stocked with food, especially since he had arrived with large numbers and without preparations made for provisioning, and would actually have left with nothing accomplished but for Paetus's fear of his archers, whose arrows actually reached his camp, and his horsemen, who appeared on the scene everywhere. Paetus therefore sent him communications about a truce and came to an understanding with him, swearing that he would leave all Armenia and that Nero would give it to Tiridates.[113] 3. The Parthian was well satisfied with these terms inasmuch as he would take possession of the country without a fight and also put the Romans under obligation for a great service done for them. 4. In addition, he had found out that Corbulo, whom Paetus had kept sending for before he was surrounded, was now approaching. He released the blockaded Romans, first securing an agreement that they would bridge the river Arsanias for him, not because he actually needed any bridges—he had crossed the river on foot—but to show them that he had power over them. Not even then did he withdraw by the pontoon: he crossed on an elephant, and the others crossed by the same means as they had before.

22.1. The agreement had just been made when Corbulo came to the Euphrates with extraordinary speed and waited there. When the two armies

---

had twenty legions and 500 ships, although unlike Corbulo he had an *imperium* that was *equal* to that of the proconsuls. He took three months to complete the task. The special command given to Corbulo, with its *maius imperium* ("greater imperium"), had during the principate previously been enjoyed only by members of the imperial family, such as Germanicus.

111 The fate of Paetus is one of the most baffling aspects of the whole Parthian campaign. As Tacitus presents the situation, which is not contradicted seriously by Dio, Paetus had led the Romans to a disaster, yet he suffered no consequences when he returned to Rome, and in AD 70, he was appointed *legatus* of Syria by Vespasian.

112 Dio summarizes very briefly the mistakes of Paetus. He alludes to the troops stationed in the Taurus Mountains, also mentioned by Tacitus (*Ann.* 15.10.3), and provides the name of the location of the camp at Rhandea, where Paetus was cut off by the Parthians.

113 Tacitus (*Ann.* 15.16.1) cites Corbulo for the claim that the Parthians were on the verge of giving up the siege when Paetus surrendered.

came together, one could have observed the enormous difference between them and between their commanders: on one side, there was rejoicing and pride over their speed; on the other, grief and shame over the agreement that had been reached. 2. Sending Monaeses to him, Vologaeses demanded that Corbulo abandon the fortress in Mesopotamia. The two men had many discussions together on that very bridge over the Euphrates, after they had removed its middle section.[114] 3. Corbulo undertook to leave the country if the Parthian also left Armenia. Both items remained provisional until Nero learned what had transpired, dealt with the second set of ambassadors that Vologaeses sent, and told them in his reply that he would give Armenia to Tiridates if he came to Rome. 4. He also relieved Paetus of his command, sent the soldiers who were with him elsewhere, and again put Corbulo in charge of the war against the same enemy. Nero intended to go with him on the campaign, but when he fell ill while offering a sacrifice, he did not dare set out on it but remained in the country.[115]

Corbulo reorganizes the army and launches an invasion of Armenia. Tiridates and Vologaeses are willing to come to terms, and Corbulo meets them at the site of the earlier Roman disaster under Paetus.

Tac. *Ann.* 15.26.1. In Corbulo's view, the Fourth and Twelfth legions, with their best fighters lost and the rest demoralized, were not battle-ready. He transferred them to Syria, and from there took into Armenia the Sixth and Thirteenth.[116] 2. This was a force with a full complement of soldiers that had been hardened by regularly and successfully facing difficult tasks. He added to it the Fifth Legion (which had been spared the disaster because it was on service in Pontus),[117] the soldiers of the Fifteenth, recently brought into the theater, and companies of elite troops from Illyricum and Egypt.[118]

114 Dio adds the information, not in Tacitus, that Monaeses was sent to discuss the terms with Paetus and that the discussions took place on the bridge. Both of these details presumably came from Corbulo's account.

115 Dio's claim that the troops were sent "elsewhere" and that Nero had planned to lead the new expedition himself is baffling. There is no other evidence for such a scheme.

116 No mention is made of the Tenth Legion (Fretensis), one of the regular legions stationed in Syria. Presumably, it was left in that province to shore up the weakened Fourth (Scythica) and Twelth (Fulminata).

117 It is puzzling that the Fifth Legion (see Tac. *Ann.* 15.9.2) had not been brought from Pontus earlier to help deal with the crisis.

118 Confusingly, Illyricum is sometimes used for the province that initially bore that name (which later became Dalmatia) and sometimes, as here, more loosely of the Danube area, including Pannonia, which became a separate province in about AD 9.

He also added all the auxiliary cavalry and infantry that he had, and the auxiliary troops of the kings that had been concentrated at Melitene (which was where he was preparing to cross the Euphrates).[119] 3. Corbulo then undertook the ritual purification of the troops and summoned them to a meeting. There he proceeded to talk in grandiose terms about his campaigns under the emperor's auspices, and his own achievements, attributing the reverses to Paetus's incompetence. And this he did with great authority, which counted as eloquence in the military man.[120]

27.1. Presently, Corbulo took the road once opened up by Lucius Lucullus,[121] clearing such obstacles as the years had thrown up. And when spokesmen came from Tiridates and Vologaeses to discuss peace, he did not rebuff them, sending back with them some centurions bearing a communiqué that was not intransigent in tone.[122] Matters had not yet reached the point where out-and-out war was necessary, it said. 2. Much had gone well for the Romans, and some things for the Parthians—and this served as a warning against pride. Accordingly, not only was it to Tiridates' advantage to receive as a gift a kingdom spared the ravages of war, but Vologaeses would also serve the interests of the Parthian race more by an alliance with Rome than by resorting to mutual damage. Corbulo was aware of the amount of internal conflict in Vologaeses' realm, the message concluded, and of the unruliness and ferocity of the tribes he ruled over, whereas Corbulo's own ruler had undisturbed peace everywhere else, and this was his only war.

3. At the same time, Corbulo pressed home his advice with some intimidation. He drove from their homes the Armenian grandees who had been the first to defect from us, demolished their strongholds, and filled the plains and highlands, and the strong and the weak, with the same terror.

28.1. Even among the barbarians, Corbulo's name did not excite animosity or the hatred felt for an enemy, and so they thought his advice reliable. Consequently, Vologaeses was not inflexible on the main issue, and even re-

119 Melitene was a town (Barr. 64 G4) and region (E4) near the Euphrates River; it controlled the crossing there at Tomisa. It was technically in Armenia Minor (Ptolemy 5.7.5) but became part of Cappadocia. After 70–71, it became the legionary base of the Twelfth Legion (Fulminata) (Joseph. *BJ* 7.18).

120 Tacitus earlier referred to Corbulo's eloquence (*Ann.* 13.8.3: "flamboyant speech").

121 The reference is to Lucullus's advance on Tigranocerta in 69 BC; his journey is vaguely described by Plutarch (*Luc.* 24.2–4).

122 Dio (62.23.1) does not mention this deputation from the Parthians but has Corbulo send a centurion to Vologaeses with a strict order to leave Armenia but also privately suggesting that he might send Tiridates to Rome.

quested a truce in certain prefectures.[123] Tiridates demanded a place and day to parley. 2. The date chosen was close, and the place was where the legions and Paetus had recently been under siege—selected by the barbarians in remembrance of a rather successful operation there. Corbulo did not shy away from it, hoping that the contrast between the two situations would only increase his prestige. Nor did Paetus's disgrace distress him, a fact made abundantly clear by the order he gave to Paetus's son, a tribune, to take some units and cover over the vestiges of that unfortunate encounter.

3. On the appointed day, Tiberius Alexander and Vinicianus Annius came into Tiridates' camp as a mark of respect for the king and also to allay any fears of a trap.[124] (Alexander was a distinguished Roman knight who had been brought in as a military administrator, and Annius was Corbulo's son-in-law, not yet of senatorial age but set in command of the Fifth Legion as a legate.) Then each leader took an escort of twenty cavalrymen. Catching sight of Corbulo, the king was the first to dismount. There was no hesitation on Corbulo's part either, and, on foot, the two clasped each other's right hand.

29.1. The Roman then praised the young man for rejecting impetuous policies in favor of a safe and secure course. After a lengthy prelude on the nobility of his family, Tiridates proceeded modestly. He would go to Rome, he said, and bring Nero a novel honor—an Arsacid as suppliant, although Parthia had suffered no reverse. It was agreed that Tiridates would set his royal diadem before the emperor's statue and take it back only from Nero's hand. And the meeting ended with a kiss.

2. Then, after a few days' interval, there was a magnificent display on both sides. On the one, cavalry was deployed by squadrons and with tribal insignia; on the other, legions were standing in columns, with gleaming eagles,

123 The elder Pliny (*HN* 6.27) indicates that Armenia was divided into 120 *praefecturae*.

124 These two men were individuals of considerable prominence. Tiberius Alexander pursued an active and important career in the politics of the empire. Born into a prominent Jewish family in Alexandria (he was the nephew of Philo), he turned his back on his faith and rose to become procurator of Judaea (46–48). After his service under Corbulo (of which this is the sole mention), he went on to become the prefect of Egypt sometime before 68 and brutally crushed a Jewish uprising in Alexandria. He declared his support for Vespasian's candidacy in 69 and offered his troops to him. He participated with Titus in the siege of Jerusalem, when he unsuccessfully tried to save the temple.

Annius Vinicianus was the son-in-law of Corbulo. He was appointed legate of the Fifth Legion even though he was not yet of senatorial age (Tac. *Ann.* 15.28.3). He in fact was the leading figure in a conspiracy against Nero in Beneventum in 66 (Suet. *Ner.* 36.1) (See Chapter VIII.)

standards, and representations of the gods, as in a temple. In their midst was a tribunal, which held a curule chair, and the chair held an effigy of Nero. 3. Tiridates went forward to it. After the customary slaughter of sacrificial animals, he took the diadem from his head and set it at the feet of the image, which stirred deep emotions in all present, emotions magnified by the vision of the slaughter and the blockade of Roman armies that still lingered before their eyes. Now, they reflected, the situation was reversed: Tiridates would go ahead to be on view for the world—and how little short of a captive was he!

30.1. Corbulo enhanced his glorious reputation by affability and by hosting a banquet. Moreover, the king would ask for explanations whenever he noticed something unfamiliar—the centurion's announcement of the start of each watch, for instance, the dinner party's end signaled by a bugle call, and the fire on the altar before the general's tent being lit from beneath with a torch.[125] Corbulo embellished everything and filled him with admiration for the old Roman traditions. 2. The next day, Tiridates requested time to visit his brothers and his mother, since he had such a long journey before him. Meanwhile, he handed over his daughter as a hostage, together with a letter of entreaty to Nero.[126]

31.1. Setting off, Tiridates found Pacorus in Media and Vologaeses in Ecbatana.[127] Vologaeses was not unconcerned about his brother, for he had requested of Corbulo, through his personal messengers, that Tiridates not be subjected to any outward appearance of servitude. Vologaeses asked that Tiridates not surrender his sword, that he not be barred from embracing provincial governors or be made to stand at their doors, and that, in Rome, he be shown as much respect as the consuls.[128] Vologaeses, of course, was

125 The night was divided into four watches, and each watch was introduced by the sound of a bugle (*bucina*). The leading centurion (*primipilus*) supervised the routine (Polybius 6.35.12), and this passage suggests that he reported the passing of each phase to the commander. The reference to the altar is obscure; a fire on the *top* of an altar would not merit surprise. Tacitus's language suggests a temporary altar set alight for some unknown ritual purpose.

126 Dio (62.23.4) suggests that Vologaeses and Monobazus, king of Adiabene, came to Corbulo and gave hostages. This seems to be contradicted by Tacitus's version.

127 Pacorus had been appointed ruler of Media Atropatene (he was the last king of the area) by his half-brother Vologaeses in AD 51. He supported Tiridates' effort to assume the throne of Armenia. Pacorus would later (about 72) suffer the humiliation of fleeing and having to ransom his harem when the Alani invaded his kingdom.

128 It was the custom of Parthians to wear the broadsword, which conflicted with the principle that no one could appear armed in the presence of the emperor. Tigranes, for example, had been required to surrender his to the lictors of Pompey (Plut. *Pomp.* 33.3).

used to the pomp of the foreigner and had no knowledge of us, people for whom the reality of power is important but its trappings irrelevant.

Tacitus ends his account of events on the Parthian border at this point.

FIGURE 8. *RIC*^{2} Nero 283, Brass Dupondius. Obverse: NERO CLAVD(ius) CAESAR AVG(ustus) GER(manicus) P(ontifex) M(aximus) T(ribunicia) P(otestate) IMP(erator), P(ater) P(atriae), "Nero Claudius Caesar Augustus Germanicus, Chief Priest, with Tribunician Power, Imperator, Father of the Country." Reverse: PACE P(opuli) R(omani) TERRA MARIQ(ue) PARTA IANVM CLVSIT, "After achieving the peace of the Roman People on land and sea he closed (the temple of) Janus." From the collection of Andreas Pangerl/ romancoins.info.

The Temple of Janus was a small building in the northeast corner of the Forum, rectangular in shape and with a double door at each end. It appears frequently on coinage of Nero down to AD 67. The reverse of the coin in Figure 8 depicts the temple, with a latticed window and a celebratory garland hung above the closed double door. The legend records that Nero closed the Temple of Janus after bringing about peace. The closing of the temple was a symbolic act to mark the cessation of war. It was a rare event. Augustus recorded that he closed it three times and that it had previously been closed only twice (*RG* 13).

The status of the Temple of Janus during Nero's reign is a major problem. The late source Orosius (7.3.7) claims that according to Tacitus's *Histories* (presumably in a part now lost) the temple was open continuously from late in Augustus's reign to Vespasian's. This is flatly contradicted by Suetonius's statement (*Ner.* 13.2, see section on Nero

As it happened, Tiridates refused to surrender his sword but fixed it to his scabbard with nails (Dio 63.2.4).

as Performer in Chapter IX) that Nero closed it during the celebrations to mark the arrival of Tiridates in Rome in 66. The closure on this occasion is not mentioned by Dio (63.1.2); the *Annals* are of course missing for that period. But some issues of the type bear the legend Tr(ibunicia) Pot(estate) XI, hence the eleventh year of Nero's reign (end of 64 to end of 65). This could mean that the temple was closed to mark the symbolic surrender of Tiridates to Corbulo in AD 63 (Tac. *Ann.* 15.29), and that out of a desire to keep the achievement before the public eye, Nero continued to issue the same type in later years.

ILS 232 (Smallwood 51b). Nero Claudius Caesar Augustus Germanicus, Imperator, pontifex maximus, holding tribunician power for the eleventh time, consul for the fourth time, Imperator for the ninth time, father of the country, with Gnaeus Domitius Corbulo as his legate with propraetorian authority, and Titus Aurelius Fulvus as his legate of the third Gallic Legion.

This inscription occurs on a stone base, one of a matching pair, the other very fragmentary (*CIL* 6742), found in Charput in Armenia Minor. The reference to Nero's eleventh tenure of tribunician power, which, unlike the consulship, occurred every year successively from succession, indicates that the inscription belongs to the period late 64 to late 65, thus after the formal submission of Tiridates to Corbulo but before Tiridates' arrival in Rome. It may have accompanied some victory monument, perhaps connected with the Third Legion.

Nero and Corbulo are mentioned (on Corbulo's propraetorian powers, see the earlier discussion on *ILS* 9108). The third individual has a link with later Roman history. Titus Aurelius Fulvus was the grandfather of the emperor Antoninus Pius. He was at this time commander of the Third Legion, Gallica ("Gallic"). It was probably raised by Caesar in 48 BC and taken over by Antony, but commanded by Octavian after Actium and transferred to Syria. After the Parthian settlement, Nero moved it to Moesia in 67 or 68, and it was still commanded by Titus Aurelius in AD 69, when he led a successful campaign against the Rhoxolani, who invaded Moesia in that year. In recognition of his achievement, Titus received the *ornamenta consularia* from Otho (Tac. *Hist.* 1.79.3). He went on to a second consulship, perhaps in AD 85, as well as the prefecture of the city (*SHA Ant. Pius* 1.2).

Dio 62.23.1. Corbulo, then, openly prepared for war against Vologaeses. Sending a centurion, he commanded Vologaeses to leave the country but confidentially advised him to send his brother to Rome, and he did manage to persuade him because he apparently was superior to the king in military strength. 2. Thus, Corbulo and Tiridates met right in Rhandea, as this location was agreeable to both—to Vologaeses because his men had shut up the Romans there but had released them under a truce, which clearly demonstrated they had been done a favor, and to Corbulo because his men would surely erase the infamy that had earlier befallen them in the place. 3. Nor was it just a matter of their making speeches there. A high stand was erected and images of Nero set on it, and Tiridates came forward and did obeisance to them under the eyes of many Armenians and many Parthians and Romans. Then, after sacrificing and uttering words of praise over them, he took the diadem from his head and set it before them.[129] 4. Monobazus and Vologaeses both came to Corbulo and gave him hostages.[130] And in commemoration of this, Nero was many times hailed as supreme commander, and he broke precedent by celebrating a triumph. 5. So Corbulo possessed a strong force and no slight reputation. He could easily have been declared emperor since people were sick to death of Nero but had unqualified admiration for Corbulo in every respect, but he made no attempt at revolution and faced no denunciation for it either. 6. In actual fact, he became even more self-restrained in every way, and in particular he willingly sent to Rome his son-in-law Annius, who was serving as his legate; and while this was ostensibly so that Annius could escort Tiridates, it was really so that Nero should have a hostage.[131] Such was Nero's confidence that Corbulo would make no revolutionary move that the general received his son-in-law as his legate even before the man had held the praetorship.

129 Tacitus (*Ann.* 15.28–30) reports the negotiations between Corbulo and Tiridates and the latter's submission to the image of Nero in the camp.

130 Tacitus says nothing of the direct meeting between Corbulo and Monobazus (king of the Adiabeni) and Vologaeses. According to Tacitus (*Ann.* 15.30.2), it is Tiridates who leaves a hostage, his daughter.

131 On Annius, see Tacitus (*Ann.* 15.28.3) and Chapter VIII.

V

BRITAIN AND GERMANY

INTRODUCTION

For most of the imperial period, Rome was preoccupied by problems in two frontier areas, the eastern, where there were almost continuous clashes with the Parthian empire, and the northwestern, where the main cause of concern was the threat posed by Germanic tribes. In the northwest, problems in Britain would sometimes eclipse those in Germany, and such was the case under Nero, when the Rhine region was relatively stable but a major crisis erupted in Britain.

BRITAIN

The great rebellion that broke out in Britain under the leadership of Boudica during Nero's reign was an event of major significance, one of the most serious cases of internal provincial dissension to occur in the early principate. The main sources—Tacitus, Dio, and Suetonius—are in agreement on one central fact: it was a catastrophe. Tacitus calls it a "cataclysmic defeat" (*Ann.* 14.29.1), Suetonius a "debacle" (*Ner.* 39.1), and Dio a "frightful disaster" (62.1). The events are described in considerable detail by Tacitus and Dio, in accounts that seem to have drawn on different sources. Both are excellent examples of those ancient narratives where the very wealth of detail creates historical problems, and where detailed knowledge stands side by side with frustrating ignorance.

Tacitus would have had available a rich, if not impartial, source of information. His father-in-law, Julius Agricola, whose biography he wrote, served on the staff of the Roman commander Suetonius Paulinus at the time (Tac. *Agr.* 5.1). It is also thought likely that for the *Annals,* though perhaps not for the earlier *Agricola,* Tacitus drew directly on the memoirs of Paulinus himself. There is no reference to a specifically British memoir by Paulinus, but we do know that he wrote a chronicle of his earlier service in Mauretania, since Pliny cites him specifically for detailed information on the Atlas Mountains (Plin. *HN* 5.14–15).

The Boudican episode highlighted the weaknesses in the Roman administration of Britannia, a Roman province since the invasion of Claudius in

MAP 4. Britannia

AD 43. These weaknesses meant that when the crisis erupted, Boudica's appeals for help and support found a receptive audience. This crisis was aggravated by the fact that at the outset the *legatus* was not in the area. His absence is in itself noteworthy, and one of the most remarkable aspects of the whole episode is that the Romans seem to have been taken entirely by surprise (Tac. *Ann.* 14.32.2). For two years after his arrival in early 58, Suetonius Paulinus had been single-mindedly engaged in reducing the recalcitrant tribes in Wales (the name properly speaking is anachronistic in this period), essential groundwork for a campaign against Anglesey. Meanwhile, in southeast Britain, where Rome had first established itself, the Trinovantes were forced to cede more and more of their land to settlers in the colony (Colonia Victricensis) established at Camulodunum (Colchester) in 49, as those settlers forcibly took more territory than they had been originally allotted. The establishment of the imperial cult and the founding of the temple to Divus Claudius added to the financial burdens. Members of the priesthood had to pay a subscription for the honor of holding office in the cult, and since at this stage the number of candidates would have been very small, the burden would have fallen heavily on a very small number.

The incident that sparked the rebellion took place not in Colchester but well to the north. In 47, there had been an attempt under the governorship of Ostorius Scapula to disarm tribes in a wide swathe of Britain (Tac. *Ann.* 12.31). The main opposition had come from Iceni, in their relatively small kingdom in Norfolk and Suffolk, with its capital possibly in Thetford. They had to be subdued militarily. It was possibly at that point that the presumably pro-Roman Prasutagus was appointed as the last Icenian king, but we have no way of being certain. The sequence of events that followed the death of Prasutagus is extremely confusing. His name has been tentatively identified (Prasto) on Icenian coinage (Allen [1976]), and his historicity is not to be doubted. But Tacitus is alone in associating his death with the beginnings of the rebellion. Suetonius sees that disaster as an accidental setback and finds no fault with Nero. Dio blames financial pressures, noting that Claudius had offered subsidies to encourage Romanization and that these were treated as loans, not gifts, and were for some reason recalled. Other Romans had apparently made loans to the Britons, which no doubt encouraged the building of lavish Roman-style country houses and the like. Among these was Seneca, who had loaned an enormous sum, which was subsequently called in. It is hard to understand why this financial pressure would have affected the Iceni more seriously than other tribes, but Dio's information may lie behind the account given by Tacitus that Prasutagus "had long enjoyed" his wealth and tried to protect it by making the emperor joint heir with his daughters. The tradition of securing at least part of one's legacy by a substantial bequest to the emperor was by then well established.

It may be that the procurator Catus Decianus was enforcing increased taxation to cover the cost of the military activities in the province, since financial issues play a big role in the accounts of both Tacitus and Dio, but this is not proven. "Provincial" procurators served in both the imperial and senatorial/ public provinces. In the early period, they were probably looked on as essentially private agents of the emperor, responsible only for overseeing financial matters relating to the imperial properties within the provinces, with no official administrative role. But this situation gradually changed, and they assumed administrative duties; in the imperial provinces, this had perhaps happened already under Augustus. The powers and responsibilities of the procurators grew, especially from the time of Claudius, and there could be tensions between the procurator and the *legatus* of the province. In AD 23, a case was brought against the procurator Gnaeus Lucilius Capito for making improper and unauthorized use of troops in Asia, a public province, when he took over the soldiers that were under the proconsul's command to enforce his own decision (Tac. *Ann.* 4.15.2). Tacitus stresses that, when governor of Aquitania, Agricola went out of his way to avoid quarrels with the procurators, implying that this approach was the exception rather than the rule (Tac. *Agr.* 9). But in the case of Britain, any increase in taxation was apparently not enough. The assets of Prasutagus and the Icenian nobility were seized through Catus Decianus's exactions. Catus may have been acting largely on his own initiative in extracting the dues, but the incorporation of the kingdom into the province, while it had financial implications in that it would result in increased revenue, surely could not have been carried out without reference to the provincial *legatus* and indeed to the emperor in Rome.

The fact that no heir to the kingdom came forward to champion the rebellion might suggest that the absence of a clear successor was at the heart of the problem. It is to be noted that, according to Tacitus, Prasutagus named his daughters as his heirs and apparently did not include his wife, which might suggest caution on his part, since she may have been known for her anti-Roman views. There is no suggestion that Boudica had a right to succeed, nor is there in fact in any of the accounts the suggestion that she made such a claim. It is noteworthy that although Tacitus refers to Cartimandua of the Brigantes as "queen" (*regina*), as at *Ann.* 12.36.1and 12.40.2, he never applies this term to Boudica (nor does Dio apply a Greek equivalent). The absence of a plausible claimant may in part explain Decianus's actions. Also, while the conduct of the procurator may well have been impolitic, or even unethical, it can surely be assumed that it was basically rational. What is astonishing, then, is Tacitus's claim in the *Annals* that Boudica was flogged and her daughters raped (*Ann.* 14.31.1), behavior that was not typical of Roman authorities even at their worst and not mentioned in Dio or Suetonius, nor, indeed, in Tacitus's shorter account in *Agricola*. It is hard to see any legal basis for this treatment, or any political advantage, and one might suspect a degree of exaggeration on Tacitus's part. It is possible that he overstated their ill treatment to create a contrast with the enlightened policy of Agricola.

The picture of Boudica in Tacitus's account is not entirely negative; in places, he seems to admire her. Of course, his admiration can be selective. In *Germania* 45, in a different context, he notes that a German tribe, the Sithones, in being ruled by a woman, had fallen to a status lower than that of slaves. No female rulers are known in Gaul, nor is any attested in Britain in the late Iron Age before the arrival of the Romans. We know of at least two powerful British female leaders during the first century AD, Boudica and Cartimandua of the Brigantes, but it would be dangerous to draw any general conclusions about the social structure of British Iron Age society, despite Tacitus's claim that the Britons were accustomed to female rulers (Tac. *Agr.* 16.1; *Ann.* 14.35.1). And it should be noted that Tacitus seems to contradict himself in asserting that the Brigantes revolted against Cartimandua because of the shame of being ruled by a woman (Tac. *Ann.* 12.40.3). He seems to refer to a second queen of the Brigantes (Tac. *Agr.* 31.4), since the description there does not quite fit Cartimandua, but the passage is part of the speech of Calgacus and may reflect a slight bending of the truth on his part.

The Icenian leader's name was probably close to the form Boudica ("Victoria"), with the "i" pronounced long (Jackson [1979]). The "a" ending reflects the fact that early Celtic languages were, like Latin, inflected. The same name, Boudica, with a single "c," is attested in an undated inscription from Lusitania (*CIL* 2.455), and a Bodicacia has been recently attested on a second-century AD gravestone from Cirencester in Britain (http://www.thehistoryblog.com/archives/35042).

The familiar form "Boadicea" seems to have resulted from misreading "u" and "c" in Tacitus's manuscript, where the text reads Boudicca. Tacitus's double "c" might reflect a "c" that has started to become voiced (moving toward a "g"), as in Modern Welsh *buddugol* = "victorious." The form Boudig(a) is found in a dedication to a tutelary goddess of Victory in Aquitania, securely dated to AD 237 (Courteault [1921]).

Reliable figures for the deaths caused by the rebellion are impossible to ascertain. The official figure of 70,000 found in Tacitus may be exaggerated, but there can be no doubt that the totals would have been considerable, especially in the sackings of Camulodunum (Colchester), Londinium (London), and Verulamium (near modern St. Albans), where the destruction has left its trace in the archaeological record. The sources do not mention other towns, but others probably were affected: there is evidence of destruction at Venta (Winchester) in this period. Also, coin hoards, a traditional symptom of serious unrest, discovered in Norfolk, Suffolk, and Cambridgeshire, may reflect these events. The rebellion ended in a major battle and the death of Boudica—by poison according to Tacitus, by illness according to Dio (which is not, of course, totally incompatible with poison); Dio adds unconvincingly that she had a grand funeral. The battle probably took place in the midlands. Precisely where is much disputed, but a location near the fort of Mancetter is generally most favored (Webster [1993], 97, 111). Boudica's last resting place is woven into British folklore, with an old candidate from as far north as the Prestatyn area in North Wales (under Gop Hill, a Neolithic mound) and a more recent one from as far south as King's Cross station, London, between platforms 9 and 10. The latter originated perhaps in 1937 with Lewis Spence (*Boadicea, Warrior Queen of the Britons*), who placed the last battle in the King's Cross area.

The immediate repercussion of the rebellion is described by Tacitus in very guarded language. He generally despised cautious governors and admired aggressive ones like Suetonius Paulinus, a vigorous man of military action with little interest in the notion of "hearts and minds." He initiated a brief period of savage reprisals, although Fulford (2008) has argued, on archaeological grounds, that this retributive policy did not apply south of the Thames, where the Roman allies may have stood firm and where there was subsequent investment and development. The most important ruler here would probably have been Tiberius Cogidubnus (or Togidubnus), who, Tacitus notes, stayed loyal to Rome down to *nostram memoriam* (Tac. *Agr.* 14.1), which could mean broadly "to our own times" or specifically "to the times of which I have a recollection," the latter of which would generally fit in nicely with the rebellion.

The procurator Catus Decianus fled to Gaul when the crisis first erupted, and his replacement Julius Classicianus found himself at odds with the policy of the *legatus*. He reported to Rome on the need for a period of reconciliation and lobbied for Suetonius Paulinus's replacement. Nero sent a freedman, Polyclitus, an individual for whom Tacitus felt considerable contempt, to mediate and report to him. Polyclitus was apparently sympathetic to Classicianus's view of the situation, but was diplomatic in the reports that were sent to Rome. Suetonius Paulinus had after all been the man of the hour, albeit an earlier hour, and had attained a huge military victory, the type of achievement much respected by Romans. His removal did not happen at first, but it seems that a face-saving way was found to redeploy him without any serious loss of prestige. It is worth noting, however, that he was apparently not in disgrace. He, or more likely his son, later held a consulship, in AD 66, and the assertion of Tacitus that Nero personally made the decision to send massive reinforcements into Britain after the final battle suggests that the strong military response was approved in Rome (Tac. *Ann.* 14.38.1). There is in fact some evidence that Suetonius's victory might have been celebrated in Rome with a special donative after his return. A lead tessera has survived with NERO CAESAR on one side and PAULLINI on the other, with the symbols of Jupiter and an eagle. Nero's eighth salutation as "Imperator" might also be related to the victory (Griffin [1976]). Suetonius Paulinus was replaced in 61 by the much less aggressive Publius Petronius Turpillianus. The medium-term effect was that the Roman advance through Britannia was held back. In the long term, it could be argued, this lull was beneficial and led to a more tactful approach of the Roman authorities in dealing with the native population. In the Flavian period in particular, there seems to have been a serious effort to encourage *civitates* to govern their own affairs on the Roman model.

SOURCES

Suetonius limits himself to two passing comments on the Boudican Rebellion.

Suet. *Ner.* 18.1. Never motivated by any wish or hope to enlarge or extend the empire, Nero even considered withdrawing the army from Britain, and only refrained from doing so because he felt ashamed at appearing to have sullied his father's glorious achievement.[1] It was only the kingdom of Pontus that he

1 No other source repeats the suggestion that Nero contemplated withdrawing from Britain, and the issue is further complicated by the fact that Suetonius gives no indication of when the decision was supposedly made. It was at the very beginning of the reign that Nero was particularly concerned to honor Claudius's memory, and at the beginning that the influence of his mother, who was also keen to sustain Claudius's legacy, was at its strongest. There are thus good arguments for placing the policy decision in 54–55, during which time the *legatus* in Britain was Aulus Didius Gallus (on whom see Tac. *Ann.* 14.29). And it is certainly the case that Rome did not make aggressive progress under Didius's stewardship. If, however, the reference to Claudius is seen as mere hypocritical posturing, the plan to withdraw could be a reaction to the Boudican rebellion (see Cappai [1992]).

transformed into a province, when Polemo ceded it[2] and also that of Cottius in the Alps when Cottius died.[3]

Suet. *Ner.* 39.1. In addition to the heinous crimes and misdeeds committed by the emperor, there were also a number of accidental setbacks. There was an epidemic in a single autumn that saw 30,000 deaths added to Libitina's account;[4] a debacle in Britain where two major towns were sacked, with a massacre of citizens and allies; and an ignominious reverse in the East, where legions were sent under the yoke in Armenia, and Syria was only with difficulty kept in submission.[5]

The governor of Britain, Suetonius Paulinus, is engaged in subduing the Druids on the Island of Anglesey (Mona) when the rebellion breaks out.

Tac. *Agr.* 14. After Veranius,[6] Suetonius Paulinus had success for two years, during which he brought the tribes to heel and strengthened garrisons.[7] Feeling confident from this, he attacked the island of Mona, which was the center of the rebels' strength, and so left his rear open to enemy opportunism.[8]

2 Polemo II ruled the kingdom of Pontus on the Black Sea from AD 38 until he was obliged to give up his kingdom to the Romans in about AD 62.

3 Claudius had conferred the title of king on Marcus Julius Cottius when he enlarged Cottius's ancestral realm in AD 44.

4 Libitina was the goddess of Funerals. The plague is possibly the one referred to also by Tacitus (*Ann.* 16.13.1–2) but without statistics. Suetonius refers to only two major centers being sacked; this may be explained by the fact that Verulamium had sufficient advance warning to evacuate a large portion of its population.

5 For the ignominious incident, see Chapter IV.

6 Quintus Veranius gained a considerable reputation in Lycia, where he was charged by Claudius with reducing the area to the status of a province. He spent five years there, engaging in a number of serious military campaigns, improving the road network, and setting up the provincial administration (*AE* 1953.251). He received the consulship in AD 49. He succeeded Aulus Didius in Britain, probably in 58, but died in office within the year.

7 Suetonius Paulinus had achieved military fame some two decades before the Boudican rebellion, when he led Roman troops in a swift march over the Atlas Mountains just before the annexation of Mauretania (Plin. *HN* 5.14; Dio 60.9.1). After his consulship (probably sometime before AD 45), we have no record of his career until he was made *legatus* of Britain in AD 58, succeeding Quintus Veranius. Although he was removed from office after the rebellion, he was not apparently in disgrace; a senator of the same name held the consulship in 66, possibly this Suetonius in a second term or his son. It is to be noted that Tacitus speaks of Suetonius Paulinus building up preexisting forts, not establishing new ones.

8 At *Ann.* 14.29.3, Tacitus speaks of Mona (Anglesey) as a "haven for refugees" (from Roman authority).

Tac. *Ann.* 14.29.1. During the consulships of Caesennius Paetus and Petronius Turpilianus, there was a cataclysmic defeat in Britain.[9] There the legate Aulus Didius had, as I noted earlier, merely held on to what he had gained,[10] while his successor Veranius, [11] after some minor pillaging expeditions against the Silures,[12] was prevented by death from pushing ahead with his offensive. Throughout his life, Veranius was famed for his austere character, but an egotism was clearly demonstrated by the final words of his will, where, with gross flattery of Nero, he added that he would have brought the province to heel for him had he lived a further two years.

2. Paulinus Suetonius then took over the governorship of Britain.[13] He was Corbulo's rival in military science and in the esteem of the people (which permits nobody to be without a competitor), and he passionately wanted to match the glory of the recovery of Armenia by crushing the foe. Accordingly, he prepared for an assault on the island of Mona, home to a strong population and a haven for refugees, and he built flat-bottomed boats to counter the precarious shallows. Thus the infantry crossed; the cavalry followed through the shoals or by swimming alongside their mounts where the waters were deeper.

30.1. Facing them on the shoreline was the enemy line, a dense array of arms and men, and among them rushed women who, like furies, wore funereal clothing, had disheveled hair, and brandished torches. Around stood Druids, their hands raised to heaven, pouring out terrible curses, and the extraordinary spectacle struck such fear into the men that they presented

9 Tacitus assigns the events of the rebellion securely to AD 61 and implies that it started early in the year, before the crops were sown (*Ann.* 14.38.2), but there seem to be too many events to fit into one year. The first to argue that the rebellion must have begun in the previous year was Asbach (1878), and his claim has been generally accepted, notably by Syme (1958), 765. Carroll (1979) has challenged Asbach's thesis.

10 At *Ann.* 12.40.1, Aulus Didius, appointed to Britain in AD 52, was criticized by Tacitus for his defensive approach (cf. Tac. *Agr.* 14.2). Didius was consul in 39 (*AE* 1973.138) and served with Claudius in Britain in 43. He was subsequently legate in Moesia, where he was awarded the *ornamenta consularia* for his role in establishing Cotys as king of the Bosporus. Between 49 and 52, he served as proconsul in Asia. Despite a previous energetic career, his term of office in Britain was marked by no major achievements.

11 On Veranius, see the discussion earlier in this chapter.

12 The Silures were an aggressive tribe in southeast Wales. They resisted Rome from AD 44, initially under Caratacus, and were eventually subdued in 74–76 by Frontinus. They were organized as an administrative district (*civitas*) in the second century, with their capital at Venta Silurum (Caerwent), and eventually became highly Romanized.

13 This is the first mention of Suetonius Paulinus in the *Annals*.

their bodies motionless to enemy weapons, as if their limbs were paralyzed.[14] 2. Then, with encouragement from their commander, and urging each other not to be alarmed at a horde of fanatical women, they charged forward, mowing down those in their way and engulfing them in their own flames. 3. A garrison was then imposed on the defeated enemy, and the groves sacred to their barbarous superstitions were cut down (for they held it morally acceptable to make their altars reek with prisoners' gore and to consult the gods with the entrails of humans). While Suetonius was thus engaged, he was brought news of a sudden uprising of the province.

British tribes give vent to their sense of grievance by joining Boudica of the Iceni in rebellion.

Tac. *Agr.* 15. Their fears removed by the legate's absence, the Britons began discussing the ills of their servitude among themselves, comparing the wrongs they had suffered and exacerbating them with the construction they put on them.[15] Nothing was gained by tolerance, they said; it resulted only in heavier impositions for readily putting up with them! In the past, they had one king each; now two were being imposed on them: the legate so he could wreak his fury on their lifeblood and the procurator on their possessions. Discord between these men who were set over them was deadly for their subjects, and concord was equally deadly. They have their tools—one

14 Druids were a Gallic priestly caste whose teachings spread from Gaul to Britain. They had been known to the Romans since Julius Caesar's campaigns in Gaul. At the time of Caesar, they were a significant branch of the British and Gallic aristocracies; they were priests, teachers, and judges, responsible for the maintenance and transmission of religious and other knowledge, such as medicine. In the imperial period, increasingly severe measures were taken against them, mainly, it was asserted, because they practiced human sacrifice but presumably also because of the fear that they would be dangerous as the focus of resistance to Rome—it may be that they stirred things up in the south of Britain when under pressure from Paulinus in Wales. They were suppressed by Tiberius (Plin. *HN* 30.13) and Claudius (Suet. *Claud.* 25.5), as well as by Nero, but they were clearly not extirpated completely, since in 69––70 they are recorded as interpreting the burning of the Capitol in Rome as marking the end of Roman domination (Tac. *Hist.* 4.54). It is to be noted that neither Dio nor Tacitus makes any reference to support from the Druids for Boudica's rebellion.

15 The arguments that follow are of course Tacitus's own creation (a historical approach far more acceptable in ancient historiography than in modern). But the complaints expressed here were no doubt those familiar to his father-in-law Julius Agricola and suggest issues that Agricola might have tried to settle. Tacitus says nothing about the specific grievances stemming from the treatment of Prasutagus's kingdom.

his centurions, the other his slaves—to inflict violence and indignities indiscriminately. Nothing escapes their cupidity, nothing their lust. In battle, it is the braver man who despoils his opponent, they said, but in this case it is mostly by cowards who have no fight in them that our homes are snatched from us, our children taken off, and troop levies forced on us, as though it is only for our native land that we do not know how to die! If the Britons count their numbers, what a meager scattering of soldiers it is that has crossed to us! This was how the Germanies shook off the yoke, and yet their defense was a river, not the ocean![16] For the Britons, the reasons for war were country, wives, and parents; for the Romans, they were greed and self-indulgence. They would retreat, as the deified Julius had retreated—the Britons had only to emulate the courage of their forefathers![17] They should not be dismayed with the outcome of one or two battles either; the successful may have more gusto, but the unfortunate have greater determination. Now, too, the gods were feeling compassion for the Britons—they were keeping the Roman general away and had his army exiled on another island. The Britons were already taking what was the most difficult step in meeting to discuss the problem. And, in fact, in such deliberations, being caught was more dangerous than taking action.

Tac. *Ann.* 14.31. Prasutagus, king of the Iceni, famed for a wealth that he had long enjoyed, had entered in his will as his heirs the emperor and his own two daughters, thinking that such an act of obsequiousness would keep his realm and household out of harm's way. The reverse turned out to be the case, so much so that the realm was pillaged by centurions and his household by slaves, as if they were spoils of war. Right at the start, Prasutagus's wife, Boudica, was flogged and his daughters raped. All the leading Iceni were divested of their ancestral property, as though the Romans had been made a gift of the entire region, and the king's relatives were dealt with as slaves.

Dio 62.1. While such children's games were being played out in Rome, a frightful disaster occurred in Britain. Two cities were destroyed, eighty thousand Romans and allies lost their lives, and the island was lost. And all this befell them at the hands of a woman, making the occurrence particularly ignominious for them. In fact, signs from the gods forewarned them of the

16 The plural "Germanies" alludes to the Germanic tribes.

17 Julius Caesar had conducted two invasions of Britain, in 55 and 54 BC, and, after receiving a nominal submission from some of the tribes, withdrew, mainly because of preoccupation with other parts of the Roman world.

disaster: at night, murmuring in a foreign tongue accompanied by laughter could be heard coming from the Senate house, as well as an uproar punctuated with wailing coming from the theater, though nobody was responsible for the utterances or the moaning. Some houses were also seen underwater in the river Thames, and the sea between the island and Gaul once took on a bloody color with the incoming tide.

2. The cause of the war lay in the confiscation of monies that Claudius had given to the leading Britons. According to Decianus Catus, procurator of the island, these sums had to be surrendered. It was over this that the Britons revolted, and also because Seneca, after lending them at their request ten million sestertii, hoping for a good return in interest, later demanded payment of the whole sum together, and used force to get it.[18]

But it was chiefly Boudica who roused them to arms and convinced them to go to war with the Romans; she was judged fit to take on their leadership and was their commander-in-chief throughout the war. She was a woman of royal stock whose spirit was greater than a woman's. She put an army together that was about 120,000 strong, and she climbed up on a platform made of earth in the Roman fashion. She was tall of build, with a grim appearance and a fierce look in her eyes.[19] She had a harsh voice and thick, golden hair that she grew down to her buttocks. She wore a large gold torque and was dressed in a multicolored tunic and over it a thick cloak fastened

18 The precise meaning of this passage is uncertain because there seems to be a problem in Dio's manuscript, but the textual difficulty does not affect the basic information that Seneca is said to have made a huge loan and then recalled it. Beneficence of this type is known elsewhere. Nero gave 200,000 sestertii to Tiridates (Dio 63.6.5). Julius Caesar reminded Ariovistus of the considerable gifts made to him by Rome (Caes. *BG* 1.43.3). In AD 58, the ruthless prosecutor Publilius Suillus denounced Seneca for a number of sins, one of which was that he had sucked Italy and the provinces dry by his unscrupulous usury. In *Vita Beata* 17.1, Seneca notes that among the imagined criticisms of the philosopher who fails to live up to his own teachings is the question, "why do you have overseas estates (*cur trans mare possides*)?" Syme (1958), 762–66, is scathing about Dio's account as a whole and argues that Tacitus was aware of the charge against Seneca but did not think it merited repetition.

19 Dio's description of Boudica probably owes more to the Roman stereotype of the barbarian queen than to her actual appearance. Thus, Candace, queen of the Ethiopians, who clashed with Augustus, was said by Strabo to be of manly appearance (and, to top it off, had only one eye [Strabo 17.1.54]). The German divinity who appeared to Nero's great-grandfather Drusus on the eve of his death and advised him to withdraw from the Elbe was said by Dio (55.1.3) to be a huge woman. Similarly, Curtius Rufus, proconsul of Africa under Claudius (and possibly the author of *The History of Alexander*), received a prediction of his governorship from a woman of "superhuman size" who appeared before him in the town of Hadrumetum (Tac. *Ann.* 11.21.1).

with a broach.[20] This was how she was always clothed. On that occasion, she was grasping a spear to strike fear into them all with this as well, and she spoke as follows:[21]

3. "You have been shown by the facts just how different freedom is from servitude. Even if some of you were earlier taken in by the tempting promises of the Romans through ignorance of which was the better option, now that you have experienced both you have discovered just how wrong you were in choosing self-inflicted despotism over your ancestral way of life, and you have learned how much better poverty with no overlord is than riches with slavery. Of all the most degrading and painful treatments possible, what have we not experienced since these men put into Britain? Have we not been stripped of most of our possessions, and all the greatest ones? Do we not pay taxes on what remains? To say nothing of all the husbandry and farming we do for them, do we not have our very bodies in bondage all year long? How much better to have been sold to other people once and for all than to bear the empty title of freedom and pay a ransom for ourselves each year! How much better to have been slaughtered and to have died outright than to be carrying around our heads with a tax on them!"

"But why did I say that? Not even death is tax-free among them! No, you are aware of how much tax we pay even for our dead. Among the rest of humanity, death sets free even those in slavery to others; only for the Romans are the dead still alive to give them income! How is it that even if none of us has money—how could we get it, and from where?—we are stripped and picked clean like men who are murdered? And why would they show moderation as time goes by if they have acted like this toward us at the start, when all men take care even of animals that are newly caught?"[22]

62.6. Upon finishing her address, she used some form of divination, letting a hare run loose from her arms, and when it ran auspiciously for them the whole crowd shouted out with joy.[23] Boudica then raised a hand toward

20 Gold torques known from the archaeological record give some validation to Dio's account.

21 The spear is clearly symbolic here, and may have been supposed to have talismanic powers. Florus (1.33.13–14), in describing the rebellion of Olyndicus in Spain in the middle of the second century BC, has him brandishing a silver spear that he said the gods had provided. In the end, it made him overconfident, and he was killed by a sentry's very human spear as he confidently approached the Roman camp.

22 The repeated emphasis on financial burdens may reflect the hardships caused by the supposed recall of money by the emperor and rich Romans like Seneca.

23 The allusion to the hare may owe much to Dio's imagination; it is reminiscent of the Roman system of divination through the flight of birds.

heaven and said: "I thank you, Andraste, and call to you as one woman to another.[24] I am not, like Nitocris,[25] a ruler of Egyptians who bear burdens, nor am I, like Semiramis, a ruler of Assyrians who engage in trade (such things we have now learned from the Romans),[26] and certainly not a ruler of the Romans themselves, as Messalina was once, and after her Agrippina and now Nero (for while he has a man's name he is in fact a woman, as is indicated by his singing, his lyre playing and his use of makeup). No, I am the ruler of Britons, who are not acquainted with farming or the trades but are thoroughly versed in warfare and regard everything as communal property, including children and wives, who therefore have the same fortitude as men. Such being the men and such the women that I rule over, I beseech you and request of you victory, salvation, and liberty in the face of men who are arrogant, unjust, insatiably greedy, and godless; that is, if one may use the term "men" of those who bathe in hot water, feed on fancy delicacies, drink neat wine, smear themselves with myrrh, sleep on soft beds and share them with boys (boys who are also beyond their prime, too!), and are slaves to a lyre player, and a bad one at that! . . .

7.1. After making such a speech, Boudica led her army against the Romans—for they were, by chance, leaderless, as their commander Paulinus had launched a campaign against the isle of Mona, which lies near Britain. Because of this, they sacked and looted two Roman cities and, as I said, caused unspeakably great bloodshed. Men captured by them suffered all manner of atrocities at their hands. 2. Their most heinous and brutal act was the following. The most noble and attractive of their female captives they hung up naked, cut off their breasts, and sowed them into their mouths so

24 The deity invoked here appears in the manuscripts of the text as either Adraste or Andraste. She is presumably identical with Andate in the next section, whom Dio identifies with Nike (Victory), but she is not otherwise attested and may be a deity specifically of the Iceni. Jullian (1899) suggests that she is the British equivalent of Andarte of the Vocontii, a Gallic tribe, and identifies her with their goddess of Victory, but the identification is essentially speculative.

25 In Dio's account, Boudica displays considerable knowledge of ancient history, and in the imaginative world of ancient historiography we are meant to suppose that her audience of mainly unschooled British peasants would have picked up the references. Nitocris was supposedly the first queen to exercise political power over Egypt, and was the last ruler of the Sixth Dynasty, according to the Egyptian writer Manetho. Herodotus (1.184) describes her as the ruler of Babylon and attributes major engineering works on the Euphrates to her. Her precise identity has been much debated.

26 Semiramis was the Assyrian queen Shammuramat, wife of Shamshi-Adad V. She was regent between 810 and 806 BC on behalf of her son. Many legendary stories are attached to her.

that they would appear to be eating them. After that, they impaled them on sharpened poles, which they ran lengthwise through the whole body. 3. And all this they would do amid sacrifices, banquets, and orgies, in their sacred areas and especially in the grove of Andate. This was their name for Victory, and they revered her most of all.

The first target of the rebels' resentment is the colonia *at Colchester.*

Tac. *Agr.* 16. Spurring themselves on with these and other such arguments, they as a body opened hostilities,[27] led by Boudica, a female member of the royal family (they make no distinction between the sexes in the matter of rulers). They hunted down the soldiers scattered among the forts, and after storming the strongholds overran the *colonia* itself, seeing it as the headquarters of their servitude.[28]

Tac. *Ann.* 14.31.2. Prompted by this humiliation and the fear of worse (since they had been formally made into a province), the Iceni took up arms. They also incited the Trinovantes to join the revolt, along with other peoples who, still not broken by oppression, had committed themselves by covert intrigues to reasserting their independence—their most bitter animosity being directed toward the veterans. 3. These had recently been settled in the colony of Camulodunum and had been driving its inhabitants from their homes and throwing them off their lands, calling them "prisoners of war" and "slaves."[29] The common soldiers were also abetting the lawlessness of the veterans—their way of life was similar, and they hoped for the same lack of constraint on themselves. 4. Furthermore, a temple erected to the deified Claudius lay before the natives' eyes like a bastion of everlasting domination, and the men chosen as its priests were pouring away whole fortunes in

27 Tacitus exaggerates when he says "as a body." The Iceni and Trinovantes were certainly involved, as were other tribes. But some remained loyal; this seems to be especially the case south of the Thames (see the introduction to this chapter).

28 Tacitus's account differs here from what he says in the *Annals*, where the rebellion *began* with the attack on the *colonia*, which is the more plausible scenario. Without proper siege equipment, the Britons would have dissipated their energies if they had concentrated their action initially against the auxiliary forts.

29 The Trinovantes settled the area of modern Essex, north of the Thames, from the late Iron Age. Under their powerful king Cunobelinus, they dominated southern Britain. Their principal fortified town, Camulodunum, was captured in AD 43 by the Romans. A legionary base was set up there, which was abandoned before 49, when Colonia Victricensis was founded. The slaves would presumably have been on the staff of the imperial procurator, who would have had responsibility for collecting taxes.

the name of religion.[30] And wiping out a colony surrounded by no fortifications did not seem a difficult undertaking—our commanders, paying more attention to aesthetics than utility, had taken too little precaution in this regard.[31]

32.1. Meanwhile, for no apparent reason, the statue of Victory in Camulodunum toppled over and turned around as though it were giving ground to an enemy. In addition, women who had been driven into a frenzy uttered prophecies that destruction was at hand. Foreign cries had been heard in their Curia, they said, and the theater had rung with wailing, while an apparition of the colony overthrown had been seen in the Thames estuary.[32] In addition, the ocean had taken on a bloody hue, and the imprint of human corpses had been left behind by the ebbing tide, all of which fed the Britons' hopes and the veterans' fears.

2. Because Suetonius was far off, however, the veterans sought help from the procurator Catus Decianus. He sent no more than 200 improperly armed men, and there was also a small group of regulars in the town.[33] The defenders had to rely on the temple building for protection. They were also impeded by clandestine accomplices of the rebellion who were trying to sabotage their plans, with the result that they dispensed with a ditch or a rampart and failed to remove the old and the women and leave only the young men in the fighting line. Showing as little caution as if they were in the midst of peace, they were surrounded by a horde of barbarians. 3. Everything else was pillaged or burned by their onset, but the temple in which the soldiers

30 The temple to the deified Claudius was supposedly decreed during his lifetime, and it is remarkable that the worship of Claudius was apparently not joined with the worship of Rome, the condition attached by Augustus during his lifetime to temples dedicated to the imperial cult ([Sen.] *Apoc.* 8). Colchester was clearly meant to be the official center of the imperial cult in Britain, and the temple almost certainly lay beneath the keep of the later Norman castle (Fishwick [1961], 161–64).

31 The ramparts of Camulodunum had been demolished by the departing Twentieth Legion in AD 49 and had not been replaced. The stone walls now seen at Colchester were built in the second century AD.

32 Colchester is in fact quite distant from the Thames estuary, casting doubt on the report.

33 It is not suprising that the procurator would have troops at his disposal in the absence of the *legatus*. Upon the death of Herod in 4 BC, the procurator of Syria, Sabinus (his full name is unknown), made use of the legion that the legate had stationed at Jerusalem and that apparently considered itself under his command. He also armed his slaves and freedmen and used them as troops. (Joseph. *AJ* 17.252–53; *BJ* 2.16–18, 40–41). There is also the case of the procurator Gnaeus Lucilius Capito, who made use of troops in the public province of Asia to enforce one of his decisions. He was subsequently deemed to have acted improperly (Tac. *Ann.* 4.15.2).

had gathered was subjected to a two-day blockade and then taken by storm. Moreover, the triumphant Britons met Petillius Cerialis, legate of the Ninth Legion,[34] who was coming to relieve the Romans, and they put his legion to flight and killed all his infantry.[35] Cerialis escaped to his camp with the cavalry and found protection within his fortifications. Alarmed by this disaster, and by the hostility of the province that his rapacity had driven into war, the procurator Catus crossed to Gaul.

Suetonius Paulinus moves south from North Wales to London.

Tac. *Ann.* 14.33.1. Suetonius, however, showing amazing determination, headed for Londinium through the midst of his enemies.[36] While it did not have the distinction of being designated a "colony," the town was nevertheless much famed for its large concentration of businessmen and salable goods. There Suetonius vacillated over whether he should choose it as his base of operations, but when he considered his small numbers, and the clear evidence of the severe penalty Petillius had paid for headstrong action, he decided on saving the overall situation by sacrificing a single town. The tearful lamentations of people begging his aid could not divert him from giving the signal to move out and taking into the body of his column only those able to accompany him. All who were held back because their sex disqualified them from fighting or because they were feeble with age or had attachments to the locality were overwhelmed by the enemy. 2. The same disaster befell the town of Verulamium, because the barbarians, who reveled in plunder and were averse to hard work, bypassed strongholds and garrisoned positions to make for the military granary—rich pickings for a looter and difficult for its

34 This is the first mention of Petillius Cerialis, a commander who would go on to have a distinguished career, holding the consulship in AD 70 and 74. In the civil war, he fought on the side of Vespasian (to whom he was related) and became *legatus* of Britain in 70 or 71, where he won acclaim for his vigorous campaigns against the Brigantes.

35 It is likely that Tacitus is mistaken in claiming that the infantry of a whole legion was eliminated. A legion comprised some 5,000 men, and the later reinforcements sent to make up for the loss numbered only 2,000. The Ninth Legion formed part of the invasion force of Britain and was stationed in Lindum (Lincoln). It was now probably broken into at least two vexillations (subdivisions), and the vexillation that Petillius brought south could well have been based at the vexillation fortress at Longthorpe near Peterborough. Hasty work there suggests a reduction of the perimeter, perhaps to accommodate the remaining cavalry after the disaster.

36 This is the earliest historical reference to London, which became an important commercial center from the beginning of the Roman presence in Britain. It was an open town without defenses or garrison.

defenders to secure.[37] It is well established that some 70,000 Roman citizens and allies lost their lives in the locations I have mentioned.[38] This was because the Britons did not take captives, sell them, or indulge in any other wartime trafficking but instead hastily resorted to slaughter, the gallows, burning, and crucifixion, accepting that they would face punishment but meanwhile taking revenge for it ahead of time.

Boudica meets the Romans in a final battle.

Tac. *Agr.* 16.1–2. Their rage in victory overlooked no sort of atrocity found among barbarians. Had Paulinus not come swiftly to the province's aid upon hearing of the uprising, Britain would have been lost, but the fortunes of a single battle brought it back to its erstwhile obedience.

Tac. *Ann.* 14.34.1. Suetonius had under his command the Fourteenth Legion,[39] the *vexillarii* of the Twentieth, and some auxiliaries from the nearby settlements—a total of about 10,000 men under arms—and he now prepared to take the field, delaying no further.[40] He selected a location where

37 Verulamium, on the south bank of the river Ver, provides a good example of the process of Romanization in a young province. It had originally been established as the capital of the Catuvellauni under their ruler Tasciovanus, father of Cunobelinus. Tacitus refers to it as a *municipium*, perhaps loosely; it may not have been granted the formal status of a *municipium* until the Flavian period, which in the hierarchy of cities meant that its residents had "Latin Rights," with limited citizenship, a status below that enjoyed in a *colonia*.

38 Dio gives the figure as 80,000. It seems likely that official figures were drawn on, and the discrepancy is not significant. The allies (*socii*) would presumably include Romanized Britons, and there may have been a considerable number of foreign non-Romans, including merchants, traders, and the like, especially from Gaul, who may or may not be included in Dio's figure.

39 The Fourteenth Legion (Gemina) was stationed at Mainz in Upper Germany (Tac. *Ann.* 1.37.3, 70.1) when it was made part of the army led by Aulus Plautius against Britain. After the initial invasion, it presumably advanced northwest through the midlands. It was eventually moved to the legionary base at Wroxeter, near what later became Shrewsbury, possibly under the governorship of Aulus Didius Gallus (AD 52–57). For its role in suppressing the Boudican rebellion, it received the new title of Martia Victrix (in place of Gemina).

40 The Twentieth Legion took part in the invasion of Britain and at the outset remained at Colchester. In AD 49, it moved to a base near Gloucester. It may well have received its title Valeria Victrix after the rebellion, since it is not attested before 60. It is worth noting that the colony at Colchester was called Colonia Victricensis (from veterans of that legion). Of course, the *colonia* may have been refounded and renamed after the rebellion.

there was a narrow defile and he had the cover of a wood to his rear, and he had ascertained for sure that the only enemy presence was before him, where an open plain guaranteed no fear of ambush.[41] 2. The legionaries therefore stood in close-ordered lines, with the light infantry deployed around them and the cavalry bunched on the wings. The troops of the Britons, by contrast, darted about in squadrons and companies all over the field in unprecedented numbers, and such was their confidence that they also brought their wives along with them to witness their victory, placing them in carts that they had set at the far edge of the plain.

35.1. Boudica rode in a chariot with her daughters before her, and as she approached each tribe, she declared that, while it was quite normal for the Britons to fight under a woman's command, she was not on that occasion seeking vengeance for a kingdom and possessions as a woman descended from great ancestors. No, she said, she sought it as one of the people, for liberty lost, a flogging received, and the sexual abuse of her daughters. The cupidity of the Romans, she said, had reached the point of not leaving people's bodies undefiled, or even old age, or girls' virginity. 2. But, she added, the gods were with them to exact their just revenge. The legion that had dared to engage had been destroyed; the others were hiding in their camp or looking around for an escape. The Romans would not stand up even to the roars and shouts of so many thousands of men, much less to their charge and their sword arms! If they themselves assessed their own troop numbers and their motives for war, she said, then in that engagement they had to win—or fall. That was the decision a woman had made—let the men live on and be slaves!

36.1. Suetonius did not remain silent at such a critical juncture either. Though confident in the valor of his men, he nonetheless delivered a mixture of exhortations and pleas, urging them to pay no heed to the barbarians' noise and empty threats—there were more women than young men visible among them, he said. Lacking fighting ability and weapons, they would immediately give ground when they recognized the arms and courage of their conquerors—so many were their past defeats! 2. Even when legions were many, he said, only a handful of men decided the outcomes of battles, and it would further redound to their glory that, small force as they were, they would win the fame of an entire army. They should just keep close order and, after discharging their javelins, continue the bloody slaughter with shield bosses and swords, and with no thought for plunder—everything would

41 The site of Boudica's last battle has been the subject of much antiquarian debate (see the Introduction). The most likely spot is near Mancetter, on Watling Street, in the midlands.

come to them when victory was won! 3. Such was the enthusiasm that followed the commander's words, and such the eagerness with which his veterans, with their long battle experience, had made ready to hurl their javelins, that Suetonius, certain of the outcome, gave the signal for battle.

37.1. At first, the legion, not taking a step, held onto the restricted terrain for its defense, but when the enemy closed in and the legionaries had used up their well-aimed javelins on them, they burst out in wedge formation. The auxiliaries' charge was equally spirited, and with lances leveled, the cavalry smashed through any stiff resistance they encountered. The rest of the Britons turned tail, escape being difficult because the wagons deployed around them blocked all the exits. And the troops did not refrain even from the slaughter of women, while pack animals that had been run through with spears also increased the pile of corpses.

The glory won that day was spectacular, equal to that of victories of old, for some reports put the British dead at not much below 80,000, with roughly 400 Roman soldiers killed and not many more wounded.[42] Boudica ended her life with poison. 3. Poenius Postumus,[43] camp prefect of the Second Legion,[44] also stabbed himself with his sword when he learned of the success of the legionaries of the Fourteenth and Twentieth. He had cheated his own legion of similar glory and violated military procedure by disobeying his commander's orders.

Dio 62.8.1. It happened that by now Paulinus had brought Mona to terms, and when he learned of the setback in Britain, he immediately sailed there from Mona. He did not wish to risk an all-out confrontation with the barbarians, as he feared their numbers and their insane rage, and he was for deferring the battle to a more favorable occasion. But since he was running short of food and the barbarians did not relax their pressure, he was obliged to face them in battle against his will.

42 For these statistics, Tacitus may well have drawn on his father-in-law, Agricola, who served in this campaign. The figure could also have been recorded in the memoirs of Suetonius Paulinus. The number 80,000 is suspicious, being identical to the figure given by Dio for the Roman and allied dead in the whole campaign (Dio 62.1).

43 The camp prefect, Poenius Postumus, was second in command to the legionary legate and became the actual commander of the troops in the absence of the legate, who was perhaps commanding a vexillation of the Second Legion at the time. Postumus is otherwise unknown.

44 The Second Legion (Augusta) was used in the Claudian invasion of Britain, under the command of Vespasian (Tac. *Hist.* 3.44), and was eventually based at Caerleon near Newport, South Wales.

2. Boudica had an army of some 230,000 men. She herself rode in a chariot, and she put the others in their various positions. Paulinus could not extend his line the whole length of hers (even if the men were formed up only one deep, they would not have reached so far—such was their numerical inferiority), 3. but no more would he risk engaging in a single body in case he were surrounded and cut to pieces. Instead, he divided his army into three parts, so they could fight in several places at the same time, and made each strong enough that it would be difficult to break through.[45]

62.12.1. After haranguing them in these and similar terms, he raised the signal to engage and the armies came together, the barbarians with a lot of shouting and with threatening battle hymns but the Romans maintaining silence and order until they came within javelin range. 2. At that point, as the enemy advanced against them at walking pace, they rushed forward on a prearranged signal and subjected them to a vigorous charge, easily breaking their ranks in the act of engagement. They were, however, surrounded by the Britons' large numbers and were fighting on all sides at the same time.

3. The conflict was multifaceted: light infantry were hurling their weapons at light infantry; heavy infantry were grappling with heavy infantry; cavalry were engaging cavalry; and the archers of the Romans were ranged against the chariots of the barbarians. The barbarians would charge the Romans at high speed with their chariots and bowl them over, but as they were fighting without cuirasses, they were themselves driven back by the arrows. The cavalryman would bowl over the foot soldier, and the foot soldier would bring down the cavalryman. 4. A number of men in tight formation would advance against the chariots, and others would be scattered by them; some Britons would converge on the archers and throw them back, and others would protect themselves at a distance. And this was happening not just in one spot but in three areas of the field at the same time.

5. They continued the struggle for a long time, both sides fired with the same defiant spirit, but finally, later in the day, the Romans triumphed, cutting down large numbers in the battle, beside the wagons and in the woods, and taking many alive. There were also numerous fugitives who made ready to fight again. In the meantime, however, Boudica died of an illness, and her people, grieving deeply over her, gave her a very costly funeral; and now, since they were well and truly defeated, they all dispersed.

45 Dio's account depicts Paulinus as having been forced into battle with little or no control over the situation. Tacitus, who admires Paulinus, assigns him much more control over the strategy that he in the end adopted. Dio's figure of 230,000 for the army of Boudica is clearly a major exaggeration.

After the battle, the Britons are subjected to severe reprisals by Suetonius, who is eventually replaced.

Tac. *Agr.* 16.2–3. A number did still remain in arms, men who were motivated by a guilty conscience over their uprising and a personal dread of the governor, who, they feared, excellent man though he was in general, might treat those who surrendered high-handedly and avenge every injury as though it had been inflicted on him personally.[46] Thus, Petronius Turpilianus was sent out, being thought a man more readily placated and all the more lenient since he was new to the outrages of the enemy.[47]

Tac. *Ann.* 14.38.1. The entire army was then brought together and kept under canvas with a view to finishing off what remained of the war. The emperor increased its strength by dispatching two thousand legionaries from Germany, along with eight cohorts of auxiliaries and a thousand cavalry, upon the arrival of which the shortages in the ninth were made good with regular legionaries. 2. The cohorts and cavalry squadrons were placed in new winter quarters, and any tribes that had been vacillating or resisting were devastated by fire and the sword. But nothing caused the enemy as much suffering as famine: they had been negligent about sowing crops, with men of all ages being diverted to the war effort, while they assumed our provisions were going to be theirs.[48] 3. In addition, these savage tribes were all the slower in inclining toward peace because of Julius Classicianus, who had been sent out to succeed Catus.[49] Classicianus, at loggerheads with Suetonius, was undermining the national interest by his personal feuds, and he had put about the idea that they should await the arrival of a new legate who would deal

46 Tacitus says nothing here about the roles of Polyclitus or Classicianus, both of whom appear in the *Annals.*

47 Petronius was consul in AD 61 and sent to Britain, probably in the same year. In 65, he had a role in exposing the Pisonian conspiracy and received the *ornamenta consularia.* In 68, Nero placed him in command of the troops assigned to counter the rebellion in Gaul, but he did not leave Italy. He was put to death by Galba.

48 Tacitus shows that the suppression of the remaining opposition after the battle took place over the winter. Since Suetonius's successor took office immediately after the termination of his consulship in AD 61, this is a central argument for the rebellion having begun in AD 60 rather than 61.

49 The increasingly public role of the procurator within imperial provinces made it inevitable that there would be occasional tensions between Julius Classicianus and the governor. Classicianus belonged to the Germanic Treveri and would perhaps have had a better understanding of the sensitivities of subject peoples. His tombstone, erected by his wife, Julia Pacata, is preserved in the British Museum (*RIB* I, 12).

humanely with those who surrendered, without an enemy's resentment or the pride of a victor. At the same time, he was sending reports to Rome that they should expect no end to the hostilities unless a successor was found for Suetonius, whose setbacks he ascribed to bad judgment and his successes to luck.

39.1. One of the freedmen, Polyclitus, was therefore sent out to review the situation in Britain, for Nero greatly hoped that, through the man's authority, not only would harmony be established between legate and procurator but the barbarians' rebellious spirit might also be pacified.[50] 2. Polyclitus proved burdensome to Italy and Gaul with his enormous retinue, and after crossing the ocean he did not fail to cut a frightening figure for our soldiers either. But to the enemy he was a joke. The spirit of freedom still burned strongly among them, and they were as yet unacquainted with the power of the freedmen. They were also amazed that a commander and an army that had brought such a great war to an end should defer to slaves. 3. Everything was toned down in the report to the emperor, however, and Suetonius was kept in charge of operations. But after losing a few vessels on the shore and the oarsmen along with them, he was commanded to pass on his army to Petronius Turpilianus (who had now left the consulship) on the grounds that a state of war still existed. Not provoking the enemy, and unprovoked by them, Turpilianus gave his listless inaction the honorable title of "peace."[51]

GERMANY

The notion of the Rhine as a frontier took shape in the period when Julius Caesar incorporated the provinces of Gallia Lugdunensis, Aquitania, and, most significantly, Belgica, and thus extended the zone of Roman authority and administration up to the river. Even then, it would be misleading to think of the Rhine as a traditional border between two nations. In Caesar's time, it did not provide a true ethnic or linguistic demarcation, since Germanic tribes had migrated from the east side (Caes. *BG* 2.4.2, 6.32.1) and some, such as the Menapii, had settlements on both sides of the river (Caes. *BG* 4.4.1–2; Strabo 4.3.4). Nor did the Romans see the Rhine as a permanent border of their empire in the northeast. Augustus aggressively sought to extend the Roman *imperium* as far as the river Elbe, and in the first part of his reign the area

50 Nothing is known of the previous history of Polyclitus, but his greed is noted in Tac. *Hist.* 1.37.5, 2.95.2. He was left in charge at Rome, along with Helios, when Nero made his trip to Greece (Dio 63.12.3).

51 It is likely that Suetonius Paulinus was replaced because of his repressive policies and that Tacitus's sneer at Petronius is unjustified (on Petronius, see the earlier discussion).

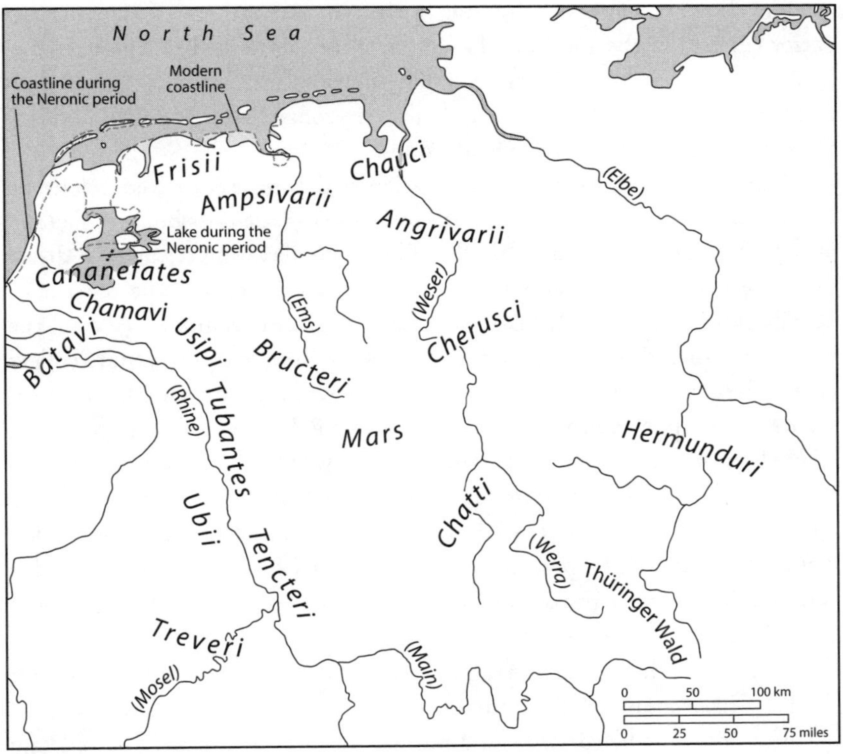

MAP 5. Approximate Locations of Germanic Tribes at the Time of Nero

saw almost continuous campaigning under Marcus Agrippa, Nero Claudius Drusus, and Drusus's brother, Tiberius. There was a process of Romanization east of the Rhine, and Velleius Paterculus talks of Tiberius almost reducing this part of Germany to the status of a tribute-paying province (2.97.4). These plans were brought to a calamitous halt with the disaster suffered by Quinctilius Varus in AD 9, when three legions were lost in the Teutoberg forest in what is now the Kalkriese region. This led Augustus to abandon his hopes of eastern expansion, and the west bank of the Rhine was organized as two military districts, Germania Inferior (lower) in the north and Germania Superior (upper) in the south. Eight legions were established in legionary fortresses along the west of the river under Augustus and Tiberius, four in each district, and the stretches between them were controlled by smaller auxiliary forts manned by non-Roman allied troops.

Upon Augustus's death, his expansionist dream was revived briefly by Germanicus, who seemed once again to be raising the possibility of Roman *imperium* extending as far as the Elbe but who also almost came to disaster. Tiberius prudently reined him in and recalled him. For the remainder of Tiberius's reign, the Rhine frontier was far from secure. In AD 28, the Frisii (Frisians) revolted, crucifying some of the Roman troops sent to collect taxes. The commander of Lower Germany, Lucius Apronius, with reinforcements from Upper Germany, traveled down the Rhine to Frisian territory, where he suffered a great defeat. The Romans were forced to retreat, and 900 of them, taken as exhausted prisoners, were put to death in the grove of their goddess Baduhenna. The true dimension of the disaster was kept hidden from the public. In Upper Germany, Lentulus Gaetulicus exercised a lax command, and tribes broke over the Rhine and caused major devastation in Gaul (Tac. *Ann.* 4. 72–74; Suet. *Tib.* 41).

Caligula conducted a campaign against the Germans from AD 39, but the garbled accounts in the sources make it difficult to evaluate his strategy. It seems that he carried out a number of raids at various points along the Rhine to discourage the German tribes from mounting expeditions into Gaul (as they had done during the previous reign) and thus cutting off supplies to the legions involved in the projected invasion of Britain. That this was his intention is suggested by the fact that his new appointment as commander of Upper Germany, the future emperor Galba, continued to campaign under Claudius and in AD 41 achieved the first military success of the new reign and received the *ornamenta triumphalia* (Suet. *Galb.* 8.1). Domitius Corbulo, appointed legate of Lower Germany, where he is attested in AD 47 (Tac. *Ann.* 11.18–20), carried out successful campaigns against the Chauci and resettled the Frisii. But Claudius cautiously ordered the garrisons on the east of the Rhine to be abandoned. The area was now stable, and Corbulo employed his troops in building a twenty-three-mile canal connecting the Rhine to the Maas. In AD 50, a plundering expedition by the Chatti in Upper Germany was suppressed by a firm and timely reaction by legate Publius Pomponius.

The Germans, along with the Parthians, preoccupied Rome for most of its imperial history, but under Nero, until his demise, a strategy of prompt and ruthless response to unrest kept the frontier reasonably secure, and military forces could be transferred from the Rhine districts to help in the dispute with Parthia (see Chapter IV). Generally, the Romans benefited from the tribal nature of German society and the inability of the Germans to coalesce under a single unified command (which also, of course, made it difficult for the Romans to establish strong alliances among them). Tacitus devotes only one small section to Germany in the surviving Neronian section of the *Annals*. To judge from what seems to be an oblique reference in *Ann.* 13.57.1, it is possible that his main source here was Pliny the Elder. According to his nephew, Pliny the Younger, the uncle undertook a history of all of Rome's German wars in order to preserve for posterity the achievements of Livia's son, Claudius Drusus (Plin. *Ep.* 3.5.4). It was earlier cited by Tacitus as the source for his account of the famous incident of Agrippina the Elder saving the bridge on the Rhine and greeting the retreating Romans (*Ann.* 1.69).

SOURCES

The Frisians attempt to encroach on Roman territory and are dealt with firmly.

Tac. *Ann.* 13.53.1. To that point, things had been quiet in Germany.[52] This was because of the shrewdness of the commanders, who, now that triumphal insignia were commonplace, were hoping for greater glory from maintaining the peace. 2. Paulinus Pompeius and Lucius Vetus were at the head of the army at that time.[53] To avoid having their men idle, Pompeius completed

52 Tacitus's last treatment of Germany went up to AD 50 (*Ann.* 12.28). In covering detailed military campaigns, he often violates the strict annalistic pattern. The events narrated here must have begun before the year to which these chapters strictly belong, AD 58. The activities of the Frisii may well relate to 57, and those of the Ampsivarii might have carried through to the following year, 59.

53 Aulus Paulinus Pompeius was a *novus homo* (in that he was the first of his line to reach the consulship), consul possibly before AD 54, and perhaps the brother of Pompeia Paulina, wife of Seneca (Tac. *Ann.* 15.60.4). From at least 54 to 56, he was legate of Lower

the embankment for containing the Rhine that had been started by Drusus sixty-three years earlier, and Vetus prepared to connect the Mosella and the Arar by constructing a canal between the two.[54] (The aim here was to enable merchandise that was transported by sea, and then taken up the Rhone and the Arar, to travel by way of the canal, and then the Mosella, to the Rhine, and from there to the ocean. With the difficulties of the journey removed, there could be a shipping connection between the shores of the West and those of the North.) 3. Aelius Gracilis,[55] governor of Belgica, looked on the project with envy, and he deterred Vetus from bringing his legions into another man's province and courting popularity in Gaul.[56] The emperor, Aelius kept telling him, would find this alarming—the argument by which honorable endeavors are often blocked.

54.1. Now, because of the prolonged inactivity of the armies, a rumor arose that the legates had been stripped of their authority to lead them against an enemy. As a result, the Frisians brought their soldiers to the bank of the Rhine by way of the woods and marshes, transporting over the lakes those who were not of fighting age.[57] There, led by Verritus and Malorix, who were the rulers of the tribe (to the extent that Germans can be ruled), they settled on unoccupied lands that had been set aside for the use of the troops. 2. They established homes, seeded the fields, and were tilling the land as though it had belonged to their fathers. At that point, Dubius Avitus, who had taken over the province from Paulinus, threatened the Frisians with a

---

Germany. In 62, he was charged by Nero with reorganizing the taxes (*vectigalia publica*) (Tac. *Ann.* 15.18.3).

Lucius Antistius Vetus was consul in AD 55 along with Nero (Tac. *Ann.* 13.11.1) and was legate of Upper Germany in the same year, to be removed a year later. His differences with the legate of Belgica may have contributed to his hasty removal. He was proconsul of Asia in 64–65 and committed suicide, along with his daughter and mother-in-law, to escape a guilty verdict (Tac. *Ann.* 16.10–11). His project was to connect the Moselle River to the Saône (Arar) and thus enable communication by river from the Mediterranean as far as the North Sea, via the Rhine and Rhone.

54 Drusus died in 9 BC, and the later work may belong to 55 AD. Vetus may have been sent to Germany in 55 upon the termination of his consulship, and his post in Rome may have been filled by a suffect consul. Tacitus (*Hist.* 5.19.2) mentions the destruction of the dam by Julius Civilis and implies that it was originally constructed to prevent flooding on the western (Gallic) side.

55 Aelius Gracilis is not otherwise recorded.

56 The eastern boundary of the province of Gallia Belgica was the Rhine, but the two military areas alongside the river were generally outside the province's jurisdiction.

57 The Frisians (Frisii) were an ancient and bellicose Germanic people who occupied the North Sea coast in what is now modern Friesland, as well as much of the adjoining territory in the coastal area between the Yssel and the Ems.

violent Roman response if they did not go back to their old location, or if they did not have a request for a new site granted by the emperor.[58] He thus forced Verritus and Malorix into undertaking the petition.

3. The two left for Rome, where, while waiting for Nero, who was busy with other concerns, they saw the sights usually shown to barbarians, including the theater of Pompey, which they entered in order to observe the size of the population.[59] While they were idling around there (for, being ignorant, they found no pleasure in the performances), they made inquiries about the audience in the seating area and the class distinctions there (which seats were for the knights, and where the Senate sat). They also noticed some people in foreign dress in the senators' seats and, when they asked who they were, were told that this was an honor accorded to ambassadors of peoples who were particularly noted for their courage and their friendship with Rome.[60] The two then announced that there were no people alive superior to the Germans in combat and loyalty, and they went down and sat among the senators. 4. This was taken in good part by the onlookers, who saw in it a primitive impulse and an honorable spirit of competition.

Nero conferred Roman citizenship on both men but ordered the Frisians to leave the territory. And when they disobeyed, auxiliary horsemen were suddenly sent into their midst, and these, capturing or killing all who put up a spirited resistance, left them no alternative.

The Ampsivarii unsuccessfully try to form an alliance against the Romans.

Tac. *Ann.* 13.55.1. The Ampsivarii,[61] a stronger tribe, took over those same lands not only through their own resources but also from having the sympathy

58 Dubius Avitus was one of the first senators to come from Gaul, originating from Vasio (modern Vaison-la-Romaine), the hometown also of Nero's praetorian prefect Burrus (and the historian Pompeius Trogus). After his praetorship, he served as legate of Aquitania (Plin. *HN* 34.47) and held the consulship in AD 56. He received command of Lower Germany in 57/58.

59 The theater of Pompey was the first built of stone in Rome, constructed on a grand scale by Pompey between 55 and 52 BC and restored several times after that.

60 Suetonius (*Claud.* 25.4) tells the same story but relates it to the Claudian period and identifies the ambassadors seen by the Germans as Parthians and Armenians. The privilege of a seat among those reserved for the senators in the theater orchestra had been granted to the Massilians from an early period. Augustus forbade foreign ambassadors access to the orchestra (Suet. *Aug.* 44.1), a prohibition that seems from this reference to have been lifted.

61 The Ampsivarii were a Germanic tribe living between the lower Ems (Amisia) and the Weser. They were not mentioned by Tacitus in his *Germania*. They stayed loyal to Rome after the Varan disaster in AD 9.

of the neighboring peoples—they had been driven out by the Chauci[62] and, now homeless, were begging only for a safe exile. They were also helped by a man called Boiocalus, who was famous among those peoples and was also loyal to us. Boiocalus declared that he had been put in irons on Arminius's orders during the Cheruscan uprising;[63] that he had later served under the leadership of Tiberius and Germanicus; and that he was now further adding to his fifty years of faithful service by bringing his people under our sway. 2. And it was such a small portion of the plain, he said, serving only to have the flocks and herds of the soldiers occasionally driven into it![64] Of course, they should hold in reserve refuges for their animals while men go hungry—but not so much as to prefer empty desert to friendly peoples! These fields once belonged to the Chamavi,[65] he continued, then to the Tubantes,[66] and after them to the Usipi.[67] As heaven had been allocated to the gods, so had the earth been granted to the race of mortals, and what was unoccupied belonged to everybody. 3. Then, looking up at the sun and invoking the other heavenly bodies, he kept asking, as though face-to-face with them, whether what they wanted to look on was empty soil. Better, he said, for them to pour the sea over it to combat these robbers of land!

56.1. Avitus was annoyed by this and replied that commands from one's superiors must be obeyed.[68] Those gods that they were invoking had decided, he said, that judgment of what was to be given and what taken away should remain with the Romans, and the Ampsivarii should accept no arbiters other than them.

Such was Avitus's official response to the Ampsivarii; to Boiocalus personally, he said he would grant him land in memory of their friendship. Boi-

62 The Chauci were a powerful tribe, noted for their aggressiveness, in the area of the lower Weser.

63 The Cherusci were the tribe of Arminius, occupying the area of the middle Weser; their rebellion had led to the Varan disaster fifty years earlier, in AD 9. After the disaster, Tiberius commanded in Germany for two years and Germanicus in AD 13–16.

64 Boiocalus's words here are bitter and ironic. He is suggesting that the area to be taken by the Romans for their animals was enormous and that they would happily use land to graze their animals while the people starved.

65 The Chamavi, perhaps a subdivision of the Marsi, lived east of the Batavians in the area of the Issel.

66 The Tubantes occupied the right bank of the north Rhine.

67 The Usipi, or Usipetes, were also from the region of the north Rhine.

68 Tacitus uses the word *commotus* (here "annoyed") to describe Avitus's reaction to the request of Boiocalus. It means that he was somehow stirred, and some assume here that he was sympathetic, but such a reaction would not be consistent with the action that he pursued.

ocalus dismissed the offer as a bribe for his betrayal, adding: "We may be short of land to live on, but not land to die on." And with that they parted, with bad feeling on both sides.

2. The Ampsivarii now called on the Bructeri, the Tencteri, and tribes even further afield to become their allies in the war. Avitus wrote to Curtilius Mancia, legate of the upper army,[69] requesting that he cross the Rhine and appear in force to their rear, and Avitus himself led his legions into the land of the Tencteri,[70] threatening them with destruction unless they dissociated themselves from their allies' cause. 3. And so the Tencteri withdrew, and the Bructeri now faced the same intimidation.[71] When the rest also proceeded to abandon a dangerous campaign that was not their concern, the tribe of the Ampsivarii was left isolated and withdrew to the Usipi and Tubantes. Driven from their lands, too, they made for the Chatti and then the Cherusci. In their long migrations, they were regarded successively as guests, as indigents, and as enemies on foreign soil, and on that soil all their fighting men fell, while those not of military age were distributed as plunder.

War breaks out between the Hermunduri and Chatti, and the Ubii suffer a natural disaster.

Tac. *Ann.* 57.1. That same summer, a great battle was fought between the Hermunduri and the Chatti.[72] Both were trying to appropriate by force a river that was a rich producer of salt and that formed the boundary between them.[73] In addition to their love of deciding everything by warfare, the tribes also had a deep-seated superstition that this region was particularly close to heaven and that nowhere were mortals' prayers heard by the gods in closer proximity. (Hence, they believed, it was through divine indulgence that, in that river and those woods, the salt was produced not, as among other peoples,

69 Curtilius Mancia was suffect consul, probably in AD 55; he seems to have succeeded Lucius Vetus in 56, after Vetus had served for only one year. Domitia Lucilla, grandmother of Marcus Aurelius, was Curtilius's granddaughter and inherited his estate (Plin. *Ep.* 8.18.4).

70 The Tencteri were located on the east bank of the Rhine, perhaps in the general area of Cologne, and were noted for their horsemanship (Tac. *Germ.* 32.2–3).

71 The Bructeri were located in northwest Germany, in the area of the river Lippe.

72 The Hermunduri were an ancient Germanic people in the area around Thuringia and northern Bavaria, and were generally well disposed toward the Romans. The Chatti, located in the area of the upper Weser, were Rome's most powerful German enemy in the Julio-Claudian period.

73 The river over which they disputed has been variously identified, the Werra and the Saale being the leading contenders.

from the evaporation of tidal overflows but from water poured over a pile of burning trees.[74] Its crystallization was thus the result of two elements that are opposites, fire and water.) 2. The war went in favor of the Hermunduri and was all the more ruinous for the Chatti in that both peoples vowed to sacrifice the enemy battle line to Mars and Mercury in the event of victory, a vow that meant the extermination of horses, men, and all living things.[75]

In this case at least, the threats made by the enemy recoiled on themselves. 3. Not so with the community of the Ubians, allied to us, which was afflicted with an unforeseeable disaster.[76] Fires emanating from the earth engulfed farms, cultivated land, and villages far and wide, and were carried right to the walls of the recently established colony. They could not be extinguished, not by rainfall and not by water drawn from the river or any other source, until a number of peasants, at a loss for a remedy and angry over the calamity, began to hurl stones at them from a distance. Then, as the flames came to a halt, the peasants came closer and proceeded to drive them off like wild animals by beating them with clubs and other instruments. Finally, they stripped the clothes from their bodies and threw these on, and the dirtier and more soiled they were, the more effective they were in dousing the fires.

74 Tacitus may here have misunderstood a process described by Pliny (*HN* 31.73), where evaporation was accelerated by burning wood.

75 Tacitus (*Ann.* 1.61.2–3) reports that Roman officers were sacrificed after the Varan disaster.

76 The Ubii were a tribe friendly to Rome, resettled from the east to the west bank of the Rhine by Agrippa in 38 BC. Their capital was the site of the later Cologne, founded in AD 50 as Colonia Claudia Ara Agrippinensium to honor Agrippina, who had been born there. It was an unusual settlement in that the original inhabitants shared the privileges of the new settlers (Tac. *Germ.* 28.4; *Ann.* 1.57.2, 12.27.1).

VI

THE GREAT FIRE

INTRODUCTION

The major fire that broke out in Rome in AD 64 marked an important turning point in Nero's reign and had political repercussions that went far beyond the immediate effects of the fire itself. By 64, Nero had already exhibited erratic and autocratic behavior. But up to that point, there is no evidence of general disapproval. The devastation of the fire caused an enormous drop in his broader popularity, and the huge cost of reconstruction would almost certainly have alienated the wealthier classes in Italy and farther afield.

Rome had been subjected to continuous fires from at least the time of the first recorded one, after the sack of the city by the Gauls in 390 BC. The crowded nature of the city, with multistory buildings containing much flammable material, made such occurrences inevitable. But the fire of AD 64 stands out for its scale and ferocity. It broke out on the night of July 18–19 south of the Palatine, in the shops, with their flammable booths, that crowded the area of the Circus Maximus, and it spread north on the eastern side of the Palatine as far as the Esquiline. It came in two waves, lasting nine days in all. It supposedly reduced to rubble three of the fourteen districts into which Augustus had organized the city (allowance must be made for exaggeration), and only four districts escaped entirely. Temples, private homes, shops, and tenements all succumbed to the flames. Among the buildings destroyed was Nero's new palace, known as the Domus Transitoria. The Campus Martius was apparently not affected, and its buildings were opened to homeless inhabitants of the city.

Nero seems to have behaved admirably. He tried to prevent the blaze from spreading by creating firebreaks, which may have led to the suspicion that he was pulling down buildings to get land he needed to expand his own palace. He made provision for those who had lost their homes, took a personal interest in the rebuilding program, and took the opportunity to introduce a new building code in Rome in order to prevent a repetition of the disaster in the future. He reimposed the height limit earlier imposed by Augustus but since then generally ignored. He regulated timber construction

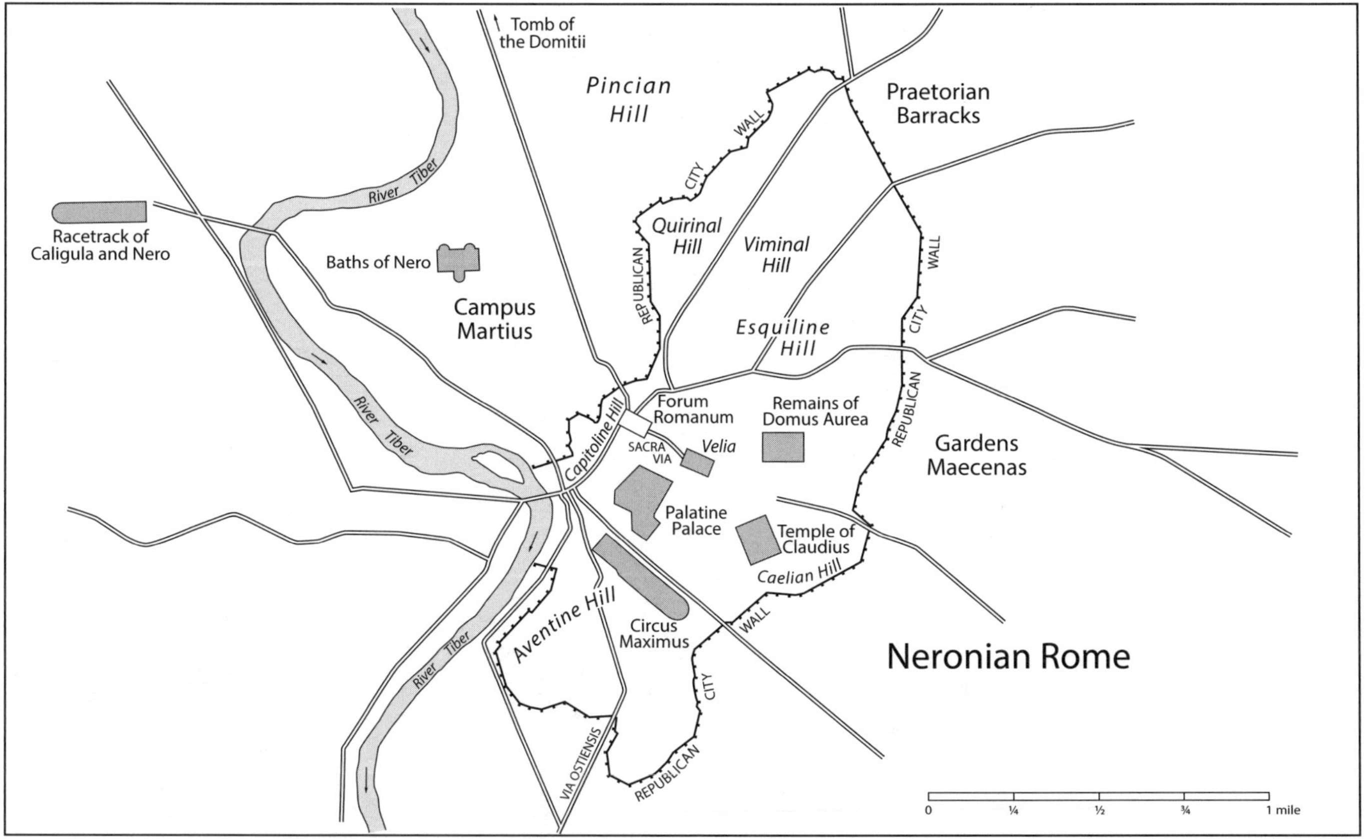

MAP 6. Neronian Rome

and prescribed the use of fire-resistant stone. Streets were to be wider and regular, and tenements were to be made less congested by the construction of internal courtyards and porticos on the outside. He also provided aid. He had supplies transported from Ostia and other towns and reduced the price of corn. Debris was carried away without cost. In fact, it was placed out of bounds, presumably to discourage looting, especially for gold and silver, and then taken down the Tiber by now-empty corn ships. The supply of public water was controlled by supervisors. The building of porticos was financed in part by Nero's personal funds. Private individuals were encouraged to invest in construction. The jurist Gaius records a Neronian measure that enacted that any wealthy Latin (that is, someone with limited citizen rights) who invested half his assets in building at Rome would obtain full citizenship. This measure might well have been introduced just after the fire.

The rebuilding of large parts of Rome was extremely costly, and the unpopularity this caused was aggravated by the expropriation of land for the grandiose palace, the Domus Aurea (Golden House), with its extensive parkland, that Nero planned for the center of the city. The poor would no doubt have been seriously affected, since proper planning to discourage overcrowding would lead to a shortage of accommodations and pressure to increase rents. Moreover, the fire followed on the heels of the costly campaigns in Britain and against Parthia, inevitably creating a serious financial crisis. Tacitus goes on to describe the ruthless measures that Nero undertook to acquire money in Italy and the provinces. The free grain distribution had to be suspended for a while. Some troops were not paid. Pliny the Elder seems to imply that there was widespread confiscation in Africa, when the six landowners who owned half the province were put to death by Nero (Plin. *HN* 18.35), and temple treasures were melted down. There was further devaluation of the coinage, the number of aurei to the pound of gold being increased from forty (or perhaps forty-two) to forty-five and denarii to the pound from eighty-four to ninety-six.

The general discontent resulted in a public receptive to rumors that Nero had instigated the fire and planned to give the rebuilt city the name Neropolis (Suet. *Ner.* 55). Belief in his guilt seems to have become firmly established by the end of the first century, but Tacitus is insistent that the question of Nero's involvement has to remain open. The serious reservations expressed by Tacitus, if not by the other sources, about Nero's responsibility, at least for the initial phase of the fire, cast serious doubt on the case against him. There was a full moon at the time, hardly a convenient condition for arson, and in any case neither outbreak started in the area that Nero would develop for his Domus Aurea. The energetic measures he took to prevent the spread of the fire, as described by Tacitus, speak against the notion of its being deliberately set. Also, the fire destroyed Nero's Domus Transitoria (Tac. *Ann.* 15.39.1). There were widespread reports of arsonists and of people who were hindering the efforts to fight the flames, and these individuals were widely believed to have been Nero's agents—they may well have been looters, and it is of course not out of the question, even if unlikely, that they were Christians. Adding to this belief that Nero was the instigator was the fact that after six days the fire was under control but suddenly broke out again, near the estates of Nero's minister Tigellinus. Contributing to this negative image was the claim that Nero recited his own poetry with the burning city as his backdrop; here, again, Tacitus, unlike Suetonius (*Ner.* 38.2) and Dio (62.16.1–2), is cautious, observing that the claim began as a rumor (*Ann.* 15.39.3). In a context later than the fire, after the Pisonian conspiracy, Dio records that Nero entered the orchestra of the theater and recited some Trojan compositions of his own (62.29.1). Tacitus probably refers to this incident in his account of Nero's poetic recital in the theater at the Quinquennial Games in AD 65 (*Ann.* 16.4.2). Could these compositions be the source of the rumor?

The most dramatic consequence of the fire was the persecution and horrific treatment of the Christians.

SOURCES

A disastrous fire occurs, the responsibility for which is assigned generally to Nero; Tacitus alone expresses uncertainty.

Plin. *HN* 17.5. These were nettle trees . . . ,[1] and when we were young, Caecina Largus, one of the city's notables, would show them off in the grounds of his house.[2] They lasted (since we have discussed the great longevity of trees) until the fire of the emperor Nero and with attention would have remained green and youthful had not that particular emperor speeded up the death of trees as well.[3]

1 Pliny's *lotoe* are generally identified as the Celtis Australis, commonly known as the European nettle tree, which has a sweet, edible fruit and is unconnected to the common nettle.

2 The individual described here is probably Gaius Caecina Largus, who held the consulship with Claudius in AD 42. In the previous section, Pliny has identified the house with the trees as belonging to Lucius Licinius Crassus, consul in 95 BC, and Caecina had presumably acquired it from him. The house, located on the Palatine, had been coveted, especially for the six trees in question, by Crassus's colleague as censor, Gnaeus Domitius Ahenobarbus, great-great-great-grandfather of Nero.

3 The trees were presumably damaged by the fire, attributed here to Nero, and then destroyed during Nero's reconstruction.

Octavia 831–33. *Nero*: Let the roofs of Rome soon collapse beneath my flames, and let fires and falling buildings overwhelm the guilty population—and loathsome want, too, and cruel hunger and grief!

Tac. *Ann.* 15.38.1. A disaster followed, whether accidental or plotted by the emperor is unclear (for the sources have both versions), but it was worse and more calamitous than all the disasters that have befallen this city from raging fires.[4]

Suet. *Ner.* 38.1. But Nero spared neither his people nor his city's walls. When someone said in the course of a general conversation, "After I die let the earth catch fire,"[5] he replied, "No, while I am alive." And he clearly made that happen.

Dio 62.16.1. Nero thereupon set his heart on something he had probably long been wishing to do, namely to destroy in his lifetime the whole city and his whole realm; at least he, too, declared Priam to have been incredibly fortunate in having witnessed the simultaneous destruction of both his country and his kingdom. . . . 17.3. There was not a curse that the people did not utter against Nero, although they did not state his name, avoiding it by merely cursing "those who had set fire to the city."

The fire breaks out.

Tac. *Ann.* 15.38.2. It started in the part of the Circus adjacent to the Palatine and Caelian hills. There, amid shops containing merchandise of a combustible nature, the fire immediately gained strength as soon as it broke out and, whipped up by the wind, engulfed the entire length of the Circus. This was because there were no dwellings with solid enclosures,

4 Fires had been a serious problem throughout Rome's history. Two as recent as Tiberius's reign were mentioned earlier by Tacitus (*Ann.* 4.64.1, 6.45.1). Tacitus stands alone in expressing doubt about Nero's complicity in the fire of AD 64. Suetonius and Dio report only negative information about Nero, and the references in the *Octavia* and in Pliny the Elder imply sources that saw Nero as responsible. But the fact that Tacitus opens his narrative with this question suggests that it was a contentious one in his own day. It is to be noted that in Tacitus's account of the Pisonian conspiracy the tribune Subrius Flavus gives as one of the reasons for his opposition to Nero the claim that the emperor was an arsonist (Tac. *Ann.* 15.67.1–2; see Chapter VIII). Josephus (*AJ* 20.151) does not include the fire in his list of Nero's crimes, but the list is cursory and confined to transgressions against individuals.

5 The saying is anonymous but apparently widely known in antiquity. Dio (58.23.4) puts it in the mouth of Tiberius when contemplating the succession of Caligula.

no temples ringed with walls, and no other obstacle of any kind in its way.

The devastation is horrific, and there are reports of human agency.

Tac. *Ann.* 15.38.3. The blaze spread wildly, overrunning the flat areas first and then climbing to the heights before once again ravaging the lower sections. It outstripped all defensive measures because of the speed of its deadly advance and the vulnerability of the city, with its narrow streets twisting this way and that, and with its irregular blocks of buildings, which was the nature of old Rome.[6]

4. In addition, there was the wailing of panic-stricken women; there were people very old and very young; there were those trying to save themselves and those trying to save others, dragging invalids along or waiting for them; and these people, some hanging back, some rushing along, hindered all relief efforts. 5. And often, as they looked back, they found themselves under attack from the flames at the sides or in front, or if they got away to a neighboring district, that also caught fire, and even those areas they had believed far distant they found to be in the same plight. 6. Eventually, unsure what to avoid and what to head for, they crowded the roads or scattered over the fields. Even though escape lay open to them, some chose death because they had lost all their property, even their daily livelihood; others did so from love of family members whom they had been unable to rescue. 7. And nobody dared fight the fire: there were repeated threats from numerous people opposing efforts to extinguish it, and others openly hurled in firebrands and yelled that they "had their instructions." This was to give them more freedom to loot or else they were indeed under orders.

Suet. *Ner.* 38.1. As if he were offended by the unsightliness of the old buildings and by the narrow, winding streets, he set fire to the city, and did it so openly that a number of ex-consuls caught servants of his on their estates with kindling and torches in their hands and did not touch them.[7] Further-

6 Livy (5.55.2–4) suggests that the chaotic plan of Rome in the time of Augustus resulted from the hasty reconstruction that followed the Gallic destruction. "Heights" would have included the Palatine Hill, as we know from Pliny.

7 It is to be noted that in blaming Nero for the destruction Suetonius says that his contempt for the ugliness of the city was only a *pretext* ("as if") presumably covering up the more serious charge that he needed the land for his own palace. Tacitus and Dio do no more than hint that the arsonists could have been acting on Nero's orders. Suetonius here is much more explicit in asserting that they were his agents.

more, some granaries in the area of the Golden House whose land he particularly coveted were demolished by military engines—because they were built with stone walls—and then set alight.

2. For six days and seven nights, it was a raging cataclysm, with the plebs forced to seek shelter among the monuments and tombs.[8] In addition to huge numbers of apartment blocks, there also went up in flames at that time homes of generals of old, still decorated with enemy spoils; temples of the gods promised in vows and consecrated by the kings, or later in the days of the Punic and Gallic wars; and anything else memorable or worth seeing that had survived from antiquity.

Dio 62.16.2. In secret, he sent men all over the place pretending to be drunk or up to some other mischief and had them set one, two, or more fires in various areas of town.[9] The result was that people were totally perplexed, unable to find how the calamity started or how to end it, though they did observe and hear many strange things. 3. There was nothing to be seen other than a lot of fires, as in a military camp, and nothing to be heard in people's conversations except "Such and such is on fire," "Where?" "How?" "Who started it?" and "Help!" Extraordinary bewilderment gripped everybody everywhere, and they began to run around in different directions like madmen. 4. Some people while helping others would learn that their own homes were burning; others would learn that theirs had been destroyed before they were even told they were on fire. Some would run out of their buildings into the alleyways with the notion that they could do something to help from outside, and others would run in from the streets thinking they would accomplish something even inside. 5. The shrieking and wailing of children, women, men, and the old all together was endless, so that between the smoke and the uproar it was impossible to see anything or have any idea of what was happening; and as a result one could see some standing there speechless, as if they were dumb.

6. Meanwhile, many who were carrying out their personal effects, and many, too, who were stealing those of others, would wander into each other and trip over their bundles. They could not go forward, but neither could they stand still; they would push, and be pushed, bowl others over, and be bowled over themselves. 7. Many were suffocated, and many were crushed, so that none of all the misfortunes that can befall people in such a predicament

8 The reference may be to the opening of the Campus Martius and the buildings of Agrippa, as reported by Tacitus (*Ann.* 15.39.2). While Tacitus speaks of welfare measures taken by Nero, Suetonius sees people left to their own devices.

9 Tacitus describes the fire as beginning in a specific place, and he provides precise topographical details. Dio has the fire beginning in different parts of the city.

failed to overtake them. They had no chance of escaping anywhere easily, and anyone who survived an immediate crisis died when he fell into another.

17.1. Nor did these things all take place on one day; they occurred over several days and nights. Many houses were destroyed because of the lack of help, and many were also set alight by the very people who came to lend a hand.[10] This was because the soldiers, especially those on night watch, had their focus on looting and not only failed to put out fires but even started fresh ones.

Tac. *Ann.* 15.39.1. Nero was at Antium at the time, and he did not return to the city until the fire was approaching that building of his by which he had connected the Palatine residence with the Gardens of Maecenas.[11] But stopping the fire from consuming the Palatine residence, Nero's house, and everything in the vicinity proved impossible. 2. However, to relieve the homeless and fugitive populations, Nero opened up the Campus Martius, the monuments of Agrippa, and even his own gardens, and he erected makeshift buildings to house the destitute crowds.[12]

There is a rumor that Nero had performed a poem during the fire.

Tac. *Ann.* 15.39.2. Vital supplies were shipped up from Ostia and neighboring municipalities, and the price of grain was dropped to three sestertii.[13] 3. These were measures with popular appeal, but they proved a dismal failure, because the rumor had spread that, at the very time that the city was ablaze, Nero had appeared on his private stage and sung about the destruction of Troy, drawing a comparison between the sorrows of the present and the disasters of old.

10 Dio suggests that the acts of incendiarism were random and without deep motive.

11 Augustus established his home on the Palatine Hill, and it became the preferred location for subsequent emperors (giving words for "palace" in various languages). Maecenas left his Esquiline gardens to Augustus in his will. Nero started to build a fine residence, the Domus Transitoria, in the valley between the Palatine and Esquiline. This would be rebuilt as the Golden House.

12 A number of buildings had been erected by Agrippa in the area: the Saepta, where the tribes voted; the Diribitorium, where the votes were counted; the Thermae; the Porticus Vipsania (built by his sister [Dio 55.8.4]); and the Pantheon.

13 In addition to keeping an open mind about Nero's responsibility for the fire, Tacitus is more willing than the other sources to give him proper credit for the measures that he undertook for the welfare of the victims.

Suet. *Ner.* 38.2. Nero looked out over this conflagration from the tower of Maecenas, delighting in the "beauty of the flames," as he put it, and he sang "The Capture of Troy," dressed in his stage costume.[14] 3. Moreover, to lay his hands on as much plunder and spoils as he possibly could, he undertook to remove the cadavers and debris at no cost, while allowing none to approach the remnants of their own property; and with contributions that he not only received but actually demanded, he came close to draining the provinces as well as the fortunes of individuals.

Dio 62.17.2. While such things were going on in various spots, the wind caught the flames and drove them together against the remaining buildings. The result was that nobody thought any longer about personal property or houses. All the survivors stood in any seemingly safe spot and looked at what appeared to be a number of islands or many cities all ablaze at the same time. 3. No longer were they distressed over the loss of their possessions but now lamented the public calamity and reflected on how once before most of the city had been devastated like that, by the Gauls. Such were the feelings of everybody else, many of them in their distress actually jumping into flames.

18.1. Not so Nero, who climbed to the highest point of his palace, from which most of the conflagration could best be seen, and, putting on his lyre player's costume, sang what he called "The Destruction of Troy" but what was actually perceived as being "The Destruction of Rome."[15]

The fire is finally suppressed, only to break out again. The extent of the devastation is vast.

Tac. *Ann.* 15.40.1. Finally, after five days, the blaze was brought to a halt at the foot of the Esquiline.[16] Buildings had been demolished over a vast area so that the fire's unremitting violence would be faced only with open ground and bare sky. But before the panic had abated or the plebs' hopes had revived, the fire resumed its furious onslaught, though in more open areas of the city. As a result, there were fewer human casualties, but the destruction of temples

14 The tower of Maecenas was located in the Esquiline garden given by Maecenas to Augustus (see Tac. *Ann.* 15.39.1). Dio in the next passage refers more vaguely to the "highest point" of the palace.

15 The major discrepancies in the accounts of Nero's supposed performance cast serious doubt on the likelihood of their deriving from a reliable source.

16 Suetonius (*Ner.* 38) says that the fire lasted six days and seven nights. An inscription (*CIL* 6.826, copied but now lost) gives a period of nine days (*urbs per novem dies arsit*). It is possible that the second outbreak lasted for three days.

and of porticos designed as public amenities was more widespread. 2. And that particular conflagration caused a greater scandal because it had broken out on Tigellinus's Aemilian estates;[17] and it looked as if Nero was seeking the glory of founding a new city, one that was to be named after him.[18] In fact, of the fourteen districts into which Rome is divided, four were still intact, three had been leveled to the ground, and in the seven others a few ruined and charred vestiges of buildings were all that remained.[19]

41.1. To put a figure on the houses, tenement buildings, and temples that were lost would be no easy matter. But religious buildings of the most time-honored sanctity were burned down: the temple that Servius Tullius had consecrated to Luna;[20] the great altar and sanctuary that the Arcadian Evander had consecrated to Hercules the Helper; the temple of Jupiter Stator offered in a vow by Romulus;[21] the palace of Numa; and the shrine of Vesta holding the Penates of the Roman people.[22] Other casualties were rich spoils taken through our many victories; fine specimens of Greek art; and antique and authentic works of literary genius. As a result, though surrounded by the great beauty of the city as it grew again, older people still remember many things that could not be replaced. 2. There were those who observed that this

17 The precise location of Tigellinus's Aemilian estates is uncertain. Tacitus seems to imply that the fire broke out in a new area that had not previously been affected.

18 Suetonius, as noted, provides the name of the putative city: "Neropolis" (*Ner.* 55).

19 Augustus divided the city of Rome into fourteen districts, identified by numbers, in 7 BC. The description "charred vestiges" is clearly an exaggeration. Even within the areas affected, the Capitol (Tac. *Ann.* 15.44.1) and the Forum (Tac. *Ann.* 16.27.1) seem to have suffered little, if any, damage, and there was regular activity in the Circus by at least April of the following year, when games were celebrated there during the Festival of Ceres; the Temple of Ceres was clearly standing (Tac. *Ann.* 15.53.1; Suet. *Ner.* 25.2). The Domus Tiberiana on the Palatine survived (Tac. *Hist.* 1.27.2), the Temple of Apollo was the destination after the triumphant return of Nero from Greece in late 67, and there is reference made, immediately after the fire (Tac. *Ann.* 15.44.1), to the Sibylline books (discussed later) kept there. The districts that seem to have escaped were Regio XIV Trans Tiberim, Regio I Porta Capena to the southwest of Mons Caelius, VI Alta Semita on the Viminal and Quirinal, and VII Via Lata in the north. Those devastated were XI Circus Maximus, X Palatium, and IV Templum Pacis (=Suburra). Pliny (*HN* 12.94) speaks of the shrine of Augustus on the Palatine as having been destroyed by fire but does not connect this with the Neronian fire.

20 The Temple of Luna was on the Aventine. Only here is its construction attributed to Servius Tullius, but he is recorded as the founder of the Temple of Diana in the same area (Livy 1.45.2; Dion. Hal. 4.26).

21 The Temple of Jupiter Stator was supposedly dedicated by Romulus after a reverse at the hands of the Sabines (Livy 1.12.6).

22 The Temple of Numa and that of Vesta were located close to one another and are often referred to together (Plut. *Num.* 14.69; Ov. *Tr.* 3.1.27).

fire started on July 19, which was the date on which the Senones captured and burned the city.[23] Others have taken their interest so far as to compute equal numbers of years, months, and days between the two fires.[24]

Dio 62.17. The disaster that the city experienced then was without parallel earlier or later, apart from the Gallic sack. The entire Palatine Hill, the theater of Taurus, and some two-thirds of the rest of the city went up in flames, and the loss of life was incalculable.

Nero exploits the destruction caused by the fire to construct an extravagant palatial complex, the "Golden House" (Domus Aurea), and to regulate building within the city.

Suet. *Ner.* 31.1. However, being more prodigal in his building than in any other area , he [Nero] constructed a house that ran all the way from the Palatine to the Esquiline.[25] This he initially called the Domus Transitoria, but later, after it had burned down and been rebuilt, he renamed it the Golden House.[26] With regard to its dimensions and splendor, it would suffice to

23 Rome was sacked by the Gauls, specifically the Senones, who had migrated from Gaul into Italy in the fourth century BC, on July 19, 390 BC (Livy 5.41; Dio 62.17.3).

24 The calculation is that between 390 BC and AD 64, 454 years had elapsed; that is, 418 years plus 418 months plus 418 days.

25 Throughout his reign, Nero demonstrated an enthusiasm for building, and a number of his structures predate the fire, such as the grand market (Dio 61.18.3) that he erected near the Temple of Claudius on the Caelian Hill (Chapter III) or the great baths complex erected in the Campus Martius. Also, before the fire, Nero had sought to combine the imperial palace on the Palatine Hill and the Gardens of Maecenas on the Esquiline with the Domus Transitoria ("The Passage House").

26 The Golden House was an extravagant residence located in what was in effect a royal park, set around an artificial lake, the whole complex covering perhaps some 125 acres (50 hectares). The "Golden" element in the name is of uncertain origin; it may refer to the gilding of the building or, more abstractly, to its heralding a new "golden age." It might alternatively allude to the imagery of Nero, identified as the sun. The palace extended from the Palatine to the Caelian Hill, where it incorporated the platform of the projected Temple of Claudius, converting the eastern flank of that platform to a fountain (*nymphaeum*), supplied by a feeder from the Aqua Claudia aqueduct. To the north, it incorporated the Gardens of Maecenas on the Esquiline. The main entrance was from the Forum through a colonnaded vestibule, where a colossal bronze image of Nero was erected. The complex was unfinished at Nero's death, and the structures were largely demolished. The Temple of Claudius was eventually built, and the artificial lake became the site of the "Colosseum" (properly the Amphitheatrum Flavium). The giant bronze statue (whose base has been archaeologically excavated) was refurbished to represent Sol ("Sun"). With the help of a team of twenty-four elephants, it was moved to a new location during Hadrian's reign. The

note the following features. Its vestibule was such that it contained a colossal statue of him that stood 120 feet high, and so spacious was it [this vestibule] that its triple portico was a mile long.[27] Likewise, the pool was the size of a sea and was surrounded with buildings made to appear like cities, and there were also tracts of land of different sorts—tilled fields, vineyards, and woods—with large numbers of domestic and wild animals of all kinds.

2. In the other areas of the structure, everything was overlaid with gold and studded with precious stones and mother-of-pearl. The dining rooms had ceilings made of ivory panels that could rotate for flowers to be scattered from above, and were fitted with pipes for dispensing perfume. The principal dining room had a dome that, day and night, was continuously revolving like the heavens, and there were baths running with seawater and sulfurous water.[28] When he [Nero] had finished the house in this style and was dedicating it, his approval of it was limited to the statement that he had at last begun to have shelter fit for a human being.

Tac. *Ann.* 15.42.1. In fact, Nero took advantage of the homeland's destruction to build a palace. It was intended to inspire awe not so much with precious stones and gold (long familiar and commonplace in the life of luxury) as with its fields and lakes, and with woods on one side, replicating wild country, and with open spaces and views on the other. The architects and engineers were Severus and Celer, who had the ingenuity and audacity to attempt to create by artifice what nature had denied and to amuse themselves with the emperor's resources.[29] 2. For they had undertaken to dig a navigable channel from Lake Avernus all the way to the mouth of the Tiber, taking it along the desolate

---

best surviving evidence for the house is the dining complex built on the Oppian, the southwest spur of the Esquiline, not mentioned in any literary source. It consisted of a long, colonnaded structure, on at least two levels, with symmetrical five-sided courts at both sides of a magnificent domed octagonal dining hall. One hundred forty-two rooms have been identified. Two of the rooms by the octagonal hall provide some of the very earliest examples of cross vaults in Roman architecture. The remains underlie the substructures of the later baths of Trajan.

27 Pliny (*HN* 34.45–47) informs us that the statue was created by the sculptor Zenodorus, who specialized in large-scale commissions. Pliny himself saw a model of it and noted its resemblance to the emperor.

28 This remarkable structure was presumably part of the complex underlying the baths of Trajan just noted. Suetonius's description is somewhat ambiguous, since it is not made clear whether the whole room or only the dome above it rotated.

29 These two individuals are otherwise unknown.

shoreline or through the barrier of the hills.[30] In fact, one comes across no aquifer here to provide a water supply. There are only the Pomptine marshes, all else being cliffs or arid ground—and even if forcing a way through this had been possible, it would have involved an extreme and unjustifiable effort. But Nero was ever one to seek after the incredible. He attempted to dig out the heights next to Avernus, and traces of his futile hopes remain to this day.[31]

43.1. As for space that remained in the city after Nero's housebuilding, it was not built up in a random and haphazard manner, as after the burning by the Gauls. Instead, there were rows of streets properly surveyed, spacious thoroughfares, buildings with height limits, and open areas.[32] Porticos had been added, too, to protect the façade of the tenement buildings.[33] 2. These porticos Nero undertook to erect from his own pocket, and he also undertook to return to their owners the building lots, cleared of debris. He added grants, prorated according to a person's rank and domestic property, and established time limits within which houses or tenement buildings were to be completed in order for claimants to acquire the money.[34]

THE CHRISTIAN PERSECUTION

After his account of the Great Fire and of Nero's response to the crisis that it created, Tacitus goes on to describe one of its more dramatic consequences. People started to hold the emperor responsible for the disaster, and he in turn sought scapegoats, finding ideal candidates in the already unpopular Christians. What follows is possibly the most famous passage of Tacitus, in which he

30 Agrippa in 37 BC had linked the Bay of Naples to Lake Avernus to provide safe anchorage for his fleet. The construction of a canal linking it to Rome would have been a gigantic undertaking. Suetonius (*Ner.* 31.3) also refers to its construction, observing that it would have been 160 Roman miles in length (about 147 statute miles), wide enough to allow large ships (*quinqueremes*) to pass one another. It was to be constructed using gangs of convicted criminals.

31 Suetonius (*Ner.* 31.3) speaks of Nero beginning the construction of an extended pool from Misenum to Avernus, which was to be roofed over and lined by colonnades, and of the canal to link Avernus with Ostia.

32 Augustus had attempted to impose limits on the height of buildings, apparently without much success. Nero's limit seems to have exceeded sixty feet, since Trajan later reduced the height to that amount (Aur. Vict. *Epit.* 13.13). Nero's regulations may have been no more successful, since Juvenal (3.269) alludes to the excessive building heights in his day.

33 Suetonius (*Ner.* 16.1) also notes the porticos and adds that the fires could be fought from their flat roofs.

34 The scheme seems not to have proceeded speedily. Suetonius (*Vesp.* 8.5) refers to the fact that much of the city still had not been rebuilt when Vespasian returned there in 70 and allowed the vacant sites to be confiscated and built on.

describes the arrest and conviction of the Christians and the horrific punishments inflicted on them, arguably the first Christian "persecution." So horrific was their treatment that it elicited popular sympathy.

This section of Tacitus, and he is the only ancient source for the events, is of enormous historical interest, yet it is plagued by problems, and at least as early as the late nineteenth century it was rejected in its entirety as an interpolated Christian forgery (Hochart [1885]). This extreme view is not now generally accepted by scholars. The language and style is perfectly Tacitean, without any of the exaggerations that one might expect in a forged piece. Also, while the passage is clearly anti-Neronian, the Christians do not emerge from it in a particularly good light. The author, whether Tacitus or another, believes that they are innocent, but he is clearly hostile to them. Hence, if this passage is an interpolation added sometime before the end of the fourth century (when the Christian writer Sulpicius Severus cites it), it would have to be an almost unbelievably brilliant piece of deception by a true master forger who was prepared to create a negative image of his own cause in order to throw the skeptical reader off the scent.

While the passage seems undoubtedly Tacitean (as argued most recently by Shaw [2015]), it must be acknowledged that it poses some intriguing difficulties. First, while *argumenta ex silentio* are never definitive, in this case they seem particularly compelling. Neither Suetonius nor Dio, both of whom provide detailed accounts of the fire, refer to any subsequent mistreatment of the Christians. They are adamant, of course, that Nero was responsible for the fire, and they would perhaps not want to muddy the waters about the guilt by suggesting that another party was suspected. But this would not have precluded their introducing the Christians as scapegoats, as Tacitus does. Suetonius (*Ner.* 33–38) goes out of his way to list examples of Nero's cruelty but says nothing about the repercussions for the Christians, and his only reference to the sect in his *Life of Nero* is in a quite different context. There, among *meritorious* actions of the emperor, he lists what appear to be routine police measures for maintaining public order, which included action against the Christians along with the banning of *pantomimi* and restrictions on the behavior of charioteers (Suet. *Ner.* 16.2). He also makes a point of saying that in public shows Nero never had anyone put to death, even condemned criminals (Suet. *Ner.* 12.1). Dio says nothing about the Christians in the Neronian period, even though he does record the widely held view that Nero had caused the fire and describes the bitterness that this belief engendered. Perhaps even more astonishing is the silence of Christian writers. There was a strong tradition that Peter and Paul were martyred during Nero's reign, and Nero is accordingly depicted as a leading Antichrist. But no

Christian writer before Sulpicius Severus, who quotes this passage of Tacitus in the early fifth century, makes reference to any large-scale slaughter following the fire. Tertullian, Lactantius, Jerome (*Vir. Ill.* 5; *Chron.*), and Eusebius all refer to Nero generally as a persecutor. The supposed fates of Peter and Paul made this inevitable, and in the history of martyrdoms they would naturally take pride of place. But it is surely astonishing that *not a single Christian writer* makes any mention of what they would surely have viewed as the first large-scale martyrdom. The case of Eusebius is striking since his *Ecclesiastical History* is in effect an exhaustive history of martyrdoms in every corner of the empire, some significant but others fairly minor from a historical (not, of course, from an individual) perspective, yet no mention whatsoever is made of the first recorded mass execution of believers. Even Peter and Paul could hardly have *totally* eclipsed an event of such symbolic importance in the city of Rome itself. That Tacitus's *Annals* might not have been known to the Christian writers is perhaps not surprising. The *Annals* seem to have had little impact on immediately succeeding generations. The like-named third-century emperor Tacitus supposedly imagined that he was descended from the historian and ordered that copies of his works should be made in order to rescue him from the neglect (*incuria*) of readers (*SHA Tacitus* 10.3). But Christian tradition also knew nothing of Tacitus's source, variously identified by modern scholars as Fabius Rusticus, Cluvius Rufus, or Pliny the Elder. The earliest surviving Christian author to mention Nero generally as a persecutor is Melito of Sardis, who, in his *Apology* directed toward Marcus Aurelius in about AD 161 (preserved by Eusebius [*Hist. Eccl.* 4.26.9]), claimed that Nero and Domitian made false accusations about the Christian doctrine. Tertullian later identifies Nero as the first persecutor (*Apol.* 5.3–4; *Scorp.* 15.3) but says nothing of the fire or of a large-scale massacre and directs his reader to check the historical record, while noting that he consulted the "Lives of the Caesars" (*vitas Caesarum legimus*).

The First Epistle to the Corinthians by Clement of Rome, a leading member of the first-century "church," to the extent that we can use that word, is often cited in this context. Written to the Christians in Corinth in connection with a dispute there, the letter is generally considered authentic (the supposed *Second Epistle* is not now attributed to him). A bishop in the early church at Rome, Clement refers to the deaths of Peter and Paul as occurring *dia zelou* ("through jealousy") and relates how, also through jealousy, members of the elect suffered and women were persecuted, "Danaids and Dircai" suffering terrible torments (*I Clem.* 5.2–6.2). The last has been taken to refer to stage reenactments, with Christians taking the role of mythological figures (Coleman [1990]). But the manuscript text of this passage, especially the reference to Danaids and Dircai, is disputed. Also, we cannot be sure to which reign Clement is ascribing these punishments, nor is it made clear that they were in fact taking place in Rome. Moreover, the punishments described are quite different from those related in the *Annals*, and there is no hint of a connection with the fire. The persecutions are ascribed to "jealousy," and if we look at this passage in the context of Clement's letter as a whole, we see that he has been describing the baneful effect of envy and jealousy on the Jewish community through the ages, which might imply problems of internal divisions or Jewish–Christian tensions.

There are also some internal difficulties with the account of the Christians in the *Annals*. It is not well integrated into the narrative. Nero's scheme to deflect blame from himself is introduced, and then the topic is dropped, with no indication of any permanent or long-term effects on the perception of Nero's guilt or on Nero's reputation generally. Indeed, the whole section of Chapter 44 from "But neither human resourcefulness . . . " to " . . . one man's cruelty" could be eliminated from the *Annals* with no loss of sense or continuity. There is also some degree of confusion in the narrative, difficult to explain, even making allowance for Tacitus's cryptic style. Tacitus makes it clear that Nero made up the accusations against the Christians; his language, "found culprits" (*subdidit reos*), leaves no doubt that the charges were bogus. Yet, once the investigations were under way, it is implied that some Christians admitted to being arsonists, without any explanation of this apparently illogical turn of events. Most disturbingly, there is also something very curious about the way that Pontius Pilate is introduced into the narrative. He is simply described as "procurator" without reference to the "province" for which he had a degree of responsibility (strictly, Judaea was not a true *provincia* but part of, and subordinate to, the province of Syria). This is a very curious way to introduce him. Pilate is well known to Christian tradition as the governor of Judaea at the time of the crucifixion, but to the Roman reader of Tacitus's day he was not known nearly well enough to "need no introduction." One might seek to explain Pilate's introduction by an earlier reference to his rather chaotic governorship in one of the earlier lost books of the *Annals*, but a key role for Pilate there is more or less ruled out by Tacitus's dismissive comment in the *Histories* about events in Judaea in Tiberius's reign with the famous line "under Tiberius all was quiet" (*sub Tiberio quies*) (*Hist.* 5.9.2). The very mention of Pilate's administration as the context for the death of Christ is in itself very surprising; it is a detail about Christ that would not be of great interest to the Romans but would be highly important to a Christian reader. But, most significantly, Pilate is described as holding the office of "procurator." This term was not used for the equestrian governors of administrative districts like Judaea at the time of the crucifixion;

that is, in the reign of Tiberius. It is not in fact found in that sense until later, when it is used by Claudius. Before then, such governors were known as "prefects" (*praefecti*). We know that Pilate was no exception to this rule, because in a building inscription discovered at Caesarea in Judaea he is explicitly identified as *praefectus* (*AE* 1963: 104). Thus, the reference to Pilate, of much more interest to a Christian reader than to a pagan Roman, contains a serious and elementary historical anachronism. But we can in fact cite another example of the very same error. The *lingua franca* of early Christianity was Greek, and Greek is accordingly the language of the New Testament Gospels. At some point, the Gospels began to be translated into Latin, culminating in Jerome's Latin Vulgate version of the New Testament at the beginning of the fifth century, in which Jerome corrected the current Latin versions. Augustine (*Doct. Christ.* 2.16) notes vast numbers of Latin versions of the scriptures, but we are in almost total ignorance about when and where the process of translation first began. There is a general consensus that a Latin version of the New Testament, the *Vetus Latina*, had been produced by the end of the second century, possibly in Rome or North Africa (Metzger [1977], 286). In these pre-Jerome Latin versions of the New Testament, at Luke 3.1, where in the Greek text Pontius Pilate's office is described by the neutral Greek word *hegemon* ("leader"), the *Vetus Latina* translates the term with the phrase *procurante Pontio Pilato* ("when Pontius Pilate was acting as procurator"). Thus, the notion that he held the office of *procurator* was part of the Latin Christian tradition. This strengthens the possibility that at least the sentence "The man who gave them their name, Christus, had been executed during the rule of Tiberius by the procurator Pontius Pilatus" (Tac. *Ann.* 15.44.2) is a Christian interpolation.

While there was undoubtedly prejudice against the Christians under Nero, as is confirmed by Suetonius, it could hardly be the case that the Christian community in Rome was large enough to have been the object of such intense popular hatred, despite the claims of Lactantius. It has been argued that Nero's wife Poppaea, whom Josephus (*AJ* 20.195) describes as god-fearing (*theosebes*), was pro-Jewish and encouraged persecution of the Christians. But, if so, that aspect of the event was ignored by Tacitus. And when Tacitus speaks of the "large number" who were put to death, that, at the very least, has to be an exaggeration. There is of course the difficulty that, in the early stage of Christianity, the distinction between Christian and Jew was not a clear-cut one for the Romans. Thus, in the previous reign, Suetonius (*Claud.* 25.4) reports that Claudius expelled Jews from Rome because of the disturbances at the instigation of "Chrestus," presumably a reference to clashes between Christian and non-Christian Jews. Tacitus's description of Christianity as a "pernicious superstition" marked by "shameful offenses" and "hatred of mankind" is reminiscent of what he says of the Jews at *Hist.* 5.5.1: "The customs of the Jews are base and abominable. . . . [T]oward every other people they feel only hate and enmity." It has been argued that there is confusion between Christians and zealous Jews who might have been responsible for the fire. But Tacitus, who in his early career had been a *quindecemvir,* a priestly office that would have involved a fairly high degree of sophistication about religious matters, seems to have no trouble seeing the Christians as a distinct and identifiable sect.

It is no surprise that this chapter of the *Annals* is one of the most intensely studied passages of classical literature.

SOURCES

To deflect anger over the fire, Nero selects the Christians as scapegoats.

Tac. *Ann.* 15.44.1. Such were the precautions taken as a result of human reasoning. The next step was to find ways of appeasing the gods, and the Sibylline books were consulted.[35] Under their guidance, supplicatory prayers were offered to Vulcan, Ceres, and Proserpina, and there were propitiatory ceremonies performed for Juno by married women, first on the Capitol and then on the closest part of the shoreline.[36] (From there, water was drawn, and the temple and statue of the goddess were sprinkled with it.) Women who had husbands also held ritual feasts and all-night festivals.[37]

But neither human resourcefulness, nor the emperor's largesse, nor appeasement of the gods could stop belief in the nasty rumor that an order had been given for the fire. To dispel the gossip, Nero therefore found culprits, on whom he inflicted the most exotic punishments.[38] These were people hated for their

35 According to tradition, the Sibylline books, oracles written in Greek verse, had been brought to Rome in the reign of Tarquinius Priscus. A board of fifteen was responsible for their interpretation. The original collection was destroyed in a fire in 83 BC, and a new official collection was undertaken by Augustus. From 12 BC, the texts were deposited in the library located in the Temple of Apollo on the Palatine, and they seem to have avoided destruction by the fire.

36 The choice of Vulcan, god of fire, is to be expected. The roles of the goddesses are less evident, though not surprising, and variously explained. The Temple of Ceres and Proserpina was by the Circus Maximus, where the fire first broke out.

37 Ritual feasts (*sellisternia*) involved the propitiation of the goddesses at formal banquets set before their images. The goddesses were seated. In the equivalent ceremonies involving male gods, the figures reclined (*lectisternia*).

38 Unfortunately, Tacitus gives no indication of the time that had supposedly elapsed between the fire and the punishment of the Christians. Nor is it clear which authority the Christians were brought before. A number of candidates have been suggested, the

shameful offenses,[39] people whom the common people called Christians.[40] 3. The man who gave them their name, Christus, had been executed during the rule of Tiberius by the procurator Pontius Pilatus. The pernicious superstition had been temporarily suppressed, but it was starting to break out again, not just in Judaea, the starting point of that curse, but in Rome as well, where all that is abominable and shameful in the world flows together and gains popularity.

4. And so, at first, those who confessed were apprehended, and subsequently, on the disclosures they made, a huge number were found guilty—more because of their hatred of mankind than because they were arsonists.[41] As they died, they were further subjected to insult. Covered with hides of wild beasts, they perished by being torn to pieces by dogs, or they would

---

most likely being the prefect of the city, whose office was reinvigorated by Augustus and whose holder initially exercised summary justice in dealing with minor criminal cases and through time assumed responsibility for more serious cases. Another possibility would be the *praefectus vigilum*, the officer in charge of the imperial fire service, who could deal with cases of arson. Ofonius Tigellinus, Nero's sinister praetorian prefect, has also been suggested. There is also much controversy over whether there was legislation making Christianity itself a crime in this period.

39 "Shameful offenses" may refer to claims of cannibalism and infanticide, familiar in writers of the second century AD. This passage may suggest that as early as the Neronian period there was a belief that such practices were common among Christians. It has been argued that Tacitus may have heard accounts of the Christians from his friend Pliny, who famously investigated them under Trajan.

40 The original reading of Tacitus's manuscript was *Chrestiani*, which was corrected to *Christiani* by the erasure of the "e" and the addition of "i." Whether this was by the same or a later hand in the manuscript is disputed; it is also argued that the change was by the same hand and later modified by a later hand, perhaps because of the Christus in the next sentence (Woodman [2004], 325, n.53). *Chrestiani* may possibly be the form by which early Christians were commonly known by the Romans, perhaps through confusion with the Greek word *chrestos*, "worthy" or "good." Suetonius (*Claud.* 25.4) refers to "Chrestos." Tertullian (*Apol.* 3.5; *Ad nat.* 1.3.9) and Lactantius (*Div. inst.* 4.7.5) refer to mispronunciation of the word.

41 This passage has been much discussed by modern scholars. Tacitus seems to say that, through the information provided by those who confessed, others were arrested, and this happened more because of who they were than because they were arsonists. This strongly implies that the first group, unlike the second, did confess to arson, although some scholars argue that they confessed to being Christians. The issue is further confused by the difficulty that *convicti* ("were found guilty"), the generally accepted reading, is in fact an emendation of the reading *coniuncti* ("were associated with them"), found in the single Medicean II manuscript from which all the other extant copies of the latter books of the *Annals* are derived. It may well be that the fire started by accident but that some Christians believed that it was the fire expected to mark the second coming (promised in the Book of Revelation, written later, of course), and they might accordingly have felt the impulse to help it along. They might then possibly be identified with those unknown individuals who were adding to the flames (see Suet. *Ner.* 38.1; Tac. *Ann.* 15.38.7; Dio 61.17.1).

be fastened to crosses and, when daylight had gone, set on fire to provide lighting at night. 5. Nero had offered his gardens as a venue for the show, and he would also put on circus entertainments, mixing with the plebs in his charioteer's outfit or standing up in his chariot. As a result, guilty though these people were and deserving exemplary punishment, pity for them began to well up because it was felt that they were being exterminated not for the public good but to gratify one man's cruelty.

45. Meanwhile, Italy had been completely devastated to raise Nero's funds; the provinces had been ruined, and so had the allied peoples and the so-called free communities.

Suetonius speaks generally of the punishment of the Christians by Nero among a number of public order acts.

Suet. *Ner.* 16.2.2. Under Nero's rule, many offenses were severely dealt with and checked, and there were many new ordinances. A limit on expenditures was set. Public dinners were reduced to *sportulae*. It was forbidden for cooked food, with the exception of legumes and vegetables, to be sold in taverns, whereas earlier there was no sort of fare that was not on offer.[42] The Christians, devotees of a new and abominable superstition, were subjected to punishment.[43] The charioteers, who had assumed the right, long enjoyed with impunity, of wandering about cheating and robbing people for fun, saw their amusements disallowed.[44] Fan clubs of *pantomimi*, along with the actors themselves, were banished from the city.[45]

42 No other source speaks of sumptuary restrictions under Nero. In looking to his client's welfare, the patron was expected to provide food, originally in a small basket (*sportula*), though later this was sometimes replaced by a cash donation (Juv. *Sat.* 1.95–96; Mart. *passim*). There was a fear that cookshops could become the focus of disorders. Suetonius (*Claud.* 38.2) records an identical law under Claudius (which Claudius had relaxed) and claims that under Tiberius even pastries were banished (*Tib.* 34.1).

43 Suetonius's prejudice against Christianity as a dangerous superstition is echoed in Tacitus. But Suetonius silently passes over their horrific suffering as described by Tacitus, which includes the kind of detail that normally had great appeal for the biographer.

44 We have no other information on the restrictions on charioteers.

45 *Pantomimi* performed through dance and gesture, without spoken parts, and usually performed scenes from tragedy, while mimes generally performed scenes from low life, with much recourse to buffoonery. Tacitus tends to use the two terms interchangeably.

Tacitus (*Ann.* 13.25.4) reports that the *pantomimi* were banished from Italy in AD 56 after disturbances among their supporters in the theater (which Tacitus attributes largely to measures undertaken by Nero himself); they had been allowed back by 60 (Tac. *Ann.* 14.21.4).

Lactantius says nothing of a persecution following the fire.

Lactantius *De mort. pers.* 2.5–7. When Nero was now emperor, Peter came to Rome and, after performing a number of miracles (which he was able to do thanks to the power conferred on him by the goodness of God himself), he converted many to the righteous religion and founded a faithful and stable temple to the Lord. News of this was brought to Nero, who could see that large numbers, not only in Rome but everywhere, were abandoning the worship of idols and crossing over to the new religion and rejecting the old one. Being a detestable and vicious tyrant, he rushed to destroy the heavenly temple and eradicate the righteous religion, and first of all he persecuted the servants of God, crucifying Peter and murdering Paul.[46]

Eusebius was born shortly after 260. He became bishop of Caesarea and was favored by the emperor Constantine. He died before 340. He was the author of a number of works in Greek. His Ecclesiastical History (primarily a history of martyrdom) was first written in the early fourth century and went through a number of rewritings.

Eusebius *Hist. Eccl.* 2.25.1. When Nero's rule was well established, he steered into unholy practices and girded himself to attack even the religion of the god of all things. To give a written account of what sort of depraved person he became would not be appropriate for the present study. In fact, though, since many have transmitted to us a record of his doings in painstakingly accurate narratives, 2. it is possible for anyone who so wishes to see from them the loutish qualities of the bizarre man's insanity. Driven on by this,

46 Lactantius sees the focus of the Neronian persecution as the martyrdom of Saints Peter and Paul, with no mention of the fire. The martyrdom of these two saints is a primary tenet of Christianity. The earliest explicit statement that they died in Italy comes from the late second century, in a letter of Dionysius of Corinth quoted by Eusebius (*Hist. Eccl.* 2.25.8). Dionysius, whose *floruit* is given by Eusebius as AD 171, claimed that they were both martyred in Rome at the same time. Furthermore, Gaius, a Roman priest who was active during the term of Pope (St.) Zephyrinus (199–217), is similarly quoted by Eusebius (*Hist. Eccl.* 2.25.6–7), claiming that he could point out the "trophies" (*tropaia*, presumably the sepulchers or shrines) of the Apostles who founded the church (in the case of Peter) at the Vatican or (in the case of Paul) on the Ostian Way. They are clearly well-established landmarks. The chronologies of the final years of Peter and Paul are much debated by scholars, but for our purposes precision is not necessary. It is clear that by the end of the second century, a tradition of their martyrdom had become firmly established in the Christian church, and this earned Nero the reputation of Antichrist, and he seems to have been given a pass for the atrocities that followed the fire. The death of Paul, whose final years are better documented, is generally placed in AD 58–60, hence *before* the fire.

he brought about the destruction of countless men one after the other and then plunged so deeply into impious murder as not to keep his hands off his closest relatives and friends: by various forms of death, he did away with his mother as well as his brothers and wife, along with innumerable others related to him, as if they were personal or public enemies.

3. But in all this there was this one thing missing from his record, namely being the first emperor to be proved an enemy of the divine religion. 4. The Roman Tertullian again makes this observation, in these words: "Check your histories; there you will discover that it was the emperor Nero who first persecuted this creed, especially when he was ruthless toward all in Rome after he brought the whole of the East into subjection."[47] We are proud of having such a man as the originator of our punishment, since anyone knowing him can tell that only something that was a great good would have been condemned by Nero.

5. Having thus proclaimed himself to be in the forefront of those fighting against God, Nero was stimulated to slaughter the apostles. So it is recorded that, under him, Paul was beheaded in Rome itself and that Peter was likewise crucified there, and the report is confirmed by the fact that the names of Peter and Paul have survived to this day in the cemeteries there.[48]

47 Tert. *Apol.* 5.3. Tertullian's text has been mistranslated from Latin into Eusebius's Greek here. He actually said, "There you will discover that it was Nero who first persecuted with the imperial sword this creed which was especially arising in Rome." Tertullian certainly knew of Tacitus, since in this work (the *Apology*) he refers to his name in a wordplay as "the most loquacious of liars" ("Tacitus" means "silent"). Presumably, Tertullian was familiar with Tacitus's *Histories* or the minor works, rather than the *Annals*.

48 Eusebius speaks of the persecution of the Christians in general terms, as does Tertullian, with no reference to the fire or to the horrific punishments meted out in Tacitus's narrative. The only specific references Eusebius makes are to the martyrdoms of Peter and Paul.

VII

THE EMPEROR'S WIVES

INTRODUCTION

The transition of the Roman state from republic to principate represented a major constitutional adaptation at the state level. At a more personal level, the evolution of the household of the *princeps* was in its way no less remarkable. Like the principate as a whole, the imperial household developed out of the precedents established in the republic and reflected the hierarchy and structure of the earlier institution. By a gradual process, the *domus* (household) presided over by the *princeps* became an idealized microcosm of the state over which he presided. And as the state became more overtly monarchical than republican, its ruler more emperor than *princeps*, the *domus* evolved into an *aula*, or court, administered by a body of freedmen whose powerful presence was a humiliating and offensive reminder that real power had passed from the purview of the traditional powerful classes into the hands of personal appointees of the emperor.

The need for appropriate balances and *modi operandi* presented a great problem for each successive emperor and possibly an even greater one for the members of his family, especially the women. For the emperors, a valuable precedent had been set by Augustus, and it is probably fair to say that throughout the whole of imperial history none could boast the success of Augustus himself. The same might arguably be said of Augustus's wife, Livia, who, although prohibited from holding public office, deftly exercised enormous influence as the emperor's consort, probably more skillfully than any subsequent imperial wife; she had less success as an imperial mother, although her failure in this sphere was well replicated by Agrippina later. The women of Nero's court, accordingly, are well worth studying in this period of political change and evolution. But the reign of Nero also provides another dimension that adds a special level of fascination to the topic. The women who play a major role in his life, at both the upper and lower levels of the social scale, happened to be individuals with powerful personalities and determined wills. Initially, this could be said to be the consequence of circumstances; later it seems to have reflected Nero's perhaps unconscious choice. His relationship with them was a psychologically complex one, of subservience followed by a resentment that could result in violence and even death. One may wonder to what extent Nero's determination to define himself as artist and performer was a declaration of independence from the powerful female figures who had played such a dominating role in his life.

Octavia

Octavia was the daughter of Claudius and Messalina, and was probably born in early AD 40. At the age of two, she was betrothed to Lucius Junius Silanus Torquatus, great-great-grandson of Augustus (Tac. *Ann.* 12.3.2; Suet. *Claud.* 27.2; Dio 60.5.7). Through the machinations of Agrippina, she was betrothed to Nero in AD 49 (Tac. *Ann.* 12.9.1) and married to him in 53 (Tac. *Ann.* 12.58.1; Suet. *Ner.* 7.2). There seems to have been little affection between the two, and Nero developed a strong attachment to the freedwoman Acte and later to Poppaea Sabina. On the pretense that she was barren and had committed adultery with a slave, Nero divorced Octavia and banished her to Campania (Tac. *Ann.* 14.60.1, 4; Suet. *Ner.* 35.2). She was later accused of adultery with the prefect of the fleet Anicetus and confined on the island of Pandateria, where she was put to death in June 62 (Tac. *Ann.* 14.63–64; Suet. *Ner.* 35.2).

Poppaea

Poppaea Sabina was born about AD 31 to a family that had roots in Campania, the daughter of Titus Ollius and the elder Poppaea Sabina, the mother reputed to be the most beautiful woman of her day. The family distinction was matched by its wealth (Tac. *Ann.* 13.45.2). Poppaea's father was brought down through his association with Sejanus, and consequently Poppaea Sabina was named after her renowned maternal grandfather, Gaius Poppaeus Sabinus. She was married first to the equestrian Rufrius Crispinus, praetorian prefect from at least 47 to 51. Rufrius would go on to a number of distinctions, followed by exile to Sardinia after the Pisonian conspiracy and then enforced suicide. In AD 58, Poppaea began an affair with Marcus Salvius Otho, the future emperor, and married him. Suetonius says that she was already mistress of Nero when she married Otho. Suetonius claims that Otho became so jealous that he tried to prevent her from meeting Nero, who obliged them to divorce. In the *Histories* (1.13.3), Tacitus suggests that Nero used Otho as a front man in his affair until he could divorce Octavia (Plutarch [*Galb.* 19.2] also claims this), but he suspected that Otho was indulging in Poppaea himself. (Dio [61.11.2] suggests they were both happy to share her.) In the *Annals*, Tacitus claims that it was Otho who initially roused Nero's interest in her, either through naïve enthusiasm or by deliberately pandering to her to extend his own influence. Alone of the sources, Tacitus suggests that Poppaea deliberately encouraged Nero (Tac. *Ann.* 13.46), although Plutarch, while not going that far, claims that she enjoyed the rivalry (Plut. *Galb.* 19.4). Both Tacitus and Suetonius agree that Nero got rid of Otho by sending him to govern Lusitania, where he acquitted himself with some distinction (Tac. *Hist.* 1.13.3; Suet. *Otho* 3). Poppaea's marriage to Nero was supposedly obstructed by Agrippina, and Poppaea supposedly urged him to a drastic remedy (Tac. *Ann.* 14.1), but after the death of Agrippina it was in fact another three years before Nero divorced Octavia and married the by now pregnant Poppaea.

In 63 AD, Poppaea gave birth to a daughter, who was given the title of Augusta but lived only four months (Tac. *Ann.* 15.23.1; Suet. *Ner.* 35.3). In 65, Poppaea was again pregnant but, according to Tacitus (*Ann.* 16.6.1), died after Nero, in an outburst of anger, kicked her in the stomach during the pregnancy (Tacitus rejects a claim that she was poisoned). Suetonius (*Nero* 35.3) says that Nero kicked her to death, when she was pregnant and ill, for berating him for staying too long at the races. Dio (62.27.4) says that he jumped on her, perhaps accidentally. She was not cremated, the usual Roman practice, but embalmed and placed in the tomb of the Julii (Tac. *Ann.* 16.6.2), and received divine honors.

Poppaea is depicted as the epitome of wild excess. Tacitus says that she had every advantage in life except decency (*Ann.* 13.45.2). She was said to put golden slippers on the mules that drew her carriage and to bathe daily in the milk of 500 asses to preserve her beauty (Dio 62.28.1; Plin. *HN* 11.238, 28.183), and she even had a perfume named after her that rich women avidly wore (Juv.6.461–64). In reality, she seems to have been a woman of some ability, with a range of interests. One of these was Judaism, and she met its representatives (Joseph. *Vit.* 16; *AJ* 20.195) and involved herself in Judaean administrative issues (Joseph. *AJ* 20.252). Tacitus concedes that her conversation was engaging and that she had a sharp wit (Tac. *Ann.* 13.45.2). Nero seems to have sought her counsel during the Pisonian conspiracy (Tac. *Ann.* 15.61.2; see Chapter VIII).

Statilia Messalina

After the death of Poppaea, Nero seems to have sought marriage with Antonia, the oldest daughter of Claudius, but she refused him and he put her to death, claiming an involvement in the Pisonian conspiracy as a pretext (Tac. *Ann.* 15.53.3–4; Suet. *Ner.* 35.4; see Chapter VIII). Instead, his next wife was Statilia Messalina, a much-married woman with a distinguished family pedigree.

Acte

Acte was an imperial slave from Asia (Dio 61.17.1), and her relationship with Nero was a major one in his life. Suetonius (*Ner.* 28.1) claims that Nero was prepared to marry her and that he bribed some ex-consulars to testify that she was of royal blood. Agrippina saw the affair as a threat to her own influence over her son, and for that reason Seneca and Burrus encouraged it (Tac. *Ann.* 13.12–13). She remained loyal to Nero to the end, and interred his remains. She became prosperous, owning many slaves and property at Puteoli and Velitrae.

SOURCES

Agrippina maneuvers the betrothal of Nero and Octavia.

Suet. *Claud.* 27.2. He [Claudius] gave Antonia in marriage to Gnaeus Pompeius Magnus and, after him, to Faustus Sulla, both very well-born young men. Octavia, previously engaged to Silanus, he gave to his own stepson, Nero.

AD 49

Tac. *Ann.* 12.3.1. Using their family connection as a pretext, she [Agrippina] made frequent visits and so captivated her uncle that she was preferred to her rivals and, though not yet a wife, now wielded the power of a wife. 2. For, once certain of her own marriage, she began to make greater plans and to engineer a marriage between Domitius, the son she had had by Gnaeus Ahenobarbus, and Claudius's daughter Octavia. This could not be brought off without some criminal act. Claudius had promised Octavia to Lucius Silanus and had brought the young man, already distinguished, popularity with the masses by granting him triumphal insignia and staging a magnificent gladiatorial show in his honor.[1] But there seemed no difficulty in ma-

1 Lucius Junius Silanus, born about AD 26/27, was the son of Marcus Junius Lepidus, consul in 19, and Aemilia Lepida, daughter of Julia the Younger. He was thus the great-great-grandson of Augustus and enjoyed a career that matched his family connections. He was briefly the prefect of the city. After his betrothal to Octavia (cf. also Dio 60.5.7, 31.7; Suet. *Claud.* 24.3, 29.1), he accompanied Claudius to Britain; when the campaign came to an end, he went ahead of Claudius to Rome to report the victory and was awarded triumphal honors (*ornamenta triumphalia*) (cf. also Suet. *Claud.* 24.3; Dio 60.23.1, 31.7). During the triumph, he climbed the steps of the Capitol at Claudius's side. In 48, a year before his death, he held a praetorship, during which, with financial backing from Claudius, he put on a splendid gladiatorial show (cf. also Dio 60.5.8, 31.7).

nipulating the mind of an emperor whose favor and animosity were always implanted and programmed by others.

4.1. Now Vitellius, who screened his servile intrigues behind his title of censor, and had the ability to foresee the rise of despotic regimes, began to associate himself with Agrippina's schemes in order to win her favor.[2] He brought charges against Silanus, whose sister, Junia Calvina, was indeed attractive and precocious (and she had also been Vitellius's daughter-in-law shortly before).[3] 2. It was on this that the allegations were based, with Vitellius putting a sordid interpretation on an affection between the siblings that, while indiscreet, was not incestuous. And Claudius lent an ear, more prepared to listen to innuendo against a son-in-law because of his love for his daughter. 3. Silanus, who was ignorant of the plot and happened to be praetor that year, was suddenly removed from the senatorial order by an edict of Vitellius, despite the fact that the list of senators had long been drafted and the census purification performed. At the same time, Claudius broke off the engagement, and Silanus was forced to resign his magistracy, the one remaining day of his praetorship being conferred on Eprius Marcellus. . . .[4]

8.1. On the wedding day, Silanus took his own life.[5] Either he had reached that point buoyed with hopes of staying alive or he chose the day to increase public resentment. His sister Calvina was banished from Italy.[6] Claudius went further, calling for ceremonies in conformity with the laws of King Tullus, with expiatory rites celebrated by the pontiffs in the grove of Diana, and it brought general amusement that this was the time chosen for punishment and expiation for incest![7] 2. But not to have a reputation only for evil deeds,

2 The mechanics of bringing down Silanus were handled by Lucius Vitellius, father of the future emperor. He was Claudius's strongest ally in the Senate. In AD 47–48, he was censor, and one of his duties was to scrutinize the Senate membership to weed out those guilty of moral turpitude.

3 Vitellius did not invent the rumors. The *Apocolocyntosis* says that Junia Calvina was a woman of great charm, called "Venus" by everyone else but "Juno" (sister and wife of Jupiter) by her brother (Sen. *Apocol.* 8.2). She had in fact been married to Vitellius's son, Lucius Vitellius, brother of the later emperor.

4 Suetonius (*Claud.* 29.2) reports that Silanus was forced to step down on December 29. His place was taken by Eprius Marcellus, consul of AD 62 and 74, a notorious accuser who had amassed great wealth.

5 The wedding in question is that of Claudius and Agrippina. Suetonius (*Claud.* 29.1) confirms that Silanus died on the day of the ceremony. Dio (60.31.8) unambiguously characterizes the death as murder.

6 Calvina was recalled some ten years later, after the death of Agrippina, and lived into Vespasian's reign.

7 Tullus Hostilius, Rome's third king, prescribed expiatory rites for Horatius after he killed his sister.

Agrippina successfully petitioned for remission in the case of Annaeus Seneca's exile, and a praetorship for him along with it.[8] She thought this would have public approval in view of Seneca's literary fame, and she also planned to have Domitius's early years mature under such a teacher. Moreover, they could profit from the man's advice in their imperial aspirations, for (it was believed) Seneca would be loyal to Agrippina through remembrance of her benefaction and hostile to Claudius because he was piqued by the wrong he had suffered.

9.1. It was decided that there should be no further delay, and the consul designate Mammius Pollio was induced with lavish promises to put forward a motion in which Claudius would be entreated to sanction the engagement of Octavia to Domitius.[9] At the age of the two of them, this was not inappropriate, and it would open the way to greater things. 2. Pollio made the proposal in terms not dissimilar to those recently employed by Vitellius. Octavia was then engaged,[10] and, in addition to his previous family connection, Domitius now became the emperor's promised son-in-law and Britannicus's equal—all because of his mother's intrigues and the machinations of those who, having accused Messalina, feared retribution from her son.

Nero marries Octavia.

AD 53

Tac. *Ann.* 12.58.1. In the consulship of Decimus Junius and Quintus Haterius, Nero, now aged sixteen, married Claudius's daughter Octavia.[11]

Nero becomes besotted with Acte.

8 This is the first reference in the extant books of the *Annals* to the famous writer and philosopher, who from then until his death in AD 65 would play a prominent role in Nero's reign. He had been exiled to Corsica in 41 on the charge of being the lover of Caligula's sister, Julia Livilla. On his earlier life, see Chapter I.

9 As consul designate, Mammius Pollio was called on first to give his opinion on a question, but was not obliged to limit his remarks to that question. His suffect consulship presumably fell later in that year (AD 49). Vitellius had stressed the political advantages that would come about if Claudius should marry Agrippina, and similar arguments were probably made on this occasion.

10 The betrothal took place in AD 49. Nero probably was born in AD 37, Octavia in about AD 40.

11 In January 53, Nero had in fact almost certainly just passed his fifteenth birthday and was in his sixteenth year. After Nero's adoption by Claudius, Octavia became his sister, and Dio (60.33.2[2]) reports that she had to be adopted by another family before she was legally allowed to marry him.

AD 55

Tac. *Ann.*13.12. Meanwhile, the power of the mother was gradually weakened. Nero had fallen in love with a freedwoman called Acte[12] and at the same time had enlisted as his confidants Marcus Otho and Claudius Senecio, good-looking young men (Otho came from a consular family,[13] and Senecio had an imperial freedman for a father).[14] Acte had wormed her way deeply into the emperor's affections—without the mother's knowledge, and later despite her attempts to oppose it—by assisting his extravagances and by secret meetings of a dubious nature. Not even the emperor's older friends objected to seeing a young girl satisfy his urges, with no one harmed, since—whether by some stroke of fate or because the illicit is always more appealing—Nero detested his wife Octavia, a noblewoman of proven virtue, and there were fears that, if disallowed that indulgence, he would go on a rampage of unlawful sex with illustrious ladies.

Tac. *Ann.* 13.18.3. His mother's wrath, however, could be appeased by no munificence.[15] She became close to Octavia, and often held clandestine meetings with her friends, appropriating cash from all sources, which— her congenital rapacity apart—she considered an emergency fund. She gave a warm welcome to tribunes and centurions, and showed respect for the names and virtues of such nobles as still survived, as if she were searching for a leader and a party.[16]

12 On Acte, see Chapter III.

13 Marcus Salvius Otho was born April 28, 32, into a family originated from Ferentium in Etruria. His immediate forebears were active and ambitious. His grandfather was the first member of the family to reach the Senate. His father, Lucius, who was thought by some to be Tiberius's illegitimate son, was consul in AD 33, and after exposing a conspiracy against Claudius was enrolled by that emperor into the Patricians. About the career of the Otho of Tacitus's narrative, we know only of his earlier quaestorship, which he must have held early in the Neronian period, and his acceptance into the Arval brotherhood. He reputedly acquired a taste for hedonism from his early years, despite his father's efforts to flog it out of him. His self-indulgent lifestyle quickly endeared him to Nero (Suet. *Otho* 2; Tac. *Hist.* 1.13.3). Otho was now twenty-three years old. On the marriage between his former wife, Poppaea, and Nero, see later in this chapter.

14 Claudius Senecio will reappear in AD 65, when he becomes involved in the Pisonian conspiracy (see Chapter VIII).

15 Agrippina grew alarmed after what she saw as the murder of Britannicus (see Chapter III), and Nero's attempts to win her over with extravagant gifts were to no avail.

16 This is a fairly explicit statement that Agrippina had intended to mount serious political opposition to Nero. She supposedly saw Octavia as a popular figurehead around whom support might be rallied (perhaps Agrippina realized that she could not play that role herself). She also appears to have attempted to strengthen her position in the Senate

The situation is further complicated when Nero falls in love with Poppaea Sabina.

Tac. *Ann.* 13.45.1. A no less scandalous case of immorality that year proved to be the start of deep troubles for the state. One Sabina Poppaea lived in the city.[17] She was the daughter of Titus Ollius, but she had adopted the name of her maternal grandfather, Poppaeus Sabinus, who had an illustrious history and was preeminent as an ex-consul who had also celebrated a triumph.[18] For Ollius had been brought low by his friendship with Sejanus even before holding the high offices.[19] 2. This lady had to her credit everything but decency. Her mother had surpassed all women of her generation in beauty and had bestowed on her both distinction and good looks, and Poppaea's finances were in line with the renown of her family. 3. She had refined conversation and was not dim-witted. She had a modest air and a salacious lifestyle. She rarely made an appearance in public, and when she did so it was with face partially veiled so as not to satisfy men's glances or because that suited her appearance. She had no concern for her reputation, making no distinction between husbands and lovers. She was not controlled by feelings, either her own or another's, ever redirecting her sexuality to where material benefit was in evidence. 4. So it was that, while she was living married to a Roman knight, Rufrius Crispinus, by whom she had had a son,[20] Otho seduced her by his youth and his luxurious lifestyle, and by the fact that he

---

and, perhaps more significantly, among members of the praetorian guard. She had recognized the importance of this institution from an early stage and had gradually replaced officers with candidates of her choice, a policy that bore fruit (albeit not of great benefit in the end) when Burrus informed Nero that the guard would not participate in her assassination in AD 59 (see Chapter III).

17 Tacitus dates the beginning of the affair between Nero and Poppaea to AD 58. His portrayal of Poppaea is thought to owe much to Sallust's portrayal of Sempronia (*Cat.* 25), one of the followers of Catiline. She, too, was well-read and witty, but also lacking in restraint and decency.

18 Poppaeus Sabinus was a *novus homo*, consul in AD 9. In about 11, he was sent to Moesia, and was probably responsible for organizing the region as a separate province. In 15, Achaea and Macedonia were added to his command. He won the *ornamenta triumphalia* for his campaigns against Thrace. He died on service in 35.

19 None of the accounts of Sejanus mentions friendship with Titus Ollius. Suetonius (*Ner.* 35.1) reveals that Titus had held the quaestorship.

20 Suetonius (*Ner.* 35.5) claims that Nero ordered the slaves of Poppaea's son to murder him while he was fishing; he had supposedly entertained hopes of becoming emperor (not unreasonably, his relationship to Nero being that of Tiberius to Augustus). There is also a tradition that Nero stabbed him (*Octavia* 744–47).

was a notoriously close friend of Nero's. The affair was quickly followed by marriage.[21]

46.1. Otho now proceeded to sing the praises of his wife's looks and refinement in the emperor's presence, either because love made him incautious or to rouse Nero's passions and have the bond of their possessing the same woman increase his influence. He was often heard rising from the emperor's dinner table saying that he was going to her, that he had been granted a nobility and beauty that all wanted and the fortunate enjoyed.

2. With these and other such incitements, it did not take long. Accepting an audience, Poppaea first established herself by her sweet talk and wiles, pretending she could not control her passion and was captivated by Nero's looks. Presently, as Nero's infatuation intensified, she began to give herself airs. If kept there beyond one or two nights, she would say repeatedly that she was a married woman and could not abandon her marriage—she was bound to Otho by a quality of life that none could match. Otho was a man of magnificent spirit and refinement, she would say; in him, she could see qualities deserving the highest fortune. But as for Nero, he was bound to a chambermaid-whore in his relationship with Acte, and he had drawn from his cohabitation with a slave nothing that was not degrading and sordid![22]

3. Otho was cut off from his normal intimacy with Nero and then from his position as courtier and member of the imperial retinue. Finally, so he would not be in the city as Nero's rival, he was made governor of the province of Lusitania.[23] There he lived right up to the civil war, not in the disreputable fashion of earlier days but in an upright and virtuous manner, mischievous in his leisure time but quite self-controlled in his exercise of power.[24]

21 Tacitus in the earlier *Histories* (1.13) follows a different version, found also in Suetonius (*Otho* 3), Plutarch (*Galb.* 19.106), and Dio (61.11.2), that Nero had already begun his affair while Poppaea was married to her first husband, Crispinus, and that her relationship with Otho was merely a front to facilitate Nero's meeting with her, a situation complicated when Otho fell in love with her, as a consequence of which he was exiled. Tacitus seems here to be correcting his earlier view with a more plausible scenario.

22 The term that Tacitus uses for cohabitation is *contubernium*, a technical expression for the sharing of a military barracks and applied to the union of two slaves. Acte was in fact a freedwoman.

23 This province, in western Spain, was normally governed by a man of praetorian rank, but Otho had held nothing higher than the quaestorship and was at this time only twenty-six. Suetonius (*Otho* 3.1) suggests that Otho hosted the banquet that immediately preceded the murder of Agrippina and thus, by implication, did not go to Lusitania until after the murder. Plutarch (*Galb.* 20.1) suggests that Seneca advised sending him there.

24 Otho stayed in office for ten years (AD 58–68), governing well and effectively, and led the way in placing his support behind Galba.

Nero decides to murder his mother.

Tac. *Ann.* 14.1. During the consulship of Gaius Vipstanus and Gaius Fonteius, Nero put off no longer the fiendish act he had been mulling over for quite some time.[25] His rule was established well enough to bolster his confidence, and his love for Poppaea was burning hotter every day. Poppaea could not hope to be married herself, or for Octavia to be divorced, while Agrippina lived, and with frequent taunts and occasional teasing she would jeer at the emperor, calling him "the ward" and saying that he was subject to the orders of others and, so far from wielding power, did not even have his own freedom.[26] 2. Why else was her wedding being put off? she asked. Nero must be displeased with her looks and her triumph-celebrating forebears![27] Or was it with her fertility and the sincerity of her feelings?[28] No, it was fear that, as his wife, she would reveal the insults heaped on the senators and the resentment felt by the people over his mother's arrogance and greed.[29] But if Agrippina could countenance only a daughter-in-law who hated her son,[30] she concluded, then Poppaea should return to her marriage to Otho—she would go anywhere in the world where she would only *hear* the vilification of the emperor and not be personally witnessing it while also sharing his perils.[31] 3. Tearfully directed with the artfulness of an adulteress, these and other such comments were beginning to strike home, and no one tried to stop them. Everybody wanted to see the mother's power destroyed, and none thought the son's hatred would harden to the point of his murdering her.

After the murder of his mother, Nero eventually moves to get rid of Octavia.

25 The abrupt announcement of the plan to murder Agrippina comes as something of a surprise. She has been absent from the *Annals* since 13.21.

26 On the implausibility of the words put in Poppaea's mouth here, see Chapter III. Syme (1958), 536–37, finds comic elements in her upbraiding of Nero.

27 In fact, only Poppaea's maternal grandfather, Poppaeus Sabinus, had been granted triumphal insignia, for victories in Thrace under Tiberius.

28 Poppaea had borne a son to Rufrius Crispinus; Octavia was childless.

29 The logic seems to be that as long as Poppaea was in competition with Agrippina, Nero would regard her attacks against his mother as intended simply to undermine her position.

30 After the death of Britannicus, Agrippina was drawn much closer to Octavia (Tac. *Ann.* 13.18.2), so the charge of her supporting those "hating her son" would have struck home.

31 The implication is that Otho has already been sent out to Lusitania. According to Suetonius (*Otho* 3.1), however, he hosted the final banquet for Agrippina on the eve of her murder (see Chapter III).

AD 62

Tac. *Ann.* 14.59. His fear now removed,[32] he proceeded to hurry on his marriage to Poppaea,[33] which had been delayed by such anxieties, and to remove his wife, Octavia (who, for all her modest demeanor, was offensive to him because of her father's name and her popularity with the people).[34]

60. Receiving the decree of the Senate, Nero saw that all his crimes were accepted as good deeds, and so he drove out Octavia, claiming she was barren.[35] He then married Poppaea. She had long been Nero's bedfellow, controlling him first as her adulterer and subsequently as her husband, and now she pushed one of Octavia's servants into accusing her mistress of a love affair with a slave. A man called Eucaerus, an Alexandrian native who was an expert flute player, was marked out as the defendant. Octavia's maidservants were interrogated under torture and, though some were so overcome by the severity of their ordeals as to make false statements, more of them resolutely defended the virtue of their mistress (and, when Tigellinus pressed her, one replied that Octavia's private parts were more pure than his mouth).[36]

Suetonius's account of the events is even more laudatory of the conduct of Octavia's household. Dio's version reflects far less well on it, since he claims that

32 Nero had seen Rubellius Plautus (see Chapter III) as a potential rival. Hence, he had felt obliged to execute him so as to feel safe to divorce the popular Octavia and be free ("this fear now removed") to marry Poppaea.

33 Suetonius (*Ner.* 35.3) reports that the marriage to Poppaea took place on the twelfth day after the divorce from Octavia. Tacitus's reference to speed is very surprising. The year is AD 62. At the very beginning of this book of the *Annals*, Tacitus tells us that Nero is under pressure in 59 to bring forward the marriage and to remove his mother, who is proving such an obstacle, yet this scenario is not borne out by the narrative that follows.

34 By this time, Nero had been married to Octavia for more than nine years. She was a Claudian by birth, and the suggestion may be that, as a Claudian by adoption, Nero resented the Claudian name, or perhaps she reminded him of what had been done to Claudius.

35 Adultery was not of course a capital crime, but the adultery of the emperor's consort could be construed as *maiestas*. Hence, the grounds for the divorce were that she was barren. Tacitus and Suetonius (*Ner.* 35.2) agree on the legal basis of the divorce, and their accounts probably go back to a common source. Suetonius, however, does not in any way attribute the measure against Octavia to the efforts of Poppaea, and assigns responsibility for the death entirely to Nero.

36 Dio identifies the loyal servant as Pythias. Tacitus often expresses admiration for humble individuals, such as Clemens, who tried to rescue his master, Agrippa Postumus (*Ann.* 2.39.1); the freedman of Octavius Sagitta, who tried to assume the blame for his master's crime (*Ann.* 13.44.4); and Epicharis, who showed such courage during the Pisonian conspiracy (*Ann.* 15.57).

all went over to the side of Poppaea with the exception of only one, Pythias, who remained loyal, uttering the preceding insult recorded by Tacitus.

Suet. *Ner.* 35.1. He quickly tired of his relationship with Octavia, and when his friends rebuked him, his reply was that her insignia as his wife should be enough for her.[37] 2. Presently, he several times tried to strangle her, but without success, and then divorced her on the grounds that she was barren.[38] When the people disapproved of the divorce and did not refrain from showing their displeasure, he also banished her, and eventually put her to death on a charge of adultery. The charge was so brazen and groundless that when everybody flatly denied her guilt under torture he made his own pedagogue Anicetus make a false statement that she had been tricked into having sex with him.[39]

Dio 62.13.4. All the other servants of Octavia joined Sabina in attacking her, because they had no regard for her now that she was in a wretched plight, and they fawned on Sabina because of the power she wielded—all except Pythias. Only Pythias would tell no lie against her, though subjected to the most cruel torture, and finally, when Tigellinus kept pressing her, she spat on him and said: "My mistress's private parts are cleaner than your mouth, Tigellinus."

Tac. *Ann.* 14.60.4. She was removed nonetheless, first under the pretext of a civil divorce, when she was given Burrus's house and Plautus's estates—two inauspicious gifts—[40] and later she was banished to Campania, where she was also put under a military guard.[41] There followed repeated and unconcealed protests among the common people, who have less prudence than others and who, because of their meager fortunes, face fewer dan-

37 Nero made a playful analogy with the insignia of triumphs, with which successful generals outside the imperial family had to content themselves.

38 There is no evidence for efforts to strangle her in any other literary source, and the claim is probably not to be taken too seriously.

39 Suetonius claims that all the servants supported her innocence. This is contradicted by Tacitus and Dio.

40 Octavia would have been entitled to a restitution of dowry after divorce, and the estates could have been part of that settlement. Nero may have inherited the house of Burrus after his death. We know that Rubellius Plautus had extensive estates in Asia (Tac. *Ann.* 14.22.5), which would have been confiscated after his death. His wife, Pollitta, had to return to the home of her father.

41 Tacitus's chronology here is superficially confusing. The removal of Octavia from Rome to her new estates would have followed her divorce, which preceded the accusation of adultery and the subsequent investigations, which presumably resulted in her being banished to Campania.

gers.[42] From this <arose the rumor> that Nero had regretted his outrageous conduct and recalled his wife Octavia.[43]

61.1. Then the people joyfully climbed the Capitol and at last paid homage to the gods. They threw down Poppaea's statues, lifted effigies of Octavia on their shoulders, scattered flowers over them, and set them up in the Forum and temples.[44] There was even praise for the emperor, and they once more competed with each other in their homage to him. They were already filling the Palatium with their numbers and their shouting when companies of soldiers were sent forth who broke up the gathering and dispersed them with beatings and drawn swords. The changes they had brought about with the riot were reversed, and Poppaea's honors were reestablished.

2. Ever vicious in her hatred, she was now wild with fear of increased violence from the mob or a change of heart in Nero because of the mood swing of the people, and she flung herself at his knees. Her situation was not such that she was fighting for her marriage, she said, although that meant more than her life to her. No, she said, that very life had been put in extreme jeopardy by Octavia's clients and slaves, who called themselves "the plebs" and had the audacity to commit in peace acts that scarcely took place in war. 3. That armed insurrection had been directed against the emperor; all it had lacked was a leader, and one would easily be found once things got under way![45] That woman, at whose nod, even in her absence, rioting was set in motion, now had only to quit Campania and come to the city in person! 4. And what had been Poppaea's wrongdoing, anyway? What offense had she caused anyone? Could it be because she was going to give the house of the Caesars legitimate offspring? Did the Roman people prefer the scion of an Egyptian flute player to be brought to the empire's highest post?[46] In short, if it was in his interests, he should bring home the woman who controlled him, but

42 Popular protests in Rome in support of the politically mistreated seem not to have had beneficial long-term results. Protesters on this occasion might usefully have recalled how in AD 29 people had encircled the Curia in support of the elder Agrippina and her son. Both of them died not long afterward (Tac. *Ann.* 5.4.2).

43 As transmitted in the manuscript, the text is inconsistent, since it states that Nero brought back Octavia, which is contradicted in the next section (14.61.3), where Octavia is still in Campania and Poppaea fears a change of heart on Nero's part. The emendation making such information a rumor is accepted here. It provides a basis for Poppaea's concern.

44 The reference is to the practice of strewing the roads with flowers during triumphs. See Ovid *Tr.* 4.2.50.

45 Poppaea's logic is not persuasive; she seems to be attributing the popular protests to actions of the clients and slaves of Octavia. Also, by her logic, the movement directed against herself has been transferred to a movement against the emperor.

46 Tacitus seems to be suggesting here that Poppaea believed the story about Eucaerus.

of his own will rather than under duress—or else he should take thought for his own safety. The initial disturbances had been settled through fair retribution and gentle correctives, she said, but if the people lost hope of Octavia being Nero's wife, they would give her another husband!

62.1. Her address, with its varying tone, and adapted to stir up both fear and anger, both terrified and incensed her listener. But suspicion was too weak in the case of the slave and had been undermined by the interrogation of the maidservants. It was accordingly decided that a confession should be obtained from someone on whom a charge of subversion could also be pinned. 2. And for that, a good choice seemed to be Anicetus, the perpetrator of his mother's murder. He was, as I noted, prefect of the fleet at Misenum, and while he had enjoyed some slight favor after committing the crime, he had then become the object of a deepening hatred, for the agents of our nefarious acts are viewed as a standing reproach.

3. Summoning Anicetus, Nero reminded him of his earlier service. He alone had taken measures for his safety against a scheming mother, the emperor told him, and now he had the opportunity to do no less a favor by clearing away a hateful wife. No violence, no weapon was required—he need only admit adultery with Octavia. Though these would remain secret for the moment, Nero promised him great rewards and a delightful retirement property, threatening him with death if he refused. 4. With his deranged viciousness and a facility he demonstrated in his earlier crimes, Anicetus fabricated even more than he had been ordered to and made a confession before friends whom the emperor had brought together as though for an advisory council. He was then banished to Sardinia, where he endured an exile that was far from impoverished, and died a natural death.

63.1. Nero issued an edict in which he declared that the prefect had been seduced by Octavia, who had hoped thereby to enlist the support of the fleet. Then, forgetting the barrenness of which she had been accused shortly before, he added that she had undergone an abortion through guilt over her sexual excesses, and this had become known to him.[47] He then shut her away on the island of Pandateria.[48] 2. No woman in exile ever inspired more pity in those who saw her. Some could still recall Agrippina's banishment

47 Suetonius (*Ner.* 35.2) mentions only the charge of adultery. Certainly, during the republic it is known that abortion *per se* was not illegal, although the attendant circumstances might make it so (as in Cic. *Clu.* 11, where abortion is procured through bribery in order to prevent inheritance). There is no evidence that abortion itself was illegal in the imperial period before the time of Septimius Severus (*Dig.* 47.11.4).

48 The elder Agrippina, the wife of Germanicus, was similarly banished to Pandateria. According to Dio, Julia Livilla, daughter of Germanicus, was banished in AD 41 on suspicion of adultery with Seneca and put to death not long afterward (Dio 60.8.5), and the

by Tiberius, and there was also the more recent memory of Julia, banished by Claudius. But those women had with them the strength of age; they had seen some happy days and could find comfort for the brutality of the present in the recollection of better fortunes in the past.[49] 3. For Octavia, her wedding day was, first of all, tantamount to a funeral, when she was escorted to a home in which she would encounter only grief, her father being snatched from her by poison, and her brother, too, immediately after. Then came the maidservant who was more powerful than her mistress;[50] then Poppaea, whose marriage served only to destroy the wife; and finally the accusation more agonizing than any death.

64.1. So, in her twentieth year, the girl, surrounded by centurions and soldiers, had been removed from the living by the presentiment of her doom, but not yet could she enjoy the tranquility of death.[51] After a few days' interval, the order for her death was given.[52] She declared that she was now a widow and merely a sister,[53] and she appealed to Nero by calling on their common kinsmen the Germanici and, finally, on the name of Agrippina, in whose lifetime she had endured a marriage that, while unhappy, had not carried a death sentence.[54]

2. She was chained up, and the veins were cut in all her limbs; and because the blood, arrested by her fear, flowed too slowly, her life was terminated by the steam of an overheated bath. An act of even more atrocious savagery followed: her head was cut off and taken to Rome, where Poppaea viewed it.

3. In thanks for this, offerings were decreed at the temples—but how long shall I go on relating such events? Any who learn about the tribulations of those times from me, or from other authors, can take it for granted that,

---

implication here is that she also went to Pandateria. It is to be noted that the banishment to Pandateria of Julia, daughter of Augustus (cf. Tac. *Ann.*1.53.1), is not mentioned.

49 In fact, Julia Livilla was only twenty-three at the time of her banishment.

50 The maidservant is Acte; see the note on 13.12.

51 There is a mistake here. Octavia was older than Britannicus, who was born on February 13, 41, and she had been betrothed to Silanus in that same year (Dio 60.5.7). She had to be older than twenty in 62, the year of her death. Figures in manuscripts are very prone to error. It is also possible that Tacitus exaggerates her youth to increase the pathos (see Gallivan [1974]).

52 Suetonius (*Ner.* 57.1) states that her date of death was the same as Nero's (generally accepted as June 9).

53 Octavia had been adopted by another family to make her marriage to Nero possible; thus she was not strictly his sister.

54 Octavia's grandfather, the elder Drusus, had been posthumously awarded the title of Germanicus (Suet. *Claud.* 1.3). Nero's link with Drusus came through his mother and her father, Germanicus, son of Drusus. Octavia's link was through her father, Claudius, son of Drusus. Nero could also claim it through his adoption by Claudius.

whenever the emperor authorized exile or assassination, prayers were always offered to the gods, and that the former indicators of success had now become those of public disaster. And yet I shall not keep silent about any senatorial decree that marked new stages of obsequiousness or extremes of servility.

Poppaea marries Nero and bears him a daughter, who dies, and Poppaea herself dies two years later.

Tac. *Ann.* 15.23.1. In the consulship of Memmius Regulus and Verginius Rufus, a daughter was born to Nero by Poppaea, and he welcomed her with a joy transcending that of a mortal, naming her Augusta and conferring the same title on Poppaea.[55] Her birth-place was the colony of Antium, where Nero himself had been born.[56] 2. The Senate had earlier commended Poppaea's pregnancy to the protection of the gods and had undertaken vows in the name of the state, which were now multiplied and discharged. There was also a period of thanksgiving, with decrees issued authorizing a temple to Fertility and a contest modeled on the rite of Actium.[57] Statues in gold of the goddesses of Fortune were also to be set on the throne of Capitoline Jupiter, and circus entertainments were to be held at Antium in honor of the Claudian and Domitian families,[58] like those for the Julian at Bovillae.[59]

3. But these were all transitory: the baby was dead within four months. And then came more sycophancy, as they voted the child divine honors, com-

55 The year is 63. The title of Augusta was first conferred on Livia, after the death of Augustus. Agrippina was the first wife of the emperor to receive it while her husband was still living. This case is the first time that the title of Augusta was granted to an infant. She was called Claudia Augusta (*CIL* VI.1.2043.11).

56 Antium was the site of an imperial villa (see Chapter I). It was also the birthplace of Caligula. The Arval record for this year shows vows fulfilled on January 12 for the safe delivery by Poppaea, which provides a general period for the birth (Smallwood 24.20).

57 To celebrate his victory at Actium, Augustus had founded Nicopolis and instituted quinqennial games there on the model of the Olympic Games. Nero may have been reviving an already established institution. It is possible that Augustus had established such games in Rome (Dio 53.1.4); Suetonius (*Cal.* 23.1) speaks of Caligula banning Actium celebrations.

58 At Antium, the worship of Fortuna was of two sister goddesses, the Fortunae Antiates, thought to represent the fortune of war and the fortune of peace. Oracles were given from the statues. Caligula was warned by them to beware of his assassin, Cassius Chaerea (Suet. *Cal.* 57.3); in the great tradition of such oracles, he got him mixed up with someone else.

59 Bovillae was a town in Latium south of Rome on the Appian Way. It was a colony of Alba Longa, which was the ancestral home of the Julian family (founded by Iulus, the son of Aeneas). In AD 16, Tiberius erected a monument at Bovillae to the *gens Iulia,* along with a statue of Augustus (Tac. *Ann.* 2.41.1).

plete with couch, temple, and priest. And Nero himself was as immoderate in grief as he had been in joy.[60]

FIGURE 9. *RIC*[2] Nero 44, Gold Aureus. Obverse: NERO CAESAR AVGVSTVS, "Nero Caesar Augustus." Reverse: AVGVSTVS AVGVSTA, "Augustus Augusta." From the collection of Andreas Pangerl/romancoins.info.

> At some point after the Great Fire of 64, Nero reformed his coinage, and the aureus illustrated in Figure 9, on the basis of its weight, confirmed by the mature portrait, belongs to that postreform period. The reverse depicts the emperor in a toga, wearing a radiate crown (with sun's rays) and holding a scepter in his left hand. On the right side stands his consort, veiled and draped. She holds a dish (*patera*) in her right hand and a cornucopia in her left. She is usually taken to be Poppaea, but an identification with Statilia is not to be ruled out.
>
> Note that the SC legend, found on earlier precious metal coinage of Nero and possibly suggesting respect for the Senate, has been dropped.

Tac. *Ann.* 16.6.1. After the end of the games, Poppaea died, the victim of a chance outburst of anger in her husband, from whom she received a kick during pregnancy. Though some authorities record it—more from animosity than belief—I would not give credit to poison.[61] Nero wanted children, and was captivated by love for his wife. 2. Her body was not cremated, the normal

60 Nero's action had a precedent of sorts in that, after the death of his sister Drusilla, Caligula decreed divine honors with a personal shrine and a priesthood of twenty, both men and women (Dio 59.11.1–3).

61 The same story about the kick in the stomach is related by both Suetonius (*Ner.* 35.3) and Dio (62.27.4), neither of whom mentions the theory, rejected by Tacitus, that Nero poisoned her.

Roman practice.[62] It was embalmed, after the fashion of foreign royalty, by being filled with aromatic spices, and then taken into the mausoleum of the Julii.[63] There was, however, a state funeral, and Nero himself, on the rostrum, eulogized Poppaea for her beauty, for having been the mother of a now deified child, and for other gifts of fortune, which he represented as virtues.[64]

7. Poppaea's death brought sadness in public but joy to those with a memory of the past, because of her promiscuity and ruthlessness.[65]

Suet. *Ner.* 35.3. Poppaea, whom he married eleven days after his divorce from Octavia, he loved as no other. And yet he killed her, too, by kicking her to death while she was pregnant and ill for having reprimanded him when he came back late from his chariot racing.[66] By Poppaea he had his daughter Claudia Augusta, but lost her while she was still an infant.

Dio 62.28.1. This Sabina was so given to extravagant luxury (as will be fully demonstrated in the briefest space) that she had the mules that drew her carriage shod with gilded shoes and 500 recently foaled asses milked every day so she could take baths in the milk. She was extremely concerned about her beauty and the radiant quality of her physical presence, and for this reason when she once saw herself not looking good in a mirror she prayed she would die before she grew old. 2. Nero so pined for her after her death that, when he discovered there was a woman who resembled her, he at first sent for her and kept her with him. Later, however, he castrated a freed slave boy (whom he called Sporus), 3. since he, too, bore a resemblance to Sabina,[67] and treated him like a wife in every way. After some time had passed, he married the boy,

62 Pliny (*HN* 7.187) in fact states that cremation was not an old Roman custom but an expedient adopted to dispose of corpses after wars, and that it only later became the practice in Rome.

63 Pliny (*HN* 12.83) claims that more spices were burned at Poppaea's funeral than Arabia produced in a year. Poppaea's remains were deposited in the Mausoleum of Augustus, constructed by Augustus on the Campus Martius, the destination for members of the Julio-Claudian family who died in good grace. The physical shell of the structure has survived to today and has been in continuous use, serving in a variety of capacities, from concert hall to bullring.

64 It was customary for the eulogy of a departed woman to be delivered by a younger male member of the dynasty, a precedent perhaps established in 69 BC with Julius Caesar's eulogy to his aunt Julia. The eulogy to Livia was delivered by Caligula.

65 Josephus (*AJ* 20.195) gives a different picture of Poppaea as a pious woman (*theosebes*), who interceded with Nero on behalf of a Jewish deputation from Jerusalem.

66 Suetonius is alone in suggesting that she provoked Nero to violence by her nagging.

67 Nero's continued devotion to Poppaea is reflected also in Dio's claim (63.9.5) that Nero would perform parts of a tragedy wearing masks and that all the female masks would

although he [Nero] was already married to a freedman called Pythagoras, and he conferred a dowry on him by contract. And their marriage was generally celebrated, and especially so by the Romans.

63.26.3. In everything else, Nero's actions were just as they usually were. He was happy with the reports because he was hoping to defeat Vindex, and most importantly because it seemed that he had gained a plausible excuse for raising money and committing murders. He also continued with his extravagances, and after the completion and beautification of the shrine of Sabina, he consecrated it in magnificent fashion, adding to it an inscription stating that it was the women who erected it to the deified Sabina-Aphrodite.[68] 4. And in this he told the truth, since it had been built with money that had been for the most part purloined from the women.

Sometime after the death of Poppaea, Nero marries his third wife, Statilia Messalina.

Suet. *Ner.* 35.1. Apart from Octavia, Nero took two other wives: Poppaea Sabina, who was the daughter of a former quaestor and had earlier been married to a Roman knight; and Statilia Messalina, a great-great-granddaughter of Taurus, a man who had twice been consul and had also celebrated a triumph.[69] To procure Messalina, he put to death her husband, the consul Atticus Vestinus, while the man was still in office.[70]

---

have the likeness of Poppaea, so that, though dead, she could take part in the performance.

68 Tacitus reports (*Ann.* 16.21.2) that the Senate bestowed divine honors on Poppaea; she thus joined Livia, Caligula's sister Drusilla, and Nero's daughter Claudia as a deified woman. The context of Dio's statement here is 68, at the time of the rebellion of Julius Vindex (see Chapter X). Poppaea had died in 65, and the shrine was presumably decreed at the same time as her deification. Its scale and splendor are indicated by the fact that it took three years to build. It is possible that it was located at Naples (see Kragelund [2010]).

69 Statilia was the daughter of Titus Statilius Taurus, consul in AD 44, and was a descendant of the great Augustan general Titus Statilius. Born sometime between AD 30 and 40, she was married four times before Nero, according to the Scholiast on Juvenal 6.434, but we know nothing about her first three husbands. In 63/64, she married her fourth husband, Marcus Iulius Vestinus Atticus, consul in 65, the year of the Pisonian conspiracy (see Chapter VIII). Tacitus (*Ann.* 15.68.2) records Vestinus's death in the context of the conspiracy, asserting Vestinus's innocence and alleging that Nero was motivated by personal animosity and rivalry over Statilia.

70 According to Tacitus, Nero was already Statilia's lover when she married Vestinus (*Ann.* 15.68.3), although after Poppaea's death Nero had supposedly sought marriage with Antonia, daughter of Claudius. Statilia outlived Nero, and she was sought as a wife by Otho (Suet. *Otho* 10.2).

VIII

CONSPIRACIES

INTRODUCTION

By its very nature, the background to any conspiracy in the past is something that was meant to be kept secret, and as a consequence it poses particular challenges for the historian. When we add the general difficulty of properly understanding events of distant antiquity, we must face the inevitability that disentangling the truth about conspiracies in Julio-Claudian Rome is a nearly impossible task. There is a certain irony in the case of the conspiracy that erupted in April 65, the Pisonian conspiracy, named after the man who emerged as its figurehead. This incident receives the most detailed treatment of any in the extant writings of Tacitus, occupying twenty-six chapters of the *Annals*, organized as a coherent unit displaying some of Tacitus's best narrative writing. Indeed, Woodman (1993) has pointed out its resemblance to a dramatic presentation in both language and structure. Tacitus's account is supplemented by evidence from Dio and a brief notice in Suetonius. And the conspiracy provides a relatively rare instance where an ancient historian reveals his source, in this case two of them, since Tacitus specifically cites Fabius Rusticus and the elder Pliny, both of whom were contemporaries of the events. Less explicitly, he cites those who were exiled as a result of the conspiracy and who reported on it when they returned. Yet the whole episode remains frustratingly obscure.

From what we can glean from Tacitus, it seems at first sight that this was a conspiracy that should have succeeded, in the way that the conspiracy against Caligula succeeded in AD 41. It did, admittedly, like its predecessor, lack the backing of a powerful army commander from a province that hosted substantial legionary forces, but, again like its predecessor, it attracted elements inside the praetorian guard. In fact, one of the guards' two prefects and no fewer than seven of the twelve tribunes who would have commanded the twelve cohorts of the guard were either involved or suspected of involvement, and only two tribunes, Veianus (Tac. *Ann.* 15.67.4) and Gerellanus (Tac. *Ann.* 15.69.1), are depicted as totally loyal adherents of Nero.

There do seem, however, to have been differences between the two conspiracies. On the positive side, the Pisonian plot was, for all its chaos and incoherence, a more realistic conspiracy than the one that toppled Caligula. There was no impractical idealism, no ambition to replace a corrupt imperial system with a revitalized republic. The closest one gets to that is the senator Plautius Lateranus, who was supposedly patriotic and motivated by a love of the *res publica,* but this must not be confused with the republican form of government, and no desire to turn back the clock is ascribed to him by any of the sources. Lateranus, like the others, was prepared to replace one emperor with another more acceptable one (in fact, Piso, the candidate chosen to replace Nero, was in many respects oddly reminiscent of the emperor). But in order for a conspiracy to succeed, it needs organized, disciplined, and focused leadership. Behind the assassination of Caligula, we can suspect the hand of the powerful freedman Callistus, and perhaps even of Claudius himself. Behind the attempted coup to which Piso's name has been attached, there was no strong driving force; certainly none was provided by Piso himself. As a crew, the conspirators were distinctly motley, embracing praetorians, senators, equestrians, and even a freedwoman. Security was lax in the extreme, with a casual regard for concealing the preparations and for limiting the number of people in the know. The freedwoman Epicharis, although rightly admired for her outstanding courage, was woefully irresponsible and shockingly indiscreet in trying to recruit a friend who was not to be trusted. The plot was exposed on its intended eve when the senator Scaevinus behaved very injudiciously and aroused the suspicions of his freedman.

Tacitus states that the plot did not originate with Gaius Calpurnius Piso, but he does not explain with whom it did originate. Dio does not even mention Piso's role in it. Apart from what we can glean from the *Annals,* our knowledge of Piso is derived mainly from a panegyric in 261 hexameters, the *Laus Pisonis.* The author of this tract, who describes himself as a youth under twenty, is unknown, as is the date of the poem. Recent suggestions range from AD 39/40 (Champlin [1989]) to late in Nero's reign (Green [2010]), but there is a general consensus that the recipient is the Piso of the conspiracy. Tall, handsome, and generous, he is cited by Martial (12.36.8–9) as an example of a generous patron. Affable, eloquent, and cultured, he seems superficially to have had all the right qualities, but he lacked firmness of character and had little capacity for practical affairs. This impression given by Tacitus is echoed by the *Laus Pisonis,* which refers to his skill at ball and board games (185, 190), and the fact that he writes light verse and plays the lyre (163–77). He also had a liking for luxury, and his properties included a villa at Baiae. When sent into exile by Caligula, he was given ten slaves but asked for more (they were granted) (Dio 59.8.8).

Piso belonged to a family that was still powerful and distinguished, and he does not seem to have suffered from the notoriety of his earlier kinsman

Gnaeus Calpurnius Piso, who committed suicide in AD 20 for his supposed role in Germanicus's murder. Another kinsman, though the connection is unclear, would have been Lucius Calpurnius Piso Licinianus, who was adopted by Galba and executed shortly afterward (Tac. *Hist.* 4.48.1). Piso's precise relationship to the other members of the family is uncertain. It is just possible that he was the son of Lucius Calpurnius Piso "Augur" (consul 1 BC) or Lucius Cornelius Piso "Pontifex" (consul 15 BC), but we are told that he acquired his wealth through a maternal inheritance (Scholiast on Juvenal 5.114). The apparent absence of a specific strong family connection might normally be a major obstacle to a leading role in a conspiracy, and it is quite possible that Tacitus more clearly explained Piso's qualifications in the chapters now missing from Caligula's reign.

At some point in 37, Caligula married Piso's wife, Livia Orestilla (or Cornelia Orestina; the name is uncertain). Suetonius reports Caligula's quip that he acquired his wife in the manner of Augustus and Romulus, referring to the fact that they had both snatched their brides from their original husbands (Livia was previously married to Tiberius Claudius, and Hersilia was married to a Hersilius before she married Romulus) (Suet. *Cal.* 25.1; Dio 59.8.7). Piso's co-option into the Arval brotherhood in place of Caligula's father-in-law, Silanus, on May 24, 38, may have been a reward for his compliance in giving up his wife. Caligula seems to have tired of his new bride very quickly and soon divorced her—after a few days, according to Suetonius, who adds that he later banished her on the grounds that she took up with Piso again within two years of the marriage. Dio (59.8.7) claims that Piso was included in the exile. The Scholiast on Juvenal 5.114 notes that he was recalled by Claudius and also mentions his consulship (date unknown). He may have held governorships, but he certainly had no major military command, and he seems to have had no major role in civil matters either.

Tacitus has serious reservations about his character and seems to have believed that his apparent public virtues were something of a façade. In the narrative of the conspiracy, he devotes relatively little space to him, focusing in fact more on people who may not even have been part of the plot, such as Seneca or the consul Marcus Julius Vestinus. If the reservations of Tacitus are well founded, Piso seems to have been far from the ideal candidate to be the figurehead of a conspiracy. To many, he must have seemed too much of a clone of the man he was replacing, with his affability, his penchant for the theater, and even his penchant for the wives of friends. He was certainly no leader of men. He refused to allow the coup to happen at his villa at Baiae, in part because it would look as though he had violated the laws of hospitality, and the plot was finally wrecked by his dithering when he lost his nerve and felt unable to make a direct response to the praetorians and to the people. Some of the collaborators seem to have entertained serious reservations about him. Piso himself felt that he had a rival in Lucius Silanus, the last living member of Augustus's line. Vestinus was believed to have Republican sympathies and might have thrown his support behind a different claimant, so he was not informed of the plot. There were rumors that Subrius, a tribune of the guard, despised Piso as much as he did Nero, because Piso had performed as a tragic actor on the stage, and because he planned to eliminate Piso after the assassination and replace him with Seneca. Given that the senatorial conspirators and the praetorian officers gave their support to a man whose moral qualities were so questionable and about whom some of them had such serious reservations, it is perhaps not surprising that the conspiracy very quickly crumbled.

The absence of a strong central motive, beyond antipathy toward Nero, and the absence of a forceful, widely accepted, leader, were clearly obstacles to the conspiracy's success. It also cannot have been helped by the dubious morality of some of the participants, along with their questionable motivations. Afranius Quintianus had been insulted in a lampoon. The praetorian prefect Faenius Rufus was afraid that his colleague Tigellinus was gaining more influence than himself. The poet Lucan resented the fact that Nero was suppressing his verses because of artistic jealousy. Only Plautius Lateranus and the freedwoman Epicharis seem to have been motivated by any sense of ideal, although Tacitus's claim that Epicharis was concerned not only about Nero's crimes but also about the reduced constitutional role played by the Senate does not sound convincing. There was so little substance to the plot that, according to Tacitus, there was a widespread belief that there had been no conspiracy, that the whole affair was merely a fabrication of Nero to get back at men he feared or envied (a possibility that probably should not be dismissed out of hand). Many of the participants displayed arrant cowardice. Scaevinus and an associate were arrested. They then revealed the names of their partners, which had a snowballing effect. Scaevinus, for instance, denounced Claudius Senecio and Lucan; Senecio then betrayed his friend Annius Pollio; and Lucan implicated his own mother. As the conspiracy collapsed, Faenius Rufus, who was not at first exposed, tried to save his own skin by making a point of interrogating others ruthlessly; then he in turn was denounced by his fellow conspirators. Tacitus is scathing about two of the senatorial conspirators: Scaevinus's "mental powers had been weakened by his excesses," and Quintianus "was notorious for his effeminacy" (Tac. *Ann.* 15.49.3–4).

As a consequence of the exposure of the conspiracy, nineteen individuals were put to death or committed suicide and thirteen were exiled. The most famous of the victims was Seneca. While Agrippina was alive, Nero had been happy to have Seneca and Burrus as powerful allies. With her death, he felt very much more his own man. Upon the death of Burrus in AD 62, Seneca found himself isolated, and his enemies exploited that isolation, criticizing his enormous wealth and provoking Nero's jealousy by pointing out that Seneca's estates were finer than the emperor's. They also suggested that he was trying to garner personal popularity, and most gallingly they harped on his successes in oratory and reputation as a poet, the latter role only pursued to try to outdo Nero, an issue that would have been particularly sensitive to the emperor. With some justification, they pointed out his disapproval of Nero's passions: of his love of chariot racing and of his desire to sing before an audience. They would have found a receptive audience when they urged Nero to be his own man and to cut himself off from his old teacher. Seneca was politically shrewd and realized that he could do little to change things, and he sought to withdraw into private life. He offered to hand over his estates to the emperor and to devote himself to intellectual pursuits. Although Tacitus suggests that by this time Nero's feelings had reached the level of contempt, he cloaked this under a veil of flattery and made a great pretense of still needing Seneca, and no doubt he did in a sense, possibly feeling that his association with the famous philosopher and man of letters added a veneer of respectability to his reign. Although Seneca did not then gain his sought-after retirement, he did withdraw somewhat, avoided large groups, and stayed outside the city as much as possible, citing ill health or intellectual activities (Tac. *Ann.* 14.52–56).

Following the Fire of Rome in AD 64 and the ill will aroused by Nero's subsequent measures, Seneca asked to be allowed to retire to the country, and when his request was refused, he feigned a muscular illness and did not leave his bedchamber, living on wild fruits and spring water. This led to rumors that Nero had tried unsuccessfully to have him poisoned through his own freedman Cleonicus (Tac. *Ann.* 15.45.3). He lost his life as a consequence of this conspiracy, but it is by no means clear what he knew of it.

Nero also expected the consul Vestinus to be implicated, but this did not happen. He was ordered to commit suicide in any case. The indirect consequences were even more bloody, and a number of prominent Romans died through judicial murder in the course of the following year, AD 66, including Petronius, Nero's famous "arbiter of good taste" (*arbiter elegantiae*), and the distinguished philosophers Thrasea Paetus and Barea Soranus. Yet it should also be borne in mind that, for all the distinction of his opponents, Nero could also count on the support of prominent Romans, which included a future emperor, Nerva, and a senator and epic poet, Silius Italicus (Plin. *Ep.* 3.7).

The origins of the conspiracy are traceable to events three years earlier.

Tac. *Ann.* 14.65.1. That same year, Nero was believed to have murdered by poison two of his most powerful freedmen[1]—Doryphorus for his opposition to the marriage to Poppaea,[2] and Pallas for living too long in possession of immense riches.[3] 2. Romanus[4] had laid secret charges against Seneca of collaboration with Gaius Piso but was himself more effectively brought down on the same grounds by Seneca. From that arose fear on Piso's part, and against Nero there arose a conspiracy that was momentous and ill-starred.[5]

1 Tacitus thus ends Book 14 with a brief notice on the punishment meted out to prominent freedmen in AD 62.

2 Doryphorus held the post of *a libellis* (in charge of petitions). He had great influence over Nero and on one occasion received a gift of ten million sestertii from him. He was reputed to have gone through a form of marriage with the emperor (Suet. *Ner.* 29; Dio 61.5.4). In this last context, he was possibly confused with Pythagoras, about whom a similar, more detailed claim is made.

3 Pallas was formerly a slave of Antonia. Under Claudius, he took control of finances (*a rationibus*) and promoted Agrippina's marriage to the emperor as well as the adoption of Nero. Dio claims that he was worth 400 million sestertii. He received major honors from the Senate under Claudius but was dismissed by Nero in 55 (Suet. *Claud.* 28; Tac. *Ann.* 12.1.2, 25.1, 53.2, 13.2, 14.1; Dio 62.14.3).

4 The identity of Romanus is not known. He is perhaps the Tiberius Claudius Romanus mentioned in the calendar of Antium (*Fasti Antiates, CIL* X 6638 C 3, 2). The context indicates very strongly that, like Doryphorus and Pallas, he was a powerful freedman, and the abrupt introduction (if there is no gap here in the manuscript) suggests that he is a figure already familiar to the reader and that he appeared in the Claudian books of Tacitus that are now lost.

5 Tacitus expresses himself cryptically here, suggesting that Seneca was engaged in some sort of criminal collaboration with Piso, but we are not told the nature of the collaboration, with the implication, but only an implication, that it was seditious in nature. Unless the action was overtly treasonous, it is hard to see why a "collaboration" with Piso, who was relatively obscure, could have been seen as criminal. And if it were treasonous, it would surely have made Piso a marked man. Tacitus also seems to suggest that Piso's sense of insecurity compelled him to initiate the conspiracy against Nero, although in the account proper of the plot it is stressed that Piso was not the prime mover. There is also a difficulty here in that, although Piso was at least indirectly implicated in murky transactions, Nero seems to have harbored no suspicions about him but remained friendly enough with him to be a frequent visitor to his villa at Baiae. Also, it is very hard to see how Seneca could have turned the tables about collaboration with Piso on his accuser: Why would Romanus's consorting with Piso have been criminal? And what happened to Romanus?

The conspiracy gains widespread support.

Tac. *Ann.* 15.48.1. Silius Nerva and Atticus Vestinus then entered their consulship,[6] at a time when a conspiracy had begun and immediately escalated. Senators, knights, soldiers, and even women raced to enroll in it, from hatred of Nero and also because of the popularity of Gaius Piso. 2. Piso was of the Calpurnian line and was well connected with many distinguished families, because of his father's noble breeding. And he enjoyed a brilliant reputation among the lower orders thanks to his virtue, or qualities that looked like virtues. 3. For he used his oratorical ability to defend his fellow citizens, showed generosity toward his friends, and was affable in his conversation and interaction, even with strangers. He also enjoyed the fortuitous advantages of a tall physique and handsome looks. But he was far from possessing depth of character or moderation in his pleasures; he immersed himself in frivolity, luxury, and, sometimes, dissipation. And this had the blessing of most people, who, surrounded by such sweet vices, do not want to see austerity or great strictness in the supreme power.

Dio 62.24.1. However, Seneca, the prefect Rufus, and a number of other distinguished men hatched a plot against Nero, since they were unable to tolerate any longer his shameful conduct, his prurient ways, and his brutality.[7]

The conspirators have a wide range of motivations.

Tac. *Ann.*15.49.1. The conspiracy did not start from ambition on Piso's part, but I would not find it easy to say who the prime mover was or who provided the inspiration for a coup that so many espoused. 2. Its most fervent supporters proved to be Subrius Flavus, tribune of a praetorian cohort, and the

6 Marcus Iulius Vestinus Atticus was the son of an equestrian from Vienna (Vienne) in Gallia Narbonensis. His father was an intimate of Claudius and had a distinguished career. Little is known about the son outside the context of the conspiracy and his marriage to Nero's third wife, Statilia Messalina, but Claudius in his speech on the Gauls does speak of priestly offices conferred on the sons of his friend (Smallwood 369). From Tacitus's account of the conspiracy, we learn that Vestinus lived in Rome in some style, in a house overlooking the forum. He would be put to death not, according to Tacitus (*Ann.* 15.68.3), because of his involvement in the conspiracy but because Nero coveted his wife.

7 It is striking that in Dio's account no mention is made of any role for Piso. Dio gives a central role to Seneca. Although he does not explicitly identify him as the leader, by mentioning his name first he gives an impression of prominence. He also gives a more dominant role to Faenius Rufus, making no mention of his less than distinguished conduct later.

centurion Sulpicius Asper, as the resolution they showed in their deaths demonstrated.[8] 3. Annaeus Lucanus[9] and Plautius Lateranus[10] brought to it impassioned hatred. Lucanus had personal motives for anger: Nero, fatuously thinking himself his [Lucanus's] rival, was trying to suppress the fame of his poems and had forbidden him from giving them public exposure. In the case of Lateranus, a consul designate, it was no personal slight but rather patriotism that brought him into the plot. 4. Flavius Scaevinus and Afranius Quintianus, both of senatorial rank, belied their reputations in embracing such a bold enterprise from the start.[11] Scaevinus's mental powers had been weakened by his excesses, and he therefore led a life of languid indolence, while Quintianus was notorious for his effeminacy, and having been insulted by Nero in a scurrilous poem, he was now set on revenge for the humiliation.

50.1. These men were therefore dropping hints among themselves or their friends about the emperor's crimes, saying that his reign was coming to an end and that a man must be chosen to succor the ailing state; and they brought into their circle the Roman knights Claudius Senecio, Cervarius Proculus, Vulcacius Araricus, Julius Augurinus, Munatius Gratus, Antonius

8 We see an inherent weakness in the conspiracy at the outset. At 15.65, Tacitus tells us that Subrius is said to have planned to replace Nero ultimately not with Piso but with Seneca. Nothing is known about Subrius or his colleague beyond what is told in the sources about this episode. As Tacitus concedes, he gives them a prime role in the conspiracy essentially because of their later conduct, after the plot had been exposed.

9 Annaeus Lucanus is the famous poet Lucan, author of *De Bello Civili* about the conflict between Caesar and Pompey; on the paternal side, he was the nephew of Seneca. He was born in AD 39 in Cordoba in Spain, to a well-to-do family, and was brought to Rome as an infant. He became one of Nero's intimate circle and won a prize at the Neronia of AD 60 (Stat. *Silv.* 2.7.58). At some point, he is said to have held a quaestorship, although he was only twenty-six at the time of his death. The notion of artistic envy is raised elsewhere in Tacitus, as in Nero's motives for murdering Britannicus, and is no doubt exaggerated. Tacitus much admired the poetry of Lucan, and groups him with Horace and Vergil (*Dial.* 20.8).

10 Plautius Lateranus was accused of adultery with Messalina in AD 48. He was expelled at that time from the Senate but escaped the death penalty because of the reputation of his uncle Aulus Plautius, who commanded the Roman forces against Britain in AD 43 (Tac. *Ann.* 11.36.4). He was readmitted to the Senate by Nero and was consul designate at the time of the conspiracy. He was the only participant of senatorial or equestrian rank to whom Tacitus ascribes lofty motives. Juvenal (10.15) cites him as an example of the dangers of wealth and observes how his fine house on the Caelian Hill was seized on Nero's orders. It presumably became imperial property. As noted in Chapter I, the property of the Laterani was eventually given to the Church, and the name is preserved as "Lateran."

11 Flavius and Afranius are unknown outside the *Annals*. Tacitus mentions that Flavius was a close friend of Petronius, Nero's "arbiter of good taste" (*arbiter elegantiae: Ann.* 16.18.2); both shared the same languid approach to life.

Natalis, and Marcius Festus.[12] 2. Senecio had been particularly close to Nero and, since even at that time he kept up a façade of friendship, he was confronted with a multitude of dangers. Natalis was acquainted with all of Piso's secrets. For the others, fulfillment of their aspirations was being sought via revolution.

3. Military assistance was also enlisted—in addition to Subrius and Sulpicius, whom I mentioned earlier—from Gavius Silvanus[13] and Statius Proxumus, tribunes of the praetorian cohorts, and from the centurions Maximus Scaurus and Venetus Paulus.

However, their chief strength appeared to reside in the prefect Faenius Rufus.[14] His lifestyle and reputation won him general approval, but Tigellinus surpassed him in the emperor's estimation because of his barbarity and immorality.[15] Tigellinus kept hounding the man with accusations and had often frightened him by portraying him as a lover of Agrippina, bent on revenge for losing her. 4. Eventually, the conspirators were convinced, by the frequent comments he himself made, that the prefect of the praetorian guard had joined their side, and they began to discuss more readily the timing and location of the assassination. It was said that Subrius Flavus felt an urge to

12 Claudius Senecio is no doubt the person named as an ally of Nero, along with Otho, in the emperor's affair with Acte, and identified as the son of an imperial freedman (Tac. *Ann.* 13.12.1); the others on the list are unknown. Antonius Natalis and Cervarius Proculus go on to give evidence against their colleagues, in Proculus's case against Faenius, for which they are granted a pardon (Tac. *Ann.* 15.66, 71.1).

13 Gavius Silvanus came from Augusta Taurinorum (Turin) (*CIL* V. 7003). As praetorian tribune, he would have been a soldier of long service. He would be acquitted but later committed suicide.

14 Faenius Rufus was an equestrian who in AD 55 became the prefect in charge of the grain supply, thanks to the support of Agrippina (Tac. *Ann.* 13.22.1). It was an important office, and he may have been responsible for the construction of the *horrea Faeniana* (*CIL* VI 37796). He was held in generally high esteem in Rome. In AD 62, he was appointed joint prefect of the praetorians as a colleague of Tigellinus (Tac. *Ann.* 14.51.2).

15 Ofonius Tigellinus was reputedly of lowly origins, and came to be regarded as the quintessential evil counselor of Nero. From the time of Caligula, he had connections with the imperial family, and Dio (59.23.9) tells us that he was banished from Rome on the grounds of a supposed affair with Agrippina. The Scholiast on Juvenal 1.155 claims he had an affair with Agrippina and her husband, as well as with her sister and her sister's husband, and that he went into exile in Greece and became a fisherman. Claudius allowed him to return, but he was barred from the court circles. He bought land in Apulia and raised horses. Nero made him his prefect of the *vigiles* in about 60 AD, and after the death of Burrus he became, in 62, praetorian prefect, along with Faenius Rufus. He was highly honored following the conspiracy and accompanied Nero on his later journey to Greece. He was forced to commit suicide by Otho.

make the attack on Nero as he sang onstage or as he scurried here and there at night without an escort. In the latter scenario, it was Nero's isolation that had stimulated his enthusiasm, and in the other the very presence of a crowd—a fine witness to a great exploit. But a wish to avoid punishment, always an impediment to great endeavors, held him back.

The plot is compromised through the carelessness of a freedwoman, Epicharis.

Tac. *Ann.* 15.51.1. Meanwhile, a certain Epicharis had gained information about the plot—how is unclear, as she had previously had no interest in honorable causes—and as the conspirators vacillated and were deferring their hopes, and their fears, she began to incite and criticize them.[16] She finally grew tired of their inertia and, as she was spending some time in Campania, she attempted to weaken the loyalty of the officers of the fleet at Misenum and to enlist them as co-conspirators by taking the following steps.

2. Volusius Proculus was one of the captains in the fleet there. He had been one of Nero's henchmen in his mother's murder[17] but, to his way of thinking, had not received the advancement that such an important crime merited. Proculus may have been known to Epicharis for some time, or possibly the acquaintance had been recently made, but he revealed to her his services to Nero and how they had turned out to be of no benefit to him. He added further complaints and said that he would take his revenge if the opportunity arose, thus giving Epicharis hope that he could be pushed into

16 Tacitus (*Ann.* 15.48.1) speaks of "women" being involved in the conspiracy. This is not just for rhetorical effect: Lucan denounced his own mother, Seneca's wife attempted suicide, and Antonia, daughter of Claudius, was accused of involvement. But the only major role is attributed to Epicharis, whose courage is attested later in the account (*Ann.* 15.57). It is perhaps a sign of the general incompetence of the conspiracy that Epicharis somehow found out about it and then sought to recruit allies. It is frustrating that Tacitus provides so little information on her background and does not tell us who her former owner was. According to Polyaenus (*Strat.* 8.62), she was a prostitute and the mistress of Seneca's brother, Annaeus Mela, the father of Lucan. Mela killed himself when he was suspected of being an accessory to the conspiracy (Tac. *Ann.* 16.17.1–5). It is possible that Seneca and his brother had a more central role in the conspiracy than Tacitus (unlike Dio) chooses to ascribe to them, especially if Tacitus was following the version of Fabius Rusticus, and that Epicharis had found out about the conspiracy through them.

17 Proculus's name is not mentioned in the actual account of the murder, but since it was engineered by the commander of the fleet at Misenum, we must assume that he was one of the commander's subordinates. Or perhaps this passage hints at Tacitus's use of different source materials for different episodes. It seems remarkable that Epicharis would have revealed the plot to someone with this supposed background.

action and win more supporters. In the fleet, too, she thought, they would have no small help, and many opportunities, because Nero enjoyed outings on the sea in the area around Puteoli and Misenum.

3. So Epicharis went further, listing all the emperor's crimes and saying that nothing remained sacred anymore. But, she added, measures had been put in place whereby Nero could be punished for bringing down the state. Proculus need only prepare himself to do his part and bring to their cause his bravest men, for which he could expect appropriate rewards. The names of the conspirators, however, Epicharis withheld. 4. Thus, although Proculus reported to Nero what he had been told, his denunciation was worthless, for when Epicharis was called in and confronted with her informer, she easily confuted him since he had no witnesses to support him. But she was herself detained in custody, since Nero suspected that what was not demonstrably true was not necessarily false.

The mistake of Epicharis alarms the conspirators but does not galvanize them into immediate action. The conspirators agree on the details of the attack.

Tac. *Ann.* 15.52.1. Prompted by fear of betrayal, however, the conspirators decided to advance the assassination, which would now take place in Piso's villa at Baiae—Nero was taken with its charming ambience and often went there, enjoying baths and dinners, and dispensing with guards and the weighty trappings of his position.[18] Piso, however, objected, putting forward as an excuse the antipathy they would face if the sanctity of the table, and the gods of hospitality, were stained with an emperor's blood, whatever the man's qualities. It would be better for them to carry out in the city—in that detested abode built through the pillaging of Roman citizens or else in a public area—the deed they had undertaken for the good of the state.[19]

2. This was for general consumption, but Piso secretly harbored fears about Lucius Silanus. Silanus had an outstanding pedigree and had been elevated to every distinction as a result of his training under Gaius Cassius, in whose home he had been brought up, and Piso therefore feared he might seize power. And those who had no connection with the conspiracy, and

18 An additional objection to the choice of Baiae for the assassination is that the location would be eerily reminiscent of Nero's murder of Agrippina.

19 The "detested abode" is clearly an allusion to the Golden House (see *Ann.* 15.42.1 and Chapter VI), but this cannot yet have been ready for occupation; indeed, construction had only just begun on it, and Nero at the time was living in the Servilian Gardens (*Ann.* 15.55.1).

would feel sorry for Nero as the victim of a criminal assassination, would be ready to hand it to him. 3. Several people also thought that this was Piso's way of avoiding the problem of the highly intelligent consul Vestinus, who might rise up in the cause of liberty or who, choosing another as emperor, might make the state his own personal gift to that individual, for Vestinus had no part in the conspiracy, though it was on such a charge that Nero later sated his old hatred of an innocent man.

53.1. They finally decided to carry out their plan on that day of the circus games that is consecrated to Ceres.[20] Nero rarely went out, and kept himself shut up in his home and gardens,[21] but he did regularly attend the entertainments in the circus, where access to him was easier in the merry atmosphere of the show. 2. They had established a program for the plot. Lateranus would fall as a suppliant before the emperor's knees, pretending to be begging him for financial assistance. Surprising him, he would knock him over and, being a man with a strong will and large physique, keep him pinned down.[22] At that point, with Nero helpless on the ground, the tribunes and centurions, and any others who had the courage, would run up and butcher him. (Scaevinus insisted on the leading role for himself; he had taken down a dagger in the temple of Salus—or, according to others, of Fortuna—in the town of Ferentinum, and was carrying it about as though it were consecrated to some great exploit.)[23] 3. Meanwhile, Piso was to wait at the Temple of Ceres.[24] The prefect Faenius and the others would summon him from there and carry him into the camp, and Claudius Caesar's daughter Antonia would

20 The chief festival of Ceres, primarily a plebeian one, was held April 12–19. The last day, the anniversary of the founding of her temple, was the main day, when horse races were held in the Circus Maximus and foxes were let loose with burning brands attached to their tails (Ovid *Fast.* 4.681–712).

21 The gardens are the Horti Serviliani. The identification of the "home" is uncertain.

22 The story is reminiscent of that of Haterius, who grabbed Tiberius's knees in supplication, at the time of his accession, and knocked him over (Tac. *Ann.* 1.13.6).

23 The Temple of Salus stood on the Quirinal in Rome. The expression "in Etruria" follows the mention of Salus in the manuscript, assumed by editors to be a gloss, since the expression is too vague to be informative. But it may be that Tacitus wished to stress that it was not the Temple of Salus that stood on the Quirinal in Rome. This would suggest that the Etrurian temple was well known at the time. It is also possible that Tacitus was referring to a single temple but was not sure about the deity's name. The town appears in a corrupt form in the manuscript but is almost certainly Ferentium (modern Ferentino) in Etruria, famed as the birthplace of Otho (Tac. *Hist.* 2.50.1; Suet. *Otho* 1).

24 The Temple of Ceres stood near the Circus Maximus, so it must be assumed that it had been restored after the Fire of 64 (Tac. *Ann.* 2.49.1).

be with them,[25] according to the account of Gaius Plinius,[26] in order to win over the support of the mob. 4. I did not consider suppressing this version, whatever its value, although it does seem odd that Antonia should have lent her name to, and taken the risk for, such a forlorn hope. Odd, too, that Piso, whose love for his wife was well known, should have committed himself to another marriage—unless ambition for power burns hotter than all other feelings.[27]

Suet. *Ner.* 35.4. There was, in fact, no sort of family tie that he did not criminally destroy. When Claudius's daughter Antonia refused to marry him after Poppaea's death, he executed her, allegedly for fomenting revolution, and his treatment of all connected with him by any blood relationship or marriage was similar.

Carelessness of Flavius Scaevinus betrays the plot, and he and his colleague Antonius Natalis break down under interrogation.

Tac. *Ann.* 15.54.1. What is amazing is that it was all kept veiled in secrecy amid people of different families, classes, ages, and sex, and among rich and poor alike—until, that is, betrayal proceeded from the house of Scaevinus.[28]

25 Antonia was the oldest daughter of Claudius, by Aelia Paetina (Tac. *Ann.* 12.2.1). She married Gnaeus Pompeius Magnus in AD 41 and then, after his death, Faustus Cornelius Sulla (see Chapter III). After the murder of Faustus and the death of Poppaea, Nero supposedly wanted to marry Antonia (surprisingly, if she was a conspirator), and she rejected him. Suetonius (*Ner.* 35.4) suggests that this was the reason why Nero decided to put her to death, implicating her in the conspiracy as an excuse. Dio (61.1.2) confirms, without elaborating, that Nero eliminated her. Pliny, according to Tacitus here, said that after the murder of Nero it was planned that Piso would join with Antonia because of her popularity, a notion that does not convince Tacitus (nor Syme [1958], 192). Marriage to Antonia would presumably have helped remove a source of opposition to Nero. Syme describes Pliny as "credulous" and deems this account a "silly story."

26 Pliny the Elder wrote a history of the later Julio-Claudian period, and Tacitus (*Ann.* 13.20.2) cites him as the source for the claim that Burrus's loyalty was not suspect. The history was mentioned by Pliny the Younger (*Ep.* 3.5.6) and by the elder Pliny himself (*HN*, Pref 20).

27 Tacitus suggests cryptically that Piso might well have pondered marrying Antonia had the conspiracy been successful and had he been appointed as successor.

28 Tacitus here seems to have forgotten about the misjudgment of Epicharis. Plutarch (*De garr.* 7) gives a variant explanation that a conspiracy, almost certainly this one, was betrayed by a careless comment from an indiscreet conspirator (possibly Scaevinus). He assured a prisoner about to go before Nero that by the next day he would have nothing to worry about, and he was betrayed by the prisoner to the emperor.

The day before the coup,[29] Scaevinus had a long conversation with Antonius Natalis. After that, he returned home, sealed his will, and took the dagger I mentioned earlier from its sheath. Complaining that it had become blunt over time, he gave orders for it to be whetted with a stone until its point was gleaming, and this task he confided to his freedman Milichus. 2. At the same time, he took a more sumptuous dinner than usual and bestowed gifts on his slaves—freedom for his favorites, and money for others. And Scaevinus himself was downcast and clearly deep in thought, though he did make some rambling conversation to feign cheerfulness. 3. Finally, he ordered dressings for wounds and articles for arresting bleeding to be prepared, and he again put this in Milichus's charge. Either Milichus was privy to the conspiracy and remained loyal to this point or he knew nothing and now became suspicious for the first time, which is what most sources have reported.

4. On what happened next, there is agreement. When the man's servile mind thought over the rewards of treachery, and at the same time the unlimited money and power danced before his eyes, then moral obligation, the safety of his patron, and the memory of the freedom he had been given all faded away. And, in fact, he had also accepted the advice of his wife—womanly advice and quite despicable,[30] for she worked on him with a further motive, fear, noting that numerous freedmen and slaves had been present and seen the same things as he. The silence of one man would do no good, she told him, but the rewards would come to just one man—the one who turned informer first.

55.1. So, at daybreak,[31] Milichus set off for the Gardens of Servilius.[32] As he was being turned away from the door, he kept repeating that he brought important and dreadful news, and he was then escorted by the doorkeepers to Nero's freedman Epaphroditus, and by Epaphroditus to Nero.[33] He then

29 That would be April 18.

30 A general theme of the *Annals* is the inordinate influence exercised by women like Agrippina and Messalina over their husbands. This passage is an interesting insight into the fact that Tacitus did not feel that the excessive influence of women was restricted to the nobility.

31 The date would now be April 19.

32 The precise location of the Gardens of Servilius is uncertain. Nero went there on a later occasion (Suet. *Ner.* 47.1), when contemplating flight to Ostia, and they thus presumably lay between Ostia and the Palatine. Tacitus (*Hist.* 3.38.1) reports that Vitellius occupied them when he was seriously ill.

33 Epaphroditus was *a libellis* (in charge of petitions) to Nero, possibly succeeding Doryphorus, who died in AD 62 (Tac. *Ann.* 14.65.1), in that role. He was wealthy, the owner of gardens near the Anio Novus aqueduct (Front. *Aq.* 68). He would assist Nero's suicide (Suet. *Ner.* 49.3; Dio 63.27.3) and was executed for so doing by Domitian, on the

told Nero of the imminent danger, the formidable conspirators he faced, and everything else that he had heard or surmised. He also displayed the weapon that had been made ready for Nero's murder and insisted that the culprit be brought in.

2. Arrested by some soldiers, Scaevinus opened his defense with the retort that the weapon that he took to be the basis of the charge was a venerated family heirloom. He kept it in his bedchamber, he said, and it had been removed by his treacherous freedman. On numerous occasions, he had signed the tablets of his will, he added, without taking note of the dates. He had also previously made gifts of money or emancipation to his slaves[34] but had done so more generously at this time because, with his financial situation now weak and his creditors pressing, he had little confidence in his will. 3. Moreover, he had always put on ample dinners while he could enjoy his agreeable lifestyle, one not meeting the approval of moralizing critics. No dressings for wounds had been prepared on his orders, he said. It was because the other accusations were patently groundless that the freedman had added this one, for which he could be both informer and witness!

4. Scaevinus backed up his statements with complete self-possession. He actually went on the offensive, calling the man a detestable scoundrel, and with such confidence in his voice and expression that the informer's case began to fall apart. It would have done so, in fact, but for Milichus's wife reminding him of Antonius Natalis's long private conversations with Scaevinus and the fact that both were close associates of Piso.[35]

56.1. Natalis was therefore called in, and the two men were interrogated separately on the nature and subject of their conversation. Then, because their answers did not match, suspicion arose and they were put in irons. And at the sight and threat of torture, they could hold out no longer.[36] 2. The

---

grounds that one should never slay a patron, no matter how well motivated one may be (Suet. *Dom.* 14.4; Dio 67.14.4). He was a close friend of Josephus, who dedicated his *Antiquities* to him (Joseph. *AJ* 1.8, 430; *Ap.* 1.1, 2.1, 2.296). According to the Byzantine encyclopedia the *Suda*, the famed philosopher Epictetus was originally one of his slaves. We know from epigraphic evidence that Epaphroditus received honors, and these could well have been in recognition of the services he rendered in exposing this plot.

34 Legacies in a will were confirmed only when debts had been paid off. The same would apply to manumission of slaves made in a will.

35 We have to assume here that Milichus had accompanied Scaevinus when he visited Natalis. Piso's name would be expected to ring alarm bells, not necessarily because of the present conspiracy (he had not yet been named in that connection) but because he had been suspected of conspiracy some three years earlier, in AD 62 (Tac. *Ann.* 14.65.2).

36 Torture was a device regularly used to extract information from slaves. Its use on Roman citizens is strongly implied by Suetonius (*Tib.* 62.1) in describing the response of

first to break was Natalis, who had a fuller knowledge of the conspiracy as a whole and more skill as a denouncer. He first confessed with regard to Piso and then added Annaeus Seneca, either because Seneca was actually the go-between for him and Piso or because Natalis wanted to ingratiate himself with Nero (who, hating Seneca, was seeking any means to bring him down).[37] 3. Then, after learning of Natalis's disclosure, Scaevinus also showed the same weakness—or perhaps he thought that all had now been revealed and silence would do no good—and gave away the others. Of these, Lucanus, Quintianus, and Senecio long denied their guilt.[38] Later, tempted by the promise of impunity, and as a way of gaining leniency for their slowness, they named names—Lucanus naming his own mother, Aelia,[39] and Quintianus and Senecio each their best friends, Glitius Gallus[40] and Annius Pollio, respectively.[41]

Epicharis is now subjected to vicious torture.

Tac. *Ann.* 15.57.1. Now, in the meantime, Nero remembered that Epicharis was being detained on information laid by Volusius Proculus and, believing that a woman's constitution could not cope with pain, he had her subjected to body-rending torture. But no lashing, no burning, and no furious treatment

---

Tiberius to the evidence that his son Drusus was poisoned. Claudius promised to abstain from it upon his accession, but it proved an empty promise, as even senators were tortured (Dio 60.15.6); Tacitus (*Ann.* 11.22.1) records that an equestrian, Gnaeus Nonius, was tortured in connection with a plot to assassinate Claudius.

37 On Seneca, see Tac. *Ann.* 15.60.2.

38 On Lucan, see Tac. *Ann.* 15.49.2–4.

39 The anonymous *Life of Lucan* tells us that the poet's mother, Aelia (the spelling of her name is uncertain), came from Cordoba and was the daughter of one of the city's most famous orators, Acilius Lucanus. Her life would be spared (Tac. *Ann.* 15.71.5 [Acilia]). No harm came to Lucan's wife, Argentaria Polla, who lived on for many years and was active as a patron of literature (Stat. *Silv.* 2 *praef.*; Mart. 7.21–23, 10.64).

40 Glitius Gallus was perhaps connected to the general Corbulo through the latter's mother, who was first married to a Publius Glitius Gallus (*CIL* V 5345). He was banished to the island of Andros, where his wife accompanied him. His possessions were later restored to him by Otho (Plut. *Otho* 1.3; implied by Tac. *Hist.* 1.90.1).

41 Annius Pollio was also exiled. He may be the son of the Annius Pollio consul in AD 21 or 22, and the grandson of Vinicianus, consul late in Tiberius's reign, who played a prominent role in the final plot against Caligula and was later involved in the revolt of Furius Camillus against Claudius in AD 42, committing suicide when it failed (Dio 50.15.2–5). Both father and grandfather were accused of treason under Tiberius (Tac. *Ann.* 6.9.3). Glitius and Annius were not among the conspirators identified earlier; they may be among those who returned to Rome later and testified to the conspiracy (Tac. *Ann.* 15.73.2).

from her torturers—who piled on the pressure so as not to be bested by a woman—could break her denial of the charges. Thus, the first day of the inquisition was a failure. 2. On the next, she was being brought back by means of a chair (her limbs were now dislocated, and she could not stand) to face the same torments when she took the band from her breast, attached it to the chair's canopy in the form of a noose, put her neck into it, and, throwing the weight of her body into the effort, choked out what little life she had left. Thus, a freedwoman set all the more brilliant an example in such dire circumstances, protecting people unrelated, indeed almost strangers, to her—and that when male free persons, who were Roman knights and senators, were all betraying their nearest and dearest, without being subjected to torture.

Dio 62.27.3. Noteworthy, too, was a certain woman called Epicharis.[42] She had taken part in the conspiracy, and all its planning had been confided in her, but she gave absolutely nothing away despite being tortured time and again by the dreadful Tigellinus.

More participants are rounded up.

Tac. *Ann.* 15.58.1. For Lucanus, too, and Senecio and Quintianus, did not fail to tell on their accomplices, one after the other,[43] while Nero grew more and more frightened, despite having redoubled the guards with which he surrounded himself.

2. In fact, Nero virtually put the city under arrest, keeping the walls manned with military units, and the sea and river under close surveillance.[44] There were also foot and horse soldiers—with Germans in their ranks, trusted by the emperor as being foreigners—tearing about the forums and private houses, and even through the countryside and closest municipalities.[45] 3. And so neverending columns of manacled prisoners were being

42 Dio gives Epicharis a much more direct role in the events than does Tacitus. Here she is an active conspirator, and the details of the plot have been confided to her. Tacitus implies that she might have found out about it accidentally.

43 The contrast between the conduct of these men and Epicharis as just described is striking and deliberate.

44 Presumably, Nero would have strengthened the unit at Ostia and at landing places on the Tiber.

45 Germans, mainly from Batavia, constituted the main element of the emperor's private bodyguard and were distinct from the praetorians, who were a formal part of the Roman army. The Germans were recruited initially by Augustus and disbanded after the

dragged out and left waiting near the gates of the gardens. Then, when they went in to plead their case, it was not simply a matter of support for the conspirators being regarded as a crime; so, too, were a casual conversation, chance meetings, and attending a dinner or a show in their company. And all the while, in addition to the ruthless interrogation by Nero and Tigellinus, Faenius Rufus was piling on violent pressure. He had not yet been named by the informers, and to make people believe that he knew nothing, he was pitiless toward his accomplices. 4. When Subrius Flavus was standing at his side and inquired with a gesture whether he should draw his sword and assassinate Nero during the actual investigation, the same Rufus shook his head and checked the man's ardor, as he was already bringing his hand to his sword hilt.[46]

Piso now vacillates.

Tac. *Ann.* 15.59.1. After the conspiracy had been betrayed, at the time when Milichus was being given his audience and Scaevinus was hesitating, there were some who urged Piso to march into the camp or mount the rostrum and work on the feelings of the soldiery and the people. If his fellow conspirators rallied in support of his effort, they told him, nonpartisans would also follow; the coup, once started, would have great publicity, which was extremely important for revolutionary movements. 2. Against this, Nero had taken no precautions, and brave men, too, were unnerved by the unexpected—there was much less chance then of a counterattack from this stage performer, with Tigellinus and his concubines at his side! Many things that the timid think difficult are brought off just by the attempt! 3. With the numbers involved, hoping for silence and loyalty was useless when all those minds and bodies could be worked on—torture or bribery can penetrate anything! Men would come to shackle him, too, and finally put him to an ignominious death, they said. How much more creditable to die embracing his state and calling for help for its liberty! Better that the soldiers not join him and that the plebs abandon him—provided that he himself, if his life must

---

Varan disaster, but were reinstated shortly afterward. They proved to be fiercely loyal. They had shown their loyalty during the assassination of Caligula, when, unlike the praetorians, they ruthlessly sought out the murderers.

46 Tacitus is here explicit about Subrius Flavus's conduct. Elsewhere in this section, he expresses reservations. In *Ann.* 15.50.4, "it was said" that Subrius was planning to make an attack on Nero, and in *Ann.* 16.65 there "was a rumor" that he had hatched some plot with Seneca. This new dogmatism may reflect the efforts of Tacitus's source, Fabius Rusticus, to divert blame from Seneca.

be prematurely taken, make his death a credit to his ancestors and to his descendants.[47]

4. Piso was not persuaded. He spent a short time in the streets, after which he shut himself up at home and stiffened his resolve to meet the end—until the arrival of military units (men of Nero's choosing, newly recruited or recently enlisted—veterans were feared as being infected with sympathy for Piso). 5. He died by severing the veins in his arms. His will, marked by disgusting obsequiousness toward Nero, he made as a concession to his wife, whom he loved. She was of low birth, with only good looks to commend her, and Piso had taken her out of an earlier marriage to a friend of his. The woman's name was Satria Galla, the former husband's Domitius Silus. Both contributed to Piso's bad name: the man by his acquiescence, the woman by her shame.[48]

Plautius Lateranus and then Seneca are the next victims.

Tac. *Ann.* 15.60.1. The next murder that Nero registered was that of the consul designate Plautius Lateranus, and with such speed as not to allow him to embrace his children or have that short moment to choose how to die. He was rushed to a location reserved for punishments for slaves and there was butchered at the hands of the tribune Statius. Lateranus maintained all the while a resolute silence and did not reproach the tribune with involvement in the plot.

2. Next came the killing of Annaeus Seneca, for the emperor the sweetest.[49] Not that he had discovered any proof of Seneca's involvement in the

47 Tacitus's lengthy and rather rhetorical enumeration of the reasons for Piso to take action are intended to emphasize his dithering when there was still a chance, however slim, of the coup being successful.

48 Satria Galla and Domitius Silius are known only from these references. There is a suggestion that Domitius had been a *mari complaisant* in a previous affair between his wife and Piso. Otherwise, in Roman eyes there would have been no disgrace in the divorce and the remarriage.

49 Seneca dominates Tacitus's account of the conspiracy, standing at its center. Tacitus seems determined to absolve him of guilt, and his account of how he came to be implicated is unpersuasive. He says nothing, for example, of the links between Epicharis and the Annaei (discussed earlier). He makes no comment on the coincidence that Seneca had returned from Campania to be in the vicinity of Rome at the very time that the conspiracy was taking place. In Tacitus's account, Seneca shows a courage and dignity in someone who was probably not part of the plot, in contrast to the behavior of the titular protagonist Piso. Tacitus's description of Seneca and his wife is sympathetic, far more than that of Dio, which suggests that they were drawing on different sources.

conspiracy, but after the failure of the poison, he could now go to work with the sword.[50] 3. In fact, Natalis alone had implicated Seneca, and only to the extent of saying that he had been sent to visit him when he was ill and to express dissatisfaction over his refusing Piso access to him. It would be better, Natalis had said to him, if the two men developed their friendship by meeting on cordial terms, and Seneca's reply had been that conversations between the two, and frequent meetings, were of advantage to neither, but his own life depended on Piso's safety.[51] 4. Gavius Silvanus, tribune of the praetorian cohort, was instructed to report these details to Seneca and ask if he acknowledged such to be Natalis's words and his own reply.[52] Seneca, perhaps intentionally, had been returning from Campania that day and had made a stop at his country estate four miles from Rome. The tribune came to this spot as evening was coming on, and he surrounded the villa with some military units. Then, as Seneca was dining with his wife, Pompeia Paulina,[53] and two friends,[54] he [the tribune] brought him the emperor's message.

50 The true role of Seneca in the conspiracy is uncertain. Dio (62.24.1) presents him as a ringleader. Tacitus leaves the question of his involvement open. We know that Tacitus used two different sources for the conspiracy, Pliny the Elder and Fabius Rusticus, and the uncertainty could reflect his sources, since Fabius Rusticus was an admirer of Seneca and would have been concerned with depicting him in positive terms. The detailed and sympathetic description of the last hours of Seneca is probably an indication that Tacitus leaned heavily on Fabius. The only witness against Seneca provided by Tacitus is Antonius Natalis (*Ann.* 15.60.3), supposedly the contact man between Piso and Seneca, and Tacitus raises the possibility that his evidence may have simply been intended to ingratiate himself with Nero.

It can be argued that in his writings Seneca voices abhorrence of assassination (*Clem* 1.26.1; *Ben.* 2.20.2) and enunciates the principle that the philosopher should not be involved in the elimination of the tyrant (*Constant.* 8.5). But Seneca is someone who somehow always reconciled his lofty Stoic ideals with his own political and material advancement.

51 On the surface, this last statement might seem to indicate complicity in the plot and hope that it would succeed. The implication here of depending on someone's safety may, however, just be a distortion of a formulaic greeting, on the lines of the standard Roman expression *si valeas, bene est, ego quoque valeo* ("if you're well, that's good, I'm well too").

52 Gaius Silvanus is of course one of the conspirators. His involvement here throws into higher relief the contrasting courage of Seneca.

53 Pompeia Paulina was probably the sister of Pompeius Paulinus, consul in about AD 54 and legate of upper Germany in 56 (see Tac. *Ann.* 13.53.1), and was the daughter of an identically named equestrian from Arelate (Arles) (Plin. *HN* 33.143), to whom Seneca addressed *De Brevitate Vitae.*

54 It may be that one of the friends present at the banquet was Fabius Rusticus the historian and that Tacitus used his firsthand account. The other could have been the friend and doctor Statius Annaeus, who is mentioned as being present during Seneca's final banquet (Tac. *Ann.* 15.64.3).

61.1. Seneca replied that Natalis had been sent to him, that he had expressed dissatisfaction on Piso's behalf that Piso had been kept from visiting him, and that he had then excused himself for this on the grounds of ill health and his love of the quiet life. He had no reason to put the life of a private individual ahead of his own safety, he said, nor was he temperamentally prone to obsequiousness—and nobody knew that better than Nero, who had more often had experience of his outspokenness than his servility![55]

2. These remarks of Seneca's were reported by the tribune to Nero while he was with Poppaea and Tigellinus—the emperor's closest advisers in his savage periods.[56] Nero asked Silvanus whether Seneca intended to commit suicide. The tribune then asserted that he had recognized no signs of apprehension, and no distress in his language or expression. He was therefore told to go back and deliver the death sentence. 3. Fabius Rusticus records that the tribune did not return the way he had come but made a detour to the prefect Faenius.[57] Having told Faenius about Nero's orders, he asked whether he should obey them, and was advised by him—with that fatal cowardice now common to all—to carry them out. 4. For Silvanus, too, was one of the conspirators, and he was now increasing the number of crimes he had plotted to avenge. He did spare himself from saying or seeing anything, however, sending one of the centurions to Seneca with the announcement of his final obligation.

62.1. Undaunted, Seneca called for the tablets of his will.[58] The centurion refused, and Seneca, turning to his friends, declared that, since he was barred

55 Seneca's response is rather convoluted, but he seems to suggest that he would have no reason to put the well-being of a *private* individual (that is, anyone other than the emperor) before his own, and that his career had shown that he would not say that just to flatter Piso. Seneca makes the claim at *Clem.* 2.2 that he was not obsequious. Tacitus seems to be at pains simply to record Seneca's words without commenting on how convincing, or otherwise, he found them.

56 Under Augustus, a formal *consilium principis* (council of close advisers) was appointed by lot to sit as a group and advise the *princeps*. This system of lots was abandoned by Tiberius, and later emperors chose members, which could include equestrians, at their own discretion. Whether Tacitus intends to suggest that the formal *consilium* included Tigellinus and Poppaea is difficult to say; he may have an informal grouping in mind. This is the last appearance in Tacitus of the living Poppaea.

57 The reference to Fabius Rusticus is significant, since it is an indication that Tacitus was using him as his source for the death of Seneca. Tacitus (*Ann.* 13.20.2) comments that Fabius "tends to eulogize Seneca," to whose friendship he owed his success. This particular incident serves again to show the general cowardice of those involved in the conspiracy, in contrast to the conduct of Seneca.

58 The expression seems to suggest that the tablets on which his will appeared had already been written, and the context implies that Seneca wants to add codicils to leave legacies to the friends who are present with him.

from repaying them for their services, he was leaving them the one thing he still had but the one that was also the best: the model of his life.[59] If they kept that in mind, he said, they would gain a reputation for good character as their reward for loyal friendship. 2. At the same time, he alternated normal conversation with sterner, coercive tones in order to halt their tears and revive their courage. Where were their philosophical tenets, he asked, and where that rationality they had pondered on for so many years to counter impending misfortune? For who had been unaware of Nero's ruthlessness? After killing his mother and his brother, nothing else remained but to add the murder of his guardian and tutor.[60]

63.1. After these words, which had the air of a public address, Seneca embraced his wife. Then, softening a little, despite his present resolve, he asked and entreated her to limit her grief and not keep it up forever—she should find honorable solace for the loss of her husband in reflecting on the life of virtue that he had lived. Her firm response was that she, too, had decided to die, and she demanded for herself the executioner's blow.[61] 2. Seneca was not opposed to her noble decision, and his love also prompted him not to leave the woman he cherished above all to be maltreated. "I showed you how to make life more palatable," he said, "but you prefer the glory of death, and I shall not begrudge you the fine example. For such a courageous end, let us both have the same resolve, but may your leaving have the greater fame." After that, they cut their arms with the same stroke of the

59 Seneca seems to have assumed that his will would be valid. Tacitus (*Ann.* 6.29.2) lays out the principle that in the case of suicide committed before condemnation, a will would remain valid, and Seneca apparently had faith that such a provision would apply. The centurion perhaps believed that the entire estate would be seized by the emperor and that allowing Seneca to add codicils might raise unnecessary legal complications. Dio (62.25.3) says that he had earlier assigned all his property to the emperor to aid in the rebuilding of Rome, but that is clearly an exaggeration, since he still at the very least had his country estates.

60 Tacitus, possibly relying on Fabius here, does not comment on the hypocrisy that would be apparent from Seneca's own comment on Agrippina's murder. He was similarly restrained when noting that Seneca even wrote the letter that Nero sent to the Senate justifying her murder. He reports that Seneca suffered much opprobrium for that (*Ann.* 14.11.3). There is no record of his making any protest when Nero supposedly murdered Britannicus, and, surprisingly, he is not reported as saying anything here about the death of Octavia, an outrage that had occurred when he had lost his influence over Nero and could not be held to blame.

61 In Dio's account (62.25.1), which is much less favorable toward him, Seneca forced his wife to open her veins with him, but, because he died first, she was able to survive. Seneca does refer to the affection that she felt for him in the only mention of her that he makes (Sen. *Ep.* 104.2).

blade.[62] 3. Seneca's aging body, emaciated by his spare diet, allowed only slow escape for the blood, and so he also severed the veins in his legs and at the backs of his knees. Worn down by the cruel torment, and not wishing to break his wife's spirit with his suffering or have himself lapse into indecision through seeing her agonies, he persuaded her to retire to another bedroom. And since his eloquence still remained even in his very last moments, he summoned his scribes and dictated a long work to them. As this has been published in his own words, I refrain from paraphrasing it.[63]

64.1. Nero, in fact, had no personal grudge against Paulina, and fearing a surge of animosity over his cruelty, he ordered her suicide to be stopped.[64] Prompted by the soldiers, her slaves and freedmen bandaged her arms and stanched the bleeding, though whether she was unconscious is unclear. 2. (For, the public being ever ready to believe the worst, there was no shortage of people who thought that she had sought the renown of dying with her husband as long as she feared that Nero was implacable, but fell victim to life's charms when offered a more favorable prospect.) To her life, she then added only a few years, maintaining a laudable fidelity to her husband's memory, and with face and body so pale and white as to show that much of her life force had been sapped away.[65]

3. Meanwhile, Seneca's death was slow and drawn out. He begged Statius Annaeus,[66] who had proved himself a steadfast friend and skillful doctor over a long period, to bring out the poison that was used for executing those condemned in the public court of Athens and that had been prepared sometime before.[67] When this was brought, Seneca drained it, but in vain—his limbs were already cold, rendering his body immune to the poison's effects.

62 The death of Seneca is portrayed in the noblest of terms, and, in fact, nowhere else does Tacitus give such a detailed and moving account of someone's death. One can of course be cynical and say that, since he knew that his survival was impossible, Seneca exploited his death to earn a noble place in history.

63 Dio (62.25.2) adds that he took the precaution of having his last words placed out of the reach of Nero.

64 No explanation is given for how the incident could have been reported to Nero and how his order for the suicide to be prevented could have been carried out in sufficient time.

65 Tacitus makes no reference to the less flattering account that appears in Dio.

66 Statius Annaeus is otherwise unknown, but his name suggests that he might have been a client of Seneca, probably his former slave, who acquired his old master's name after manumission.

67 By Athens Seneca alludes to the famous death of Socrates, on which Seneca expatiated, calling hemlock the "elixir of immortal life" and noting that Socrates discussed the nature of death at the end (*Prov.* 3.12); it seems that Seneca had long envisaged Socrates' death as a prototype for his own.

4. Finally, he went into a pool of hot water, spattering the slaves closest to him, and adding the comment that with that liquid he was making a libation to Jupiter the Liberator.[68] He was then taken into the bath, where he suffocated in the steam. He was cremated with no funeral ceremony. Such was the instruction he had left in his will when he was—even at the height of his wealth and power—thinking about his end.

65. There was a rumor that Subrius Flavus had formulated a secret plan with the centurions, of which Seneca was not unaware.[69] The plan was that, after Nero had been assassinated through Piso's initiative, Piso would also be killed, and the imperial command would be transferred to Seneca, an innocent man and chosen for supreme power on the basis of his renowned virtues. In fact, there was also a saying of Flavus in circulation that the disgrace remained the same if a lyre player was removed and a tragic actor succeeded him (for while Nero sang with the lyre, Piso did so in tragic costume).[70]

Dio 62.25. To tell of all the others who lost their lives would be a great undertaking. In Seneca's case, he also wanted to end the life of his wife, Paulina, saying that he had convinced her both to despise death and also to wish her life's end to be simultaneous with his, 2. and so he slit her veins too. His death, however, was lingering, and he was helped to his end by the soldiers and died before her. Thus, Paulina survived him.[71] Nevertheless, Seneca did not set to work on himself before revising the book he was writing and storing the others with certain people, as he was afraid that they would be destroyed if they came into Nero's hands. 3. Such was the man's death, despite

68 It was the custom to close Greek banquets with an offering made to Zeus Sôter ("Zeus the Savior"). The expression Jupiter Liberator is found on Neronian coins and in old calendars (*CIL* 1.2, 274; see Chapter IX). Valerius Maximus (2.6.8) reports that it was the custom to pour a libation from the poisoned cup to Mercury for a safe passage to the next world.

69 The issue of Seneca's complicity in the plot is much disputed, and no resolution of the question is likely to be forthcoming. Given the poor security surrounding the conspiracy and the fact that Epicharis, possibly an associate of Seneca's family, found out about it, it seems unlikely that Seneca could have been completely in the dark.

70 That such a saying was attributed to Flavus is probably not to be doubted. It presumably reflects the fatal lack of enthusiasm that the conspirators felt for Piso. It is, however, difficult to believe that Seneca himself was privy to some such arrangement. The *Laus Pisonis* (166) refers to Piso's skill with the lyre, but he presumably did not play it in public. The Scholiast on Juvenal 5.109 refers to Piso performing in tragedies in costume (see the introductory section).

71 Dio's account of Paulina's experience strips it of the nobility of Tacitus's version. Dio suggests that because Seneca predeceased her, Paulina simply changed her mind. Tacitus claims that Nero intervened to stop her bleeding.

the fact that he had left Nero's court on the grounds of poor health and had freely given him all his property, allegedly for the emperor's building program. Seneca's brothers also perished later.

Further executions follow.

Tac. *Ann.*15.66.1. The soldiers' part in the conspiracy no longer remained secret either, as the informers were burning to denounce Faenius Rufus, whom they could not bear both as conspirator and inquisitor. So, as he was pressured and threatened, Scaevinus said with a smile that no one knew more than Faenius himself, and he urged him to do such a fine emperor a favor of his own accord.[72] 2. Faenius had no reply to this, nor was he silent; instead, he stumbled over his words and was clearly panic-stricken. Then, after a concerted effort by the other conspirators, particularly the Roman knight Cervarius Proculus, to have him convicted, he was, on the emperor's orders, seized and put in irons by Cassius, a soldier who was in attendance because of his remarkable strength.

67.1. Presently, the tribune Subrius Flavus was brought down by the same men's denunciation. At first, he tried to make difference in character his defense, arguing that a soldier such as he would not have associated with unarmed and effeminate individuals for so great a deed. Then, under pressure, he seized on the glory of confessing. 2. Interrogated by Nero on the reasons that brought him to forget his military oath, Subrius declared: "I hated you, but none of your soldiers was more loyal to you while you deserved our affection. I started to hate you when you became the murderer of your mother and wife,[73] and a charioteer, actor, and arsonist." 3. I have given the man's very words because, while they were not published like Seneca's, the powerful, rough-and-ready sentiments of a military man were no less worth recording.

It was well known that nothing in that conspiracy was more painful to Nero's ears, for while he was ready to commit crimes, he was unused to being told what he was doing. 4. Flavus's execution was entrusted to the tribune Veianius Niger. Niger ordered a pit to be dug in a neighboring field, and Flavus criticized it for being shallow and narrow. "Not even this accords with military standard," he remarked to the soldiers standing around him. When

72 Presumably, Scaevinus is urging Faenius to take the initiative and confess before he is accused.

73 The resentment over the murder of Nero's mother, Agrippina, is perhaps surprising. She did not command the same general popularity as Octavia, but she was apparently held in high regard by the praetorian guard. It is to be noted that there is no reference to the fate of Britannicus.

he was told to be firm in stretching out his neck, he replied, "I just wish your blow could be as firm!" The tribune was trembling a lot and had difficulty decapitating him with two blows. He then bragged about his callousness to Nero, saying Flavus had been killed by him with a "stroke and a half."

68.1. The next instance of fortitude was provided by the centurion Sulpicius Asper, who, when Nero asked why he had conspired to murder him, briefly replied that nothing else could be done for all his atrocities.[74] He then suffered the prescribed penalty. The other centurions did not disgrace themselves in facing execution either,[75] though Faenius Rufus did not have the same resolve and even entered lamentations in his will.

Dio 62.24.1.They wanted to be delivered from these ills[76] themselves, and they wanted to rid him [Nero] of them, as the centurion Sulpicius Asper and the military tribune Subrius Flavius, both members of his bodyguard, openly admitted even to Nero himself. 2. When Sulpicius Asper was asked by Nero the reason for the projected coup, he replied, "I could not help you in any other way,"[77] and Flavius said, "I loved you and hated you more than anyone. I loved you when I had hopes that you would be a good emperor, and I hated you because you do these and other things—I cannot be subservient to a charioteer and a lyre-player."[78] Information was laid against these men, and they were punished, and because of them, many others were, too.

The Consul Vestinus, husband of Statilia Messalina, is executed because Nero covets his wife.

Tac. *Ann.* 15.68.2. Nero was waiting for the consul Vestinus, whom he thought a violent man who detested him, to be included in the charge. However, none

74 Sulpicius's words clearly became proverbial, since they are reflected both in Suetonius, who attributes them generally to the conspirators (*Ner.* 36.2), and in Dio. It seems that they are meant to be taken ironically, that Nero had committed such atrocities that only by murdering him could Sulpicius relieve him of the great burden of guilt. The sentiment does not sound right in the mouth of a centurion, unless he was a particularly philosophical one.

75 The other centurions are presumably Maximus Scaurus and Ventus Paulus.

76 By "ills" he means Nero's shortcomings.

77 Both Tacitus and Dio attribute this rather unmilitary sentiment to the centurion Sulpicius Asper. Suetonius suggests that it was a notion expressed by several others.

78 The words supposedly uttered by Subrius Flavus (Flavius in Dio) reflect those found in Tacitus. On several occasions, Tacitus notes Subrius's aversion to Nero as a performer but suggests that he felt that same contempt for Piso and intended to get rid of Piso after the coup and replace him with Seneca.

of the conspirators had communicated their plans to Vestinus, some because of old quarrels with him, more because they thought him a reckless and difficult person. 3. Nero's loathing of Vestinus had arisen from a close companionship with him. In the course of this, Vestinus came to know well, and to despise, the emperor's cowardice, while Nero came to fear his friend's outspokenness; he had many times been the butt of his biting witticisms, which, when they have drawn largely on the truth, leave behind a bitter recollection. There was, in addition, a recent motive for his animosity: Vestinus had married Statilia Messalina, though he was not unaware that Nero was one of her lovers.[79]

69.1. Thus, with no charge and no accuser forthcoming, and as Nero was therefore unable to adopt the guise of judge, he resorted to the force of the despot, sending the tribune Gerellanus to him at the head of a cohort of soldiers. Gerellanus was under orders to take preemptive measures against the consul's designs, seizing Vestinus's "stronghold" and overwhelming his "handpicked young men." (Vestinus owned a house overlooking the Forum, and a number of handsome slaves, all of the same age.) 2. On that day, Vestinus had completed all his consular duties and was hosting a dinner party—fearing nothing or else concealing his fear—when the soldiers entered and told him he was summoned by the tribune. With not a moment's delay, he got up, and everything was hurriedly carried out at once. He shut himself in his bedroom; the doctor was in attendance; the veins were cut; and, still strong, he was carried into the bath and immersed in hot water, letting out no exclamation of self-pity. 3. Meanwhile, those who had been reclining at table with him were surrounded by guards and were not released until late at night. By then, Nero with amusement had pictured their fright as they awaited death following the dinner, and he remarked that they had been punished sufficiently for their consular feast.[80]

70.1. Nero next ordered the murder of Annaeus Lucanus. As the blood flowed, Lucanus felt his feet and hands grow cold and his life gradually slip away from his extremities, though his breast was still warm and his mental powers intact. At that point, he remembered a poem he had composed in which he had presented a wounded soldier dying a similar kind of

79 The comments about Vestinus being innocent of the conspiracy are consistent with what was said about him earlier (Tac. *Ann.* 15.52.3). Suetonius (*Ner.* 35.1) records that Nero killed Vestinus, but he says nothing about his being suspected of involvement in the plot, only that Nero wanted to marry Statilia. On Statilia Messalina, see Chapter VII.

80 Tacitus here stresses Vestinus's innocence of the charges, since Nero had no evidence that would have merited a trial, even a trial held *in camera* by the emperor, where the outcome might well have been determined in advance.

death.[81] He recited those very verses, and they were his last words. Following that, Senecio, Quintianus, and Scaevinus met their ends, in a manner at variance with their soft living of earlier days, and the remainder of the conspirators soon followed, though without any memorable deed or saying.

Further reprisals follow.

Tac. *Ann.* 15.71.1. Meanwhile, the city was filling up with funerals, and the Capitol with sacrificial animals. After the killing of a son—or of a brother, relative, or friend—people gave thanks to the gods, decorated their homes with laurel,[82] fell at the knees of Nero himself, and plied his right hand with kisses.[83] And Nero, believing this to be a manifestation of joy, rewarded Antonius Natalis and Cervarius Proculus for their speedy denunciations with a grant of impunity. Milichus, who was enriched with gifts, adopted the name "Saviour," but used the Greek word for it. 2. Of the tribunes, Gavius Silvanus died by his own hand, although acquitted; and Statius Proxumus wasted the pardon he had received from the emperor by making a vainglorious exit. Then Pompeius < . . . >, Cornelius Martialis, Flavius Nepos, and Statius Domitius were relieved of the tribuneship; the grounds were not that they hated the emperor but that they were nevertheless thought to do so. 3. Novius Priscus was given exile (for his friendship with Seneca), as were Glitius Gallus and Annius Pollio (for being discredited rather than found guilty). Priscus was accompanied by his wife, Artoria Flaccilla, and Gallus by Egnatia Maximilla (who had great wealth, which was initially left untouched but later confiscated, and both circumstances redounded to her glory).[84]

81 The poem (*carmen*) here probably refers to part of a poem. The reference may be to Lucan, *Bell. Civ.* 3.635–46, describing a sea fight in which one of the participants, Lycidas, is wounded by a grappling iron and bleeds to death, supported by his friends.

82 It was the custom to decorate the house with laurel branches to mark public or private rejoicing. Juvenal (10.65–66) similarly describes sacrifices on the Capitol and wreathing the house with laurel, on that occasion to mark the fall of Sejanus.

83 The sycophantic response to Nero's measures echoes the aftermath of the murder of Agrippina. Tacitus here lists no fewer than twenty-four victims.

84 The men listed were presumably tribunes of the praetorian guard, but no other information on them is available. Pompeius's "vainglorious exit" might have been explained in the gap that seems to follow Pompeius's name (only one element of it is given in the manuscript; all the other names have two elements). Nothing more is known about Novius Priscus. He may be identical with, or the father of, the Novius Priscus who held the consulship in AD 78 and was legate of Upper Germany in 82. Gallus may be the same Glitius Gallus who was the first husband of Vistilia, mother of Corbulo (Plin. *HN* 7.39). Gallus and Egnatia were exiled to Andros, where an inscription records them as patrons and

4. Rufrius Crispinus was also exiled, and though the conspiracy supplied the grounds, he was actually hated by Nero for having once been married to Poppaea.[85] In the case of Verginius Flavus[86] and Musonius Rufus,[87] it was the fame of their names that ensured their exile, for Verginius promoted the studies of our young people by his eloquence, Musonius by his philosophical teaching.[88] Cluvidienus Quietus, Julius Agrippa, Blitius Catulinus, Petron-

---

benefactors (*IG* 12.5.757). They returned under Galba, and Gallus's fortune was restored by Otho.

85 Rufrius Crispinus is attested as praetorian prefect in AD 47 (nothing is known of him before that), perhaps through friendship with Messalina. For his loyalty, the Senate bestowed on him the rank of praetor and 1.5 million sestertii. He was removed from his command in 51 at the urging of Agrippina but received the consular insignia (Tac. *Ann.* 11.1.3, 12.42.1). He was the first husband of Nero's second wife, Poppaea. Exiled to Sardinia, he was obliged to commit suicide in AD 66.

86 Verginius Flavus was a noted teacher of rhetoric. He wrote a book on the complete system of rhetoric, which was much admired by Quintilian (*Inst.* 7.4.40).

87 Gaius Musonius Rufus, of Volsinii in Etruria, was an equestrian, born about AD 30. A famous Stoic, he enjoyed an enormous reputation in antiquity, and Philostratus viewed him as a new Socrates (Philostr. *V.A* 4.4–5). He was a teacher of the famous philosopher Epictetus while Epictetus was a slave of Nero's freedman Epaphroditus (Epict. 1.9.29). Tacitus identifies Musonius as a teacher of Rubellius Plautus, who was murdered by Nero (*Ann.* 14.59.1), and it seems that Musonius followed him into exile. If so, he must have returned to Rome upon Rubellius's death. He was banished to Gyarus (Philostr. *V.A.* 7.16.2) but had returned by AD 69 and was much involved in the political life of the time. He tried to reconcile the conquering Flavian armies with the forces of Vitellius, but his proposals provoked only derision or boredom (Tac. *Hist.* 3.81.1). He escaped the general banishment of philosophers under Vespasian in 71 (Dio 65.13) but was later exiled, to be recalled by Titus after Vespasian's death (Jer. *Chron.* 79). He was a friend of Pliny the Younger (*Ep.* 3.11.5).

88 "Philosophical teaching" refers to Stoicism, a school that was founded in the third century BC and took its name from the Painted Stoa (arcade) in Athens. The system had considerable influence over the literate Roman upper classes, who were much attracted in particular to its philosophical tenets, especially the validation of virtue as the true good in life and the only source of true happiness. Stoics figure largely among the vocal opponents of the later Julio-Claudians, and this has led to suggestions that a "Stoic opposition" developed and was particularly prominent under Nero. But it is far from clear that Stoic dogma formed the basis for opposition. Stoic elevation of the virtuous life might in some sense preclude a public or political life, and Nero's suspicions of his kinsman and potential rival Rubellius Plautius were supposedly exacerbated by the thought that he "ostentatiously aped the Romans of old, even adopting the arrogant teachings of the Stoics which made men mutinous and ambitious" (Tac. *Ann.* 14.57.3). But much Stoic writing suggests that an accommodation could be made, and Seneca certainly taught in *De Clementia* that monarchy was not incompatible with Stoicism. In *De Beneficiis*, he claims that the best political system is that under a just king (*Ben.* 2.20), and in a letter to Lucilius he refutes the assertion that those who are philosophical are contemptuous of kings and magistrates (*Ep.* 73.1).

ius Priscus, and Julius Altinus—as though to round out the numbers and the list—were granted islands in the Aegean Sea. Scaevinus's wife, Caedicia, however, and Caesennius Maximus[89] were forbidden residence in Italy, and it was only from the sentence that they discovered they had been prosecuted. Annaeus Lucanus's mother, Acilia, was simply ignored, with no acquittal and no punishment.

72.1. Upon finishing this business, Nero held an assembly of the troops. There he distributed two thousand sestertii to every member of the rank and file[90] and made them the further gift of complimentary grain rations, which previously had cost them the market rate.[91] Then he convened the Senate, as though he were going to discuss achievements in war, and conferred triumphal honors on the ex-consul Petronius Turpilianus,[92] the praetor designate Cocceius Nerva,[93] and the praetorian prefect Tigellinus. He honored

---

Despite Tacitus's claim that Nero wanted to be rid of Thrasea because he represented virtue (*Ann.*16.21.1), the accusations lodged against him were not apparently provoked by his philosophical doctrines. He had contempt not for imperial rule but for Nero individually and personally as a ruler. It may well be that the type of person who was attracted to Stoicism was likely to have little respect for what might be perceived as an arbitrary martinet like Nero, and the demeanor of those attracted to virtue might have seemed offensive to the emperor. It is interesting that Nero particularly despises Rubellius for "being austere in appearance, and moral and reclusive in his private life" (Tac. *Ann.* 14.22.1).

89 Caesennius Maximus was a philosopher and friend of Seneca (Sen. *Ep.* 87.2). Martial (7.44.6) refers to his consulship, and to his exile in Sicily, where his friend Ovidius followed him. In Sen. *Ep.* 87.2, he is just "Maximus," and in Mart. 7.44.1 he is Maximus . . . Caesonius.

90 To put this figure in perspective, upon his accession, Nero paid out the same as Claudius, 15,000 sestertii to each (Tac. *Ann.* 12.69.2).

91 Tacitus (*Ann.* 1.17.4), in describing the charges made to legionaries at the time of Augustus's death in AD 14, says nothing about a levy for rations, which might suggest that the legionaries were exempt at this time but that praetorians still had the price of their rations deducted from their pay. It is not clear whether Nero's grant of free rations was established as a permanent measure or granted, like the donative, only as a one-time gift. Suetonius (*Ner.* 10.1) says that among the handouts at the outset of the reign there was a monthly allowance of cost-free grain for the praetorian cohorts, but he might have been speaking of a free ration for one month only (see Chapter I).

92 Petronius Turpilianus had been consul in AD 61 and was sent as legate to Britain in that year (see *Ann.* 14.29.1, 39.3). There is no indication of what his service to Nero was at this time. In 68, he was placed in command of the troops against the rebelling Gauls and Galba, but he did not leave Italy. He was put to death without trial by Galba.

93 Marcus Cocceius Nerva is the future emperor (AD 96–98), born on November 8, probably in AD 30 (Dio 68.4.2), into a distinguished family. His grandfather was a close friend of Tiberius, and his father was an eminent lawyer. Nerva had an extraordinary early career. To judge from his rewards on this occasion, he was a close confidant of Nero (he was praised by Nero as the Tibullus of the age [Mart. 8.70.7–8]), even though he had not held major office). His collaborationist role did him no apparent harm, and he was consul

Tigellinus and Nerva to the extent of placing their busts in the Palatium, in addition to their triumphal statues in the Forum. 2. Consular insignia were decreed for Nymphidius Sabinus, and since this is the first time he has come up, I shall give a brief resume, for he, too, will be part of the calamities that befell Rome.[94] He had as his mother a freedwoman who had spread her fine body around the slaves and freedmen of the emperors, and he claimed to have been fathered by Gaius Caesar for, by some chance, he was tall of stature and had a grim-looking face—or else Gaius Caesar, who lusted even after whores, did in fact have his way with Sabinus's mother, too. < . . . >[95]

73.1. After his speech among the senators, Nero also delivered an edict to the people, to which he added evidence that had been gathered together on writing scrolls, and confessions of those convicted,[96] for in fact he was being lambasted regularly in talk among the masses for having put to death famous and innocent men out of jealousy or fear. 2. However, that a conspiracy had begun, had come to fruition, and been suppressed was not doubted at the time by any with a care to discover the truth, and it was also later admitted by those who returned to the city after Nero's death. 3. But in the Senate all were debasing themselves with flattery (and the greater their sorrow, the more they flattered). During this, Junius Gallio, fearful after the death of his brother Seneca, and pleading for his life, was denounced by Salienus

---

in 71 as Vespasian's colleague, and again in 90 as Domitian's. He was chosen as emperor upon the latter's death. It seems remarkable that Tacitus feels circumscribed and unable to provide details for the service provided by Nerva, who is here coupled with the notorious Tigellinus. His contribution must have been substantial.

94 Nymphidius Sabinus was the son of Nymphidia, a freedwoman of Callistus, one of the most powerful freedmen in the courts of Caligula and Claudius. Despite Nymphidius's claim to a Caligulan heritage, Plutarch (*Galb.* 9.1) says that Caligula was a boy when Nymphidius was born and that the latter's father was actually a gladiator, Martianus. Nymphidius gained the status of equestrian, perhaps thanks to Callistus, and was prefect of an auxiliary unit in Pannonia (*ILS* 1322). It was probably at the time of the Pisonian conspiracy that he was appointed praetorian prefect alongside Tigellinus. His sense of loyalty was not profound. In 68, he promised the praetorians an enormous donative to abandon Nero and support Galba, but then sought to have them proclaim Nymphidius himself as emperor and was killed by Galba's soldiers (Plut. *Galb.* 8.1, 14–15).

95 It is assumed that there is a gap in the manuscript at the end of this chapter, since a section on Nymphidius's life and career would be expected here.

96 The trials had not been conducted in open court before the Senate but *in camera* before the emperor in the Servilian Gardens. Hence, Nero feels the need to present the evidence and provide proof that there had in fact been a conspiracy. It is possible that Tacitus had obtained testimony directly from those who returned to Rome under the Flavians, which may account in some part for the wealth of detail that he provides, despite the secrecy of the proceedings.

Clemens, who called him an enemy and a murderer.[97] Finally, Clemens was restrained by a unanimous appeal from the Senate that he not give the impression of profiting from public misfortunes to satisfy a private animosity, and not give rise to fresh savagery by dragging up things that, through the emperor's clemency, had been laid to rest or forgotten.

74.1. Decrees were then passed for gifts and thanks offerings to the gods, with special honors for the Sun for having uncovered the secrets of the conspiracy with his power (he has an old temple in the Circus, the prospective location for the coup).[98] The Games of Ceres in the Circus were also to be held with an increased number of horse races, and the month of April was to receive Nero's name.[99] A temple was to be erected to Salus in place of the one from which Scaevinus had taken his weapon.[100] 2. Nero himself consecrated the dagger in the Capitol, it bearing the inscription "To Jupiter the Avenger."[101] (Although it was not noticed at the time, this was, after the armed insurrection of Julius Vindex, taken to be an omen foretelling future vengeance.)[102] 3. I find in the records of the Senate that the consul

97 Junius Gallio was the older brother of Seneca, who dedicated his *De Ira* and *De Vita Beata* to him. Born Annaeus Novatus, he was adopted by Junius Gallio, a friend of his father, Seneca the Elder. The older Junius was expelled from the Senate in AD 32 for his obsequiousness, exiled to Lesbos, and then put under house arrest upon his return (Tac. *Ann.* 6.3.3). The younger Junius entered the Senate possibly under Caligula, and after a praetorship was proconsul of Achaea in in 51/52, when he refused to listen to the charges of the Jews against Paul (*Acts* 18.12–16). He was favored by Nero. He was consul in 55 (Plin. *HN* 31.62) and was the herald who introduced Nero onto the stage in 59 (Dio 61.20.1). He was forced into suicide in 66 according to Jerome's *Chronicle*. His accuser Clemens is otherwise unknown.

98 Tertullian (*De spect.* 1.8) says that the Circus is especially consecrated to the Sun.

99 April, the month when the conspiracy was exposed, was renamed Neroneus (Suet. *Ner.* 55). There was a precedent for this. Quinctilis (the birth month of Julius Caesar) and Sextilis (the month of Augustus's first consulate) were renamed July and Augustus, respectively, under Augustus, and under Caligula September was renamed Germanicus, which did not last any more than did Drusilleios (named after his sister Drusilla) in Egypt. We learn later that May was also renamed Claudius and June Germanicus (Tac. *Ann.* 16.12.2).

100 Tacitus's words are rather cryptic here and are complicated by our uncertainty about the location of the Temple of Salus, where Scaevinus first took down the dagger (see *Ann.* 15.53.2). If Tacitus means that the original temple was to be demolished and another more splendid one erected in its place, or even one on a similar scale but untainted by Scaevinus, he has neglected to make this clear.

101 Nero had a precedent for the dedication of the dagger in the Capitol. After the exposure of the conspiracy of AD 39, Caligula dedicated three daggers in the Temple of Mars Ultor (Suet. *Cal.* 24.3). Later, Vitellius will send to Cologne the dagger with which Otho killed himself, to be dedicated to Mars (Suet. *Vit.* 10.3).

102 On Vindex, see Chapter X. The name Vindex means "avenger."

designate Anicius Cerialis[103] proposed that a temple to the Divine Nero be erected as soon as possible, at public expense.[104] Cerialis surely made this motion on the grounds that Nero had gone beyond the limits of mortality and deserved the worship of human beings, but Nero himself vetoed it in case it could be interpreted by some as an omen of his death, for divine honors are not paid to an emperor before he has stopped living among humans.

Dio 62.27.4. Why would one bother to recount all the gifts made to the praetorians at the time of this conspiracy or the outrageous things voted to Nero and his friends? In fact, the philosopher Musonius Rufus was banished over such things.[105]

The atmosphere generated by the Pisonian conspiracy is one of mistrust and suspicion, and this contributes to the high number of deaths of perceived opponents of the regime, including Vinicianus, son-in-law of Corbulo.

Suet. *Ner.* 36.1. The violence he directed against those not members of his family was no less vicious. A comet, which is commonly thought to predict the end for very great rulers, had begun to appear for a number of nights in succession.[106] Nero was worried by the phenomenon, but he was told by

103 Dio (59.29.5) speaks of Anicius Cerialis, who was put to death with his stepson Sextus Papinius in AD 40 and died courageously, revealing nothing about the conspiracy. Tacitus (*Ann.* 16.17.6), by contrast, says that Cerialis committed suicide in AD 66, his conscience troubled by the fact that he had revealed the conspiracy to Caligula. He held a suffect consulship in that year, AD 65 (*CIL* IV.2551).

104 The proposal that a temple be erected to the Divine Nero in Rome was remarkable. Temples to the deified emperors are known outside of Rome, and even there they were normally linked with "Rome," "the Senate," or the like. A temple was dedicated to Claudius at Colchester during his lifetime, and the strangeness of this is alluded to in the *Apocolocyntis* (8.3). The unusual nature of Cerialis's motion may well explain why Tacitus goes to such great lengths to insist that he found this in the *acta senatus*, Tacitus's only specific citation from this source (otherwise mentioned only by Suetonius [*Aug.* 5]).

105 Tacitus (*Ann.*15.71.4) suggests that Musonius Rufus, the celebrated Stoic philosopher, was exiled (along with Verginius Flavus) purely as a result of Nero's artistic jealousy. Dio here suggests that Musonius had made some criticism of the obsequious response of the Senate to Nero's activities.

106 The comet recorded here is presumably the one mentioned by Tacitus just before the Pisonian conspiracy, which he places at the end of the year (*Ann.* 15.47.1). Chinese records note a "guest star" that appeared on May 3 of that year for seventy-five days. A "guest star" might be a comet, but it is more usually a nova or a variable star. Pliny (*HN* 2.92) notes a "fierce and almost continuous" comet that appeared under Nero; his description is reminiscent of Suetonius's "number of nights in succession."

his astrologer Balbillus that royalty usually expiated such portents by killing some distinguished personage and thereby turning them away from themselves and onto the heads of important people.[107] He therefore decided on the annihilation of every one of his most noble subjects and was all the more determined, and seemingly with some justification, after news of two conspiracies was made public, the first and more threatening being that of Piso in Rome and the later one that of Vinicianus,[108] which was hatched and uncovered in Beneventum.[109] 2. The conspirators defended themselves in court bound with three sets of chains. Some readily admitted the charge, and a few even made a virtue of it, saying that it was only by his death that they could assist Nero when he had brought infamy on himself by all manner of crimes. The children of the condemned were banished from Rome or put to death by poison or starvation.[110] It is on record that some were killed together at

107 Balbillus was a famous astrologer of the Julio-Claudian period, author of a work that enabled the astrological calculation of life spans. His biography is very difficult to disentangle. He may be identical with Tiberius Claudius Balbillus, prefect of Egypt in AD 55–59, a man admired by Seneca (*QNat.* 4.2.13) for his fine literary talents.

108 Suetonius's notice of the Pisonian conspiracy is very brief compared with Tacitus's detailed narrative, but in compensation he is the only literary source to allude to the conspiracy of Annius Vinicianus in 66, perhaps explained by the loss of the last books of Tacitus's *Annals* (although it is similarly not mentioned by Dio). This conspiracy may be alluded to in the Arval record on June 20, and once on an earlier date in AD 66, with celebrations for something like the "exposure of plots of evil-doers," although the text is very fragmentary (see Smallwood 25.3, 20–21). The leader seems to have been Annius Vinicianus. His father, of the same name, had been a primary participant in the conspiracy against Caligula and in AD 42 had put his support behind the rebellion of Furius Camillus, the legate of Dalmatia. He committed suicide after its failure (Dio 60.15.3). The son was appointed legate of a legion under Corbulo, who was his father-in-law, in AD 63/64 (Tac. *Ann.* 15.28.3). We know that Corbulo sent Vinicianus to Rome in AD 65 to accompany Tiridates (Dio 62.23.6), which would place him on the spot at the appropriate time for the later conspiracy. The failure of that conspiracy might well be connected with the death in 67 of Corbulo, who was summoned to Greece and ordered to commit suicide. It might also be connected with the similar summons and suicide of the brothers Scribonius Proculus and Scribonius Rufus, legates of Upper and Lower Germany, respectively (Dio 62.17.2–3). It is to be noted that Vinicianus's brother, Annius Pollio, was a victim of the aftermath of the Pisonian conspiracy.

109 It is possible that the plan was to assassinate Nero as he passed through Beneventum on the way to Greece.

110 Suetonius's comment about the "children of the condemned" is clearly an exaggeration. Even Calpurnius Piso Galerianus, son of the nominal leader of the conspiracy, survived, and we are not told that he suffered at all under Nero. He later tried to live a quiet life, not being a man of daring ambition, but was quietly put to death in 69 by Lucius Mucianus because there were rumors that he was plotting a rebellion, rumors based on nothing more than his handsome appearance and his parentage (Tac. *Hist.* 4.11.2).

one meal, along with their pedagogues and attendants, while others were prevented from acquiring their daily sustenance.

One of the most celebrated victims is Nero's arbiter elegantiae, Petronius.

Tac. *Ann.* 16.18.1. In Petronius's case, a brief background sketch is necessary.[111] His days were spent sleeping, his nights on the duties and delights of life.[112] While others had been brought fame by industry, in his instance, it was by idleness; and yet he was not considered a glutton and a spendthrift, like most who squander their fortunes, but a man of educated extravagance. The more outrageous his words and actions, which had a distinctive sort of nonchalance about them, the more acceptable they became as a demonstration of his sincerity. 2. As proconsul of Bithynia, however, and subsequently as consul, he showed himself to be a man of energy who was competent in business. Then, sliding back into his vices or through imitating vices, he was taken into Nero's small band of cronies as his "arbiter of good taste"; in his jaded state, Nero considered nothing delightful or agreeable unless it had Petronius's approval. 3. That explains Tigellinus's envy, directed against a rival who outclassed him in the science of pleasure. Tigellinus therefore went to work on the emperor's ruthlessness, to which all his other passions took second place, accusing Petronius of friendship with Scaevinus. He also bribed one of Petronius's slaves to inform on him, removed any means of defense, and imprisoned most of his household staff.

111 One of the most famous of Nero's victims was Petronius, almost certainly the Petronius who wrote Rome's oldest surviving novel, the *Satyricon*, an anarchic tale of self-indulgence peopled by grotesque and satirical caricatures (sadly, it survives only in fragments). Petronius is an individual with an enduring appeal, inspiring, as one example of many, Macaulay's characterization of Horace Walpole: "No minister in his time did so much; yet no minister had so much leisure."

Virtually nothing is known about Petronius's life, but it is now generally assumed that he is to be identified with the consul of AD 62, Petronius Niger. He may well be the Titus Petronius identified by Plutarch as one whose wit consisted in berating someone for failings the opposite to what they in reality manifested, such as mocking a spendthrift for being miserly (Plut., *De adulatore et amico* 60d–e). Pliny relates that when he knew he was going to die, Titus Petronius destroyed his wine dipper, worth 300,000 sestertii, so that Nero could not inherit it (Plin. *HN* 37.20). The praenomen of Publius, however, seems to have been confirmed in an inscription (*SEG* 39 [1989], 1180.35). As Tacitus reveals, Petronius held a governorship of Bithynia, which would have followed his praetorship. In office, it seems that he put aside his frivolous persona and became a conscientious administrator. He clearly became a key member of Nero's inner circle, and such was his polished wit that he became Nero's *arbiter elegantiae* ("arbiter of good taste").

112 The Romans regarded the night-owl person with moral suspicion, as Seneca (*Ep.* 122.2) reveals.

19.1. As it happened, Nero had set off for Campania during the days in question, and Petronius, who had gone as far as Cumae, was detained there, and he did not let fear or hope further delay him.[113] 2. He was, however, in no rush to end his life. Having cut his veins, he bandaged them and opened them again, as he felt inclined, in the meantime chatting with his friends, but not on serious matters or topics that would win him glory for his resolve. He in turn listened to their words—nothing on the immortality of the soul or the tenets of philosophers, but light poetry and playful verses. To some of his slaves, he presented gifts, to others a whipping. He started dinner and let himself drop off to sleep so that his death, though imposed, might look natural. 3. Even in his will, he did not, like most who perished, flatter Nero, Tigellinus, or any other of the powerful. Instead, he itemized in writing the emperor's depravities, naming the male prostitutes and women involved, and describing all their novel sexual acts, and sent it to Nero under seal.[114] He then broke his signet ring to prevent its later use for manufacturing danger.[115]

Nero also takes action against opponents and against the Stoic philosophers.

Tac. *Ann.* 16.21.1. After butchering so many distinguished men, Nero finally felt a deep desire to exterminate virtue itself by killing Thrasea Paetus[116]

113 It seems that Nero had gone to one of his villas in Campania and was accompanied by Petronius as far as Cumae, at which point the arrest took place. That sequence is rather strange; one wonders why they could not have waited until the final destination, and it may be that Petronius had set out later to join Nero and been intercepted at Cumae by a detachment of the guard.

114 Instead of a pompous farewell speech, Petronius wrote dirty stories about Nero, which some have identified with the *Satyricon*, but that work would surely have been too long, and in any case he is said to have provided explicit names of Nero's lovers, not found in the *Satyricon* (although admittedly much of it is lost).

115 In breaking his signet ring, Petronius may well have thought of the forged letter of Lucan that was produced after the latter's death.

116 Publius Clodius Thrasea Paetus was a native of Patavium (Padua). He married Arria, the daughter of Caecina Paetus, who rebelled against Claudius in AD 42, and the elder Arria (discussed later). Thrasea was consul in 56 and gained a reputation in the Senate for his principled stands. Even Nero grudgingly gave credit to Thrasea's qualities as judge (Plut. *Prae. Ger. Reip.* 14), and Vitellius is said to have regarded him as a model of proper conduct (Tac. *Hist.* 2.91.3).

In 59, Thrasea left the Senate chamber, when it passed obsequious resolutions following the murder of Agrippina (Tac. *Ann.* 14.12.1). He opposed the death penalty of the praetor Antistius on a charge of writing defamatory verses and won over the Senate, despite Nero's disagreement (Tac. *Ann.* 14.48.3–49). He was eventually viewed as hostile by Nero and was not allowed to join other senators in conveying congratulations to the emperor and Barea Soranus.[117] He had long nursed a grudge against both, and there were additional motives for his resentment of Thrasea: he had left the Senate when the matter of Agrippina was under discussion, as I have noted, and at the Iuvenalian Games, his services had not been conspicuous. That particular offense went deeper because at Patavium, his birthplace, Thrasea had actually sung in tragic costume at the Cetastian Games established by the Trojan Antenor.[118] 2. Furthermore, on the day that the praetor Antistius was being sentenced to death for the lampoons he composed on Nero, he successfully proposed a lighter penalty, and, after deliberately missing the meeting when divine honors were decreed to Poppaea, he had missed her funeral.[119] 3. Capito Cossutianus would not allow these things to be forgotten.[120] He was of a criminal disposition anyway, but he also resented Thrasea because it was to his influence that he owed an earlier conviction. That was when Thrasea gave assistance to the Cilician delegation that was indicting Capito for extortion.

22.1. In fact, Capito made the following accusations against him as well. At the beginning of the year, Thrasea would avoid the customary oath.[121] Though vested with a quindecimviral priesthood, he did not attend the formal prayer offerings.[122] He had never offered sacrifices on behalf of the emperor's safety or his heavenly voice. He had not entered the Curia in three

---

on the birth of his daughter (Tac. *Ann.* 15.23.4). Ultimately, Thrasea was condemned by the Senate, and the extant *Annals* break off during the account of his suicide (Tac. *Ann.* 16.35.2). He wrote a biography of Cato recorded by Plutarch (*Cat. Min.* 25.1, 37.1). His neglect of the *Iuvenalia*, noted here, is not mentioned elsewhere.

117 Quintus Marcius Barea Soranus was consul in AD 52. As consul designate, he had moved that Pallas, the freedman favored by Agrippina, be honored by the grant of the *ornamenta praetoria* and fifteen million sestertii (Tac. *Ann.* 12.53.2). He was proconsul of Asia in 61/62. His son-in-law, Annius Pollio, had already been exiled for his role in the Piso conspiracy.

118 The reference to the "Cetastian" Games is reconstructed from the totally garbled text of the manuscript; the Trojan Antenor was the traditional founder of Padua.

119 Tacitus does not mention the apotheosis in his account of Poppaea's funeral (*Ann.* 16.6), but she is identified as a *Diva* (goddess) on Neronian coinage and inscriptions, and Dio (63.26.3) mentions that Nero consecrated a temple to her.

120 Cossutianus Capito was a senator from at least AD 47. In 57, he was sentenced by the Senate for extortion in his province, perhaps Lycia-Pamphylia, although no mention is made of his playing any role in the prosecution of Thrasea (Tac. *Ann.* 16.33.2).

121 The oath to maintain the acts of the *princeps* was taken in January 1 of each year.

122 Prayers for the well-being of the state were made on January 1, and, under the republic, senators were fined for nonattendance. Enforcement, however, had become lax. It was restored by Augustus and Claudius. It appears that it had been allowed to lapse again under Nero.

years, though at one time he had attended diligently and tirelessly, conspicuously championing or opposing even quite ordinary senatorial resolutions. And, most recently, when people were racing to put a stop to Silanus and Vetus, he had preferred to spend that time on the private affairs of his clients.[123] This was already dissidence and partisanship, said Capito, and it was outright war if many dared do the same thing. . . .

23.1. As for the indictment of Barea Soranus, the Roman knight Ostorius Sabinus had already laid a personal claim to it on the basis of Soranus's proconsulship of Asia. During his mandate, Soranus had increased the emperor's resentment by his fairness and industry, and also because he had carefully cleared the harbor of Ephesus[124] and refrained from punishing the state of Pergamum for forcefully preventing Nero's freedman Acratus from making off with statues and artwork.[125] However, the charges laid were friendship with Plautus and courting popularity to induce his province to revolt. 2. The date chosen for Soranus's condemnation was that on which Tiridates was coming to accept the throne of Armenia. This was in order to shade a crime at home by turning talk to foreign affairs—or so that Nero could flaunt his imperial greatness by a kinglike act of putting illustrious men to death.[126]

24.1. The whole city poured out to welcome the emperor and see the king, but Thrasea was barred from the gathering. He was not despondent, and in fact he wrote a petition to Nero asking to be informed of the accusations against him and declaring that he would clear himself if he were given notification of the charges and an opportunity to refute them. 2. Nero quickly accepted the petition, hoping that a fearful Thrasea had written something that might promote the emperor's renown and discredit his own reputation.

123 The prosecutions were referred to earlier in this book. Lucius Junius Silanus was the last living relative of Augustus. He was brought down along with his uncle, the famous juror Gaius Cassius Longinus (Tac. *Ann.* 16.7.2). Lucius Antistius Vetus was brought down soon after (Tac. *Ann.* 16.10–11). He was Nero's partner in the consulship in AD 55 and was the father-in-law of Rubellius Plautus.

124 The harbor of Ephesus was notoriously prone to silting up because of the mud deposits of the river Cayster.

125 Acratus was a freedman of Nero who, with Carrinas Secundus, collected works of art for the emperor in Achaea and Asia to adorn the Domus Aurea. It was said that only Rhodes was off-limits to him (Tac. *Ann.* 15.45.2; Dio *Chrys.* 31.149). Tacitus links Acratus's work to the Great Fire (AD 64), which was later than Soranus's governorship (61/62), and it must be assumed that his art plundering had simply intensified, rather than begun, after the disaster.

126 Tiridates journeyed from Parthia with a large retinue and met Nero in Naples, to be accompanied from there to Rome (see Chapters IV and IX). No irony need be intended. Tacitus's reference is to the arbitrary behavior of an eastern king.

When this turned out not to be the case, it was Nero's turn to become frightened—at the prospect of the innocent man's expression, spirit, and independence—and he had the Senate convened.

Tac. Ann. *16.25–33: The Senate determines that Thrasea, Soranus, and also Soranus's daughter, Servilia, should be allowed to choose the manner of their death.*

Tac. *Ann.* 16.34.1.Thrasea was in his gardens when, as evening approached, the consul's quaestor was sent to him.[127] He had gathered together a large crowd of illustrious men and women and was focusing his attention mostly on Demetrius, a professor of the Cynic philosophical school.[128] With him, as could be judged from the earnestness of his expression, and from the more audible parts of their conversation, he was examining the nature of the soul and the separation of the spirit and the body. Then one of his close friends, Domitius Caecilianus, arrived and told him of the Senate's decision. 2. Thrasea therefore urged all present, who were weeping and protesting, to leave quickly and not incur danger themselves by association with a man doomed to die. Arria's aim was to accompany her husband to his end, after the example of her mother, Arria, but Thrasea advised her to hold onto her life and not remove the only support enjoyed by the daughter they shared.[129]

35.1. He then went to the colonnade, where the quaestor found him almost joyful because he had learned that his son-in-law Helvidius had merely

127 It was established practice for each consul to have attached to him one, and then from 38 BC two, quaestors (Dio 48.43.1). The consul presided over the trial; his quaestor would be the appropriate officer to communicate the verdict. The quaestor's mission and presence at the house seem to have been conveyed to Domitius Caecilianus, one of Thrasea's friends, otherwise unknown.

128 The Cynics in many ways were the precursors to the Stoics and had much in common with them. Demetrius was a friend of Seneca, who viewed him as the ideal learned sage. He was courageously outspoken in his opposition to Caligula, Nero, and Vespasian, who banished him (Suet. *Vesp.* 13; Dio 66.13.3). He did, however, defend Egnatius Celer, the accuser of Barea Soranus (Tac. *Hist.* 4.40.3).

129 Arria's mother had volunteered to die along with her husband, Caecina Paetus, involved in the rebellion of Scribonianus against Claudius in AD 42. When Paetus hesitated, she stabbed herself, so Pliny and Martial record, and said: *Paete, non dolet* ("It does not hurt, Paetus"), which became a byword for courage (Plin. *Ep.* 3.16.6; Mart. 1.13). The younger Arria lived and later, under Domitian, went into exile along with her daughter, both returning under Nerva. She was the mother of Fannia, who married Helvidius Priscus (Plin. *Ep.* 7.19) (discussed later).

been barred from Italy.[130] He accepted the decree of the Senate and took Helvidius and Demetrius into his bedroom. He offered the veins of both arms and, letting the blood flow freely, sprinkled it on the ground. He then called the quaestor over and said, "We are making a libation to Jupiter the Liberator. Look, young man![131] I pray the gods avert the omen, but you have been born into a time when it is helpful to toughen the mind with examples of firmness." 2. Then, as his slow death brought agonizing pains, turning to Demetrius . . . [132]

Dio 62.26. Thrasea and Soranus, who had become the leading men in terms of family, wealth, and every moral virtue, were not accused of treason, but they, too, met their ends, for being such people as they were! A philosopher, Publius Egnatius Celer, gave false evidence against Soranus.[133] Soranus had two companions, Cassius Asclepiodotus of Nicaea and the above-mentioned Egnatius of Berytus.[134] 2. Far from denouncing the man in any way, Asclepiodotus went so far as to testify to his outstanding qualities (and for doing so was exiled, though he was later recalled in the reign of Galba). Egnatius, like many involved in that sort of thing, received cash and honors for his sycophancy, but he was later sent into exile. 3. Soranus was therefore put to death for having performed magic of some kind, for which he used the services of his daughter, because the two had made a type of sacrifice when he was ill. In Thrasea's case, it was for not regularly attending the Senate, which purportedly signified displeasure with its decrees, for never listening

130 Helvidius Priscus, the son of a centurion, came from Cluviae in Samnium (modern Casoli). He entered the Senate sometime before AD 49. He may be the Helvidius who commanded a legion in Syria in 51 (see Chapter IV). He married Fannia, the daughter of Thrasea. He was plebeian tribune in 56 but held no further office under Nero, presumably because of his connection with Thrasea. After the latter's death, Helvidius was exiled, returned under Galba, and held a praetorship in 70. He continued to argue for the independence of the Senate and was exiled and eventually executed under Vespasian. At Fannia's request, a life of Helvidius was written by Herennius Senecio (a Stoic philosopher of the time of Domitian), who was executed in AD 93, in part because of his authorship of that work (Tac. *Dial.* 5; *Hist.* 4.5–6; Suet. *Vesp.* 15; Plin. *Ep.* 7.19; Dio 66.12, 67.13.2).

131 It is not clear whether these words were addressed to the quaestor (the minimum age was twenty-five) or Helvidius. The latter, however, seems to have been a plebeian tribune ten years earlier (Tac. *Ann.* 13.28.3), and he must now have been at least thirty-seven.

132 The text of the *Annals* breaks off at this point.

133 Tacitus also identifies Soranus's friend Egnatius Celer, born in Berytus (Beirut), as the chief accuser (*Ann.* 16.32.2).

134 Nothing further is known of Asclepiodotus of Nicaea.

to Nero's lyre playing, for not sacrificing to his divine voice, and for not putting on public oratorical displays, 4. although he had acted in a tragedy staged every thirty years in his hometown of Patavium. As he slit his vein, he raised his hand and said: "I make a libation of this blood to you, Jupiter Liberator."[135]

135 Tacitus and Dio were probably drawing on the same ultimate source here, to judge from the reference to Thrasea's performances in the tragedy in his hometown and to the oath to Jupiter Liberator as he died (see Chapter IX).

IX

THE EMPEROR AS ARTIST AND SHOWMAN

INTRODUCTION

Thanks to Agrippina's intervention, even before his adoption by Claudius, Nero had been put in the charge of Annaeus Seneca, now restored from exile and granted a praetorship, for his education in rhetoric and public behavior. Supervised by Seneca and Afranius Burrus, Nero, as Claudius's adopted heir, was prepared for his future role. There seems to have been little opposition to his advancement, and he fully exploited his head start over Britannicus, some three years younger (see Chapter I appendix), and met no challenge for the succession. This chapter illustrates how the young prince, even while he was being groomed for future public functions as advocate and commander, moved away from this conventional education to spend ever more time on his enthusiasm for performance, racing chariots, the passion of his father and grandfather before him, and then gradually seeking increasing publicity. His overwhelming desire to become a musical artist, composing and singing his own compositions to the cithara, would begin slightly later. This chapter follows his growing obsession with stage performance, not only as artist but also as impresario, controlling the performances of respectable private citizens as well as sporting and artistic professionals and becoming the chief entertainer of the Roman people.

SOURCES

Tac. *Ann.*13.2.1. [Afranius Burrus and Seneca] were the men guiding the emperor's youth, and (a rare phenomenon when power is shared) they acted in harmony, exercising equal influence but in different spheres, Burrus with his military interests and strict morality, Seneca with his oratorical teaching and principled cordiality.[1] The two worked together so that they could more

1 At Nero's age, the elite Roman would begin instruction in rhetoric, both systematic theory and the technique of declamation (philosophy was an option for boys of sixteen or

easily confine the unsteady age of the emperor (if he rejected virtue) to acceptable diversions.

Tac. *Ann.* 12.58.1 (AD 53). In the consulship of Decimus Junius and Quintus Haterius, Nero, now aged sixteen, married Claudius's daughter Octavia. And to gain a brilliant reputation for honorable pursuits and public speaking, he took up the cause of the people of Ilium. After an eloquent disquisition on the Roman people's Trojan descent, on Aeneas as the founder of the Julian family, and other old tales not far removed from legend, he succeeded in having the people of Ilium granted immunity from all public taxation.[2] Thanks to the same public speaker, the colony of Bononia, which had been razed by fire, was assisted with a grant of ten million sestertii. The Rhodians had their freedom restored—it had often been taken from them, or confirmed, depending on their service in foreign wars or their misdeeds in times of civil discord—and Apamea, shaken by an earthquake, was excused payment of tribute for a five-year period.[3]

Suet. *Ner.* 7.2. When he was first escorted into the Forum as a novice, Nero announced a distribution of largesse to the people and a donative to the soldiers, and after giving the praetorians notice of a march past he took the lead, shield in hand.[4] After that, he offered his thanks to his father in the Senate. Nero also spoke as advocate, for the people of Bononia in Latin and

---

older). Nero would also be expected to learn horsemanship and the skills of an army officer, in which Burrus, as commander of the imperial guard, would instruct him.

On Seneca's earlier life, see Chapter I. He would become famous for his moral writings: the twelve *Dialogues*, the tragedies, his seven books "On Benefactions," his "Natural Questions," and the progressive moral instruction to Lucilius ("Moral Letters"), but in AD 49 he had written only three *Dialogues* and perhaps some tragedies.

2 When cities of the empire sent boundary disputes with neighbors or petitions for immunity from taxation and other services to the emperor in Rome for his decision, they would be represented by a Roman advocate. Ilium (Troy) had been destroyed in 85 BC by Flavius Fimbria, the supporter of Marius and ruthless commander of the anti-Sullan forces in the East. It was restored mainly through the favor of Caesar and then Augustus, who traced their lineage back to the Trojan hero Aeneas. It had always been a privileged city. Sulla restored it and granted it freedom from tribute (App. *Mith.* 61), which Julius Caesar confirmed (Strabo 13.1.27). The remarks here indicate that it had at some point once again become tributary, and this is supported by Suetonius's statement (*Claud.* 25.3) that Claudius granted the citizens of Ilium a perpetual exemption from tax on the grounds that they were the ancestors of the Roman people (*IGR* 4.208–9).

3 Rhodes and Apamea in Asia Minor were excused taxes to compensate for the natural disaster.

4 Tacitus (*Ann.* 12.41.1) notes that the largesse was given by Claudius in connection with Nero's assumption of the *toga virilis*.

for the Rhodians and the people of Ilium in Greek, before Claudius, who was presiding as consul. His introduction to the administration of justice came when he was city prefect in the Latin festival, and there, though it had been forbidden by Claudius, the most famous advocates competed with each other to present to him not the usual inconsequential and brief cases but very important ones, and those in large numbers.[5]

Nero pursued oratory and poetry.

Tac. *Ann.* 14.16.1. But so as not to have the imperial fame restricted to theatrical skills, Nero also adopted the pursuit of poetry, gathering around him men who had some as yet unrecognized proficiency in composition.[6]

5 The ancient office of prefect of the city had become largely ritual by the late republic but was given real functions by Augustus, when the prefect was charged with maintaining order in Rome and dispensed summary justice in dealing with minor criminal cases. Through time, he was granted responsibility for more serious cases. In the later empire, the prefect became an individual of considerable importance. The office referred to by Suetonius here was a relic of the republican one, and its purpose was to take charge of the city during the *Feriae Latinae*, the celebration of Jupiter Latiaris on the Alban Hill. Magistrates were required to attend, and the prefect was expected to exercise authority in their absence. Clearly, the prefect was not expected to hear important cases, and Claudius imposed a ban on such procedures, but without much success.

6 Tacitus and Suetonius agree on Nero's enthusiasm (compare his output mentioned later), but Suetonius, with access to the imperial archives, had seen Nero's *pugillares* (notebooks), not available to Tacitus. Nero certainly had some fluency and great ambition as a poet: compare his public recitation of his own poetry and mention of his Trojan lays (to be identified with his *Fall of Troy* mentioned by both Suetonius [*Ner.* 38.2] and Tacitus [*Ann.* 15.39.3]). Add to this the prospective epic of all past Roman achievements—all the poems mentioned seem to have been narrative epics.

Three hexameters by Nero about the Tigris disappearing underground before its delta are quoted by the Scholiast on Lucan 3.261–62, showing a turn of phrase similar to Lucan's conception; a single line is quoted by Seneca (*QNat.*1.5.6). Some half verses together with one four-line fragment, denounced by Persius (1.93–102) as affected and decadent, while certainly in the style of the times and on mythological topics that appealed to Nero (Attis; the Maenads escorting Bacchus), may not have been his but display a nimble command of alliteration and perverse ingenuity in wordplay. Like other elite Romans, Nero probably composed epigrams on social occasions; if not an epigram, what was the "poem" (Suet. *Ner.* 24.2) in which he criticized Mithridates' ambitious attempt to drive a ten-horse chariot? Nero could have been expected to display his intellect and Grecizing tastes in the language arts, and his enthusiasm for singing as a citharode (see discussion later) also entailed the language art of verse composition, albeit in Greek, but the singing of lyrics was quite alien at Rome. We might equally expect young Nero, as a lad of seventeen, not just to love the speed and excitement of chariot racing as a spectator but also to want to race his own team in person; this had deep roots in the Roman tradition of public festival games, which Nero was now in a position to organize in every detail of spectacle.

These would sit with him and string together lines of verse they had brought along or that they improvised on the spot, and they supplemented Nero's own words in whatever meter he had used. (This process is betrayed by the very features of the poetry, which in its flow has no drive or inspiration or uniformity of style.) 2. Nero would also devote some time to professors of philosophy, after-dinner affairs at which he would also enjoy the conflict of opposing opinions. And there was no shortage of people wanting to be seen at the royal entertainments with their gloomy faces and expressions.

Suet. *Ner.* 52. As a boy, he sampled all the liberal arts. But his mother turned him away from philosophy, with the warning that it was a detriment to a future ruler. His teacher Seneca held Nero back from discovering the old classical orators, in order to keep him longer in his thrall, so being inclined to poetry he happily and effortlessly composed poems, nor did he, as some people think, produce other men's work as his own. His writing pads have come into my possession, as have notebooks containing some very familiar verses written in his own hand, so that it was quite obvious they were not borrowed or taken down at someone's dictation but clearly written as if he were thinking them out and devising them—there were so many erasures and words written in between or above the lines. He also enjoyed no mild enthusiasm for painting and modeling.

Suet. *Ner.* 10. He recited his poems not only in private but in the theater as well, which gave everybody such pleasure that a day of thanksgiving was decreed in honor of his recitation, and the poems that he had read were inscribed in letters of gold and dedicated to Capitoline Jupiter.

Dio 62.29.1. Nero did other absurd things, such as once coming down to the orchestra of the theater at a public show and reading some of his Trojan lays, and many sacrifices were made in their honor, as for all his other enterprises. 2. He was also preparing to record all the heroic deeds of Rome in heroic verse and was considering the number of volumes before compiling any part of them, seeking advice on that from others, especially Annaeus Cornutus, at that time well reputed for his learning. 3. And Nero almost killed the man (but instead exiled him to an island) because, when some friends were advising him to compose four hundred volumes, Cornutus said that was too many, and no one would read them. And when someone objected "Chrysippus, whom you praise and imitate, filled far more volumes," he answered, "but they are useful to the lives of mankind." Now for this Cornutus incurred exile, but Lucan was forbidden to compose poetry, because he was receiving so much praise for his work.

We can preface the evidence for Nero's games and other performances with the record of Augustus's benefactions to the people of Rome as empresario.

Augustus, *Res Gestae* 22. I gave a gladiatorial show three times on my own account and five times in the name of my sons or grandsons; at these shows about ten thousand men were in combat. I also twice presented to the people a show of athletes, summoned from all lands, in my own name, and a third time in the name of my grandson. I held games four times on my own account. And standing in for other magistrates, I held games twenty-three times. On behalf of the College of Fifteen (*Quindecimviri*), as master of their college with my colleague Marcus Agrippa, I held Secular Games when Gaius Furnius and Gaius Silanus were consuls. As consul, I was the first to hold Games of Mars, which subsequently were conducted by the consuls each year on the authority of the Senate and the law.[7] I made a present to the people of African wild beast hunts in my name or that of my sons and grandsons in the Circus, the Forum, or the amphitheaters twenty-six times, and in them about three thousand five hundred beasts were slaughtered.[8] 23. I gave the people the show of a naval battle across the Tiber, on the site of the Groves of the Caesars. . . . [I]n this conflict, thirty beaked ships, both triremes and biremes, and more smaller craft clashed with each other, and about three thousand men fought besides the oarsmen.[9]

Suet. *Aug.* 43.1. [Augustus] says that he "four times held games on his own account and twenty-three times on behalf of other magistrates who were either absent or could not meet the cost." He also at times held games in the districts and on several stages using actors speaking all languages. These performances could be held not only in the Forum or the amphitheater but also in the Circus and the *Saepta* (voting enclosures), and on several occasions

7 In the republic, the six major games of the religious calendar were financed and managed by elected magistrates, but ambitious individuals took advantage of the recognized pretexts for offering gladiatorial shows, usually to honor their deceased fathers. Augustus did not need a pretext: he gave Greek-style athletic games, as Nero would, at Rome and at Naples (the *Augustalia*); with his wealth from the Actium campaign, he financed shows not just in his own name but to maintain the popularity of his sons and grandsons. He was also a keen spectator of theatrical performances, both comedy and mime, hence his dying request for applause for playing the mime of his life successfully (Suet. *Aug.* 99.1).

8 "The amphitheaters" were temporary structures until the completion of the amphitheater of Statilius Taurus. Animals were captured in North Africa and exhibited in menageries, but sent into the arena to be killed by armed *bestiarii* (wild-animal fighters).

9 Suetonius says too little about Nero's naval games, which probably reused Augustus's old site in Trastevere.

he gave only an animal hunt. He also exhibited athletes, erecting wooden benches on the Campus Martius; likewise, he "staged a naval battle after excavating the ground around the Tiber where there is now the grove of the Caesars." On these days, he set guards in the city so that it would not be at the mercy of thugs because so few people had stayed at home.

44.1. He disciplined the utterly random and rowdy behavior of the spectators provoked by the abuse of a senator to whom no man would give a seat in the packed crowd at the very popular games at Puteoli. On this account, the Senate passed a decree that, whenever any public show was put on, the first rank of seats should be left open for the senators, and he prohibited the envoys of free and allied nations from sitting in the orchestra at Rome when he discovered that some envoys were even freedmen. 2. He separated the soldiery from the people. He assigned their own rows to husbands from the plebs and their own wedge of seats to boys, next to their slave escorts, and ordained that no one wearing rough tunics could sit in the main auditorium. He did not allow women, who had formerly followed the practice of sitting at random, to watch even the gladiators, except from the upper rows. 3. He gave only the vestal virgins a separate place in the theater, facing the praetor's box. Indeed, he completely banned the female sex from the displays of athletes. . . .

45.3. He thought every kind of person offering their services to a public show was worthy of care; he both kept and extended the privileges of athletes, banned gladiators from being presented without the chance of appeal, and removed from magistrates the right to use force on actors, permitted by an old law at every time and occasion except at the games and onstage. . . . 4. Upon a praetor's complaint, he thrashed Hylas the pantomimus in his own atrium open to the public and exiled Pylades from the city and from Italy because he had pointed at and made a show of a spectator who was hissing him.[10]

Macrobius *Saturnalia* 2.5.18. Since it was believed that Pylades had changed the old manner of that dance that was popular with our ancestors and had introduced a new kind of charm, when Augustus asked him what he had contributed to the art of the dance, he said "the air of pipes and flutes and the throng of men." 19. When Augustus was outraged because the people were rioting on account of the rivalry between himself and Hylas, Pylades retorted, "you are ungrateful, your majesty, let them be distracted with our affairs."

10 This anecdote is cited only here but closely resembles the encounter with Pylades reported by Macrobius in the next passage.

Tac. *Ann.* 1.77 (AD 14). Disorderly behavior in the theater, which had first manifested itself the previous year, at this point broke out more seriously. Not only members of the public but also soldiers and a centurion were killed—and a tribune of the praetorian cohorts was also wounded—as they attempted to stem abuse that was being hurled at the magistrates and halt disputes among the common people. 2. The fracas was discussed in the Senate, and opinions were voiced to the effect that the praetors should have the authority to thrash actors. 3. Haterius Agrippa, a plebeian tribune, vetoed the motion and received a tongue-lashing from Asinius Gallus, but Tiberius ... remained silent. The veto remained in force, however, because the deified Augustus had once expressed the opinion that actors were not subject to floggings. . . . . 4. On limiting actors' pay and combating the unruly behavior of their supporters, many decrees were passed. The most striking were the following: no senator was to enter the homes of pantomimes; Roman knights were not to escort actors when they appeared in public; and the actors were to be viewed nowhere but in the theater. Also, the praetors were to have the right to punish with exile any outrageous behavior on the spectators' part.

Nero's first year as emperor witnesses audience indiscipline and actual rioting.

Tac. *Ann.* 13.24 (55 AD). At the end of the year, the cohort usually stationed to keep watch over the games was removed. The point of this was to provide a greater impression of freedom, to lessen corruption among the military by isolating them from the permissive atmosphere of the theater, and to test whether the plebs would maintain order if their guardians were removed. ...

25.4. [Nero] also created virtual battles from unruly behavior in the theater and the factions supporting the actors (i.e., *pantomimi*) by granting amnesty and awarding prizes, and even by viewing the troubles himself, sometimes hidden but very often quite openly. Finally, with the people at each other's throats and the frightening prospect of more serious disturbances, the only remedy that was found was the banishment of the actors from Italy and the return of a military presence in the theater.

Nero's shows exhibit varieties of physical and artistic skill.

Suet. *Ner.*11.1. He presented a great number of shows of different kinds: his *Iuvenalia,* the chariot races, the staging of plays, and a gladiatorial contest. At the *Iuvenalia,* he invited even old men of consular status and elderly married ladies to perform. At the chariot races, he marked off a space for the knights separated from the rest of the audience and even raced camels in teams of four. 2. At the games, which he wanted to call "Greatest," on the grounds that they were offered to promote the eternity of Rome's empire, a great many of both ranks and sexes performed stage roles; most conspicuously, a Roman knight seated on an elephant made a circuit in the ring of the theatre. . . .

12.1. At the entertainment that he offered in the wooden amphitheater, which had been constructed in the Campus Martius within the year, he killed no one, not even condemned criminals.[11] But he put on show for combat four hundred senators and six hundred Roman knights, and some people of unblemished standing and repute, including from this category beast slaughterers and various servants for the arena. He also displayed a naval battle with sea creatures swimming in saltwater. Also, he staged Pyrrhic dances from the ranks of ephebes and offered the ephebes certificates of Roman citizenship after their regular services.[12]

Dio 61.17.2. In honor of his mother, he celebrated a huge and most extravagant festival, so that the gatherings were held in five or six theaters over many days.[13] An elephant with a rider on its back was led up to the gallery of a theater, where it ran the circuit on a rope. 3. But the most shameful and awful event was when both men and women not just of the equestrian class but of senatorial rank presented themselves in the orchestra, the racetrack, and the hunting theater as if they were the lowest and most dishonored, and some of them played the pipes, danced tragedies, acted comedies, and sang to the cithara: they drove horses, killed wild beasts, and fought single combats, some willingly but others completely against their will. 4. And men of that generation viewed the noble clans, the Furii and Horatii, the Fabii, Porcii, and Valerii, and all the others whose trophies and temples were to be seen, standing up and doing acts that they would not even have watched done by others . . . such were the ceremonies that Nero chose to offer as the initiation of his own disgrace.

In AD 59 Nero staged a special celebration of his coming of age and made this personal and private rite a pretext for bringing respectable amateurs before the public. He also inaugurated a more "high brow" set of contests in the Greek style.

11 If the wooden amphitheater was erected within a year, it shows the high priority he gave to the kinds of shows exhibited in amphitheaters, mostly gladiatorial or wild beast hunts. But another amphitheater outside Rome would collapse during his reign (Tac. *Ann.* 13.31).

12 See Suet. *Ner.* 12.3–4. A Greek type of war dance, assigned to a Greek (not Roman) age group of young men before reaching full manhood.

13 These stood in for funeral games; whether the people believed Nero's claim that his mother had tried to murder him or knew that he himself had planned her murder, they could hardly be called games in her honor.

Dio 61.19.1. For this feast (the *Iuvenalia*), everyone, even the most nobly born, were put on show.[14] 2. As an example, Aelia Catella, who was prominent in birth and wealth, and well advanced in years (she was an octogenarian), danced, and others who could not perform individually because of their age or sickness sang in the choruses. Everyone practiced whatever they could, and the most distinguished persons attended designated schools—men and women, girls and youths, old women and old men. 3. If anyone could not put on any other act, Nero demoted them to the choruses. And when some of them in shame put on masks so as not to be recognized, Nero took them away, saying that the public demanded it and displayed them to people who just before had been under their authority.

Suet. *Ner.* 12.3. He was first of all men at Rome to found a quinquennial contest, in three categories, according to Greek custom—musical, athletic, and equestrian performances—which he called the *Neronia*; and at the dedication of the hot baths and gymnasium, he provided oil to both the Senate and order of knights.[15] He appointed as masters of the whole contest ex-consuls, selected by lot, holding the power of praetors. Then he came down into the orchestra and accepted in person the crown in Latin oratory and poetry, for which all the most respected men had competed but that had been passed to him by their unanimous agreement; he paid reverence to the lyre bestowed on him by the judges and ordered it to be conveyed to the statue of Augustus. 4. At the gymnastic contest that he was holding in the *Saepta*, he offered up his first beard amid the equipment of the ox sacrifice, enclosing it in a golden pyxis embellished with the most costly pearls, and dedicated this personal relic on the Capitol. He even invited the vestal virgins to attend the athletic displays since the priestesses of Ceres were permitted to watch at Olympia.

Tac. *Ann.* 14.20. During the consulship of Nero (his fourth) and Cornelius Cossus, Quinquennial Games were established at Rome on the model of the Greek competition, and, as with nearly all innovations, opinions were mixed. . . . [16]

14 The *Iuvenalia* may still have counted as a private, not a public, occasion; this would go some way toward explaining the voluntary (probably enforced) performances by respectable citizens.

15 It was the custom in Greece to provide athletic contestants with rubbing oil.

16 Normally, it was the cities of the empire (Syracuse, Corinth, Naples) that instituted games named in honor of their Roman lords: Marcellus at Syracuse and Flamininus at Corinth.

The Quinquennial Games that Augustus established at Naples in his own name (Suet. *Aug.* 98.5), originating late in his long principate, offered Nero a model of Greek games

21. Most were actually pleased with the permissive climate, but they still cloaked it with respectable terms. Their ancestors, too, had not shunned agreeable spectacles, as far as the resources of the day allowed, they would say. And so actors had been brought from Etruria and horse racing from Thurii. With the annexation of Achaea and Asia, games were staged more elaborately, but in the last two centuries since the triumph of Lucius Mummius (146 BC), the first to put on that kind of show in the city, no Roman of decent background had disgraced himself by taking up professional acting.[17] Victory in the oratorical or poetic spheres would be an incentive for talent, and no judge would find it offensive to lend his ear to honorable intellectual activities and legitimate diversions.

In their reports of Nero's early games, as throughout the life of Nero, Suetonius and Dio both stress Nero's coercive pressure on the nobility ("invitations" to respectable middle-aged senators and ladies of their class to perform), always a source of easy indignation in the Roman elite. Suetonius adds to the reports of Nero's prodigal generosity to the audience (see Suet. Ner. *11.2) events he created for the public outside the theaters and extravagant entertainments (the elephant, the naval battle), before moving to an account of the more highbrow Greek festival to which Nero gave his own name, the* Neronia *(12.3), established in AD 60.*

Tacitus uses the Neronia, the quinquennale ludicrum, *at* Ann. *14.20–21, to offer a balance of criticism and praise (including a brief history of resistance to the construction of a permanent theater at Rome) before reporting the apparently favorable reaction of the majority to the use of theater buildings, which saved magistrates reiterated expense for temporary structures (21.2) and would benefit society through the stimulus to emulation provided by poetry and oratory (21.3). In favor of the new-style athletic and musical games, Tacitus's speakers add that participating in these (as opposed to theatrical shows) involved no serious shame or damage* (dehonestamentum) *to men's dignity and met with even stronger popular enthusiasm because the* pantomimi *had been permitted to return to the stage but were banned from sacred contests (21.4).*

Nero exploited the diplomatic visit to Rome of king Tiridates of Armenia.

---

from Italy itself. The category called "Music" covered poetry in both speech and song, as inspired by the Muses, and was extended to cover prose rhetoric.

17 Actors at Rome, like pimps, prostitutes, and undertakers, were disqualified from bearing witness in court; conservatives would thus see any performance on the public stage as dishonor (*infamia*).

Suet. *Ner.* 13.1. It is not unjustified for me to report the ceremonial entrance of Tiridates into the city among Nero's public displays. After pressing this king of Armenia with lavish promises when, on account of cloudy weather, Nero had postponed the day destined by edict for him to show the king to the people, he presented him at the most convenient time, distributing armed cohorts around the temples of the Forum, and seating himself in his curule chair by the speakers' platform in the costume of a triumphant commander, surrounded by military standards and banners.

Dio 63.1.1. In the consulship of Gaius Telesinus and Suetonius Paulinus (66 AD), two events took place, one most glorious but the other most disgraceful. Nero competed among the citharodes, and when Menecrates, his former teacher, organized a victory celebration in the circus, he drove his chariot.[18]

2. Also, Tiridates was conveyed to Rome, bringing not only his own children but also those of Vologaeses, Pacorus, and Monobazus with him, and their procession journeyed through all the lands from the Euphrates like a triumphal parade.[19] 2.1. Indeed Tiridates was in his prime of youth, strength, and beauty, and all the courtiers and his royal baggage train escorted him, while three thousand Parthian cavalry and a great number of Romans followed separately after them. 2. The cities had been splendidly decked out, and their populace also welcomed them, calling out many flattering salutations. They received all their maintenance free of charge, so that a daily charge of 200,000 [sestertii] was calculated as a public expense. And this was maintained consistently for all nine months of their journey. 3. The king rode on horseback all the way as far as Italy, and his wife rode alongside him, wearing a golden helmet in place of her veil, so as not to be seen and contravene their national traditions. But in Italy Tiridates was conveyed in a two-horse coach sent to him by Nero and reached him traveling through Picenum to Naples. 4. But he would not put aside the scimitar when he approached the emperor, despite his instructions, but fastened it with nails inside its sheath; even so, he knelt on the ground and, crossing his arms and bowing to the earth before him, called Nero master. 3.1. So Nero, admiring his action, honored him with many entertainments, and in particular a gladiatorial show at Puteoli.

18 The narrative has reached AD 66, when nothing inhibits the performing emperor: Nero competes in singing to the lyre with the professional citharodes and celebrates with another public display, as charioteer, but Tacitus's account of this episode is lost and we must depend on Dio's epitomator. Luckily, he seems to have preserved this story in full.

19 Tiridates was no doubt bringing his own children and those of his brothers, too, to be educated at Rome as hostages for his loyal behavior.

Patrobius, one of Nero's freedmen, produced it, employing such a dazzling and costly display that on one day he brought only Ethiopians onstage—men, women, and children. 2. Since there was an obligation to pay Patrobius some honor for this, Tiridates shot at some of the wild beasts from his high balcony and hit and killed two bulls with a single shot, if you can believe it.

4.1. After this, Nero escorted him to Rome and placed the diadem on his head. The whole city was decorated with lights and garlands, and huge crowds were seen everywhere, with the Forum exceptionally full. 2. The people occupied its central area, arranged by rank, wearing white garments and carrying laurel branches, while soldiers filled the rest, brilliantly armed so that their weapons and standards glittered and flashed. The tiled roofs of all the houses in the neighborhood were covered with people who had climbed up onto them. 3. Every one of these features had been prepared during the night, and now Nero, clad in triumphal costume, entered the Forum at dawn along with the Senate and his praetorian guard, mounted the dais, and sat on the ruler's throne; after this, Tiridates made his way with his retinue through ranks of heavily armed soldiers arrayed on either side. 5.1. When an immense shout arose at this, Tiridates was frightened and for a while was dumbstruck as if at the point of death. Then, when the herald called for silence, he gained courage and, swallowing his pride, submitted himself to the circumstances and necessity, no longer caring whether he said something humble when he had such prospects in view.

2. And this is how he spoke:

"Master, I, a descendant of Arsaces and brother of the kings Vologaeses and Pacorus, am thy slave. And I have come to thee, my god, bowing before thee like Mithras, and shall be whatever thou makest of me. For thou art my destiny and my fortune." 3. And Nero answered him, "You have acted well in coming here in person, so that you may enjoy my favor face to face. Indeed, what neither your father left to you nor your brothers gave and preserved for you I bestow upon you and name you King of Armenia, so that you and they may learn that I can both take away kingdoms and bestow them."

4. After this speech, he bade Tiridates go up the steps, made for this purpose, that led to the speakers' platform, and when he was seated there at his feet, Nero set the diadem on his head. At this, there were many acclamations of all kinds.

6.1. By decree, there was a theatrical festival. And the theater—not just the stage but the whole proscenium all around—was gilded, and everything that was brought on stage was also adorned with gold. This was the reason that they also called it the Golden Day. 2. The awnings spread in the sky to ward off the sunshine were purple dyed and at their center was embroidered the likeness of Nero driving his chariot, and around him golden stars glittered.[20]

3. Such was the event, and Nero gave an extravagant banquet, after which he sang to the lyre and drove his chariot in a public show wearing the uniform of the Green team and the charioteer's helmet.[21] 4. Tiridates was disgusted at this display and praised Nero's general Corbulo, reproaching him only for tolerating such a master. Nor did he conceal this feeling from Nero but said to him, "Master, thou hast a good slave in Corbulo."[22] 5. But Nero did not understand his meaning.

Plin. *HN* 33.54. Nero had the theater of Pompey covered with gold for a single day's use, the day on which he proposed to show it to King Tiridates of Armenia.

Suet. *Ner.* 13.2. As Tiridates approached up a sloping ramp, Nero let the king fall at his feet, then raised him with his right hand and kissed him. Then, at the king's request, he removed his tiara and set the diadem on his head, while a man of praetorian rank proclaimed the suppliant's words to the crowd in translation. Then Tiridates was escorted to the theater and repeated his supplication; Nero had the king seated beside him on his right. For this, Nero was hailed as *Imperator* and, after bearing a laurel branch up to the Capitol, he closed the Temple of Janus Geminus on the grounds that no possibility of war now remained.[23]

20 As Champlin ([2003], 227–29) argues, Nero had postponed the staging of this ceremony because he needed the sunshine to reflect the gold and gilded surfaces of the Forum; similarly, the purple awnings and golden image of Nero driving his chariot presented him as Apollo in his role as sun god.

21 Far from being a gentleman amateur, Nero was shamelessly professional in this partisanship.

22 Domitius Corbulo had fought Vologaeses and Tiridates for ten years and reduced them to this diplomatic face-saving ceremonial (see Chapter IV). Tiridates' admiration may well have increased Nero's resolve to execute his too talented and popular general.

23 The stress in Suetonius's account, far shorter than Dio's quoted here, is chiefly on the resemblance of the ceremony to a Roman triumph, though there is no triumphal procession entering the city. A victorious general would be hailed as *Imperator* by his troops, and normally brought a representative unit of his victorious army to a halt outside the walls before making his formal entry as *triumphator* along the processional route to the Capitol. Instead, Nero, seated on his magistrate's chair, waits for Tiridates to approach him as a suppliant, like a conquered enemy (Suetonius notes his prostration at Nero's knees). This royal submission is Nero's first counterpart to a true military triumph; he will offer another version upon his return to Rome from his year of victories in the cycle of

Suet. *Ner.* 30. Nero's lavishness on Tiridates seemed almost unbelievable. He spent 800,000 sestertii every day, and when the king left Rome, he gave him more than 100 million.

Nero began to adapt his youthful talent as a racing charioteer and his more formal development of the art of a citharode.

Suet. *Ner.* 19.3. I have brought together these acts of Nero, some of them deserving no criticism and some even modest praise, to separate them from his scandals and crimes, which I shall discuss from this point.[24]

20.1. Along with the other disciplines he studied in his boyhood days, he was also steeped in music. As soon as he reached the imperial office, he summoned Terpnus the citharode, who at that time flourished ahead of all others, and, seated day after day beside him as he sang after dinner late into the night, he, too, began to practice and train, not missing any of the devices that the artists in that skill used to employ in order to preserve or develop his voice; he even lay down wearing a lead sheet on his breast and would gargle with a clyster and vomit, and avoid apples and foods injurious to his objectives until his efforts so beguiled him that, despite having a thin and husky voice, he longed to appear on stage, regularly saying to his friends that music concealed met no respect.

Tac. *Ann.* 14.14. Nero had long had a hankering to drive a four-horse chariot, and a no less disgraceful desire to sing accompanied by the lyre like a stage

---

Greek athletic contests. The Temple of Janus was only closed when peace was restored and Rome was no longer at war.

While Corbulo had been the actual commander in Rome's victorious campaigns against the Parthians, Augustus had inaugurated the tradition that all achievements of an emperor's legate were credited to the emperor under whose auspices he had campaigned; hence, Nero is hailed as victorious commander and dedicates his laurel branch to Jupiter Capitolinus. His closing of the gates of Janus (the temple took the form of a double-gated archway) echoes a rare religious ritual that Augustus boasted of achieving three times during his long reign.

24 As he did for Caligula (*Calig.* 22), Suetonius has adopted the explicit procedure of separating those of Nero's public actions that met with his approval, or at least acceptance, from his more reprehensible behavior. But he also divides the next six chapters (*Ner.* 20–25) between Nero's passions for singing and for charioteering, assigning to each activity first a private phase of training and then a section on his more public performances. So in Chapter 20 he reports Nero's early enthusiasm and vocal training methods with Terpnus and then breaks off to begin again with his early enthusiasm for horses and chariot racing in Chapters 21 and 22: see Tac. *Ann.*14.14, combining Nero's two passions.

performer. Horse racing, he would say, was the sport of kings, one in which leaders of old would frequently indulge, and it was celebrated in the panegyrics of the bards and put on in honor of the gods. Furthermore, he said, singing was sacred to Apollo, and it was dressed for this activity that this outstanding, prescient deity stood not only in the cities of Greece but also in the temples of Rome. There was now no holding him, and Seneca and Burrus thought that, to prevent him from gaining both ends, they should grant him one. And so an area was fenced off in the Vatican valley for him to drive his horses without making a public spectacle of it. Soon the Roman people were actually invited to watch, and they praised Nero to the skies. . . . However, the exposure of his humiliating activities did not induce weariness of them as his advisers had expected but further stimulation.

Suet. *Ner.* 20.2. And his debut was at Naples, where the theater was shaken by earth tremors during his performance, but even so, he did not abandon singing until he had completed the aria. He sang there repeatedly over several days. When he had taken a brief rest to refresh his voice, he tired of seclusion and moved from the baths to the theater, and there, after feasting in the orchestra surrounded by a large crowd, he promised in Greek that after a little more to drink he would offer them a resounding encore. 3. He was charmed by the harmonized acclamations of the Alexandrians who had poured into Naples from the freshly arrived grain freighters, and summoned more from Alexandria. But he called up with equal enthusiasm young lads of equestrian rank and more than 5,000 of the strongest youths from the common people all around, who divided into teams and learned the types of applause—"buzzes," "rooftiles," and "potsherds"[25]—and gave their services when he sang. These were men recognizable from their thick hair and preeminent grooming, their left hands bare, without rings. Their leaders earned 400,000 sestertii.

Suet. *Ner.* 25.1. When he returned from Greece . . . his claque followed his chariot like victory celebrators shouting that they were "Augustiani" and soldiers of his triumph.

Dio 62.20.4. [Upon his entry into Rome], the city was all adorned with swags of flowers and blazing with lamps and incense, and everyone, especially the senators, shouted out together: "Hail Olympic victor, Hail Pythian victor,

25 These names may evoke the rhythms of the various types of cheering, whether continuous buzzes or staccato, on one note or undulating.

Augustus. Augustus, hail to Nero Hercules, hail to Nero Apollo.[26] You are the only victor in the circuit, the only one in all ages, Augustus. Your voice is holy, and those who hear you are blessed."

Suet. *Ner.* 22.1. He burned with a passion for horses even from his early boyhood, and most of his chatter was about chariot races, although it was forbidden. Once when he was complaining among his fellow students about the dragging of a Green charioteer[27] and his *paedagogus* scolded him, he lied that he was talking about Hector. At the beginning of his principate, however, he played every day with ivory teams on the gaming table, and he used to leave his country retreat to watch even the minor races, at first secretly and then more or less openly so that no one was left in doubt that he would be there on that day. 2. Nor did he hide the fact that he wanted the number of prizes to be increased, so that the show was extended into nightfall, with the sessions multiplied, since not even the masters of the factions would condescend to bring their teams unless it was for a whole day's run.[28]

Soon he wanted to drive himself and even be watched frequently, and after building up his experience among the slaves and common folk, he displayed himself in the Circus Maximus to the eyes of the whole crowd, using a freedman to raise the starting signal from the point where the magistrates usually did.

Both Tacitus and Suetonius give parallel treatment to the young emperor's pursuit of the two widely different skills; both build up a crescendo in the shame of publicity from initially quasi-private performances—first singing in Greek Naples, away from Rome and then later in Rome, and first watching the races but soon actually driving chariots on private grounds for a domestic audience. Roman readers did not need instruction in the techniques of chariot racing, but the art of

26 Common to all these excerpts are the organized cheers and slogans both of Nero's "Alexandrian" cheerleaders ("Augustus's men," a group he formed early in his singing career) and of his official welcome back to Rome. This is the most explicit of various occasions on which Nero encourages his own identification with Apollo.

27 The Green teams were most favored in Nero's day, and if the charioteer was dragged along the ground, it could be reinterpreted as Hector's brutal dragging by Achilles around the walls of Troy.

28 Suetonius offers a glimpse—and perhaps the only one from this period—of the all-important owners and trainers who controlled the availability of horses, chariots, and drivers for the Circus that represented the teams of each "color." Nero clearly favored the Greens (see the preceding Tiridates narrative). But while Suetonius deliberately reports both of Nero's passions in matching installments, Tacitus introduces both crazes in one sentence and then proceeds to describe the same early races in a different location.

singing to the lyre would be quite alien and require details of training methods, and this may be why Suetonius has less to say about Nero's racing career than his singing ambitions, both as citharode and as tragic hero in the genre of quasi-operatic scenes or sequences of scenes that Nero chose to perform.

Suet. *Ner.* 21.1. Thinking it very important to sing even at Rome, he revived the Neronian contest before the predetermined date, and when everybody demanded to hear his divine voice, he answered that he would give the opportunity to those so interested to do so in his park. However, when even the detachment of soldiers on duty at the time backed up the prayers of the crowd, he gladly promised he would perform it again and instantly ordered his name to be inscribed in the register of citharodes claiming a turn. Then, when his lot had been dropped in the urn with the rest, he entered in his turn, the prefects of the praetorian guard holding his lyre, followed by the military tribunes and his closest friends. 2. When he paused after completing the prelude, he used Cluvius Rufus the ex-consul to announce that he would sing Niobe, and he went on into the tenth hour and postponed the crowning and the rest of the contest to the next year to give himself more opportunities to sing.[29] And as this seemed a long delay, he did not stop repeatedly making himself public. He even hesitated whether to offer his services among the stage performers at private shows, when one of the praetors offered 1,000,000 sestertii.

3. He also sang tragedies,[30] wearing the masks of heroes and gods, and similarly of heroines and goddesses, having the masks designed to resemble his features and those of whatever woman he loved.[31] Among other scenes, he sang Canace in labor, Orestes as mother killer, Oedipus blinded, and Hercules driven mad, and there is a story that in this drama a raw recruit, who was

29 Cluvius Rufus was not only a former consul, one of the most senior men in the Senate, but a historian cited by Tacitus (*Ann.* 14.20–21) as one of his sources for Nero (see the Introduction); he may well be the chief source for Nero's behavior as a contestant in the Greek Sacred Games.

30 The key to Nero's art form is "sang." While the star dancers enacted scenes or whole mythical narratives, Nero seems to have recognized that he could not compete in dancing (Dio 62.18.1: "Nero ordered Paris, the pantomime dancer, to be executed because he had wanted to learn dancing from Paris but could not succeed"). The roles from myth or tragedy specified here might refer only to climactic scenes (the equivalent of the baroque operatic *scena ed aria*), such as the incestuous Canace's labor, though he may have extended them to a sequence of dramatic episodes.

31 Nero carries his impersonation to the level of identification. When performing as a citharode, he would wear a rich, ornate costume but no mask, and presumably when singing "Niobe" would keep his own identity while voicing the bereaved queen's emotions.

set to guard the entrances, saw Nero loaded and bound with chains, as the plot required, and ran up to bring him aid.

Dio 62.20.1. To provide a climax worthy of these performances, Nero himself came onstage and had Gallio announce his name. Caesar himself stood onstage dressed in a citharode's costume. "My lords, listen to me kindly," he said, and 2. it was the emperor who said this, playing and singing the role of Attis or the Bacchantes, while many soldiers stood on guard and all the populace that the seats could hold sat watching. And yet his voice was weak and husky, as tradition has it, so that he provoked laughter and tears from them all. 3. Burrus and Seneca stood by him, prompting like a pair of instructors, and they waved their arms and robes whenever he sang, urging the rest to do the same.

It looks as though the senior members of Nero's court and his military officers had decided to put a brave face on it and back Nero up in a performance that they must have felt was incongruous. Like Cluvius Rufus, Seneca's brother Gallio was an ex-consul; the prefects of the guard were the most senior military officers in Rome. Suetonius returns to Nero's behavior as a singing contestant in the context of his tour of the Greek games, describing it in section 23 and the first part of 24, before breaking in suddenly with a report of Nero's multiple acts of charioteering, culminating in his attempt to steer a ten-horse chariot at Olympia (although he had jeered at Mithridates in an unidentified poem for attempting this). Although he was thrown, he picked himself up, but abandoned the race before the end—and yet still was awarded the crown. (Again, our text of Tacitus has broken off before the missing narrative of the Greek tour.) But difficult as it is to disentangle Suetonius's alternation of Nero's twin enthusiasms, Dio's and Suetonius's versions are both leading up to the climax of his return to Italy and Rome itself.

Nero now turned to the fully professionalized cycles of both song and equestrian skills.

Our elite sources treat as shameful aspects of his enthusiasm both Nero's effort to switch from the status of noble amateur to professional and the fact that he entered as a contestant at Rome and in Greece, even adding criticism of his consideration of performing for payment. Suetonius reports both Nero's alleged respect for the Greeks as the only worthy critics of his art (Ner. 22.3) and the way he showed no respect for the schedules of the Sacred Games (23.1). Like Suetonius, Dio is fascinated by the implications of the emperor aspiring to compete professionally, and both authors offer detailed reports of Nero's deportment onstage and jealousy toward rival contestants, a strange mixture of apparent timidity and shameless rivalry.

Tacitus's text breaks off before the narrative of Nero's tour of Greece in AD 66–67, so we must rely on Suetonius and Dio for both his tour and his return to Rome.

Tac. *Ann.*16.4.1. Meanwhile, as the fiveyear games approached (the lustral games of AD 65), the Senate, wishing to avoid a scandal, offered the emperor victory in singing and added the crown for eloquence, in order to keep hidden a scandalous stage performance. 2. Nero, however, kept saying he had no need of the influence or the authority of the Senate: he was as good as his competitors and would win the praise he deserved from the impartial decision of the judges. He began by reciting a poem onstage. 3. Then the crowd insisted that he "put on show his entire repertoire" (these were their very words), and he entered the theater again. This time, he followed all the rules of lyre playing—not sitting when he was tired, wiping away the sweat only with the garment he was wearing, and keeping from view any emissions from his mouth or nose. 4. Finally, bending his knee and with a respectful wave of his hand to the crowd, he awaited the verdict of the judges with feigned anxiety. And the city plebs, used to encouraging the body movements even of actors (i.e., dancers), thundered its applause, in time and with orchestrated clapping.[32] One might have thought them delighted, and perhaps they were delighted, with no concern for the public disgrace.

Suet. *Ner.* 23.1. Nero entered all the contests; he ordered games scheduled for quite different seasons to be concentrated in one year, even demanding that some be repeated, and at Olympia, too, contrary to its tradition, he added a contest in music to the program. . . . 2. While Nero sang, it was not permitted to leave the theater, even under necessity.[33] Hence, some women are said to have given birth at the shows, and a number of men, when they grew weary of listening and praising him, and the gates to the city were closed, either

32 Tacitus's account of Nero competing as citharode at Rome (in AD 65) matches in detail Suetonius's report of his stage behavior (*Ner.* 23.3, where he addressed the judges most respectfully, and 24.1, where he scrupulously obeyed the code, adding only the rhythmic clapping and chanting previously associated with Nero's corps of Augustiani). To counter this picture of public rejoicing, Tacitus next reports as the more severe judgment of old-fashioned country gentlemen his personal disapproval of Nero's theatrical activities, which he sees as an offense against his class and birth and supreme office. In 16.5.2, he illustrates the consequences with audience misbehavior during these games that shocked foreign delegations, and mob rioting resulted in the deaths of knights trampled underfoot and incurred mass executions.

33 Suetonius seems to shift here from the theme of Greek contests to describing Nero's performances in general.

jumped surreptitiously from the wall or feigned death and were carried out for burial.[34] Now it is almost beyond belief how anxiously and tremulously he competed, what with jealousy of his fellow contestants and fear of the judges. He would treat his rivals as if they were on equal terms with him, slandering them in secret, at times cursing them when they encountered him, or if any were distinguished in their skill, even bribing them. 3. In addition, before he began, he would address the judges most respectfully, saying he had done everything that was required but the outcome was in the hands of Fortune, but they as expert and wise persons should exclude the accidents of Fortune. Then, when they encouraged him to be bold, he would retreat more calmly, yet not even then without anxiety, accusing their silence and modesty as grimness and ill will and saying he suspected them.

24.1. Indeed, when competing, he obeyed the code so strictly that he never dared to spit, and even wiped away his perspiring brow with his arm; in one tragic scene, he was quick to pick up his stick, which had fallen, and panicked, afraid of being disqualified for the lapse, and he was not reassured until an actor swore he had seen nothing because of the delight and cheers of the crowd. Then he declared himself victor; for this reason, he also competed as herald in all contests. To prevent any memory or trace of other sacred victors surviving anywhere, he ordered all their statues and portraits to be overthrown and dragged away by the hook and thrown into the latrines.

Dio 62.8.4. But [Nero's retinue] were such as you would expect Nero's soldiers to be, and their weapons were lyres and plectra, masks and buskins. And his victories were the kind of thing that suited such an army, and he defeated Terpnus, Diodorus, and Pammenes as if they were Philip, Perseus, or Antiochus.[35] And it seems he compelled Pammenes, old as he was, to compete (he had been in his prime during Gaius's years) so as to do violence to the statues dedicated to him. 9.1. If that were all he had done, he would have incurred mockery. But how could one endure hearing, let alone seeing, a Roman, a senator, a nobleman and high priest, Caesar Augustus the emperor, listed on the white board of contestants, practicing voice exercises, rehearsing songs, and cultivating long hair and a shaved chin, 2. tossing his garment over his shoulder at the races, walking around with one or two attendants, glaring at

34 Compare Dio 62.15.3 on the subterfuges of members of the audience who could not endure until the end of Nero's extended performances.

35 Terpnus had been Nero's teacher; the two others were probably of the older generation, but Nero's pride in his victory was as great as if he had won the famous Roman victories of the second century BC over King Philip V of Macedon, his son Perseus, or King Antiochus III ("The Great") of Syria.

his opponents and constantly uttering provocative insults at them, scared of the masters of ceremony and floggers at the games and secretly paying out cash to them so as not to be caught and flogged? But though he did all this just to win in the competitions of citharodes and tragic singers and heralds, he was defeated in the contest of Caesars.

Dio 62.12.1–2. With the excuse of needing something from them, Nero had actually taken off to Greece with him large numbers of leading citizens, so they would die there. Those in Rome and Italy he surrendered to the charge of one Helios, a member of the imperial household. The man had been given absolute carte blanche so that he could confiscate property and send into exile or execute private citizens, equestrians, and senators even before informing Nero.

And so at that time the Roman empire was simultaneously a slave to two rulers, Nero and Helios, and I cannot say which of them was worse. In general, their comportment was much the same, but in this one regard they were different: the descendant of Augustus was emulating lyre players and tragic actors, and Claudius's freedman was emulating the Caesars.

Dio 62.14.3. Nero competed in every city that held a contest, using Cluvius Rufus, a former consul, as the herald for all the heraldic duties, except at Sparta and Athens. He shunned Sparta because he thought the laws of Lycurgus were opposed to his purpose and shunned Athens because of the myth of the Erinyes. 4. His announcement was: "Nero Caesar wins this contest and crowns the Roman people and the inhabited world, which is his domain." Thus, while apparently possessing the whole world, he sang to the cithara, acted as herald, and played tragic roles.

While he was in Greece, Nero provided a concrete demonstration of his admiration for the Greeks by declaring their freedom, recorded in this inscription preserved on a marble slab in the wall of the Church of St. George at Acraephia in northeast Boeotia. The inscription comprises what are really three separate documents: (a) the edict of Nero summoning Greeks to Corinth, (b) the speech he made in Corinth about the liberation of Greece, and (c) the decree of Epaminondas of Acraephia passed by that city dedicating an altar and offering sacrifices in gratitude for Nero's gesture.

ILS 8794 (Smallwood 64, see Figure 10) The Emperor (Nero) Caesar declares:

> Since I wish to repay the most eminent of the Greeks for their goodwill and pious conduct toward me, I bid as many people as is practicable from this province to gather at Corinth on November 28th

When the crowds came together in an assembly, Nero addressed them as follows:

> Gentlemen of Greece: Even though no request made to my generous nature can be without hope, what I grant to you is something you did not even presume to request. All of you Greeks living in Achaea and in what until now has been the Peloponnese: accept the gift of freedom without taxation, something that none of you ever possessed even in your most prosperous times, as you were subservient to foreigners or to others among you. I only wish that I were granting you this gift when Greece was flourishing, so that more people would be benefiting from my favor. I therefore find fault with the present age for using up the greatness of this kindness of mine too early. Furthermore, I now grant you this favor not from pity but from goodwill, and I do it also in repayment to your gods, whose benefaction I have always experienced in my land and sea journeys, for granting me the ability to confer such benefactions. For other leaders, too, have given freedom to cities, [*erased* but Nero alone] has granted it to a province.

Epaminondas, son of Epaminondas,[36] high priest for life of the Augusti and of Nero Claudius Caesar Augustus, then spoke, moving that this preliminary decree that he formulated go to the Boule and the People:[37]

> Inasmuch as Nero, lord of the entire world, Emperor almighty, appointed to hold tribunician power for the 13th time,[38] father of his fatherland, a new Sun that has shone on the Greeks, has chosen to confer a benefit on Greece, repaying and respecting our gods who always stand by him to care for him and protect him, and as he who is the one and only most grand emperor of all time and a philhellene, [*erased* Nero] Zeus the Deliverer has restored to us what was from time

36 Epaminondas, a wealthy pro-Roman citizen of Acraephia, is known from other inscriptions in the town. He was the priest of the local imperial cult, and an ambassador sent on behalf of the Boeotian *Koinon* (Federation) to congratulate Caligula on his accession (*IG* VII.211–12).

37 The Boule was broadly a council of citizens that would oversee the regular operations of the city and prepare measures for the public assembly ("the People"). Little was known of such councils outside Attica. In Boeotia in the classical period, a municipality of full citizens was split into departments, each of which acted alternately as council.

38 The Greek word used here, *apodeigmenos*, is regularly the equivalent of the Latin *designatus*, a term used of someone assigned an office sometime before their actual tenure. It is not appropriate to the holding of tribunician power, and the town has either made a mistake or is using the expression loosely in a nontechnical sense, as conveyed in the translation.

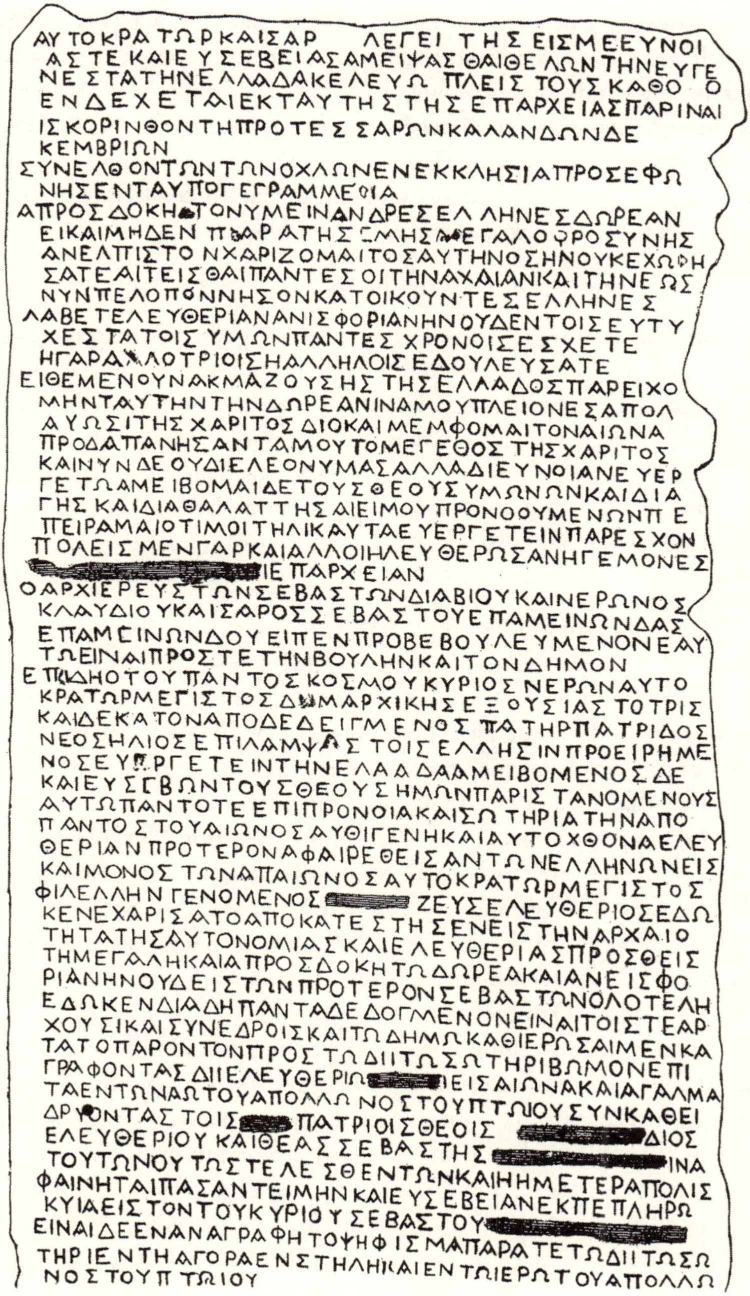

ΑΥΤΟΚΡΑΤΩΡ ΚΑΙΣΑΡ ΛΕΓΕΙ ΤΗΣ ΕΙΣ ΜΕ ΕΥΝΟΙ
ΑΣ ΤΕ ΚΑΙ ΕΥΣΕΒΕΙΑΣ ΑΜΕΙΨΑΣΘΑΙ ΘΕΛΩΝ ΤΗΝ ΕΥΓΕ
ΝΕΣΤΑΤΗΝ ΕΛΛΑΔΑ ΚΕΛΕΥΩ ΠΛΕΙΣΤΟΥΣ ΚΑΘΟ Ο
ΕΝΔΕΧΕΤΑΙ ΕΚ ΤΑΥΤΗΣ ΤΗΣ ΕΠΑΡΧΕΙΑΣ ΠΑΡΙΝΑΙ
ΙΣ ΚΟΡΙΝΘΟΝ ΤΗ ΠΡΟ ΤΕΣΣΑΡΩΝ ΚΑΛΑΝΔΩΝ ΔΕ
ΚΕΜΒΡΙΩΝ
ΣΥΝΕΛΘΟΝΤΩΝ ΤΩΝ ΟΧΛΩΝ ΕΝ ΕΚΚΛΗΣΙΑ ΠΡΟΣΕΦΩ
ΝΗΣΕΝ ΤΑ ΥΠΟΓΕΓΡΑΜΜΕΘΙΑ
ΑΠΡΟΣΔΟΚΗΤΟΝ ΥΜΕΙΝ ΑΝΔΡΕΣ ΕΛΛΗΝΕΣ ΔΩΡΕΑΝ
ΕΙ ΚΑΙ ΜΗΔΕΝ ΠΑΡ ΑΤΗΣ ΕΜΗΣ ΜΕΓΑΛΟΦΡΟΣΥΝΗΣ
ΑΝΕΛΠΙΣΤΟΝ ΧΑΡΙΖΟΜΑΙ ΤΟΣΑΥΤΗΝ ΟΣΗΝ ΟΥΚ ΕΧΩΡΗ
ΣΑΤΕ ΑΙΤΕΙΣΘΑΙ ΠΑΝΤΕΣ ΟΙ ΤΗΝ ΑΧΑΙΑΝ ΚΑΙ ΤΗΝ ΕΩΣ
ΝΥΝ ΠΕΛΟΠΟΝΝΗΣΟΝ ΚΑΤΟΙΚΟΥΝΤΕΣ ΕΛΛΗΝΕΣ
ΛΑΒΕΤΕ ΛΕΥΘΕΡΙΑΝ ΑΝΙΣΦΟΡΙΑΝ ΗΝ ΟΥΔΕ ΝΤΟΙΣ ΕΥΤΥ
ΧΕΣΤΑΤΟΙΣ ΥΜΩΝ ΠΑΝΤΕΣ ΧΡΟΝΟΙΣ ΕΣΧΕΤΕ
Η ΓΑΡ ΑΛΛΟΤΡΙΟΙΣ Η ΑΛΛΗΛΟΙΣ ΕΔΟΥΛΕΥΣΑΤΕ
ΕΙΘΕ ΜΕΝ ΟΥΝ ΑΚΜΑΖΟΥΣΗΣ ΤΗΣ ΕΛΛΑΔΟΣ ΠΑΡΕΙΧΟ
ΜΗΝ ΤΑΥΤΗΝ ΤΗΝ ΔΩΡΕΑΝ ΙΝΑ ΜΟΥ ΠΛΕΙΟΝΕΣ ΑΠΟΛ
ΑΥΩΣΙ ΤΗΣ ΧΑΡΙΤΟΣ ΔΙΟ ΚΑΙ ΜΕΜΦΟΜΑΙ ΤΟΝ ΑΙΩΝΑ
ΠΡΟΔΑΠΑΝΗΣΑΝΤΑ ΜΟΥ ΤΟ ΜΕΓΕΘΟΣ ΤΗΣ ΧΑΡΙΤΟΣ
ΚΑΙ ΝΥΝ ΔΕ ΟΥ ΔΙ ΕΛΕΟΝ ΥΜΑΣ ΑΛΛΑ ΔΙ ΕΥΝΟΙΑΝ ΕΥΕΡ
ΓΕΤΩ ΑΜΕΙΒΟΜΑΙ ΔΕ ΤΟΥΣ ΘΕΟΥΣ ΥΜΩΝ ΩΝ ΚΑΙ ΔΙΑ
ΓΗΣ ΚΑΙ ΔΙΑ ΘΑΛΑΤΤΗΣ ΑΙΕΙ ΜΟΥ ΠΡΟΝΟΟΥΜΕΝΩΝ ΠΕ
ΠΕΙΡΑΜΑΙ ΟΤΙ ΜΟΙ ΤΗΛΙΚΑΥΤΑ ΕΥΕΡΓΕΤΕΙΝ ΠΑΡΕΣΧΟΝ
ΠΟΛΕΙΣ ΜΕΝ ΓΑΡ ΚΑΙ ΑΛΛΟΙ ΗΛΕΥΘΕΡΩΣΑΝ ΗΓΕΜΟΝΕΣ
[illegible] ΙΕ ΠΑΡΧΕΙΑΝ
Ο ΑΡΧΙΕΡΕΥΣ ΤΩΝ ΣΕΒΑΣΤΩΝ ΔΙΑ ΒΙΟΥ ΚΑΙ ΝΕΡΩΝΟΣ
ΚΛΑΥΔΙΟΥ ΚΑΙΣΑΡΟΣ ΣΕΒΑΣΤΟΥ ΕΠΑΜΕΙΝΩΝΔΑΣ
ΕΠΑΜΕΙΝΩΝΔΟΥ ΕΙΠΕΝ ΠΡΟΒΕΒΟΥΛΕΥΜΕΝΟΝ ΕΑΥ
ΤΩ ΕΙΝΑΙ ΠΡΟΣ ΤΕ ΤΗΝ ΒΟΥΛΗΝ ΚΑΙ ΤΟΝ ΔΗΜΟΝ
ΕΠΙΔΗ Ο ΤΟΥ ΠΑΝΤΟΣ ΚΟΣΜΟΥ ΚΥΡΙΟΣ ΝΕΡΩΝ ΑΥΤΟ
ΚΡΑΤΩΡ ΜΕΓΙΣΤΟΣ ΔΗΜΑΡΧΙΚΗΣ ΕΞΟΥΣΙΑΣ ΤΟ ΤΡΙΣ
ΚΑΙΔΕΚΑΤΟΝ ΑΠΟΔΕΔΕΙΓΜΕΝΟΣ ΠΑΤΗΡ ΠΑΤΡΙΔΟΣ
ΝΕΟΣ ΗΛΙΟΣ ΕΠΙΛΑΜΨΑΣ ΤΟΙΣ ΕΛΛΗΣΙΝ ΠΡΟΕΙΡΗΜΕ
ΝΟΣ ΕΥΕΡΓΕΤΕΙΝ ΤΗΝ ΕΛΛΑΔΑ ΑΜΕΙΒΟΜΕΝΟΣ ΔΕ
ΚΑΙ ΕΥΣΕΒΩΝ ΤΟΥΣ ΘΕΟΥΣ ΗΜΩΝ ΠΑΡΙΣΤΑΝΟΜΕΝΟΥΣ
ΑΥΤΩ ΠΑΝΤΟΤΕ ΕΠΙ ΠΡΟΝΟΙΑ ΚΑΙ ΣΩΤΗΡΙΑ ΤΗΝ ΑΠΟ
ΠΑΝΤΟΣ ΤΟΥ ΑΙΩΝΟΣ ΑΥΘΙΓΕΝΗ ΚΑΙ ΑΥΤΟΧΘΟΝΑ ΕΛΕΥ
ΘΕΡΙΑΝ ΠΡΟΤΕΡΟΝ ΑΦΑΙΡΕΘΕΙΣ ΑΝ ΤΩΝ ΕΛΛΗΝΩΝ ΕΙΣ
ΚΑΙ ΜΟΝΟΣ ΤΩΝ ΑΠ ΑΙΩΝΟΣ ΑΥΤΟΚΡΑΤΩΡ ΜΕΓΙΣΤΟΣ
ΦΙΛΕΛΛΗΝ ΓΕΝΟΜΕΝΟΣ [illegible] ΖΕΥΣ ΕΛΕΥΘΕΡΙΟΣ ΕΔΩ
ΚΕΝ ΕΧΑΡΙΣΑΤΟ ΑΠΟΚΑΤΕΣΤΗΣΕΝ ΕΙΣ ΤΗΝ ΑΡΧΑΙΟ
ΤΗΤΑ ΤΗΣ ΑΥΤΟΝΟΜΙΑΣ ΚΑΙ ΕΛΕΥΘΕΡΙΑΣ ΠΡΟΣΘΕΙΣ
ΤΗ ΜΕΓΑΛΗ ΚΑΙ ΑΠΡΟΣΔΟΚΗΤΩ ΔΩΡΕΑ ΚΑΙ ΑΝΕΙΣΦΟ
ΡΙΑΝ ΗΝ ΟΥΔΕΙΣ ΤΩΝ ΠΡΟΤΕΡΟΝ ΣΕΒΑΣΤΩΝ ΟΛΟΤΕΛΗ
ΕΔΩΚΕΝ ΔΙ ΑΔΗ ΠΑΝΤΑ ΔΕΔΟΓΜΕΝΟΝ ΕΙΝΑΙ ΤΟΙΣ ΤΕ ΑΡ
ΧΟΥΣΙ ΚΑΙ ΣΥΝΕΔΡΟΙΣ ΚΑΙ ΤΩ ΔΗΜΩ ΚΑΘΙΕΡΩΣΑΙ ΜΕΝ ΚΑ
ΤΑ ΤΟ ΠΑΡΟΝ ΤΟΝ ΠΡΟΣ ΤΩ ΔΙΙ ΤΩ ΣΩΤΗΡΙ ΒΩΜΟΝ ΕΠΙ
ΓΡΑΦΟΝΤΑΣ ΔΙΙ ΕΛΕΥΘΕΡΙΩ [illegible] ΕΙΣ ΑΙΩΝΑ ΚΑΙ ΑΓΑΛΜΑ
ΤΑ ΕΝ ΤΩ ΝΑΩ ΤΟΥ ΑΠΟΛΛΩΝΟΣ ΤΟΥ ΠΤΩΙΟΥ ΣΥΝΚΑΘΕΙ
ΔΡΥΟΝΤΑΣ ΤΟΙΣ [illegible] ΠΑΤΡΙΟΙΣ ΘΕΟΙΣ [illegible] ΔΙΟΣ
ΕΛΕΥΘΕΡΙΟΥ ΚΑΙ ΘΕΑΣ ΣΕΒΑΣΤΗΣ [illegible] ΙΝΑ
ΤΟΥΤΩΝ ΟΥΤΩΣ ΤΕΛΕΣΘΕΝΤΩΝ ΚΑΙ Η ΗΜΕΤΕΡΑ ΠΟΛΙΣ
ΦΑΙΝΗΤΑΙ ΠΑΣΑΝ ΤΕΙΜΗΝ ΚΑΙ ΕΥΣΕΒΕΙΑΝ ΕΚΠΕΠΛΗΡΩ
ΚΥΙΑ ΕΙΣ ΤΟΝ ΤΟΥ ΚΥΡΙΟΥ ΣΕΒΑΣΤΟΥ [illegible]
ΕΙΝΑΙ ΔΕ ΕΝΑΝΑΓΡΑΦΗ ΤΟ ΨΗΦΙΣΜΑ ΠΑΡΑ ΤΕ ΤΩ ΔΙΙ ΤΩ ΣΩ
ΤΗΡΙ ΕΝ ΤΗ ΑΓΟΡΑ ΕΝ ΣΤΗΛΗ ΚΑΙ ΕΝ ΤΩ ΙΕΡΩ ΤΟΥ ΑΠΟΛΛΩ
ΝΟΣ ΤΟΥ ΠΤΩΙΟΥ

FIGURE 10. The Acraephia Decree.

immemorial the liberty that was native to us and born in our land, but which was taken away from the Greeks, and has brought us back to our ancient condition of autonomy and liberty, adding immunity from taxation to his great and unexpected gift, something that none of the earlier Augusti fully gave us; for all of this the decision has been made by the archons, the councilors and the people to consecrate at this time an altar beside Zeus the Savior, inscribing on it:

"To Zeus [*erased* Nero] the Deliverer, for evermore"

and also dedicating to [*erased* our] ancestral gods, in the temple of Apollo Ptoos, statues of [*erased* Nero] Zeus the Deliverer and the goddess Augusta [*erased* Messalina], so that when these measures have been taken in this way our city, too, may be clearly seen to have fully shown honor and reverence toward the lord Augustus [*erased* Nero's house]. The decree is to appear as an inscription on a stele both in the temple of Zeus the Savior in the Agora, and in the shrine of Apollo Ptoos.[39]

The high point of Nero's tour of Greece must surely have been the declaration that the whole of Achaea would be "liberated," given autonomy and exemption from tribute. Plutarch sees his gesture as a reprise of the famous decree of Titus Flamininus in 196 BC declaring the freedom of the Greeks in the very same city, Corinth. Plutarch observes, however, that while Flamininus used a herald, Nero proclaimed the initiative in person, from a dais in the crowded agora (Plut. *Flam.* 12.8; Suet. *Ner.* 24.2 says from inside the stadium). The inscription dates this occasion to November 28. The year is not specified but is almost certainly 67, toward the end of Nero's tour, as Suetonius indicates, but since the thirteenth year of Nero's tribunician authority would have expired on October 13, 67, we must either assume that there is a mistake in the inscription or that the tribunician year is deemed to have begun not on the anniversary of Claudius's death but on December 4, when the law to confer the authority was passed by the popular assembly, the date when it was officially celebrated in Rome (Smallwood 19.14–15, 21.21). Some have argued that the occasion should be placed in 66. According to Plutarch and Suetonius, Nero's announcement took place during the Isthmian Games. They were due

39 Mt. Ptoon was located in Boeotia. It was the site of a sanctuary of Apollo, under the administration of Acraephia. It was destroyed by Alexander and later rebuilt. Evidence of it is still attested in the archaeological remains.

to be held in 67, but they would normally take place in the spring, so presumably they would have had to be postponed until later in that same year. Acraephia proposed a decree in honor of Zeus Eleutherios Nero, Zeus the Deliverer, or Jupiter Liberator, Nero. A rare, undated coin from Corinth that may be connected to the event has the legend IUPPITER LIBERATOR (Mattingly [1920], 38).

It is of course important to realize that the decree meant much less than it might sound to modern ears. Greece was not to be detached from the empire; it would receive a very limited autonomy, most notably exemption from tribute. Also, it is to be noted that a number of important Greek cities, such as Athens and Sparta, were already "free," with the status of *civitates liberae et immunes* ("communities free and exempt from tribute"). Greece seems to have been suffering from economic hardship, as alluded to in Nero's speech, and this gesture would have given the area a considerable financial boost, as well as allowing Nero to mark his thanks for his unblemished record of victories.

In return for the loss of a public province, Sardinia was assigned to senatorial administration. The arrangement proved short-lived, as Vespasian annulled Nero's measure, alleging internal dissent in Greece (Paus. 7.7.14; Suet. *Vesp.* 8.2; Philos. *Apol.* 5.41). Moreover, the Acraephians' gratitude was short-lived: they later systematically erased the instances of Nero's, as well as Statilia Messalina's, names from the inscription (although they did overlook the one at the beginning of the decree!).

Nero returns to Rome.

Suet. *Ner.* 25.1. When he returned from Greece, Nero entered Naples, because this was the first place he had displayed his art, with white horses, having dismantled part of the wall as is the practice of Sacred Victors;[40] he entered Antium, then Alba, and then Rome in the same way, in the chariot in which Augustus had once triumphed, wearing a purple robe and a cloak

40 Sacred Victors are the victors in the four major games: Olympian, Pythian, Isthmian, and Nemean. Nero has privileged the Olympian and Pythian crowns over the two others, which are tacitly included with the other crowns. Augustus had added the Actia, held at Nicopolis to honor Apollo of Actium for the victory over Antony. By Nero's time, there were Heraia, games of Hera, at Argos. Nero is described as gathering awards from any and every local contest (except Athens and Sparta), but to be *Periodonikes* (Victor in all the games) required victory in these six contests.

adorned with gold stars and with the Olympic garland on his brow and the Pythian garland in his right hand. He was preceded by a parade of the other crowns, with their titles recording where, over whom, and with what themes of song or dramatic plots he had been victorious; his applauders followed his chariot like celebrating soldiers, shouting that they were "Augustiani" and soldiers in his triumph. 2. From there, after demolishing the entrance arch of the Circus Maximus, he proceeded through the Velabrum and Forum, making for Apollo's temple on the Palatine.[41] As he advanced, victims were sacrificed at intervals, as crocus perfume was repeatedly sprinkled over the roads and birds, crescents, and sweetmeats were piled on the crowd. He put his sacred crowns in his bedchamber around the couches, also statues of himself in the costume of a citharode, an emblem that he also struck on his coinage. 3. After that, he was so far from easing off his passion and letting it lapse that, in order to preserve his voice, he never addressed the soldiers except in absence or with a spokesman to utter his words, and he did nothing serious or in play without his voice trainer standing by him to warn him to spare his windpipe and apply a handkerchief to his mouth. And he offered his friendship or declared hostility to many according to whether they praised him more or less generously.

FIGURE 11. *RIC*[2] Nero 416, Copper As. Obverse: NERO CLAVDIUS CAESAR AVG(ustus) GERM(anicus), "Nero Claudius Caesar Augustus Germanicus." Reverse: PONTIF(ex) MAX(imus) T(ribunicia P(otestate) IMP(erator) P(ater) P(atriae), S(enatus) C(onsulto), "Chief Priest, with Tribunician Authority, Imperator, Father of the Country. By a decree of the Senate." From the collection of Andreas Pangerl/romancoins.info.

41 Demolishing the entrance arch of the Circus Maximus mimics the privilege Greek cities awarded to their victors of driving through their city's fortifications. Nero's cult of Apollo (on which compare Suet. *Ner.* 53) was turning into identification.

Suetonius here makes a rare reference to a coin type in explaining that upon his return from Greece, Nero struck a coin of himself in the garb of a citharode. Suetonius had no doubt seen the coin illustrated in Figure 11, but he was mistaken in his belief that it was not struck until AD 67. The type is a common issue from about AD 62. Moreover, it is likely that the figure on the reverse is technically Apollo, in flowing robes and playing the cithara, a harplike instrument. But an association with Nero himself was surely to be drawn, reinforced by the fact that Nero's legend carries over onto the reverse of the coin. In *Apocolocyntosis* 4, Apollo wishes Nero his own grace and musical talents. The image of the citharode may be intended to recall the statue of Apollo Citharoedos at the Palatine temple, said by some sources to have the facial features of Augustus.

Dio 62.20.1. When he entered Rome, a portion of the wall was torn down and a section of the gates broken through, because some people claimed each of these customs was observed for crowned victors of the contests. 2. And, first of all, men entered bearing the crowns he [Nero] had won, and behind them came other men, carrying placards on spears on which the name of each event and the form of the contest were inscribed with a statement that Nero Caesar was first of all Romans to win it in all of time.

3. Then Nero himself appeared on the victory chariot in which Augustus once had paraded his many victories;[42] he wore a purple garment studded with gold, he was crowned with a garland of wild olive, and he held before him the Pythian laurel. Diodorus the citharode rode with him, 4. and he went up through the racecourse and the Forum with the footsoldiers, the knights, and the Senate to the Capitol and from there to the Palatine;[43] the whole city was garlanded and glittering, and perfumed with incense, 5. and everyone, especially the senators, all cried together, "All hail, Olympic victor, all hail, Pythian victor, Augustus, Augustus."

Dio and Suetonius are working from a single source, as the many details in common indicate. This was not a Roman general returning to Italy, whose triumph would lead to the Temple of Capitoline Jupiter, but a Greek artist (technites)

42 This recall of Augustus is not mentioned by Suetonius and may be a later invention.

43 The citharode Diodorus rides in the victor's chariot as Roman generals might take their children with them.

and athlete following the custom of victorious Greek charioteers in breaking down and driving through the city walls—the "eiselastic *victory.*"[44] *This was certainly the most glamorous victory in the Sacred Games honored by cities, and hymned as the Greek model of glory by Horace* (Odes 1.1.3–6): *"[T]here are some whose delight is to gather the dust of Olympia in the race, and avoid the turning post with burning wheels, men whom the glorious palm of victory has swept up to the gods, masters of the earth." But by the end of the fifth century, nobles like Alcibiades did not drive their own chariot teams. At Rome, Nero differed from the* triumphator *not only in his unheroic musical achievements but because the* triumphator *himself traditionally did not drive in the city: he rode with a charioteer as chauffeur.*

APPENDIX

Nero as the Object of Contemporary Poetry

We saw earlier in this chapter that both Tacitus (*Ann.* 14.16.1) and Suetonius (*Ner.* 52) attest to Nero's preoccupation with composing poetry in a social setting, most likely in competitive individual recitals at drinking parties of young courtiers. While Tacitus stresses the emperor's dependence on the language and ideas of his companions, Suetonius actually took advantage of his access to imperial archives to vindicate Nero's originality by examining the emperor's notebooks, with their evidence of his revisions and corrections.

More scattered evidence confirms that the young emperor was an ambitious poet both in occasional short forms and potential epic lays, but formal poetry was probably only a default while he was thwarted from more showy performance genres. Quite soon, there were new imperial genres that could only be addressed *to* the emperor and not composed *by* him: panegyric, occasional forms of welcome or sendoff ("bon voyage"), birthday celebrations, and poems of thanks. This can be illustrated by Apollo's salute to the new golden prince in the anonymous parodic *Apocolocyntosis*, generally attributed to Seneca, and by Lucan's grandiose imitation in the proem of his epic of the civil war of the prayerful salute to Augustus in Virgil's first *Georgic*.

Hailing the New Prince: The "*Laudes Neronis*"

We are told by Lucan's late antique biographer Vacca (Rostagni; *Suetonius de Poetis*, Vacca line 40) that the young poet made his debut at Nero's epony-

44 *"Eiselastic,"* literally "drive-in." The magistrates and council of a victorious charioteer's city could vote to honor him by breaching the city walls for him to drive his chariot into the civic center.

mous festival with a poem in praise of the emperor, the *Laudes Neronis.* To understand this performance requires knowledge of Roman rhetorical training and the practice of uttering public praises, whether of dead kinsmen or living victorious generals. In the declamatory schools, boys exercised on the genre of praise (*laus, laudatio,* known today by the Greek terms encomium or eulogy). The simplest and earliest form was the *laudatio* given at a nobleman's funeral, often performed in the Forum itself by his young son. But politics naturally required official praise in the Senate or assembly of a living and powerful commander such as Pompey or Caesar. A distinguished speaker, such as Cicero, would weave his politically motivated eulogies into the fabric of a larger speech, such as his praises of Pompey in the speech supporting Manilius's law (66 BC), the more flattering praises of Caesar in the speech on the allocation of consular provinces (57 BC), or again—a pivotal moment toward the development of the principate—his praise of Caesar, now absolute autocrat as consul and dictator at Rome, for his clemency in consenting to the return of the self-exiled republican Marcus Claudius Marcellus to Italy (September or October 46 BC).

The Greeks had developed the art of composing such speeches in praise or blame (for which the same subject matter could be used negatively) not only of public figures but of the cities that offered public hospitality. But with the development of the principate at Rome, it became unwise to praise any prominent person except the autocrat, the *princeps* or "first citizen." Poets, too, who had previously praised their private patrons, as Tibullus praised Valerius Messala, gradually realized that it was essential to success that they should praise the great leader, whether as inspiration for their own verse or as a public benefactor, soon to be a god.

Praising "Caesar," the First *Princeps* in the Epics of Virgil and Ovid

Before we come to Nero, it will be helpful to survey the ways in which the first and second imperial generations, represented by Virgil and Ovid, praised Octavian, the young Caesar. Virgil's first collection, the *Eclogues,* assumes that boys would learn to read the praises of the ancient heroes—Homeric epic (*Ecl.* 4.26)—and that adults would be eager to sing the praises of generals like Virgil's early patrons Asinius Pollio and Varus (*Ecl.* 6.6ff.) However, he assumes a more indirect approach to Octavian himself, when, in the first Eclogue, the shepherd Tityrus tells Menalcas of his journey to Rome to appeal to the heroic young Caesar who restored his land to him: "[H]e will always be a god to me, a God, I say, and I will make sacrifice to him annually at the altar" (*Ecl.* 1.6–8, 42–45). Virgil's next poem, the four books of *Georgics,* is in the more solemn didactic genre, which encourages more explicit praise of the new ruler. The first book opens with an invocation to many country gods and leads up to the climax of Octavius Caesar himself (*Georg.* 1.24–42), wishing or praying that Caesar, whether he will prefer to be a god of the sea or the heavens or supervise the cities, may take pity on Italy's farmers and accept their worship.

The new "Caesar" returns in the grand dedication that opens *Georgics* 3. As poet, Virgil has brought the Muses to Rome and will celebrate games in their honor, dedicating a temple: "Caesar will be at its center for me." The formal proem could have been called *laudes Caesaris* ("Praises of Caesar") but is adapted to both Virgil's poetic ideals and the glorious victories that Caesar will bring to Rome (*Georg.* 3.46–48). Caesar Augustus brought Rome to accept his growing authority, so that by the end of his long life, forty odd years later, Ovid—born a whole generation after Virgil—would first dedicate his *Fasti*, the poem of the Roman calendar, to Augustus (*Fasti*. 2.119–32) and then, upon the emperor's death, redirect his praise and dedication to Augustus's adopted grandson, the popular Germanicus. Germanicus had written a verse translation of Aratus's astronomical poem, so the poet was able to combine praise of his new patron as both poet and prince. By now, it was expected that poetry would be dedicated to members of the imperial dynasty.

However, the first poetic *Laudes Neronis* were not identified as such. When Claudius died, Nero had just come of age, but he had more promise than achievements. So after Claudius had been piously hailed by the Senate as a God, with Agrippina as his priestess, an anonymous composition, almost certainly a mime, mocked the dead emperor's attempt to gain admission to the divine council, not an *Apotheosis* but an *Apocolocyntosis*, not a "dei-fication" but a Pumpkini-fication. But first the poet (most people believe it was Seneca himself) staged a scene in which the Fates presided over the birth of a godlike future prince who would bring the golden age to Rome—NERO. Here is their song and Apollo's blessing on them.

As the scene opens, the Fate Clotho breaks off the thread of Claudius's life and spins an exceptionally long and beautiful thread for his heir Nero, who is hailed in lyric song by Apollo himself, before the action moves to Olympus.

Apocolocyntosis 4

So spake she, winding thread on the ugly spindle
And snapped the royal duration of his brutish life.
But Lachesis, her tresses bound and adorned,
Setting a laurel garland on her locks and brow
Took up the shining fibers of the snowy fleece

To discipline with blessed hand[45]: then once drawn out
They took on a new color, making her sisters marvel;
Cheap wool now is replaced by precious metal
And golden ages emerge with fine-spun yarn,
This without end; they draw the blessed fibers out
Glad to fill up their hands; their chores are sweet
Their task speeds on unprompted, and without effort
The softened threads fall from the twisted spindle,
Surpassing Nestor's or Tithonus's lifetime.[46]
Apollo comes and gives his aid to future joys with song,[47]
Happily now plucking strings, now passing skeins
Charming with song the busy sisters to ease their efforts.
And while they warmly praise their brother's lyrics
Their hands spin ever faster and their work exceeds
The fates of men, winning praise. "Dear Fates, don't stint,"
said he,
"But let this prince outdo the measure of human life
My like in mien and grace, equal in song and voice;
He will give blessed ages to the weary, ending
The silencing of laws. Like Lucifer at dawn
Dispersing stars, or Hesperus when he rises[48]
At evening leading back the stars to the skies,
Or like Aurora when the darkness first dissolves
Bringing on the day, the sun looks on the world,
All glowing, and drives his chariot from its gate;
Such is now Caesar among us, and such a NERO
Will Rome behold, his shining face and lovely neck
Burning as he restrains his dazzling brilliance."

45 Traditionally, the Three Fates—Lachesis, Atropos, and Clotho—controlled the thread of a mortal's life: Lachesis drew out the woollen fibers to form the thread, but it was Clotho who ended the mortal's life by breaking it off.

46 The Greek prince Nestor is reported in the Iliad to have lived for four generations of men, but even he was outdone by the Trojan Tithonus, who was given immortality at the request of his lover Aurora. But she failed to ask for immortal youth, and when old age made Tithonus ever more feeble, she put him away.

47 Apollo as god of prophecy encourages the Fates, foretelling the blessings of Nero's reign.

48 Lucifer and Hesperus are two names for the same star, our Venus, whether as bringer of shade at evening or of daylight at dawn. The heavenly bodies and stars were the focus of contemporary astrology but were also traditional images for the new ruler or the glorious bridegroom in wedding poems.

Nero and Lucan

As Nero's tutor, Seneca had seized the opportunity to promote his nephew Marcus Annaeus Lucanus, bringing him back to Rome from his studies at Athens to be a companion, or perhaps a pacemaker, for the young Emperor (two years older than Lucan). Lucan began well, but they soon quarrelled, as Suetonius explains. What we cannot know is whether the two ambitious young men were still friends when Lucan came to compose the ceremonial dedication of his poem on the civil war, which was in honor of the emperor. Or was it?

Suetonius *On the Poets*: Life of Lucan, lines 7–19

At the beginning of his youth . . . he [Lucan] was recalled by Nero from Athens and added to his group of friends, and was even honored with the quaestorship. He did not, however, remain in favor. This was because Lucan took offense when Nero summoned a meeting of the Senate and left in the middle of a recitation of his. He believed that Nero had done this only to chill the impact of his recital and did not spare abuse of the emperor or provocative actions, so much so that once he declaimed in the public latrines, with a very loud fart, a half-line of Nero's verse, "you would think it had thundered beneath the earth," which put his fellow occupants to flight. He even savagely tore apart both Nero and his most powerful friends in a notorious poem.

Lucan, *On the Civil War*, 33–66

But if the fates could find no other path
For Nero's coming, and lasting kingdoms for the gods
Come at great cost, and heaven was subject to its Thunderer
Only when savage giants were overwhelmed in war,
Ye gods, we now complain no more; those crimes,
That evil, are welcome on these terms; let Pharsalus[49]
Fill her grim plains with corpses and the Punic dead[50]
Be satiated with our blood; let Munda[51] last of all
His battles be engaged; let, Caesar, the starvation

49 Caesar's victory over the Pompeian forces at Pharsalus in Thessaly (48 BC) decided the outcome of the civil war.

50 The remaining republican forces regrouped in Roman Africa, the former Punic kingdom of Carthage. They were defeated at Thapsus and evacuated Utica in 46 BC.

51 In 45 BC, Pompey's son Gnaeus tried to rally the republicans but was defeated at Munda in Spain.

Of Perugia and Mutina's hardships[52] join these fates,
The fleets that cruel Leucas[53] will submerge, wars with slaves
Fought under Aetna's fires;[54] yet still Rome owes
A mighty debt to all this civil violence,
Because it was for you the wars were won.
When late in time your duty is completed
And you pursue the stars, preferring heaven's palace
You will be welcomed and the vaults rejoice,
Whether you choose to wield the scepter of power
Or you rejoice to mount the fiery car of Phoebus[55]
Crossing with wandering fire the earth, that need not fear
A change of sun-god, every deity shall give way.
Nature shall yield you power to decide your choice
Of godhead,[56] and your capital to command the world.
But do not choose your place in northern spheres
Nor in the steamy vault of distant Southern winds
From which to gaze aslant upon your city Rome.
If you should load one portion of the enormous ether,
Its pole will feel your burden. Keep to the center
The weight of balanced heaven; let all that region
Of sky be clear and empty, and no clouds obstruct
Coming from Caesar. Then let all mankind discard
Its weapons, cherishing itself, and every nation
Show mutual love; let peace throughout the world
Control the iron doors of Janus's house of war.[57]

52 Lucius Antonius occupied Perugia and resisted siege by Octavian/Augustus in 41 BC, but this occurred after Octavian's conquest of Mutina in 43.

53 Again out of chronological sequence: The promontory of Leucas stands for Actium, where Octavian triumphed over Antony and Cleopatra's forces.

54 Sextus Pompey, in control of Sicily (hence the reference to Mt. Etna), enfranchised slaves to serve in his new navy but was defeated by Octavian and Agrippa at Naulochus in 36 BC.

55 "Phoebus" stands for the sun god who in the myth told in Ovid's *Metamorphoses* was bound by his oath to let his son Phaethon drive his chariot; Phaethon lost control, with disastrous consequences.

56 Unlike Phaethon, Nero's control of the chariot will be welcomed by all the gods, and Nature herself will give Nero a choice not, as in Virgil's address to Octavian, between becoming a god of earth or sea or sky but of the position he will occupy after his apotheosis and *katasterismos* (transformation into a constellation).

57 Janus's house of war is the Temple of Janus Quadrifrons in the Forum, whose gates were shut only when Rome was free of war and enjoyed victorious peace.

To me, you are god already, and if as poet
I take you in my breast, I would have no desire
To trouble Apollo, when the god inspires the caves
Of Cirrha, or turn Bacchus away from Nysa.[58]
You are enough to give me power for Roman songs.

Panegyric usually compared princes or bridegrooms to the stars, but Lucan's god goes further, presenting Nero as his own avatar among men. In other respects, the verse is a highly repetitious sample of conventional panegyric, combining allusions to divine blessing and guaranteed earthly success.

Seneca's nephew, the poet Marcus Annaeus Lucanus, won fame and the emperor's goodwill with a (now lost) encomium, the "Praises of Nero" (*Laudes Neronis*), at the prince's first literary festival, the *Neronia* of AD 60. But the goodwill was soon destroyed by mutual jealousy, and within his civil war epic there is a huge contrast between a literal interpretation of Lucan's panegyric dedication of his poem to Nero and his subsequent indignation in Book 7, especially the denunciation (7.407–60) of the loss of republican liberty to dynastic tyranny. A number of recent scholars have read the passage translated here as heavy irony, presumably calculated to appeal to Nero's enemies while escaping the emperor's notice. But these fine phrases, however extravagant, closely follow the tradition started by Virgil's opening dedication of the *Georgics* to Octavian.

58 Apollo . . . caves of Cirrha: Bacchus . . . Nysa. The two gods of inspiration each have a cult site, Apollo's being Cirrha near Delphi, mentioned in the first book of the *Iliad*, and Dionysus's Nysa in the hinterland of Afghanistan.

X

DEATH

INTRODUCTION

The loss of the final section of Tacitus's *Annals* has deprived us of his account of Nero's final years and death, and the events of the months immediately leading up to that death are consequently sometimes difficult to disentangle. As a compensation of sorts, the final hours of Nero are probably the best documented of those of any historical figure of ancient Rome, and the chapters devoted to it by Suetonius show the biographer composing what comes close to a piece of straightforward historical narrative, generally acknowledged as his finest piece of writing. It can be supplemented by the vivid account by Dio and by Plutarch's *Life of Galba*. The constant echoes suggest that a single source was used.

From late in AD 66, Nero was in Greece. In Rome, a number of prominent individuals were prosecuted for treason. More ominously, at this time, or early in 67, Domitius Corbulo, the architect of Nero's victory over the Parthians, was summoned to Greece and ordered to kill himself. The reasons behind this last development are far from clear, but it was presumably associated with the conspiracy of Corbulo's son-in-law Annius Vinicianus, which was brought to light in 66 (see Chapter VIII). In his final years, Nero seems to have appointed men without distinguished family backgrounds—Vespasian, put in command of the Jewish War; and Fonteius Capito and Verginius Rufus, appointed as legates in Lower and Upper Germany, respectively—suggesting that his nervousness had extended beyond the borders of Italy and that he felt it too risky to appoint to high office men with sufficiently distinguished families to rival him for the principate.

For all his precautions, Nero's ultimate downfall was precipitated in a part of the world from which he could hardly have anticipated serious threats. During his final sojourn in Greece, dissatisfaction grew more serious in Rome, where his freedman Helios, left in charge, urged the emperor to come back and was ultimately obliged to go Greece and make his appeal in person. Nero returned in early 68, going first to Naples and then to Rome, which he entered to a rapturous popular reception. Not long after that, he went back to Naples, and while there, in March 68, he heard of a revolt, not among the powerful legates in Syria or on the Rhine but in fact in Gaul. The instigator was Julius Vindex, a member of the old royal house of Aquitania, whose father had entered the Roman Senate. The son was legate of a Gallic province, almost certainly Gallia Lugdunensis, from at least 67; disaffected by Nero's behavior, he organized a widespread Gallic rebellion. Vindex would have had only a handful of soldiers at his disposal, and, before rebelling, he sought the support of other governors (their negotiations were leaked to Nero). Clearly, while Gaul might have been able to raise a considerable body of troops, it could not provide sufficient military backing to ensure success. Once the revolt was under way, Vindex appealed to Servius Sulpicius Galba, governor of Hispania Tarraconensis, to assume its leadership, promising him 100,000 men. Galba had had a distinguished record and was a worthy candidate. On April 2 or 3, Galba was acclaimed as "Caesar" by his troops in Nova Carthago (Cartagena) in Spain. He refused the title, which the troops had no authority to confer, and instead styled himself as the "Legate of the Senate and the People of Rome," a recognition that imperial power could be conferred only in Rome.

Nero initially seems not to have taken the revolt of Vindex very seriously, and he gave proper attention to developments only when Galba became involved. Petronius Turpilianus, who had shown his mettle in crushing the Pisonian conspiracy, was sent north to muster an army, which would embrace the Fourteenth Legion and a unit raised among the marines at Misenum. At the end of April, Nero assumed sole consulship. In the meantime, Vindex laid siege to Lugdunum (Lyon) and, probably early in May, was confronted by the commander of Upper Germany, Verginius Rufus. When Rufus learned of the rebellion, he had at his disposal his own forces in Upper Germany (the Fourth Legion, Macedonica; the Twenty-second, Primigeneia; and the Twenty-first, Rapax), and he was able to call on detachments from the four legions in Lower Germany. He advanced into Gaul but was held up at Vesontio (Besançon), which had declared for Vindex. The two leaders met for a parley. They may well have come to an agreement for joint action against Nero, but discipline in the two armies broke down and they clashed (Dio 63.24). Twenty thousand of Vindex's men were killed, and he committed suicide.

The precise chronology of events after the death of Vindex is difficult to determine. That death should have been a heartening development for Nero, but, if anything, it marked a further deterioration in his situation, since Verginius's troops turned their backs on the emperor and urged Verginius to assume the principate. He refused, but did not commit himself to Nero; instead, he said the decision should be left to the Senate and Roman people (Plut. *Galb.* 5.2; Dio 63.25.2). Galba now made contact with Verginius, suggesting that they join forces. Vigorous action from Rome, and a courageous and determined response on Nero's part, might still have salvaged the situation and saved his position; as Tacitus points out, he was brought down not by military upset but by "reports and rumors" (*Hist.* 1.89.2). He proved incapable and seems to have ranged manically between wild optimism and utter despair. Events unfolded beyond his control, and the chaos spread. The legate of the Third Legion in Africa, Clodius Macer, defected and led what seems to have been his own independent revolt, issuing his own coinage and raising fresh troops.

As was the case during the successions of Caligula, Claudius, and Nero, and would be so on many later occasions, it was the praetorian guard that finally decided matters. It seems remarkable that in the early months of AD 68 Nero does not appear to have made any serious effort to shore up the loyalty of the guard, even though, as Tacitus notes, their natural inclination was to stand by their allegiance to him (*Hist.* 1.5.2). But loyalty will always be sorely tested by expedience, and they were essentially bribed to transfer their loyalty elsewhere. Of the two prefects, Tigellinus is not assigned any substantial role, and events were set in motion by his colleague, Nymphidius Sabinus. Nymphidius began suborning the praetorians against Nero, and overnight the emperor's units abandoned him. Nymphidius went to the praetorian camp and with the promise of a large donative won them over to Galba's cause. The Senate followed this up by declaring Nero a public enemy and Galba emperor.

With a few companions, Nero fled to the house of Phaon, only a few miles from Rome, where he learned of the Senate's actions and put an end to his own life as soldiers hunted him down. His funeral was arranged by his mistress Acte, who remained loyal to the end.

SOURCES

A rebellion, which Nero underestimates, breaks out in Gaul.

Suet. *Ner.* 40.1. The world had endured a ruler like this for slightly less than fourteen years when it finally abandoned him,[1] and it was the Gauls, led by Julius Vindex,[2] then propraetorian governor of that province,[3] who started it. . . .

1 Nero came to power on October 13, 54. The Gallic rebellion broke out in early March 68, thus thirteen years and six months after the accession, and he died some three months later.

2 Nothing is known of Julius Vindex beyond what the literary sources tell us in connection with this particular episode. Suetonius speaks vaguely of the "Gauls"; in fact, only the Treveri and Lingones withheld their support from Vindex (Tac. *Hist.* 4.69.2 and 4.17; Plin. *HN* 4.106), although the city of Lugdunum (Lyon) did not join him (Tac. *Hist.*1.51.5, 65).

3 Gallia Lugdunensis was an imperial province; the legates, however senior, held their position *pro praetore* as subordinates to the emperor, who held *imperium proconsulare.*

40.4. He learned of the revolt of the Gallic provinces at Naples on the very same date on which he had murdered his mother, and he accepted the news with such calm and nonchalance that he even gave rise to a suspicion that he was happy since it meant an opportunity had arisen for him to plunder very rich provinces under the laws of war.[4] Then, going immediately to the gymnasium, he watched the athletic competitions with the most unrestrained enthusiasm. At dinnertime, too, when he was interrupted by a more alarming dispatch, his anger was limited to threatening punishment for those who had rebelled. In fact, for eight days in succession, he took no steps to write to anyone or issue any instructions or commands, and covered the whole matter with a pall of silence.[5]

41.1. He was finally prompted by Vindex's many abusive proclamations to call on the Senate in a letter to avenge him and the state, offering a throat ailment as his reason for not appearing in person.[6] But nothing hurt him as much as being scoffed at as a poor lyre player and being called Ahenobarbus rather than Nero, and in fact he declared that he would drop his adopted name and resume his family name, which was actually being used against him as an insult.[7] As for the other aspersions, the only argument he would use to refute them as being groundless was that he was being ridiculed for ineptitude in an art that he had spent so much effort to develop and perfect, and he would repeatedly ask individuals if they knew anyone better in it than him.

2. However, under pressure from the messages that kept coming to him one after the other, he [Nero] returned to Rome in panic;[8] and en route his spirits were raised slightly by a trivial omen. He noticed, sculpted on a monument,

4 Suetonius's information allows us to date this event quite precisely, since we are earlier told that Nero murdered his mother after luring her to Campania to celebrate the Quinquatrus, the festival of Minerva, which began on March 19 (Tac. *Ann.* 14.4.1; Suet. *Ner.* 34.2). Making allowance for the time it took for the information to reach Nero, we can place the beginning of the Gallic rebellion about a week before that date.

5 Nero's apparently apathetic response to the news from Gaul may not be as irresponsible as Suetonius seems to suggest. There were no legions housed there and no reason to doubt the loyalty of the legions in Germany.

6 It is not clear what help Nero was seeking from the Senate. The letter would not have contained an appeal for direct intervention in Gaul, since the "Three Gauls" (*Tres Galliae*) in which the unrest arose were all imperial provinces. The reference to vengeance would suggest that he asked them to declare Vindex a *hostis*, a public enemy.

7 The issue of Nero's name had long been a sensitive one. In AD 51, after his adoption by Claudius, Britannicus reputedly addressed him as Domitius, his preadoption name. Nero is said to have taken offense and to have sought revenge by trying to persuade Claudius that Britannicus was illegitimate (Tac. *Ann.* 12.41.3; Suet. *Ner.* 7.1; see Chapter I).

8 Nero presumably returned to Rome from Naples late in March. His delay proved a costly mistake. By miscalculating the urgency of the problem, he lost authority in Rome.

the figure of a Gallic warrior who had been defeated by a Roman soldier and was being dragged along by him by the hair, and, at the sight of it, he jumped for joy and raised a prayer of thanks to heaven. But not even then did he make any address to the Senate or people; instead, he summoned a number of leading men to his home and, after hurried deliberation with them, spent what remained of the day leading them around to view some water organs of a new and unprecedented sort. These he demonstrated one by one, discussing the mechanical principles and difficulty of operation of each, and he then declared that he would soon put them on show in the theater "if Vindex permitted it."

Dio 63.22.1. Such was Nero's life and such his rule, and I shall tell also of how he was undone and fell from power. While he was still in Greece, the Jews revolted, an event that could be foreseen, and he sent Vespasian against them.[9] The people of Britain, too, and the Gauls, both overburdened by taxation, were becoming ever more distressed and resentful.[10] There was a certain Gaul, Gaius Julius Vindex, an Aquitanian whose forefathers were of royal stock and who, thanks to his father's influence, was a Roman senator. Both physically strong and intelligent, he possessed military experience and great courage in the face of any challenge. He also had a deep love of freedom and considerable ambition, and he was the most preeminent of the Gauls.

2. This man Vindex brought together the Gauls,[11] who had greatly suffered, and were still suffering, under Nero in the frequent monetary tax levies, and, going up onto a tribunal, he delivered a long harangue against Nero, saying that they should revolt against him. They should make a stand against the emperor with him, he said, "because he has plundered the entire Roman world, because he has destroyed the best of the Senate, because he has had sex with his mother and murdered her, and does not even keep up a semblance of sovereignty. . . ."

9 The great Jewish rebellion broke out in spring or summer AD 66. It was sparked by the conduct of the procurator Gessius Florus, who removed substantial sums from the temple treasury. This led to a refusal to carry out the daily sacrifice to the emperor. The legate of Syria, Cestius Gallus, tried to assert control of Jerusalem in the autumn but was forced to withdraw. Command in Judaea was now given to Vespasian, who at the time was accompanying Nero in Greece. In 67, Vespasian brought Judaea under his control, with the exception of Jerusalem. Military activities were much disrupted by the confusion that followed Nero's death, and Jerusalem was finally taken by Vespasian's son Titus in spring or summer 70.

10 There is actually no indication of serious unrest in Britain until after the death of Nero, when the rebellious Venutius seized much of northern Britain. The notion of widespread dissatisfaction in Gaul is also something of an exaggeration.

11 Dio, like Suetonius, implies that the whole of Gaul lined up behind Vindex, but this was not really the case.

24.4a. As the revolt went on, Vindex committed suicide. He was very depressed over the dangers the soldiers with him had faced and angry with heaven over his failure to reach the great goal at which he had aimed: bringing down Nero and freeing the Romans. . . . [12]

25.1. Rufus was deeply saddened by his death but unwilling to accept the supreme power, although his men frequently pressed him to do so and he might easily have succeeded in achieving it.[13] He was a man of action, he had a strong and eager military force, and his soldiers pulled down and destroyed Nero's statues while they called Rufus "Caesar" and "Augustus." . . .

2. . . . It was with difficulty that he persuaded them to leave the matter of the emperorship to the Senate and people, but it is unclear whether he did so because he did not think it correct for soldiers to confer power on anyone (he said that it was for the Senate and people to do this) or because principle was everything for him and he felt no desire for the absolute power that others moved heaven and earth to gain.[14]

26.1. Nero learned of the Vindex affair in Neapolis while watching the gymnastic contest after his lunch; he showed no distress but jumped up from his seat and challenged one of the athletes.[15] He did not rush back to Rome either but simply sent a letter to the Senate and asked to be excused for not coming, alleging that he had a sore throat (as though even at that point he wanted to sing them a song!).

Galba joins the rebellion.

Suet. *Ner.* 42.1. When he subsequently[16] learned that Galba and the Spanish provinces had also revolted,[17] he fainted and, in a befuddled state, lay

12 Dio in fact glosses over the circumstances of Vindex's death. He had lost 20,000 soldiers in battle.

13 Verginius Rufus was born in northern Italy, not far from Comum (Como) (Plin. *Ep.* 2.1), in AD 14 or 15. He was consul in 63 and was appointed to the command in Upper Germany in 67 at Mainz.

14 Plutarch (*Galb.* 10.2) claims that after Nero's death the soldiers were again insistent that Verginius Rufus seek the principate, but that he opted to support Galba.

15 Suetonius (*Ner.* 40.4) and Dio both place Nero in Naples when word of the rebellion reached him and are close in detail, stressing his nonchalance, although Suetonius has him go to the gymnasium afterward.

16 The sequence of events as described indicates that Nero learned of the defection of Galba after he arrived in Rome. Dio (64.6.5[2]) reports on the age and career of Galba, saying that he had lived seventy-two years and twenty-three days, out of which he ruled nine months and thirteen days. This places his renunciation of allegiance in early April.

17 The defection of Galba, legate of Tarraconensis, would have marked a dramatic turning point in the rebellion. We are also told by Suetonius (*Otho* 4.1) that Otho, legate

speechless and virtually unconscious for a long time. When he came to, he ripped his clothing and beat his head, and announced that he was done for. His nurse tried to console him and reminded him that similar things had also happened to other leaders, but he replied that he was different from the others in suffering something unheard of and unprecedented—losing his imperial power while still alive. 2. Even so, he did not abandon or curtail any aspect of his extravagant and idle ways—quite the reverse, in fact. When some good news came from the provinces, he used the setting of a most extravagant feast to sing, and even accompany with gestures, bawdy songs—which became widely known—that made fun of the leaders of the revolt.[18] And he would furtively slip into the seating area of the theater and send a message to some performer who was stealing the show that "he was taking advantage of the emperor's preoccupation with his affairs."

43.1. Right at the start of the revolt, it is thought that Nero had in mind many measures that were horrendous but not out of character:[19] to send men out secretly to replace and kill those commanding armies and governing provinces on the grounds that they all had the same conspiratorial intentions;[20] to slaughter all exiles everywhere and all Gauls in the city of Rome

---

of Lusitania, was the first to declare his support for Galba, and Aulus Caecina Alienus, quaestor of Baetica, quickly joined him (Tac. *Hist.* 1.53.1).

18 It is not clear what positive news from the province Suetonius has in mind. Plutarch (*Galb.* 6.1) claims that after Galba's decision many provincial governors rebelled, most of them lining up with Galba. The only welcome news that Nero is likely to have received is that of the death of Vindex at Vesontio. This is not dated but may well have occurred sometime in late April or early May (some place it as late as June).

19 Suetonius's words "right at the start of the revolt," as well as the references to the Gauls, suggest that he has in mind Nero's plans at the outset of Vindex's rebellion, not Galba's defection, and Suetonius's claim here is somewhat contradicted by the reports of apathy. We should be very cautious of assertions thus worded ("had in mind many measures"), since we are essentially being told of Nero's supposed intentions rather than any concrete actions.

20 Certainly, after the Pisonian conspiracy in 65, Nero would have been particularly sensitive to the dangers posed by rebellious legates, but there is no basis for the claim that the legionary commanders and provincial governors were united in a conspiracy. In Upper Germany, Verginius Rufus was at worst indecisive, and there was certainly no outward rebellion. In Lower Germany, the legate Fonteius Capito was later put to death by Galba, which suggests that he remained loyal to Nero (Tac. *Hist.* 1.7.1; Plut. *Galb.* 15.2). Tiberius Iulius Alexander, governor of Egypt, acknowledged Galba as emperor in a decree on July 6, 68, but we cannot be sure that he supported the rebellion at the outset. Lucius Clodius Macer, the legate of Legio III in Africa, led an independent rebellion in Africa, issuing coins and raising a second legion. He gained no further support, and he was put to death by Galba. There is no evidence that any of the other legates threw their support behind Galba or launched their own independent rebellions.

(the exiles so they would not join the rebels, and the Gauls so they would not become accomplices and abettors of their countrymen); to leave the Gallic provinces to be pillaged by the armies; to poison the whole Senate at dinner parties; and to set fire to the city after letting wild animals loose on the people to make defending themselves against the flames more difficult.

2. He was put off these ideas less by qualms of conscience than lack of hope of realizing them, however, and thinking a military campaign necessary, he deprived the consuls of their office and entered the consulship himself in place of the two of them,[21] claiming that the Gallic provinces could be brought into subjection only by a consul.[22] When, having assumed the fasces, he was leaving the dining room after dinner, leaning on the shoulders of some friends, he announced that as soon as he set foot in his province he would go before the eyes of the soldiers unarmed and do no more than shed tears, and the next day, when the rebels had been brought to regret their actions, he would, a happy man among his happy men, sing victory odes—which he really should already be composing!

47.1. Meanwhile, news came that the other armies had defected, and Nero tore up the letter that had been brought to him while he was at lunch.[23] He overturned the table and hurled to the ground two drinking cups that he loved to use and that he called "Homeric" because they were engraved with scenes from Homer's poems. He took poison from Locusta, set it in a golden box, and then crossed into the Servilian Gardens. There, after sending the most loyal of his freedmen to Ostia to prepare a fleet, he made overtures to the tribunes and centurions of the praetorian guard to join him in his flight.[24] 2. Some, however, showed reluctance and others positively refused, one of them even crying out, "Is dying really such a terrible thing?"

21 Suetonius's information is borne out by Pliny (*Pan.* 57.2), who states that at the end of his reign Nero took over the consulship. It might ordinarily have been expected to run to the end of the year. The *ordinarii* for 68 were Tiberius Catius Asconius Silius Italicus and Pubius Galerius Trachalus. It may be that only Italicus was removed, since fragmentary inscriptions record Nero as consul with Trachalus as his colleague (VI 9190, 8639).

22 The situation is more complex than is described here. Suetonius (*Galb.* 9.2) suggests that Nero had issued orders for Galba's death *before* the rebellion; Plutarch (*Galb.* 4.2) suggests that Vindex had written to Galba before the rebellion to sound him out and that Galba had not communicated this information to Nero. These maneuverings are not plausible and may represent attempts by Galba to justify his actions afterward.

23 Suetonius, after describing Nero's reaction to the crisis, returns to a more narrative structure, bringing us up to the day before his death, probably June 8. "The other armies" is a rhetorical exaggeration.

24 Plutarch (*Galb.* 2.1–2) claims that the praetorians were bribed by Nymphidius Sabinus to renounce Nero.

He then turned over various plans in his mind: he could head to the Parthians or Galba as a suppliant or go out into the streets dressed in black and implore forgiveness for his past transgressions as poignantly as he could, and if he failed to change people's attitudes he could beg them at least to be granted the prefecture of Egypt. There was later discovered in his desk a speech designed for this purpose, but it is thought that he was put off delivering it by fear that he would be torn to pieces before reaching the Forum.

Suet. *Galb.* 9.2. Presiding in court at New Carthage,[25] Galba learned of the rebellion of the Gallic provinces when the governor of Aquitania earnestly appealed to him for help, and on the heels of that came a dispatch from Vindex urging him to take up the liberation of the human race and become its leader.[26] After no long hesitation, he accepted that role with both fear and hope, as he had intercepted orders for his death that had been secretly sent by Nero to his procurators.

11.1. These great dangers were heightened by the death of Vindex, which shocked Galba deeply and left him feeling quite desolate and not far from taking his own life.[27] But when, following that, messengers arrived from Rome and he learned that Nero was dead and everyone had sworn allegiance to him,[28] he dropped the title of "governor" and assumed that of "Caesar." He donned his general's cloak and, with a dagger hanging from his neck before his chest,[29] began his march[30] and did not resume wearing the toga until he had put down

25 New Carthage (Nova Carthago, modern Cartagena) had been founded by the Carthaginians in 242 BC and was taken by Scipio Africanus during the Hannibalic War in 210 BC. It acquired the status of a *colonia* during the principate. Pliny the Elder (*HN* 3.18) shows how Tarraconensis was divided into seven judicial districts, one of which was centered at New Carthage.

26 It is uncertain whether the governor of Aquitania was seeking help for or against Vindex. Julius Cordus was governor there at the beginning of AD 69, but we do not know for certain that he was a Neronian appointee. As noted, Plutarch (*Galb.* 4.2) refers to Vindex's approach to several governors, including Galba, *before* the actual rebellion. The reference here seems to be to a second approach.

27 Vindex seems to have committed suicide after the battle at Vesontio (Besançon). Plutarch (*Galb.* 6.4) gives a different account: that Galba wrote to Verginius suggesting a pact.

28 "Everyone" is a considerable exaggeration. The praetorians had to be bribed.

29 The military cloak (*paludamentum*) was in this period restricted to the *princeps*. The dagger (*pugio*) was traditionally the emblem of proconsular authority; it was also carried by the prefect of the praetorian guard. Thus, Vitellius loses his *pugio* and the power of life and death over citizens upon abdication (Suet. *Vit.* 15.4). Dio (64.3.4) says that Galba was ridiculed for wearing a large sword at his side for the whole journey to Rome, despite his age.

30 Tacitus (*Hist.* 1.6.1) describes Galba's journey to Rome as a slow and difficult one, and claims that he faced much opposition; it probably took from late June to September.

those who were plotting against him—Nymphidius Sabinus, prefect of the praetorian guard in Rome,[31] and Fonteius Capito[32] and Clodius Macer,[33] governors in Germany and Africa, respectively.[34]

Dio 63.27.1. However, when he was told that Galba had been hailed as emperor by his troops and that Rufus had deserted him, he [Nero] became very afraid. He personally began to make preparations at Rome, and he also dispatched Rubrius Gallus and a number of others against the rebels. 1a. However, when he learned that even Petronius, the man he had sent against the rebels with most of the army, had sided with Galba, he no longer had any hope in an armed solution.[35]

2. Abandoned by all alike, he then began planning to murder the senators, burn the city to the ground, and sail for Alexandria, suggesting that "even if we fall from power, this modest artistry will keep us alive there."[36] He had reached such a stage of irrationality as to believe he could live as a private citizen and even by playing the lyre.

2b. He was on the point of doing this when the Senate recalled Nero's personal bodyguard, entered the camp, declared him a public enemy, and chose Galba to replace him as emperor.

Nero flees Rome.

31 Nymphidius Sabinus was the son of Martianus, a gladiator, and Nymphidia, an ex-slave, although he claimed Caligula as his father (Tac. *Ann.* 15.72.4). He was made prefect after the Pisonian conspiracy but deserted Nero for Galba, who distrusted him and appointed Cornelius Laco in his place. Nymphidius then attempted a coup in his own name and was killed by the praetorians.

32 Fonteius Capito was consul in AD 67 and *legatus* in Lower Germany from early 68. Plutarch (*Galb.* 15.2), like Suetonius here, assumes his guilt, but Tacitus (*Hist.* 1.7.1–2) is more cautious. Dio (64.2.3) seems to say that Capito tried to seize power on his own account.

33 Clodius Macer was the legate of the Third Legion in Africa. His motives in 68 are unclear. He seems to have acted only after Nero's death, on the advice of Calvia Crispinilla, Nero's former mistress, who had been sent to Africa. He began to use the corn supply as a weapon (Tac. *Hist.* 1.73). He raised an additional legion in Africa: the First Legion, Liberatrix Macriana (Tac. *Hist.* 2.97.2).

34 These were by no means the only victims of Galba. Tacitus mentions other names, and Dio (64.2.3, 3.2) says that seven thousand members of the guard were slaughtered in the Rome area and that the remaining units were decimated. He also reports that others were put to death by people acting in Galba's name.

35 Dio agrees with Suetonius (*Ner.* 42.1) that it was the threat that Galba posed that made Nero begin to panic.

36 Dio speaks of the specific intention to sail to Alexandria. Suetonius (*Ner.* 47.1) does not exclude that possibility: he has Nero planning to make his way to the fleet at Ostia.

Suet. *Ner.* 47.3. He therefore shelved further consideration until the next day. He awoke about the middle of the night, and upon discovering that the soldiers on guard had gone, he leaped from his bed and sent around for his friends.[37] Receiving no response from anyone, he went to their rooms with a few attendants. But everyone's doors were closed and no one answered, so he returned to his bedroom, only to find that even the watchmen had now run away from there and had even stolen the bedclothes and made off with the box of poison.[38] He immediately tried to find the *murmillo* Spiculus or any other trained killer by whose hand he could die,[39] but finding no one, he said "So do I have neither a friend nor an enemy?" and ran out as if to hurl himself into the Tiber.

48.1. Checking this impulse, however, he now felt the need of some secluded hiding place where he could pull himself together, and his freedman Phaon offered his villa close to town,[40] between the Salarian Way and the Nomentan Way, at about the fourth milestone.[41] Just as he was, barefooted and wearing only a tunic, Nero threw on a cloak faded in color, covered his head, and, with a napkin held to his face, mounted a horse. He had four people in attendance, Sporus being one.[42] 2. He was immediately frightened by an earth tremor and lightning that flashed before his eyes, and he heard

37 Suetonius's narrative has now taken us to the day of Nero's death, probably June 9. If we are to believe Eutropius (7.15.1), Nero was at this point in the palace, on the Palatine Hill.

38 The watchmen (*custodes*) might be the German guard, who would be Nero's very last line of defense, the unit that had remained loyal to Caligula up to the very end. Their defection would symbolize Nero's total exposure.

39 Tiberius Claudius Spiculus was a member of Nero's bodyguard (*CIL* X 6690). Plutarch (*Galb.* 8.5) records that he was put to death by the mob. *Murmillo* was one of the regular terms for a heavily armed gladiator. He fought with a sword, wore a helmet, and, on the left leg, greaves, and a long oval or square shield covered his entire body.

40 Phaon is a rather murky figure, attested as a freedman possibly inherited by Nero from his aunt Domitia Lepida.

41 In the previous section, Nero indicated a wish to leave via Ostia. But the Via Salaria led to the northeast and Ostia lay in the opposite direction. A secondary road, the Via Nomentana, branched off from it in the direction of Nomentum (modern Mentana). Phaon's villa lay within the fork.

42 Sporus was the notorious freedman of Nero who so closely resembled his late wife Poppaea Sabina that the emperor had him castrated and used him as a sexual surrogate. During his Greek tour of AD 66–68, Nero even married him and gave him the name Sabina (Dio 62.28.2; Suet. *Ner.* 28.1). He was later supposedly used as a sexual partner by Nymphidius Sabinus (Plut. *Galb.* 9.3) and by Otho (Dio 64.8.3). He committed suicide under Vitellius rather than appear in a rape scene onstage (Dio 65.10.1). Aurelius Victor (*Epit.* 5.7) has him help Nero deliver the fatal blow.

the shouting of soldiers coming from a nearby camp predicting destruction for him and success for Galba.[43] He also heard one of the travelers he met saying, "These men are after Nero" and another asking "Is there any news about Nero in the city?" His horse was then startled by the stench from a cadaver that had been thrown onto the road, his face became uncovered, and he was recognized and saluted by a former member of the praetorian guard.

3. When they reached the turnoff, the horses were set loose, and, with difficulty, Nero made his way through brush and brambles along a path across a reed bed, where a piece of clothing had been laid down for him to walk on, and reached the wall at the back of the villa. There, the aforementioned Phaon urged him to take refuge temporarily in a cavity where some sand had been removed, but he said he would not go underground alive. As he was waiting briefly for a secret entrance to the villa to be made ready, he scooped up with his hand some water from a nearby pool to have a drink and said: "This is Nero's cool drink."[44]

4. His cloak having been torn by the bramble bushes, Nero then picked out the twigs stuck in it, and entering on all fours the closest small room, through a narrow passageway that was dug for him, he lay down on a bed equipped with an ordinary mattress and an old bedspread thrown over it. He was tormented by hunger and renewed thirst, and though he refused some coarse bread that was offered to him, he did drink a little tepid water.

Dio 63.27.3. When he realized that he had been deserted even by his bodyguards—while he happened to be sleeping in a garden—he tried to make his escape. He put on some shoddy clothes, climbed onto a horse that was of no better quality than the clothes, and, while it was still night and with his head covered, rode the animal toward an estate belonging to Phaon, an imperial freedman, in the company of Phaon himself, Epaphroditus, and Sporus.[45]

43 A particularly vivid and dramatic detail, intimating that as Nero was leaving he heard the praetorians acclaim Galba (in his absence) as their new emperor. Plutarch (*Galb.* 7.2) suggests that Icelus reported that the praetorians acclaimed Galba before Nero had died.

44 The pool was presumably warm and brackish, and Nero was speaking ironically. Pliny (*HN* 31.40) claims that Nero originated a scheme whereby he boiled water, presumably to get rid of impurities, and then placed the water in a glass vessel and cooled it in snow. Suetonius's account may be slightly garbled, as in the next section he again has Nero drinking tepid water and eating poor bread. In Dio's version, Nero makes his comment about his famous cool drink when he is eating this bad bread and drinking the bad water.

45 Suetonius's account (*Ner.* 48.1) differs very slightly from Dio's; he claims that Nero had *four* people in attendance, one of whom is identified specifically as Sporus, and Phaon's presence is implied.

28.1. While he was doing this, there was such a dreadful earthquake as to give the impression that the whole earth was being shattered and that all the souls of the people killed by him were springing up together against him.[46] He was, they say, despite his precautions, recognized and saluted as emperor by one of the people who met him, and he turned off the road and hid in some reed-covered spot.[47] There he remained until daybreak, lying on the ground so he would have the least chance of being spotted. Every passerby he assumed had come to get him; he trembled at every sound, thinking it was someone searching for him; and if a dog barked anywhere, a bird twittered, or a twig or branch was shaken by a breeze, he was terribly agitated. Because of these things, he could have no rest, and he dared not speak to any of those present in case somebody else heard; he just bemoaned and bewailed his fate to himself. He turned over various thoughts, particularly how he used to pride himself on his multitude of attendants and was now lurking there with three freedmen. Such was the script that the divine power now prepared for him: he would no longer be playing other mother killers and vagabonds but now only playing himself. And then he would regret his reckless deeds, as if he had the power to nullify any of them. Such was the tragic role that Nero was acting out, and the verse on which he time and again reflected was, "A pitiful death both husband and father urge upon me."[48] After quite some time, since no one could be seen looking for him, he went into the cave and there, feeling hungry, ate bread of a sort he had never eaten before and, feeling thirsty, drank water of a sort he had never drunk before. So badly upset was he over this that he commented, "This has to be that purified water of mine!"[49] 29.1. Such were his circumstances, and meanwhile the people of Rome were sacrificing and feeling overwhelming joy, and some were even wearing caps like freedmen. And they voted Galba the rights of the imperial power.

Nero kills himself.

Suet. *Ner.* 49.1. Everyone around him then urged him to free himself as soon as possible from the imminent humiliation. In response, he gave orders for a hole to be dug before his eyes that he judged appropriate for his own body

46 Both Dio and Suetonius (*Ner.* 48.2) allude to the earthquake, with Suetonius adding the dramatic detail that at the same time he heard the praetorians acclaim Galba.

47 Suetonius (*Ner.* 48.2) specifies that it was an old member of the praetorians who greeted Nero. Both sources refer to the presence of reeds near Nero's last resting place.

48 This line comes from a tragedy that is now lost.

49 See Suet. *Ner.* 48.3.

size, and at the same time for marble fragments that could be found anywhere to be brought, as well as water and wood for attending to his corpse. He wept as each stage was completed, repeatedly saying: "What an artist dies in me!"[50]

2. During the delays thus caused, a letter was brought to Phaon by a messenger. Nero seized it and, when he read that he had been adjudged a public enemy and that a search for him was under way so that he could receive the traditional punishment, he asked what sort of punishment this was.[51] Told that a man, stripped naked, had his neck inserted in a forked prop and had his body beaten with sticks until he was dead, he was terrified and grabbed two daggers that he had brought with him. Then, after checking the edge of each, he put them away with the excuse that his "fated hour had not arrived." 3. At one moment, he was encouraging Sporus to begin the lament and breast-beating, at the next begging for someone to help him take his life by setting an example, and now and then he would reproach himself for his weakness by saying, "It is shameful and a disgrace that I am alive. This is unbecoming for Nero, unbecoming. . . . In such circumstances, sangfroid is needed. Come on, pull yourself together!" By now, the horsemen were approaching with orders to bring him in alive. Realizing this, he exclaimed in terror, "The noise of swift-footed horses clatters around my ears"[52] and, with his secretary Epaphroditus helping, he drove a knife into his throat.[53]

4. He was still semiconscious when a centurion burst in and set a cloak over the wound, pretending he had come to help. All Nero said was "too late" and "this is loyalty." With these words, he expired, his eyes protruding and fixed in a stare, making those who saw him shudder with fear. The first and major demand he had made of his companions was that no one should take possession of his head but that he, by whatever means, should be cremated in one piece. Icelus, Galba's freedman, allowed this (he had been clapped in irons at the start of the revolt and had been released not long before this).[54]

50 Arguably one of the most famous utterances of antiquity, and Dio (63.29.2) testifies to its celebrity at the time. Syme ([1971], 109; and [1958], 41) takes the statement to refer to his showmanship; Champlin ([2003], 51) believes the allusion to be specifically to Nero as architect, but a more general allusion to Nero's artistic talent seems more in keeping with the context.

51 The declaration of Nero as *hostis* ("public enemy") would mean that he lost the protection enjoyed under the law.

52 Nero here quoted (in Greek) Homer (*Iliad* 10.535).

53 Epaphroditus was a freedman of Nero (see Chapter VIII). He was clearly already powerful by AD 65, when we first hear of him, since it was to him that the freedman Milichus first betrayed the conspiracy of Piso (Tac. *Ann.* 15.55.1). Aurelius Victor (*De Caes.* 140) also has him help Nero deliver the fatal blow (see *ILS* 9505).

54 Icelus, a freedman of Galba, stayed in Rome when the latter went to Spain. He was imprisoned, presumably when Galba declared his revolt. He traveled to Spain to give

50.1. Nero's funeral expenses amounted to two hundred thousand sestertii, and he was clothed in robes embroidered with gold,[55] which he had worn on the first of January.[56]

His nurses, Egloge and Alexandria,[57] along with his concubine, Acte, buried his ashes in the family mausoleum of the Domitii, which is set on the Hill of the Gardens and is visible from the Campus Martius.[58] In that monument lies his sarcophagus of porphyry, which has an altar of Luna standing on it and is surrounded by a wall of Thasian stone.

57.1. He died in his thirty-second year (on the same date that he had murdered Octavia),[59] and thus prompted so much joy among the people that the plebs ran about the whole city wearing caps of freedom. Even so, there were still those who over a long period decked his tomb with spring and summer flowers, and on some occasions put on view on the rostrum his effigies, dressed in the toga praetexta, and at other times his edicts, as if he were still alive and would soon return to inflict serious harm on his enemies.[60]

Galba the news of Nero's death, completing the journey in seven days. He was given the gold ring of the equestrian order by Galba and the equestrian name Marcianus (Plut. *Galb.* 7.1; Tac. *Hist.* 1.13.1), and is said to have had excessive influence over the new emperor (Plut. *Galb.* 20.3). His greed was notorious (Tac. *Hist.* 1.37.5, 2.95.3). He was executed by Otho, publicly, as befitted his freedman status (Tac. *Hist.* 1.46.4).

55 The cost of the funeral was so high that Bradley (1978) *ad loc.* has suggested that he might have been granted a public funeral, although if so we might have expected that to excite some comment.

56 Suetonius may well be alluding here to the ceremony on January 1 where the Senate and magistrates took vows to uphold the acts of the *princeps* and his predecessors. The use of the pluperfect tense "had worn" instead of the imperfect suggests that the reference here is not to Nero's regular practice but to his action on one specific occasion.

57 A Claudia Egloge is mentioned in an inscription apparently found on the site of Phaon's villa (*CIL* VI 34916). Otherwise, nothing is known of either nurse.

58 The Hill of the Gardens was a common name for the Pincian Hill in Rome because of the large number of gardens there, originally laid out by Pompey, Lucullus, and Sallust.

59 Generally, June 9 is accepted as the day of Nero's death, based mainly on Jerome's testimony (*Chron.* 36) that he ruled for thirteen years, seven months, and twenty-eight days; Reece (1969) has argued for June 11.

60 Suetonius is willing to acknowledge that the reaction to Nero's death was mixed. Tacitus (*Hist.* 1.4.1) observes that the news of the death prompted a range of emotions in every class of society as well as among the troops and their commanders serving on the legions. He adds that the praetorians were disinclined to abandon him and had to be persuaded to do so (Tac. *Hist.* 5.1). Tacitus (*Hist.* 1.78.2) and Plutarch (*Otho* 3.1, 5.1) also say that Otho considered ways of honoring Nero as a measure to attain popularity and that he set up statues to him. As a mark of respect, people would greet Otho as Nero Otho. Vitellius carried out sacrifices to his shade, an act that won him popularity in some quarters (Tac. *Hist.* 2.95).

2. Furthermore, when the Parthian king Vologaeses sent emissaries to the Senate regarding the renewal of the alliance, he made earnest appeals for the memory of Nero to be honored.[61] In fact, twenty years later, when I was a young man,[62] someone whose background was obscure came forward, making out that he was Nero,[63] and so favorably received was the name among the Parthians that the man received enthusiastic support and they were only with difficulty brought to surrender him.

Dio 63.29.1. They conducted an all-out search for Nero, and for a time had no idea where he might have gone, but then, when they found out, they sent riders after him. Upon observing that these were approaching, Nero ordered those present to kill him, and when they would not obey, he groaned and said: "I alone have no friend and no enemy." The riders having meanwhile closed in on him, he then killed himself, making that often-quoted comment: "Oh Zeus, what an artist dies in me." And as he was expiring in great pain, Epaphroditus finished him off.

61 The pact between Rome and Parthia that Nero had engineered in 63 was later renewed, as we know from Tacitus (*Hist.* 4.51, confirmed by Suet. *Vesp.* 6.4). Tacitus states that after Vespasian heard of the demise of Vitellius, a delegation came from Vologaeses offering him support in the form of forty thousand archers. Vespasian, having no need of them, instructed the delegates to proceed to Rome to meet the Senate, with the assurance that he regarded the empire as at peace.

62 This passage is of considerable interest, being one of the relatively few instances where the ancient source will speak of his own connection to a historical event. Similarly, when discussing the motives of Caligula for building the bridge at Baiae, Suetonius speaks of what he heard from his grandfather "when I was a boy" (*Cal.* 19.3).

63 The phenomenon of the false claimant is a relatively common one in the period. Clemens, a slave of Agrippa Postumus, claimed to be his master (Tac. *Ann.* 2.39–40; Suet. *Tib.* 25.1–3; Dio 57.16.3–4).

There were three Nero claimants. The first appeared in AD 69. His origins are not clear. Tacitus says he might have been a slave from Pontus or an Italian freedman, and was a fine musician with a good voice. He occupied the island of Cynthus in the Aegean and caused consternation in Asia and Greece. The rebellion was suppressed when Calpurnius Asprenas, on his way to the governorship of Galatia-Pamphylia, escorted by a naval squadron, put in on the island (Tac. *Hist.* 2.8–9; Dio 64.9.3; Zonaras 11.15.45). A second, Terentius Maximus, an accomplished lyre player who physically resembled Nero, appeared under Titus and ultimately sought refuge with Artabanus of Parthia, who seriously pondered supporting his claim (Dio 66.19.3b–3c).

Suetonius seems to speak of a third, in about AD 88. It could be that this claimant is in fact candidate number two, Terentius, but this would mean that Suetonius made an error of eight years, unlikely at the best of times, inexplicable for an event of which he had personal knowledge; see Syme ([1958], 518).

Nero lived for thirty years and nine months, and ruled for thirteen years and eight months of that time.[64] He was the last of the descendants of Aeneas and Augustus, which was clearly shown by the death, just before his own, of the laurels planted by Livia as well as the breed of white chickens.[65]

Plut. *Galb.* 2.1. As noted earlier,[66] when Nero's situation became completely hopeless and it was clear that he was about to run off to Egypt,[67] the court commander Nymphidius Sabinus, in company with Tigellinus, persuaded the troops—as if Nero were no longer there but had already fled—to declare Galba emperor. 2. For this, he promised a reward of 7,500 drachmas for each member of the guard (the "palace" or "praetorian" guard, as they are called) and 1,250 for soldiers serving abroad, and that was an amount impossible to raise without inflicting countless more ills on all mankind than Nero did.[68] 3. This spelled immediate death for Nero, and shortly afterward for Galba: the one the troops abandoned to get the money, and the other they murdered when they failed to get it.[69] Then, as they searched for someone

64 On the length of his reign, see the appendix to Chapter I.

65 There was a tradition that an eagle dropped a white chick with a laurel branch in its mouth into Livia's lap. She rescued the small bird and raised it, and planted the sprig. A brood of white chicks was born, and a grove of laurels sprang up, from which the *triumphatores* subsequently collected the sprigs, which they carried in their hands and made into crowns. Dio alone comments on their perishing at this time (Suet. *Galb.* 1; Plin. *HN* 15.136–37; Dio 48.52.3–4).

66 Plutarch presumably made the earlier statement in his lost *Nero*.

67 The notion of the emperor leaving to start a new life in Egypt is something of a trope. Dio (63.27.2) also says that Nero planned to go to Alexandria (after killing the senators), and Suetonius (*Ner.* 47.2) says that his last plan was to be allowed to be prefect of Egypt. But this was also said of other Roman leaders. Caesar was supposed to be planning to move the seat of government to Alexandria (or Ilium) (Suet. *Jul.* 79.3; Nic. Dam. *Caes.* 20 [FrgHist 90, F 130.20]), and Octavian made a similar charge about Antony (Dio 50.4.1). Philo (*Leg.* 250) says that there was a rumor of such a plan being held by Caligula, and Suetonius (*Cal.* 8.5, 49.2) reports Caligula's intention to move to Alexandria or to Antium. Alexandria was of course the epitome of luxury, and to suggest such an intention was an easy way to discredit one's enemies.

68 There was a serious inflation in the cost of winning the favor of the praetorians. Augustus in his will left 250 denarii to each of the praetorians and 75 to each of the legionaries. Tiberius did the same, and Caligula added 250 for each praetorian (Dio 59.2.1–3). Claudius gave 3,750 (Suet. *Claud.* 10.4) or 5,000 (Jos. *Ant.* 19.247), and Nero gave the same as Claudius. The offer from Nymphidius, the praetorian commander, is well above these totals, but of course he was trying to persuade the praetorians not just to pledge their support but actually to rebel, which must command a premium.

69 Tacitus (*Hist.*1.5.1) confirms that the payment was not made. The praetorians suffered heavily fighting for Otho against Vitellius, and after Otho's defeat at Bedriacum

who would give them that amount, they destroyed themselves in revolts and treasonous acts before they managed to get what they wanted. To provide an accurate and detailed account of these happenings is the task of history, but I, too, should not pass over noteworthy items in the acts and incidents of the Caesars' lives.[70]

4.1. Nero's unscrupulous henchmen were cruelly and savagely plundering the provinces for him, and Galba had no way of bringing help; but that he was clearly in sympathy with the provincials' distress and legitimate grievances did somehow provide a measure of consolation and comfort as they were being condemned and sold into slavery. And when poems were being composed against Nero, and being circulated and sung everywhere, he did not forbid it or share the henchmen's indignation, and for that he was held in even greater affection by the people.

2. In fact, Galba was by now well-known to them, since it was in the eighth year of his term as governor that Junius Vindex, a commander in Gaul, revolted against Nero. It is said that even before the revolt was out in the open, letters came to him from Vindex, and that although Galba had no confidence in them, he did not report or denounce the man either. (Other officials did send Nero letters that had been written to them and did their best to undermine the coup, but later they took part in it and thereby admitted to having been traitors to their own cause no less than his.) However, when Vindex openly declared war, he wrote to Galba, calling on him to assume the imperial power and offer himself to a strong body that was seeking a head; that is, to the Gallic provinces—they already had a hundred thousand men under arms, he said, and could arm many thousands more.[71]

5.1. After that, Galba, with a proclamation, set a day on which he would make individual grants of freedom to those who wanted them, and idle chatter and circulating rumors brought together large numbers of men eager for revolution.[72] Indeed, he had hardly appeared on the dais when they all with

---

(modern Calvatone, near Cremona) they were disbanded and Vitellius formed a new corps (Tac. *Hist.* 2.67; Suet. *Vit.* 10.1).

70 Plutarch is making the point that some information that properly belongs to history is not out of place in biography.

71 A hundred thousand men sounds like an exaggeration, but Plutarch (*Galb.* 6.3) says that 20,000 died at Vesontio (Besancon), and he could also have added the troops that laid siege to Lugdunum (Lyon).

72 Galba died on January 15, 69. Dio ($64.6.5^2$) says that he reigned for nine months and thirteen days. By inclusive counting, this makes the date of Galba's proclamation April 3, 68. Suetonius (*Galb.* 10.1) places the acclamation after Galba's speech; in Plutarch, the soldiers are more spontaneous.

one voice declared him emperor. 2. He did not immediately accept the title, however, but after speaking out against Nero and lamenting the most notable of the men executed by him, he agreed to devote his care and attention to the fatherland, taking not the title "Caesar" or "Emperor" but that of "General of the Senate and people of Rome."[73]

3. That Vindex's maneuver in petitioning Galba to take on imperial power was sound and well calculated was confirmed by the proof given by Nero. He pretended to despise Vindex and to consider the situation in Gaul unimportant, but, as soon as he heard about Galba's move (he happened to have taken his bath and was at lunch), he overturned the table.[74] That notwithstanding, when the Senate voted to declare Galba a public enemy, Nero wanted to make a joke and show bravado before his friends. He therefore declared that, needing money as he did, a calculation for the future had occurred to him that was not gloomy: while what belonged to the Gauls would only come to him as plunder when they were subdued, Galba's property was already available to be used and sold since he had been declared an enemy. He [Nero] accordingly ordered Galba's property put up for sale, and when Galba heard the news, he proclaimed the sale of Nero's property in Spain and found many purchasers who were more eager to buy it.[75]

6.1. Many were now abandoning Nero, and nearly all of them joined Galba. The only ones to follow their own plans were Clodius Macer in Africa and Verginius Rufus in Gaul (where Rufus commanded the German troops), though they did not take the same path.[76] 2. Clodius was in a quandary: because of his brutality and greed, he had been engaging in robbery and murder, and it was clear that he could neither hold onto his command nor give it up.[77] Verginius, commander of the most powerful legions, who often saluted him as emperor and pressed him to take the title, said that he

73 Suetonius (*Galb.* 10.1), Dio (63.29.6), and coin issues agree with Plutarch that Galba declared himself to be subject to the wishes of the Senate and people, and that he received his titles only after the Senate had confirmed them.

74 Suetonius (*Ner.* 42.1) says that Nero collapsed and lay in a faint.

75 Only Plutarch says that the Senate declared Galba a public enemy, as Nero in his turn would later be declared. As a *hostis*, Galba would lose his property; no other source says that it was sold. Galba could presumably turn the argument around and claim that Nero was in fact a *hostis* and should accordingly lose *his* possessions. The Spanish assets would presumably have included properties that Nero acquired from the estates of Seneca and Lucan, both of whom died as a consequence of the Pisonian conspiracy.

76 Apart from the names provided here by Plutarch, only Otho and Alienus are known. Tiberius Alexander in Egypt recognized Galba as emperor on July 6, less than a month after Nero's death.

77 Plutarch is hostile toward Clodius Macer, as are all the other sources.

would not personally take on the emperorship but no more would he countenance it being given to anyone else not chosen by the Senate.[78]

7.1. By now, it was summer, and in early evening Icelus, a freedman, arrived from Rome after a six-day journey.[79] Told that Galba was resting on his own, he marched swiftly to his room and, despite the attendants, opened the door and went in. He reported to Galba that, when Nero was still alive but not being seen in public, the army first, and then the people and the Senate, had declared Galba emperor, and shortly afterward a report had come of Nero's death. He personally had not believed the report, said Icelus, but had approached the body and after seeing it lying prostrate had set off on his journey.

POSTSCRIPT

Nero died in June 68 and thus gave up his earthly existence. But he still, in a way, maintained a presence, and he has continued to do so for almost two thousand years. Within a very short time of his death, impostors came out of the woodwork, and he could continue to plague his fellow Romans by proxy. The natural passage of time brought an end to the phenomenon of the Nero impersonator. But many incidents of his life had been so shockingly outrageous that the impression left on the collective imagination could never be erased: the murder of his mother, the execution of his young wife, the violent kicking to death of her successor, the Great Fire of Rome, alongside his musical performance during it, and his own melodramatic suicide. All of these monstrous yet seductively colorful episodes combined in the person of one single individual have made him strangely irresistible. To these we have to add Nero's reputation as the first persecutor of the Christians and as the murderer of the two great pillars of the church, Saints Peter and Paul, with Nero expected to return to earth one day in person as the Antichrist.

Suetonius (*Ner.* 55) claims that Nero had a yearning for *perpetua fama* ("perpetual fame"). If so, he was one of those lucky people who more than achieve their ambitions. His earliest extant posthumous appearance before a public audience is likely to have been within a generation of his death, in

78 At some point, *probably* before Nero's suicide, some of the legions that Nero moved to north Italy offered their support to Verginius Rufus (Tac. *Hist.* 1.9.3). Verginius refused it, but there were persistent rumors that he wanted to be emperor (Tac. *Hist.* 1.8.2, cf. 2.7.1).

79 Nero committed suicide in June, probably on the ninth. It is not clear why Icelus was in Rome. Suetonius (*Ner.* 49.4) says he was imprisoned at the beginning of the revolt and that after his release he allowed Nero's body to be buried. This last point conforms to Plutarch's information that he had seen the dead body.

the tragedy *Octavia*, where Nero murders his mother and his wife (assuming *Octavia* was composed in the Flavian period and was composed to be performed). He has never left the stage since. Nearly a hundred dramatic representations of Nero have been identified, and some of his appearances have been especially striking, as in Racine's *Britannicus*. The sheer flamboyance of his persona has made him a particular favorite in operas, notably in the works of Monteverdi (*L'incoronazione di Poppea*, 1643) and Handel (*Agrippina*, 1709). In the late nineteenth century, there were even circus shows based on his story. By the twentieth century, he had inevitably made his way into film, the Italian production *Nerone* (1909) apparently the earliest. For contemporary audiences, however, at least for the older members of that audience, the most memorable reincarnation must surely be that of Peter Ustinov in the 1951 film adaptation of the Nobel laureate Henryk Sienkiewicz's great epic novel *Quo Vadis* (recently turned into a musical, performed in Trier, Germany, in 2005). Ustinov's brilliantly camp performance in the 1951 film, aided, no doubt, by the scantily clad Deborah Kerr, the barbarian princess converted to Christianity and condemned to be fed, oddly enough, to a bull, reputedly inspired a whole generation of star-struck secondary school students to abandon French and chemistry and become classicists instead.

BIBLIOGRAPHY

ABBREVIATIONS

Ancient authors and their works, and the titles of periodicals, are referred to by the standard abbreviations. Some additional abbreviations are also listed.

AE	*L'Année épigraphique*
AJA	*American Journal of Archaeology*
AJP	*American Journal of Philology*
Barr.	Talbert, R. 2000. *Barrington Atlas of the Greek and Roman World*. Princeton, NJ: Princeton University Press.
CIL	*Corpus Inscriptionum Latinarum*
CQ	*Classical Quarterly*
HSCP	*Harvard Studies in Classical Philology*
HZ	*Historische Zeitschrift*
ICS	*Illinois Classical Studies*
ILS	*Inscriptiones Latinae Selectae*
JRS	*Journal of Roman Studies*
MH	*Museum Helveticum*
MRR	Broughton, T.R.S. 1951–1952. *The Magistrates of the Roman Republic*. New York: American Philological Association.
PBSR	*Papers of the British School at Rome*
RIB	*Roman Inscriptions in Britain*
RIC^2	Sutherland, C.H.V., and R.A.G. Carson. 1984. *The Roman Imperial Coinage*, volume 1, revised edition. London: Spink and Son.
SEG	*Supplementum Epigraphicum Graecum*
Smallwood	Smallwood, E.M. 1967 (reprinted 2010). *Documents Illustrating the Principates of Gaius, Claudius and Nero*. Cambridge: Cambridge University Press.
TAPA	*Transactions and Proceedings of the American Philological Association*

GENERAL WORKS

Barrett, A.A. 1996. *Agrippina: Sex, Power and Politics in the Early Empire*. New Haven, CT: Yale University Press.

Bradley, K.R. 1978. *Suetonius' Life of Nero: An Historical Commentary*. Brussels: Latomus.

Buckley, E., and M.T. Dinter, eds. 2013. *A Companion to the Neronian Age*. Malden, MA: Wiley-Blackwell.

Champlin, E. 2003. *Nero*. Cambridge, MA: Harvard University Press.

Elsner, J., and J. Master, eds. 1994. *Reflections of Nero: Culture, History and Representation*. London: Duckworth.

Griffin, M.T. 1992. *Seneca, a Philosopher in Politics*. Second edition. Oxford: Clarendon.

Griffin, M.T. 2000. *Nero, the End of a Dynasty*. Second edition. London: Routledge.

Krüger, J. 2012. *Nero*. Cologne: Böhlau Verlag.

Shotter, D. 2005. *Nero*. Second edition. London: Routledge.

Syme, R. 1958. *Tacitus*. Oxford: Oxford University Press.

TRANSLATIONS

Damon, C. 2012. *Tacitus: The Annals*. London: Penguin.

Edwards, C. 2000. *Suetonius: Lives of the Caesars*. Oxford: Oxford University Press.

Hurley, D. 2011. *Gaius Suetonius Tranquillus: The Caesars*. Indianapolis: Hackett.

Woodman, A. 2004. *Tacitus: The Annals*. Indianapolis: Hackett.

Yardley, J., and A. Barrett. 2008. *Tacitus: The Annals, the Reigns of Tiberius, Claudius and Nero*. Oxford: Oxford University Press.

CHAPTER I: THE MAKING OF THE EMPEROR

Blake, M.E. 1959. *Roman Construction in Italy from Tiberius through the Flavians*. Washington: Carnegie Institution of Washington.

Brunt, P. 1975. "Two Great Roman Landowners." *Latomus* 34:619–35.

Carlsen, J. 2006. *The Rise and Fall of a Roman Noble Family: The Domitii Ahenobarbi, 196 BC–AD 68*. Copenhagen: University Press of Southern Denmark.

Coarelli, F. 1984. *Lazio*. Rome: Laterza.

Sansone, D. 1986. "Atticus, Suetonius and Nero's Ancestors." In C. Deroux, ed., *Studies in Latin Literature and Roman History* 4 (*Collection Latomus* 196). Brussels: Latomus, 269–77.

Sumner, G. 1981. "Review of K.R. Bradley, *Suetonius' Life of Nero*." *Phoenix* 35:378–81.

CHAPTER II: THE NEW EMPEROR

Braund, S.H. 2009. *Seneca, De Clementia*. Oxford: Oxford University Press.

Hind, J.G.F. 1971. "The Middle Years of Nero's Reign." *Historia* 20:488–505.

Hind, J.G.F. 1975. "Is Nero's Quinquennium an Enigma?" *Historia* 24:629–30.

Lepper, F.A. 1957. "Some Reflections on the Quinquennium Neronis." *JRS* 47:95–103.

Levick, B.M. 1983. "Nero's Quinquennium." In C. Deroux, ed., *Studies in Latin Literature and Roman History* 3 (*Collection Latomus* 180). Brussels: Latomus, 211–25.

Müller, S. 2009. *Das Hellenistische Königspaar in der medialen Represäntation-Prolemaios II und Arsinoë II*. Berlin: De Gruyter.

Murray, O. 1965. "The Quinquennium Neronis and the Stoics." *Historia* 14:41–61.

Syme, R. 1971. *Emperors and Biography*. Oxford: Oxford University Press.

Thornton, M.K. 1973. "The Enigma of Nero's Quinquennium." *Historia* 22:570–82.

Thornton, M.K. 1989. "Nero's Quinquennium; the Ostian Connection." *Historia* 38:117–19.

CHAPTER III: ENEMIES WITHIN

Baltussen, H. 2002. "Matricide Revisited: Dramatic and Rhetorical Allusion in Tacitus, Suetonius and Cassius Dio." *Antichthon* 36:30–40.

Devillers, O. 1995. "Tacite, les sources et les impératifs de la narration: Le récit de la mort d'Agrippine (Annales XIV, 1–13)." *Latomus* 54:324–45.

Levick, B., and S. Jameson. 1964. "C. Creperius Gallus and His Gens." *JRS* 54:98–106.

Luke, T. 2013. "From Crisis to Consensus: Salutary Ideology and the Murder of Agrippina." *ICS* 38:207–28.

O'Gorman, E. 1997. "The Curse of Agrippina: Tacitus Annals 14." *Omnibus* 33:8–10.

O'Gorman, E. 2000. *Irony and Misreading in the Annals of Tacitus*. Cambridge: Cambridge University Press.

Piecha, R. 2003. "Wenn Frauen baden gehen . . . Agrippinas Ende bei Tac. *Ann.* 14, 1–13." In M. Schauer and G. Thome, eds., *Altera Ratio: Klassische Philologie zwischen Subjektivität und Wissenschaft*. Stuttgart: Steiner, 120–35.

Stahr, A.W.T. 1867. *Agrippina: die Mutter Neros*. Berlin: J. Guttentag.

Steele, C. 2007. *Death in Ancient Rome*. New Haven, CT: Yale University Press.

Townend, G.B. 1960. "The Sources of the Greek in Suetonius." *Hermes* 88:98–120.

Uden, J. 2003. "Drama and Suspense in Agrippina's Last Days." *Classicum* 29:2–7.

CHAPTER IV: PARTHIA

Ash, R. 2006. "Following in the Footsteps of Lucullus?: Tacitus' Characterisation of Corbulo." *Arethusa* 39:355–75.

Campbell, B. 1993. "War and Diplomacy: Rome and Parthia, 31 BC–AD 235." In J. Rich and G. Shipley, eds., *War and Society in the Roman World*. London: Routledge, 213–40.

Gilmartin, K. 1973. "Corbulo's Campaigns in the East: An Analysis of Tacitus' Account." *Historia* 22:583–626.

Grajetzki, W. 2011. *Greeks and Parthians in Mesopotamia and Beyond, 331 BC–224 AD*. London: Bristol Classical Press.

Kennedy, D.L. 1996. "Parthia and Rome: Eastern Perspectives." In D.L. Kennedy, ed., *The Roman Army in the East*. Ann Arbor: Journal of Roman Archaeology, Supplement, 67–90.

Lerouge, C. 2007. *L'image des Parthes dans le monde gréco-romain*. Stuttgart: Steiner.

Shayegan, M.R. 2011. *Arsacids and Sasanians*. Cambridge: Cambridge University Press.

Vervaet, F.J. 1999. "*CIL* IX 3426: A New Light on Corbulo's Career, with Special Reference to His Official Mandate in the East from AD 55 to AD 63." *Latomus* 58:574–99.

Vervaet, F.J. 2000. "Tacitus, *Ann.* 15.25.3: A Revision of Corbulo's *imperium maius* (AD 63–AD 65?)." In C. Deroux, ed., *Studies in Latin Literature and Roman History* 10 (*Collection Latomus* 254). Brussels: Latomus, 260–98.

Wheeler, E. 1997. "The Chronology of Corbulo in Armenia." *Klio* 79:383–97.

Wiesehöfer, J., ed. 1998. *Das Partherreich und seine Zeugnisse*. Stuttgart: Steiner.

CHAPTER V: BRITAIN AND GERMANY

Allason-Jones, L. 1989. *Women in Roman Britain*. London: British Museum Publications.

Allen, D.F. 1976. "An Icenian Legend." *Britannia* 7:276–78.

Asbach, J. 1878. *Analecta Historica et Epigraphica Latina*. PhD dissertation, Bonn University, 8–16.

Benario, H.W. 1986. "Legionary Speed of March before the Battle with Boudica." *Britannia* 17:359–62.

Bulst, C.M. 1961. "The Revolt of Queen Boudica in AD 60." *Historia* 10:496–509.

Cappai, C. de F. 1992. "Suet. 'Nero' 18 e il progetto neroniano di evacuazione della Britannia." *Quaderni Urbinati di Cultura Classica* 41:137–45.

Carroll, K.K. 1979. "The Date of Boudica's Revolt." *Britannia* 10:197–202.

Courteault, P. 1921. "An Inscription Recently Found at Bordeaux." *JRS* 11:101–7.

Dyson, S.L. 1971. "Native Revolts in the Roman Empire." *Historia* 20:239–74.

Fishwick, D. 1961. "The Imperial Cult in Britain." *Phoenix* 15:159–73.

Fulford, M.G. 2008. "Nero and Britain: The Palace of the Client King at Calleva and Imperial Policy towards the Province after Boudica." *Britannia* 39:1–13.

Gambash, G. 2012. "To Rule a Ferocious Province: Roman Policy and the Aftermath of the Boudican Revolt." *Britannia* 43:1–15.

Griffin, M.T. 1976. "Nero's Recall of Suetonius Paulinus." *Scripta Classica Israelica* 3:138–52.

Jackson, K. 1979. "Queen Boudica?" *Britannia* 10:255.

Jullian, C. 1899. "Note gallo-Romaines, Sainte Victoire, Victoria, Andarte." *Revue des Études Anciennes* 1:46.

Webster, G. 1993. *Boudica*. London: Batsford.

Wedeck, H.E. 1955. "The Question of Seneca's Wealth." *Latomus* 14:540–44.

CHAPTER VI: THE GREAT FIRE

The Fire

Dando-Collins, S. 2010. *The Great Fire of Rome*. Cambridge, MA: Da Capo Press.

Holson, P. 1976. "Nero and the Fire of Rome: Fact and Fiction." *Pegasus* 19:37–44.

Hülsen, Ch. 1909. "The Burning of Rome under Nero." *AJA* 13:45–48.

Newbold, R.F. 1974. "Some Social and Economic Consequences of the AD 64 Fire at Rome." *Latomus* 33:858–69.

Scheda, G. 1967. "Nero und der Brand Roms." *Historia* 16:111–15.

Yavetz, Z. 1975. "Forte an dolo principis (Tac. *Ann.* 15.38)." In B. Levick, *The Ancient Historian and His Materials: Essays in Honour of C.E. Stevens*. Farnborough: Gregg, 181–97.

The Christians

Beaujeu, J. 1960. "L'incendie de Rome en 64 et les Chrétiens." *Latomus* 19:65–80, 291–311.

Coleman, K.M. 1990. "Fatal Charades: Roman Executions Staged as Mythological Enactments." *JRS* 80:44–73.

Cook, J.G. 2010. *Roman Attitudes toward the Christians*. Tübingen: Mohr Siebeck.

Frend, W.H.C. 1965. *Martyrdom and Persecution in the Early Church*. Oxford: Blackwell.

Fuchs, H. 1950. "Tacitus über den Christen." *Vigiliae Chistianae* 4:65–93.

Heubner, H. 1959. "Zu Tac. *Ann.* 15,44,4." *Hermes* 87:223–30.

Hochart, P. 1885. *Études au sujet de la persecution des Chrétiens sous Néron*. Paris: E. Leroux.

Jülischer, A. 1976. *Itala: Das Neue Testament in altlateinische Überlierferung*, vol. 3: *Lukas-Evangelium*. Second edition. Berlin: De Gruyter.

Koestermann, E. 1967. "Ein folgenschwerer Irrtum des Tacitus (*Ann.* 15.44, 2ff.)?" *Historia* 16:456–69.

Metzger, B.M. 1977. *The Early Versions of the New Testament*. Oxford: Oxford University Press.

Michelfeit, J. 1966. "Das Christenkapitel des Tacitus." *Gymnasium* 73:514–40.

Shaw, B. 2015. "The Myth of the Neronian Persecution." *JRS* 105:73–100.

Toynbee, J., and J. Ward Perkins. 1956. *The Shrine of St Peter and the Vatican Excavations*. London: Longmans.

The Golden House

Ball, L. 2003. *The Domus Aurea and the Roman Architectural Tradition*. Cambridge: Cambridge University Press.

Hemsoll, D. 1990. "The Architecture of Nero's Golden House." In M. Henig, ed., *Architecture and Architectural Sculpture in the Roman Empire*. Oxford: Oxford University Committee for Archaeology.

Hoffmann, A., and U. Wulf. 2004. *Die Kaiserpaläste auf dem Palatin in Rom*. Mainz: von Zabern.

Knell, H. 2004. *Bauprogramme römischer Kaiser*. Mainz: von Zabern.

CHAPTER VII: THE EMPEROR'S WIVES

Barrett, A.A. 2016. "Women in the Court of Nero." In S. Bartsch-Zimmer, C.K. Freudenburg, and C. Littlewood, eds., *Cambridge Companion to the Age of Nero*. Cambridge: Cambridge University Press, forthcoming.

Gallivan, P.A. 1974. "Confusion Concerning the Age of Octavia." *Latomus* 33:116–17.

Holztrattner, F. 1995. *Neronis potens, Die Gestalt der Poppaea Sabina in den Nerobüchern des Tacitus: Mit einem Anhang zu Claudia Acte* (Grazer Beiträge Supplementband 6). Horn: Berger.

Kragelund, P. 2010. "The Temple and Birthplace of Diva Poppaea." *CQ* 60:559–68.

Mayer, F.A. 1982. "What Caused Poppaea's Death?" *Historia* 31:248–49.

CHAPTER VIII: CONSPIRACIES

Brunt, P.A. 2009. "Stoicisim and the Principate." *PBSR* 43:7–35.

Champlin, E. 1989. "The Life and Times of Calpurnius Piso." *MH* 46:101–24.

Gärtner, H.A. 1996. "Senecas Tod in der Pisonischen Verschwörung." In R. Faber and B. Seidensticker, eds., *Worte, Bilder, Töne: Studien zur Antike und Antikerezeption*. Würzburg: Königshausen und Neumann, 143–57.

Green, S. 2010. "(No) Arms and a Man: The Imperial Pretender, the Opportunistic Poet and the *Laus Pisonis*." *CQ* 60:497–523.

Ker, J. 2009. *The Deaths of Seneca*. Oxford: Oxford University Press.

O'Gorman, E. 2006. "Alternative Empires: Tacitus' Virtual History of the Pisonian Principate." *Arethusa* 39:281–302.

Pagán, V. 2004. *Conspiracy Narratives in Roman History*. Austin: University of Texas Press.

Rees, R. 2013. "The Lousy Reputation of Piso." In A.G.G. Gibson, ed., *The Julio-Claudian Succession*. Leiden: Brill, 95–106.

Rudich, V. 1993. *Political Dissidence under Nero: The Price of Dissimilation*. London: Routledge.

Toynbee, J.M.C. 1944. "Dictators and Philosophers in the First Century A.D." *Greece and Rome* 13:43–58.

Woodman, A.J. 1993. "Amateur Dramatics at the Court of Nero: *Annals* 15.48–74." In T.J. Luce and A.J. Woodman, eds., *Tacitus and the Tacitean Tradition*. Princeton, NJ: Princeton University Press, 104–28.

CHAPTER IX: THE EMPEROR AS ARTIST AND SHOWMAN

Fantham, R.E. 2013. "The Performing Prince." In E. Buckley and M.T. Dinter, eds., *A Companion to the Neronian Age*. Malden, MA: Wiley-Blackwell, 17–28.

Hall, E., and R. Wyles. 2008. *New Directions in Ancient Pantomime*. Oxford: Oxford University Press.

Kennell, N. 1988. "*NERON PERIODONIKES*." *AJP* 109:139–51.

Lada-Richards, I. 2013. "*Mutata Corpora:* Ovid's Changing Forms and the Metamorphic Bodies of Pantomime Dancing." *TAPA* 143:105–52.

Mattingly, H. 1920. "Some Historical Roman Coins of the First Century A.D." *JRS* 10:37–41.

Morford, M.P.O. 1985. "Nero's Patronage and Participation in Literature and the Arts." *Aufstieg und Niedergang der Römischen Welt* 2.36.6:2003–31.

Yawetz, Z. 1969. *Plebs and Princeps*. Oxford: Oxford University Press.

CHAPTER X: DEATH

Arand, T. 2002. *Das schmähliche Ende: Der Tod des schlechten Kaisers und seine literarische Gestaltung in der römischen Historiographie*. Berlin: Lang.

Meier, M. 2008. "Qualis artifex pereo–Neros letzte Reise." *HZ* 286:561–603.

Morgan, M.G. 1993. "The Three Minor Pretenders in Tacitus' *Histories*." *Latomus* 52:769–96.

Reece, B.R. 1969. "The Date of Nero's Death." *AJP* 90:72–74.

Sansone, D. 1993. "Nero's Final Hours." *ICS* 18:179–89.

Tuplin, C. 1989. "The False Neros of the First Century." In C. Deroux, ed., *Studies in Latin Literature and Roman History* 5 (*Collection Latomus* 206). Brussels: Latomus, 364–404.

Woods, D. 2009. "Curing Nero: A Cold Drink in Context." *Classics Ireland* 16:40–48.

INDEX

The index is restricted to items in the primary texts (including inscriptions and papyri). Notes are not indexed. Romans are normally indexed by *nomen* (if it is known), but well-known individuals, especially the emperors, are indexed under their familiar names, such as Seneca, Caligula.

Agrippina the Younger, mother of Nero, 3–12, 14, 16, 20, 22–24, 27, 42–44, 46, 48–50, 53, 55–59, 61–73, 75–76, 131, 174–76, 180, 184–85, 198, 226
Acerronia, Polla, 64, 66, 68
Acilia (Aelia), mother of Lucan, 205, 219
Acte (freedwoman), 57–58
Actium, 186
Adiabene/Adiabeni, 98–100
Aelia Catella, 239
Aelius Gracilis, 144
Aeneas, 74, 232, 281
Afranius Quintianus, 197, 206, 217
Agermus, Lucius, 66–68, 71
Agrippa, Julius, conspirator, 218
Agrippa, Marcus Julius, son of 'Herod' Agrippa, 83
Agrippa, Marcus Vipsanius, friend of Augustus, 5, 70, 142, 156, 235
Alexandria/Alexandrians, 181, 245, 274, 279
Ampsivarii, 145–47
Anicetus, 61, 65, 67–69, 182, 184
Anicius Cerialis, 222
Annaeus Cornutus, 234
Annaeus, Statius, 212
Annius Pollio, 217
Annius Vinicianus, 113, 117, 223
Antiochus, king of Commagene, 83, 89, 96, 250
Antistia, wife of Plautus, 51
Antistius (praetor), 226
Antistius Vetus, Gaius, 10
Antistius Vetus, Lucius, 32, 54, 143–44, 226–27
Antium, 6, 18, 33, 61, 63, 156, 186, 255
Antonia the Elder, 4
Antonia the Younger, 16
Antonia, daughter of Claudius, 51, 174, 201–2
Antonius Natalis, 197–98, 203–5, 209–10, 217
Apollo, 245–46, 254, 256, 261–64
Appian Way, 4
Arar, river, 144
Araxes, river, 90
Aristobulus, king of Chalcis, 83, 96
Armenia/Armenians, 27–28, 80, 82–85, 87, 89, 92–93, 95–108, 110–12, 117, 125–26, 227, 241–43
Arminius, 146
Arrius Varus, 86
Arsacids, 86, 95, 97, 113
Arsanias, river, 105, 110
Artaxata, 90, 92
Artoria Flaccilla, 217
Asconius Labeo, 30–32
Asia, 51, 53–54, 227, 240
Asinius Gallus, 237
Assyrians, 131
Attus Clausus, 11
Augustus, emperor, 8, 10, 16, 25, 34, 40, 70, 76, 82, 235–37, 239, 250–51, 255, 257, 281
Aurelius Fulvus, Titus, 116
Avernus, lake, 160

Baiae, 63, 65, 200
Bauli, 63, 65
Belgica, 144
Blitius Catulinus, 218
Boiocalus, 146–47
Boudica, 128–32, 136–38
Britain/Britons, 124–31, 133–38, 140, 269

Britannicus, 8–14, 16–18, 20–21, 32, 38, 44–50, 60–61, 76
Bructeri, 147
Burrus, Sextus Afranius, 17, 45, 49, 51–53, 66–67, 71, 82, 182, 231, 245, 248

Caecina Largus, Gaius, 152
Caedicia, wife of Scaevinus, 219
Caelian Hill, 153
Caesar, Gaius, grandson of Augustus, 10
Caesar, Lucius, grandson of Augustus, 10
Caesennius Maximus, 219
Caesennius Paetus, Lucius, 100–13, 126
Calavius Sabinus, 102
Caligula, emperor, 4–7, 12, 18, 20, 26, 220, 250
Calpurnius Piso, Gaius, 195–96, 198, 200–2, 204–5, 207–10, 213, 223
Campania, 63, 71, 73, 182–83, 199, 209, 225
Campus Martius, 36, 48, 156, 236, 238, 279
Camulodunum, 132–33
Caninius Rebilus, 37
Capito Cossutianus, 226–27
Capitol/Capitoline Hill, 74, 107, 166, 183, 217, 221, 239, 243, 257
Cappadocia, 86, 88, 95, 100–1, 104, 107
Carrinas Celer, 32
Casperius (centurion), 99
Cassius Asclepiodotus, 229
Cassius, Gaius, 91, 200, 214
Celsus, Marius, 109
Ceres, 166, 201, 221, 239
Cervarius Proculus, 197, 214, 217
Cestius, Gaius, 109
Chaldaeans, 70
Chatti, 147–48
Chauci, 146
Cherusci, 146–47
Christians, 167–70
Cilicia, 86, 226
Circus Maximus, 8, 11, 13, 76, 153, 168, 186, 201, 221, 235, 241, 246, 256
Claudians, 11
Claudius Senecio, 6–8, 10, 12–14, 17–20, 25–27, 33, 38, 45, 49, 51, 58
Clodius Macer, Lucius, 274
Cluvidienus Quietus, 218
Cluvius Rufus, 57, 247, 251
Coeranus, 54
Commagene, 104
Corbulo, Gnaeus Domitius, 54, 84–90, 92–104, 106–7, 109–14, 116–17, 126, 243
Corinth, 251
Cornelius Flaccus, 89
Cornelius Lentulus, Cossus, 239
Cornelius Martialis (tribune), 217
Cornelius Sulla, Faustus, 51–53, 174
Cornelius Scipio Salvidienus, Servius, 12, 18
Cottius, Marcus Julius, Alpine king, 125
Creperius Gallus, 64
Curia, 26, 72, 133, 226
Curtilius Mancia, 147

Decianus Catus, 121, 129, 133–34, 139
Demetrius, 228–29
Diana, 175
Didius Gallus, Aulus, 126
Domitia Lepida, aunt of Nero, 4, 7, 12, 16
Domitius Ahenobarbus, Gnaeus, father of Nero, 5–6, 16, 24, 30, 33, 59, 174
Domitius Ahenobarbus, Lucius, grandfather of Nero, 4–5
Domitius Caecilianus, 228
Domitius, Statius (tribune), 217
Domus Transitoria, 159
Doryphorus, freedman, 195
Druids, 126
Drusus, son of Tiberius, 53
Drusus, brother of Tiberius, 144
Dubius Avitus, 144, 146–47

Ecbatana, 114
Egnatia Maximilla, 217
Egnatius Celer, Publius, 229
Egypt/Egyptians, 111, 131, 183, 273, 281
Eleusinian Mysteries, 70
Epaminondas of Acraephia, 252
Epaphroditus, 203, 276, 278, 280
Epicharis, 199–200, 205–6
Esquiline Hill, 157, 159
Eucaerus, 181
Euphrates, river, 83, 94, 98, 102–4, 106–7, 110–12, 241
Evander, 158

Fabius Rusticus, 57, 210
Faenius Rufus, 53, 196, 198, 201, 207, 210, 214–15
Flaminian Way, 52
Flavius Nepos (tribune), 217
Flavius Scaevinus (senator), 197, 201–5, 207, 214, 217, 219, 221, 224
Fonteius Capito, 274
Fonteius, Gaius, 180
Fortune (goddess), 39, 186, 201, 250
Forum (Rome), 4, 49, 76, 183, 206, 216, 220, 232, 235, 241–42, 256–57, 259, 273
Frisians, 144–45
Funisulanus Vettonianus, 102
Furies, 70, 126
Furnius, Gaius, 235

Galatia, 88, 101
Galba, emperor, 229, 270, 273–74, 276–78, 281–84
Gaul/Gauls, 53, 129, 134, 140, 144, 157, 161, 267–69, 271–72, 283–83
Gavius Silvanus (tribune), 198, 209–10, 217
Gerellanus, 216
Germanicus, 4, 9–10, 44, 67, 70, 146
Germany, 53, 88, 139, 143, 274
Glitius Gallus, 205, 217
Golden House, 155, 159–60
Graptus, freedman, 52

Haterius Agrippa, Decimus, 237
Haterius Antoninus, Quintus, 18, 176, 232
Helvidius Priscus, 228–29
Herculeius, 68
Hercules, 158, 246–47
Hermunduri, 147–48
Hyrcania/Hyrcanians, 94, 97

Iberia/Iberians, 93
Icelus, 278, 284
Iceni, 127–28, 132,
Illyricum, 111
Insteius Capito, 86, 89
Iuvenalia, 226, 237, 239

Janus, 243, 263
Judaea, 167
Julius Altinus, 219
Julius Atticus Vestinus, Marcus, 189, 196, 201, 215–16
Julius Augurinus, 197–98
Julius Caesar, Gaius, 25, 69, 128, 140
Julius Classicianus, 139
Julius Densus, 32, 42
Junia Calvina, 175
Junia Silana, 9, 50, 73
Junius Gallio, 220, 248
Junius Silanus, Gaius, 235
Junius Silanus, Lucius, 174–75, 200, 227
Junius Silanus Torquatus, Decimus, 18, 176, 232
Juno, 166
Jupiter, 36, 158, 186, 213, 221, 229–30, 234

Legerda, 94
Legion: Second, 137; Third (Gallica), 101, 116, 267; Fourth (Scythia), 101–2, 111; Fifth (Macedonica), 101, 103, 111, 113; Sixth (Ferrata), 84, 101, 111; Ninth, 134; Tenth (Fretensis), 101; Twelfth (Fulminata), 101–2, 111; Thirteenth, 111; Fourteenth (Gemina), 135, 137; Fifteenth, 109, 111; Twentieth (Valeria Victrix), 135, 137
Lepidus, Marcus, 58
Libitina, 125
Licinius Gabolus, 73
Licinius Nerva Silianus, Aulus, 196
Locusta, 46–47, 49, 272
Lollia Paulina, 73
Londinium, 134
Lucan, poet, 197, 205–6, 216, 219, 262, 264
Luccius Telesinus, Gaius, 241
Lucius Verus, emperor, 19
Lucrine, lake, 64
Lucullus, Lucius, 87, 112
Luna, 158, 279
Lusitania, 179

Maecenas, Gardens of, 156
Magi, 70
Malorix, 144–45
Mammius Pollio, Lucius, 176
Marcius Barea Soranus, Quintus, 226–27

Marcius Festus, 198
Mardi, 93
Mars, 85, 148, 235
Massilia, 51–53
Maximus Scaurus, 198
Media, 80, 95, 114
Melitene, 112
Memmius Regulus, Publius, 186
Mesopotamia, 111
Messalina, 8–9, 17, 33, 131
Milichus, 203–4, 207, 217
Minerva, 72
Misenum, 61, 63, 69, 184, 199–200
Mnester, 70
Mona, island, 125–26, 131, 137
Monaeses, 99–100, 111
Monobazus, king of Adiabene, 100, 117, 241
Moselle, river, 144
Mulvian Bridge, 52
Mummius, Lucius, 240
Munatius Gratus, 197–98
Musonius Rufus, 54, 218, 222

Naples/Neapolis, 71, 241, 245, 255, 265, 268, 270
Narcissus, 16
NERO
- Agrippina, 3–12, 14, 16, 20, 22–24, 27, 42–44, 46, 48–50, 53, 55–59, 75–76, 131, 174–76, 180, 184–85, 198, 226; murder of, 61–73
- *Ahenobarbus*, name used scornfully, 12, 268
- Antium, 33
- arts, interest in, 3, 26
- birth, 5–6
- Britannicus, 8–14, 16–18, 20–21, 32, 38, 60–61, 76; murder of, 44–50
- Caligula, seizure of estate, 7
- chariot driving, 26, 168, 188, 214–15, 237, 241, 243–46, 255–57, 261
- Christians, persecution of, 166–70
- Claudius, emperor, 6–8, 10–14, 17–20, 21, 25–27, 33, 38, 45, 49, 51, 58
- consulship, 13, 32
- Cornelius Sulla, Faustus, 51–53, 174
- Curia, 26, 72, 133, 226
- Domitia Lepida, aunt, 4, 7, 12, 16
- Domitius Ahenobarbus, Gnaeus, father, 5–6, 16, 24, 30, 33, 59, 174
- Domitius Ahenobarbus, Lucius, grandfather, 4–5
- emperor, 17, 24, 38
- Fire of Rome, 152–59
- Germanicus, 4, 9–10, 44, 67, 70, 146
- Golden House (Domus Aurea), 159–61
- Graptus, freedman, 52
- introduction to Roman public, 8–9
- Messalina, wife of Claudius, attempt on Nero's life, 8
- Neronia, 239, 247
- Octavia, daughter of Claudius, 18–20, 48, 50, 180–85, 188–89, 232, 279; marriage to, 174–77; execution of, 185
- Olympia/Olympic Games, 239, 245, 249, 256–57
- omens, 5–6, 9, 11–12, 19, 50–51, 73, 76, 91, 222–23, 268–69, 275–77
- physical characteristics, 3
- Pisonian conspiracy, 195–208
- Poppaea Sabina, 58–59, 178–83, 185–89, 195, 202, 210, 218, 226; marriage to, 186; death of, 187–88
- public performance (poetry and lyre playing), 36, 74, 131, 157, 213, 215, 225, 230, 233–34, 239, 243–45, 247, 249–51, 268, 274
- Pythagoras, freedman (married to), 189
- Pythian Games, 245, 256–57
- Rubellius Plautus, Gaius, 50–51, 53–55, 182, 227
- Secular Games, participation in, 8
- Seneca, 3, 11–12, 25, 28, 33, 38, 45, 49, 53, 57, 61, 66–67, 72, 82, 129, 176, 195–96, 205, 220, 231, 234, 245, 248, 262; death of, 208–17
- snake/snakeskin, 6, 8–9
- Sporus, slave boy (married to), 59, 188–89, 275–76, 278
- Statilia Messalina, 173, 189, 216
- Thrasea Paetus, 51, 72, 225–28; death of, 228–29
- *toga virilis* granted early, 12–13

Nerva, emperor, 219–20
Nisibis, 99
Novius Priscus, 217
Numa, 158
Nymphidius Sabinus, 220, 274, 281

Obaritus, 68
Octavia, daughter of Claudius, 18–20, 48, 50, 174–77, 180–85, 188–89, 232, 279
Octavia, sister of Augustus, 4
Ollius, Titus, 178
Olympia/Olympic Games, 239, 245, 249, 256–57
omens and prodigies, 5–6, 11–12, 19, 50–51, 73, 76, 91, 102–3, 128–30, 133, 222–23, 229, 268–69, 275–77
Ostia, 38, 156, 272
Ostorius Sabinus, 227
Otho, emperor, 177–80

Pacorus, 114, 241–42
Palatine Hill, 153, 156, 159, 256–57
Palatium, 27, 62, 183, 220
Pallas, freedman, 10, 17, 51–52, 58, 195
Pandateria, 184
Papian Law, 35
Parthia, Parthians, 18, 74, 82–83, 87–88, 92, 94–95, 97–98, 100, 102–3, 105–8, 110–13, 117, 241, 280
Paul, apostle, 169–70
Pelago, eunuch, 54
Penates, 158
Peter, apostle, 169–70
Petillius Cerialis, 134
Petronius, Arbiter Elegantiae, 224–35
Petronius Priscus, 217–18
Petronius Turpilianus, Publius, 126, 139–40, 219, 274
Phaon, 267, 275–76, 278
Pharasmanes, king of Iberia, 89, 96
Plautius Lateranus, 33, 191, 197, 201, 208
plebians, 36, 72–73, 155, 157, 168, 183, 207, 236–37, 249, 279
Pliny the Elder, 202
Poenius Postumus, 137
Polemo, king of Pontus, 96, 125
Polyclitus, freedman, 140
Pompeia Paulina, 209, 212–13
Pompeius Paulinus, Aulus, 143–45
Pompey, 82, 109, 174
Pomptine marshes, 161
Pontus, 101, 103, 111, 124
Poppaea Sabina, 58–59, 178–83, 185–89, 195, 202, 210, 218, 226
Poppaeus Sabinus, Gaius, 178
praetorian guard, 33, 35, 43, 46, 67, 69, 71, 84, 116, 196, 198, 209, 219, 222, 232, 237, 242–43, 247, 267, 272, 274, 276, 281
Prasutagus, king of the Iceni, 128
Proserpina, 166
Proxumus, Statius (tribune), 198, 217
Puteoli, 200, 236, 241
Pythias, freedwoman, 182

Quinquatrus, 63, 65, 72
Quinquennial Games, 239, 249

Radamistus, 82, 89
Red Sea, 94
Rhandea, 110, 117
Rhine, river, 144, 147
Rhone, river, 144
Romulus, 158
Rubellius Plautus, Gaius, 50–51, 53–55, 182, 227
Rubria, 58
Rubrius Gallus, 274
Rufrius Crispinus, 218

Salienus Clemens, 220–21
Sallust, Gardens of, 52
Sallustius Passienus Crispus, Gaius, 8
Salus, 201, 221
Saturnalia, 45
Secular Games, 8, 235
Sejanus, 10, 178
Senate, 10, 12–13, 27, 30, 33, 36–38, 66, 70–71, 73–75, 84, 91, 107, 129, 145, 181, 186, 219–21, 226, 228–29, 232, 235–37, 239, 242, 249, 257, 262, 268–70
Seneca, 3, 11–12, 25, 28, 33, 38, 45, 49, 53, 57, 61, 66–67, 72, 82, 129, 176, 195–96, 205, 208–17, 220, 231, 234, 245, 248, 262
Senones, 159

Servilius, Gardens of, 203, 272
Sibylline Books, 166
Sigillaria, 59
Silius, Gaius, 9, 17
Silures, 126
Simbruine Lakes, 50–51
snakes/snakeskin, 6, 8–9
Sohaemus, 83
Sophene, 83
Sosibius, 12
Sporus, slave boy, 59, 188, 275–76, 278
Statilia Messalina, 173, 189, 216
Statilius Taurus, Titus, 159, 189
Stoics, 53
Sublaqueum, 50
Subrius Flavus, 196, 198–99, 213–15
Suetonius Paulinus, Gaius, 125–26, 131, 133–40, 143–44, 241
Suillius Nerullinus, Marcus, 10
Sulpicius Asper, 196–98, 215
Syria, 85–86, 88, 96, 98–101, 103–4, 107, 109, 111, 125

Taurus Mountains, 103, 110
Tencteri, 147
Tertullian, 170
Thames, river, 129, 133
Thrasea Paetus, Publius Clodius, 51, 72, 225–29
Tiber, river, 51, 160, 235–36, 275
Tiberius Alexander, 113
Tiberius, emperor, 4, 6, 10, 18–19, 25–26, 40, 52, 142, 146, 167, 185, 237
Tigellinus, 53, 152, 158, 181–82, 193, 198, 206–7, 210, 219–20, 224–25, 267, 281
Tigranes, 95, 97–100, 108
Tigranocerta, 92, 94, 99–100, 103, 110
Tiridates, 87, 89–90, 92, 95, 97, 108–14, 117, 227, 241–44
Trajan, emperor, 23–24
Trinovantes, 132
Troy, Game of, 8, 11
Troy/Trojans (Ilium), 152, 156–57, 226, 232–34
Tullius, Servius, 158, 175

Ummidius Quadratus, Gaius, 85–87, 96
Ubians, 148

Valerius Capito, 73
Vardanes, 83
Veianius Niger, 214
Venetus Paulus, 198
Veranius, Quintus, 125–26
Verginius Flavus, 218
Verginius Rufus, 186, 270, 274, 283
Verritus, 144–45
Verulamium, 134
Verulanus Severus, 95, 98
Vespasian, emperor, 269
Vesta/Vestal Virgins, 58, 158, 236, 239
Vettius Bolanus, 98
Vindex, Gaius Julius, 189, 221, 266–70, 273
Vipstanus Apronianus, Gaius, 180
Vitellius, Lucius, 175–76
Vologaeses, 83, 86–87, 92, 94–95, 97–100, 102, 104–5, 107–8, 110–12, 114, 117, 241–42, 280
Volusius Proculus, 199–200, 205
Vulcacius Araricus, 197–98
Vulcan, 166